Your Official
America Online®
Tour Guide

5th Edition

Your Official **America Online**® Tour Guide

5th Edition

Jennifer Watson
and Dave Marx

AOLPress

Dulles, VA

Your Official America Online® Tour Guide,
5th Edition

Published by

AOL Press

An imprint of IDG Books Worldwide, Inc.

An International Data Group Company

919 E. Hillsdale Blvd., Suite 400

Foster City, CA 94404

www.aol.com (America Online Web site)

ISBN: 0-7645-3420-3

Printed in the United States of America

10 9 8 7 6 5 4 3

1VH/QY/QS/QQ/IN

Distributed in the United States by IDG Books Worldwide, Inc. and America Online, Inc.

For general information on IDG Books Worldwide's books in the U.S., please call our Consumer Customer Service department at 800-762-2974. For reseller information, including discounts and premium sales, please call our Reseller Customer Service department at 800-434-3422.

Library of Congress Cataloging-in-Publication Data

Watson, Jennifer.

    Your official America Online tour guide / Jennifer Watson and Dave Marx.–5th ed.

      p.   cm.

    Includes index.

    ISBN 0-7645-3420-3 (alk. paper)

    1. America Online (Online service) I. Marx, Dave. II. Lichty, Tom. Official America Online tour guide. III. Title.

QA76.57.A43 L534   1999

025.04–dc21   99-053630

 is a trademark of America Online, Inc.

 is a registered trademark or trademark under exclusive license to IDG Books Worldwide, Inc. from International Data Group, Inc. in the United States and/or other countries.

Welcome to AOL Press™

AOL Press books provide timely guides to getting the most out of your online life. AOL Press was formed as part of the AOL family to create a complete series of official references for using America Online as well as the entire Internet — all designed to help you enjoy a fun, easy, and rewarding online experience.

AOL Press is an exciting partnership between two companies at the forefront of the knowledge and communications revolution — America Online and IDG Books Worldwide. AOL is committed to quality, ease of use, and value and IDG Books excels at helping people understand technology.

To meet these high standards, all our books are authored by experts with the full participation of and exhaustive review by AOL's own development, technical, managerial, and marketing staff. Together, AOL and IDG Books have implemented an ambitious publishing program to develop new publications that serve every aspect of your online life.

We hope you enjoy reading this AOL Press title and find it useful. We welcome your feedback at AOL keyword: **Contact Shop Direct** so we can keep providing information the way you want it.

AOLPress

About the Authors

Jennifer Watson is one of the foremost experts on America Online, authoring over ten books on learning and mastering AOL. Her invaluable compilation of keywords prepared and shared with America Online's membership became the bestselling *AOL Keywords* (now in its third edition). Jennifer followed that up with the popular *AOL Companion,* a collection of AOL tips and tricks now in its second edition, and *AOL E-Mail,* a guide to making the most of e-mail on AOL. Jennifer also coauthored the three previous editions of *The Official America Online Tour Guide* with Tom Lichty, her friend and mentor. In addition to her writing, Jennifer had the privilege of teaching America Online members and staff how to use AOL effectively and efficiently in her roles as a community leader and founder of an online training academy. Jennifer received her undergraduate degree in social psychology from the University of Michigan, a field that serves her well in understanding and explaining the new social climate on AOL and the Internet. Jennifer lives in Ann Arbor, Michigan, with her dog Kippi, an adorable Alaskan Malamute.

Dave Marx is the coauthor of *AOL E-Mail* and a major contributor to Jennifer Watson's *AOL Keywords* and *AOL Companion* titles. Dave's early journalism training lead to a career in broadcasting and music production, and he's zigzagged from technical titles to writing, producing, and back again. After many years as a broadcast engineering supervisor and recording engineer, Dave found a new world of communications on America Online. Initially applying his background in computers, technical communications, and end-user education, he spent over a year and a half as a Tech Live Advisor, helping members use AOL's features and software. For three years, he held leadership positions as a course developer and instructor in Jennifer's training academy. He is now working full-time as a writer and editor in the worlds of print and online publishing

Credits

America Online

Technical Editors
Jonathon Bell, Jeff Kimball

Cover Design
Michael Rossi, DKG Design, Inc.

IDG Books Worldwide

Acquisitions Editor
Kathy Yankton

Development Editor
Sara Salzman

Technical Editor
Kristen Tod

Copy Editor
Ami Knox

Project Coordinators
Linda Marousek, Joe Shines

Quality Control Specialist
Laura Taflinger, Chris Weisbart

Graphics and Production Specialists
Mario Amador, Jude Levinson, Ramses Ramirez, Victor Varela, Dina F Quan

Book Designer
Evan Deerfield

Illustrator
Mary Jo Richards

Proofreading and Indexing
York Production Services

For Tom Lichty,
America Online's
original Tour Guide

Foreword

When we founded America Online, Inc., our objectives were simple. First, we wanted to make going online easy and convenient. Second, we wanted to make it something that would be central to people's lives.

It's clear that we've succeeded. Our focus on improving people's everyday lives is undoubtedly the main reason that AOL continues to be the world's leading online service, with a worldwide community of more than 20 million users.

More important, AOL has indeed taken a place at the center of these members' lives. Every day, millions of AOL users communicate by e-mail and Instant Messages. They check hundreds of millions of stock quotes, spend millions of dollars shopping online, book travel, order tickets, find restaurants, choose a movie, get directions, read the news, get help on homework, do their banking, get loans, access information about their health, play games, download music, and run their businesses.

And our recently introduced 5.0 software offers new features that make AOL an even more integral part of our members' lives — including new conveniences that our members themselves have chosen. What could be more exciting than getting, saving, and storing pictures through our new You've Got Pictures? And what could be more central than keeping track of your life right online with My Calendar — not to mention getting updates on events and activities of interest to you? Even more exciting is the fact that 5.0 offers the first step to the future of computing — with its AOL Plus broadband features and coming ability to send and receive e-mails on Palm Pilots.

But even all these opportunities don't begin to scratch the surface of what you can do on AOL. That's why Jennifer Watson, the author of *AOL Companion* and *AOL Keywords* and coauthor of two previous editions of this book, has joined with Dave Marx, the coauthor of *AOL Email*, to turn out yet another edition of *Your Official America Online Tour Guide*. Jennifer's a longtime AOL community leader and currently coordinates AOL's online training center for community leaders and content providers, and Dave's a former AOL Tech Live adviser.

They know their way around the AOL service — including the 5.0 version. And they draw on that experience to offer you a virtual tour guide to the best that AOL can offer: the unique and feature-rich communications opportunities, the many convenience features, the unmatched range and quality of shopping partners, the extensive range of first-class financial services, the multitude of news and information sources, the entertainment guides — and most important, the living breathing community of members.

My hope is that with the new *Your Official America Online Tour Guide*, you'll find AOL at the center of your life as well — bringing you new value, convenience . . . and fun.

Steve Case
Chairman and CEO, America Online, Inc.

Preface

We can still remember our first timid moves into the world of America Online. A poke here in search of a stock quotation, a jab there for some computer/tech knowledge. It didn't take long to find out there was something else afoot here. There were people. Real people who were reaching out in every direction, straining to make contact. You could feel the tendrils of emotion hidden behind simple black-on-white text and sense the hurt and frustration when our first clumsy attempts at communication failed to convey our intended meaning. It was all so ephemeral, yet more real than many of our face-to-face interactions. We just *had* to master it and become full-fledged members of this brave new community.

Of course, there was information, and news. We learned our way around search engines and into Gopher and FTP space while the World Wide Web was first being spun. We tried every resource and tried out a ridiculous number of free programs before we had any reason to fear viruses. And we searched. If it was a research library, it was the noisiest library around. We could chat with our friends, pass notes under the table, shout questions at the top of our lungs, all while our electronic desktops were cluttered with search tools and buried under page after page of information.

And we loved it, and nurtured it, and championed it to the world. And as we labored to make our chat rooms and forums friendlier and more comprehensive and easier to navigate, the folks back in Virginia were creating better and better software and systems and finding more and more ways to make the online experience rewarding for the membership. And despite the technical glitches and growing pains, we saw AOL grow from 200,000 members to a million, five million, and four times five million.

It's hard to believe how mature, confident, and polished AOL has become over the years, but it has. We know that the America Online you are now first discovering will be as exciting for you as it has been for us. If the past is any measure of the future, you, too, will look back in a few years and marvel at how far you and AOL have come together.

Who Should Read This Book?

Are you an AOL member, or are you considering a membership? Then this book is for you! We present a broad overview of the many features and areas that make up AOL's software and services. We know it will be valuable to everyone, but it will be most valuable to the new member. In the space allotted, we can't possibly explore the richness and depth of AOL in the kind of detail that we would like. Even so, we hope to paint a picture that will leave you eager to dive in and make AOL your home, or open your eyes to new possibilities and understanding.

What Hardware and Software Do You Need?

This edition is written about America Online software version 5.0 for Windows 95 and Windows 98. The software requires a PC-compatible Pentium-class computer with at least 16MB RAM; 30MB available hard disk space; 640×480, 256 color or better display (optimized for 800×600); 14.4 Kbps or faster modem; and either the Microsoft Windows 95 or Windows 98 operating system.

How This Book Is Organized

Your Official America Online Tour Guide takes you on a step-by-step journey, loosely modeled on a travel guide. It is organized into four parts: the preparations and information needed before the journey begins; sending and receiving e-mail; meeting fellow AOL members; and a grand tour of AOL's programming channels and online areas. Three appendices and a glossary follow the main text to provide detailed background information on software installation and configuration, keyword shortcuts, and online terms.

Part I: Embarking on Your Online Journey

Part I begins with a broad description of AOL and the service it offers, and introduces readers to the creation of the screen names and passwords they need in order to sign on and use the service. As reader's online travels will bring them in contact with people of all descriptions online safety, parental concerns and online etiquette come next. Readers are then taken on a tour of the main AOL window so they'll know how to find their way around during the course of their journey. Attention is also given to the basics of common Windows features, which will be essential for a pleasant journey. Finally, the reader learns of the many ways he/she can find additional help and information, both offline and online.

Part II: Communicating with the World

This part is dedicated solely to e-mail, one of the pivotal features of AOL E-mail is the first mode of online communication most members will use. Mastery of e-mail and its many features empowers members for the journey yet to come.

Part III: Meeting the Locals

Once the reader is familiar with e-mail he/she can begin to explore the many other modes of online communication — Chat, Instant Messages, Message Boards, and Internet Newsgroups.

Part IV: Site-Seeing and Souvenirs

Now that our travelers are comfortable on the "streets" of AOL and know how to mingle with the natives, we can begin our grand tour of the sights and sites that make up AOL's programming channels. We visit software libraries to collect downloads, browse the online shopping bazaar, and pay a visit to every programming channel. Finally, our seasoned traveler are shown how to search and explore on their own.

Windows and Macintosh Conventions

This book primarily covers the Windows AOL version 5.0 software; the Mac AOL version 5.0 software was not yet available for evaluation when we were writing this book. When we present information for other versions or for the Mac, we clearly communicate this in the text. If you don't see a notation regarding other versions, please assume we're discussing Windows AOL version 5.0.

Key combinations

AOL offers plenty of keyboard shortcuts for quicker, easier use. Whenever possible, we give relevant key combinations for various features in the text. For instance, Ctrl+M is the keyboard shortcut to open a new Write Mail window. In this example, "Ctrl" refers to the key labeled "Ctrl" on your Windows keyboard (usually located in the lower-left corner). The + symbol indicates you should hold down the Ctrl key while typing the following letter, which is M in this case. A list of all key combinations available with the AOL software is available in Chapter 3.

Navigating Through This Book

Every chapter begins with a Quick Look, a list of key points covered in the text and a brief introduction. The chapters conclude with Independent Explorations, a signpost suggesting further travels. Within each chapter we will call your attention to important concepts and information through the use of the following icons and headings:

Tips provide you with extra knowledge that separates the novice from the pro.

Notes provide additional or critical information and technical data on the current topic.

Definitions explain terms and concepts.

Cross-Reference icons indicate places where you can find more information on a particular topic.

Find It Online icons direct you to a location on AOL or the Internet.

Acknowledgments

First and foremost, we thank you, the members of America Online. You are why we joined AOL, why we became involved, and why we wrote this book. You've created a special community to be proud of.

A very special thank you to Tom Lichty for authoring the first four editions of *The Official America Online Tour Guide*. While this edition is a completely new version, it is based on many of the principles he taught us and so many others in those earlier editions. We also thank him for his moral support and encouragement of this edition.

Thank you to George Louie, who has offered support to Jennifer throughout every book she's ever written. George is also the original coauthor of the glossary that appears at the back of the Tour Guide. Thank you, George!

Thank you to the fine folks at IDG Books Worldwide, who continue to impress us with their professionalism and excellence: Kathy Yankton, Sara Salzmann, Colleen Dowling, Andy Cummings, and Ami Knox.

Lastly, thank you to the many people at America Online who helped us with our questions: Amy Burk, Don Crowl, Ariana Deegan, John Dyn, Bob Greenlee, Kathy Harper, Thomas Jarmolowski, Jeff Kimball, Thomas Kriese, Gary Lampal, Katie Leon, Dick Prouty, Katy Rosaaen, Damian Saccocio, Peter Shiau, Janine Smith, Mary Swick, Jenn Thompson, Annie West, and Shuwu Wu.

Contents at a Glance

Preface ix
Acknowledgments xiii

Part I: Embarking on Your Online Journey 1
Chapter 1: Deciding Where to Go 4
Chapter 2: Traveling with Safety and Courtesy 26
Chapter 3: Finding Your Way 50
Chapter 4: Stopping to Ask for Directions 70

Part II: Communicating with the World **83**
Chapter 5: Getting Your Mail 86
Chapter 6: Sending Your Mail 106
Chapter 7: Moving Beyond E-Mail Basics 124

Part III: Meeting the Locals **147**
Chapter 8: Staying in Touch with Friends and Family 150
Chapter 9: Making New Friends 178

Part IV: Site-Seeing and Souvenirs **201**
Chapter 10: Unearthing Treasures 204
Chapter 11: Shopping the Electronic Bazaar 232
Chapter 12: Seeing the Sites: Business 252
Chapter 13: Seeing the Sites: Pleasure 280
Chapter 14: Finding Places and Things 308
Chapter 15; Finding People 324

Appendix A: Booking Passage to America Online 335
Appendix B: Setting Your Preferences 359
Appendix C: Finding Shortcuts with Keywords 391
Glossary 405

Index **425**

Contents

Preface ix
Acknowledgments xxiii

Part I: Embarking on Your Online Journey   1

Chapter 1: Deciding Where to Go 4

About Your Journey 5
     AOL and the Internet 5
     What You Can Expect to See and Do 6
     About Your Tour Guides 12
Planning Your Journey 13
     Passports and Identity Papers 13

Chapter 2: Traveling with Safety and Courtesy 26

Can You Drink the Water? 27
     Online Safety 27
     Terms of Service 30
     Notify AOL 31
Keeping Your Family Safe 33
     Parental Controls 33
     Kids Only 41
When in Rome 43
     Netiquette 43

Chapter 3: Finding Your Way 50

Pressing Buttons and Peering into Windows 51
     Mouse Clicks and Keyboard Shortcuts 51
     Buttons, Icons, and Hyperlinks 53

Windows and Scroll Bars 54

Close, Maximize, Restore, Minimize, Resize, and Move 55

Menus, List Boxes, and Drop-Down Lists 56

List Boxes 57

Drop-Down Menus and Drop-Down Lists 58

Text Entry Boxes 58

The AOL Window **59**

Welcome Screen. 59

Menus 60

Toolbar 62

Navigation Bar 62

Keywords and URLs **63**

Favorite Places **65**

Chapter 4: Stopping to Ask for Directions **70**

Offline Help. **71**

Software Help. 71

Phone Support 72

More Books 72

Online Help. **73**

Welcome to AOL 73

QuickStart 73

AOL Help (Member Services). 75

Live One-on-One Help 77

Member Help Rooms 77

Members Helping Members 78

Help Classes 79

Computing Help. 79

Part II: Communicating with the World   83

Chapter 5: Getting Your Mail. **86**

What Is E-Mail? **87**

Reading Your First E-Mail. **87**

Scanning Your Online Mailbox 87

Reading Your New E-Mail. 89
Old Mail 92
Dealing with Junk Mail. 93
E-Mail Addresses on AOL and the Internet. 95
The Address Book 97
A Tour of the Mail Center. 99

Chapter 6: Sending Your Mail 106

Sending Your First E-Mail. 107
Courtesy Copies. 110
Blind Courtesy Copies 111
Replying to E-Mail. 112
Reply to All. 113
Quoting 114
Forwarding E-Mail 115
Checking Status of Sent Mail 116
Unsending Mail 117
Attaching Files 117

Chapter 7: Moving Beyond E-Mail Basics 124

Saving and Organizing Your E-Mail. 125
Personal Filing Cabinet. 126
Offline Mail 129
Spell Checking 130
Mail Extras. 132
Colors & Style. 132
Smileys 133
Photos 133
Hyperlinks 133
Stationery 133
Mail Controls. 134
Styled Text. 136
Signatures 138
Inserting Pictures and Graphics 140
Picture Gallery 142
AOL NetMail. 143

Part III: Meeting the Locals   147

Chapter 8: Staying in Touch with Friends and Family 150

Instant Messages 151

Sending and Receiving Instant Messages 152

Turning Off Instant Messages 155

AOL Instant Messenger 156

Buddy List 157

Who Are Your Buddies? 158

Setting Up Your Buddy List 158

Using Your Buddy List 159

Chats and Conferences 160

Finding Communities 162

Anatomy of a Chat 164

Chatting 166

Creating Your Own Chat Room 168

Logging a Chat 169

Auditoriums 170

My Calendar 171

Chapter 9: Making New Friends 178

Message Boards 179

Finding Communities 180

Reading Messages 181

Finding Messages 183

Setting Message Board Preferences 185

Posting Messages 188

Newsgroups 190

Finding Communities 191

Subscribing to Newsgroups 192

Reading Messages 193

Setting Newsgroup Preferences 194

Finding Messages 197

Posting Messages 197

Downloading Messages 198

Part IV: Site-Seeing and Souvenirs   201

Chapter 10: Unearthing Treasures 204

What Are Files? 205
How to Download. 205
File Libraries 207
Download Center 209
    Searching for Files 210
    Browsing Files 212
Viruses and Trojan Horses. 213
Download Manager 214
Automatic AOL 216
Uploading Files 217
You've Got Pictures. 219
FTP 225

Chapter 11: Shopping the Electronic Bazaar 232

Shopping Online. 233
Customer Service 236
AOL Shopping Guarantee. 237
Safety 238
AOL Quick Checkout. 239
Money 241
Gift Reminder Service 242
Shopping Through the Classifieds 243
AOL Shop Direct 247
Shopping Outside of AOL. 247

Chapter 12: Seeing the Sites: Business. 252

Welcome 253
News Channel. 254
    News Search. 255
    CBS News. 255
    Speak Out. 256
    U.S. and World 256

Business News 256

Health News. 257

Entertainment News 257

Life 257

Politics 257

Newsstand 257

Weather 257

Local. 258

Classifieds. 258

News Ticker 258

International Channel **259**

News 260

Business 260

Cultures 261

Fun & Games 262

Travel 262

Country Information 262

Global Meeting Place 263

Personal Finance Channel. **265**

Quotes, Charts, News & Research 265

Departments. 266

Financial and Brokerage Centers 267

WorkPlace Channel **268**

Start-Up Businesses 268

Career Center. 269

Computing Channel. **270**

c|net. 271

Help and Education 271

Communities 272

Download Center. 272

Research & Learn Channel **273**

References 273

Explore a Subject 274

Ask-a-Teacher 274

Education and Courses. 275

Local Channel **276**

Chapter 13: Seeing the Sites: Pleasure. 280

Sports Channel 281

Scoreboard 281

Grandstand 282

Travel Channel 283

The Independent Traveler 284

Cruise Critic 285

Preview Travel 286

Entertainment Channel 287

AOL MovieFone 288

Entertainment Asylum 289

Games Channel 289

The Game Parlor 290

Xtreme Games 291

Game Shows Online 291

Interests Channel 292

Auto Center 293

Home & Garden 293

Pets 294

Food 294

Lifestyles Channel 295

Women 296

Ages & Stages 296

Gay & Lesbian 297

Shopping Channel 298

Health Channel 298

allHealth.com 299

Thrive Online 299

Families Channel 300

Parent Soup 301

Moms Online 301

The Genealogy Forum 302

Kids Only Channel 303

Teens Channel 304

Chapter 14: Finding Places and Things 308

    Searching and Browsing for Information 309

    AOL's Search Tools 311

        AOL Search 311

        Channel Searches 313

        Local Searches 315

        Keyword Search 316

    Searching Outside of AOL 318

        Netscape Netcenter 318

        Search Engines 319

Chapter 15: Finding People 324

    Member Directory 325

    Yellow Pages 327

    White Pages 329

    E-Mail Finder 330

Appendix A: Booking Passage to America Online 335

Appendix B: Setting Your Preferences 359

Appendix C: Finding Shortcuts with Keywords 391

Glossary 405

Index 425

Chapter 1
Deciding Where to Go

Chapter 2
Traveling with Safety and Courtesy

Chapter 3
Finding Your Way

Chapter 4
Stopping to Ask for Directions

CHAPTER

1

DECIDING WHERE TO GO

Quick Look

▶ **What's New in AOL 5.0**   **page 8**

AOL version 5.0 offers many new features and improvements, including more and longer screen names, e-mail signatures, and You've Got Pictures. Choose What's New in AOL 5.0 from the Help menu inside the AOL software for more details.

▶ **Screen Names (Passport and Identity Papers)**   **page 13**

Create up to seven screen names on one AOL account. Screen names can also be up to 16 characters long now. Use Keyword: **Screen Names** to create, delete, and restore screen names.

▶ **Passwords**   **page 17**

Passwords are the key to your AOL account, and should be created and used carefully. The more difficult your password is, the harder it is for another person to guess. You can change passwords any time you are online at Keyword: **password**.

▶ **Master Rights**   **page 20**

You can grant other screen names on your AOL account Master Rights, giving them the capability to create and delete screen names, set Parental Controls, and change your billing status.

Chapter 1

Deciding Where to Go

CHAPTER ITINERARY

Learning what you can see and do on America Online

Creating a distinctive new screen name

Discovering how to create a secure password

Learning how your family members can share your America Online account

Welcome aboard, everyone! We're so happy you've chosen to join us for your tour of America Online. We're your guides, Jennifer Watson and Dave Marx, and we can't wait to see the looks on your faces as we show you the wonders and marvels of America Online. Please get comfortable in your seats and get ready to enjoy the view from the special picture windows of our custom-built virtual tour bus.

About Your Journey

Our virtual tour bus will be making stops at every major feature and service on America Online. We'll show you how to find your way around town and locate a helping hand, how to keep yourself and your family safe in a sometimes bewildering and hazardous environment, and how to use e-mail. We'll also show you how to interact with fellow members in chat rooms, on message boards, and in Instant Messages. You'll learn to download and exchange computer files and photos, shop in an electronic mall, and maintain a stock portfolio. We'll also take you on a grand tour of AOL's channels, from Computing to Games, Health News to Personal Finance, Sports to Travel, and more than a few others in between. Just when you think we're done, we'll also show you how to search for people and information throughout AOL and the Internet.

A tour of America Online can never quite be complete. No matter what we show you on this tour, we're only scratching the surface of what AOL has to offer. We'll do our best to point you towards the best-known highlights and some of the hidden gems; but because AOL keeps growing and changing, no matter what we show you, there will always be more for you to discover on your own. By the time we reach some destinations, they will have morphed beyond recognition or fallen by the wayside and new, exciting features and areas will pop up behind us, before the exhaust from our tour bus has blown away in the breeze. Every day well over 10,000 new members join AOL. It's safe to predict that by the time we celebrate the end of the twentieth century, AOL will have welcomed its twenty *millionth* member, making AOL's population one hundred times larger than it was in 1992. This growth wouldn't have been possible if AOL weren't constantly adding new and improved features to its software and service, enriching the information and communities offered by its channels and forums, and building alliances with major media companies, merchants, and other organizations.

AOL and the Internet

America Online means many things to many people. By itself, AOL is a community of over 18 million members — individuals, families, and companies. Even if you never pass its city

Cross-Reference

We define all these new terms throughout the book. If you stumble across a term that you just have to understand now, look it up in our glossary at the end of the book.

Cross-Reference

If you're not yet a member of America Online, flip to Appendix A for instructions on signing up.

limits, AOL is the kind of diverse, thriving metropolis that can be a home to people of all interests and sensibilities. You can meet and interact with groups of your fellow AOL members in chat rooms; on public message boards; in live, one-on-one Instant Messages; and, of course, through e-mail. AOL's community is so large and its offerings so diverse that you might never be tempted to stray beyond its comforting borders. That would be a shame, though.

America Online is also part of a much wider world, the international computer network known as the Internet. Although AOL is by far the largest "city" on the Internet, it is still only a small part of that world. All the wonders and riches of the Internet are available to AOL's members at no additional charge. You can exchange e-mail and view World Wide Web sites anywhere on the globe, and you might even be able to reach astronauts in orbit through the Internet. Occasionally, the pathways of the Internet can be a bit more crooked than AOL's, and the customs and sensibilities may be somewhat different. Even so, AOL and the Internet make up a global community where nearly any need for information and interaction can be quickly satisfied.

What You Can Expect to See and Do

We've already given you a few hints about what's in store on our journey, but while we're driving to our first destination, we have enough time to go into a little more detail about what lies ahead.

Learn New Things and Explore Old Interests

AOL is overflowing with information on an incredible array of topics, from business and finance to health and hobbies. Whether you're looking for formal lessons, or want to browse around on your own or join a community dedicated to your favorite pastime, AOL has something for you.

Your search can start right at the top with AOL's Welcome screen, where you'll find all of AOL's information organized into 18 channels, each one focused on an area of interest to AOL's members (see Figure 1-1).

Let's Get Technical for a Second

In a technical sense, America Online is a proprietary online service, which uses its own customized systems. You must use AOL software to make use of the AOL service. This allows AOL to tightly integrate its many features so that you can chat, exchange e-mail, surf the World Wide Web, download files, check your stock portfolio, and much more all at the same time, and with great ease and simplicity.

AOL operates the world's largest Internet-access network. You can access AOL from over 140 countries around the world, and once you connect to AOL, you're also connected to the entire Internet. Connect via telephone line and modem, an Internet-connected local area network, another Internet service, a Palm Pilot PDA, or any of the emerging broadband systems using cable TV or DSL telephone service. Even when you don't have access to a computer running AOL software, you can still access your AOL e-mail and AOL buddies via any computer connected to the World Wide Web, thanks to AOL NetMail, and AOL Instant Messenger.

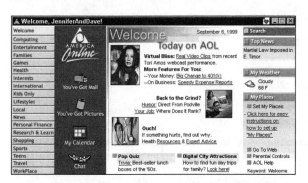

Figure 1-1. The AOL Welcome screen offers 18 channels to broaden your interests and harbor your hobbies.

We'll be visiting each of these channels on our tour, but let's list them here, so you have some idea of what's to come: Computing, Entertainment, Families, Games, Health, Interests, International, Kids Only, Lifestyles, Local, News, Personal Finance, Research & Learn, Shopping, Sports, Teens, Travel, and WorkPlace.

What's New in AOL 5.0

America Online introduced many new features and improvements in AOL 5.0. Here is a list of the best new features:

- ▶ Screen names up to 16 characters long.

- ▶ Accounts hold up to seven screen names at one time.

- ▶ The Welcome screen offers customizable links through the My Places feature.

- ▶ You've Got Pictures lets you view, organize, and share photos.

- ▶ My Calendar tracks appointments, dates, and personal events.

- ▶ E-mail signatures, which you can automatically append to the bottom of e-mail messages you send.

- ▶ Access to recently deleted e-mail for up to 24 hours.

- ▶ Import/export Personal Filing Cabinets and Address Books.

- ▶ Auto AOL sessions work for multiple screen names without disconnecting.

- ▶ Get member profiles from Instant Messenger windows.

- ▶ Long filenames preserved in the Download Manager, libraries, and attached files.

- ▶ Enhanced content when accessing AOL via Broadband.

- ▶ Improved search capabilities to help you find exactly what you want.

Meet New People and Strengthen Old Ties

Can you really make new friends on AOL? Your tour guides, Jennifer and Dave, are living proof. We met right here on America Online, teaching others how to build and operate online communities. *Community* is an important word around AOL. It means that online areas not only deliver information and services, but also create places where people can meet, get to know each other, and share their knowledge and interests.

Community is not just about chance encounters in chat rooms (although chat rooms are a great way to meet people from all over the world). Message boards on topics of every description give people a chance to share their questions, answers, and thoughts with people of like interest. Live events bring thousands of people together for interviews with movers, shakers, and stars — you can ask the guest questions and share the experience with a small group of friends or other AOL members. Once you've created ties, Instant Messages and Buddy Lists help strengthen those ties (see Figure 1-2).

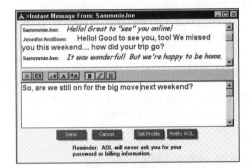

Figure 1-2. An Instant Message brings a far-off relative a whole lot closer.

Instant Messages are private, one-on-one live chats, and Buddy Lists tell you which of your friends is online at the moment. Together these features give you a sense of always being connected to your friends and loved ones. When you see that a friend has signed on to AOL, just send them a quick Instant Message greeting. Before you know it, you'll both be caught up on the latest news, and the two of you can keep sharing thoughts and ideas for as long as you're both online. What's more, it costs much, much less than a phone call since it's all included in your monthly AOL membership!

Finally, there's e-mail, the silent giant of AOL. More than 67 million e-mail messages are exchanged over AOL every day! Millions of members join AOL just so they can hear that famous voice say, "You've got mail!" E-mail can tie together far-flung families, friends, and business associates in a way the telephone or post office never could. You can address one message to dozens or even hundreds of people and instantly share news, views, and even photos with relations all over the world, at absolutely no extra charge. What's more, you may start hearing back from them within minutes!

Manage Your Finances and Spend Money

Everyone has a nest egg to build and bills to pay, and those jobs get more complicated with each passing day. Make your life a little easier. With AOL, you can trade stocks, manage your bank accounts, pay bills, shop for a home, apply for a mortgage, obtain insurance quotes, and get help with financial aid for your college-age children, all without leaving the comfort of your home!

AOL's Personal Finance Channel, the center for all these activities, is where you will find more financial information than you could possibly use. Track your investments with an online stock portfolio, open an online brokerage account, calculate interest on a loan, or find lessons in nearly every aspect of home finance — all through AOL.

Now that AOL has helped make you richer, it can help you spend your money a bit more wisely. AOL is the biggest shopping destination on the Internet (see Figure 1-3).

Figure 1-3. AOL Shopping Channel — shop 'til you drop, without leaving your seat.

Shop for everything for your home, from appliances for the kitchen to a Zip drive for your computer. For that matter, let AOL help you shop for your next home, too! From clothing to chocolates, flowers to furniture, and toys to televisions, there's little you can't buy or comparison-shop for online. Are you going places? Through your AOL connection, you can get airline tickets, theater tickets, movie tickets, and concert tickets, and, if you do your banking online, you can even pay for parking tickets. People are rightfully wary about spending money in the strange new world of electronic shopping, but AOL and its retailing partners go to great lengths to gain and maintain your trust. Your credit card information is carefully protected,

AOL's Certified Merchants Program promises the highest standards of customer service and quality, and AOL stands directly behind those merchants with its own money-back guarantee.

Keep Up-to-Date

When you go online, consider yourself wired to an ever-changing world. How does AOL help keep you up-to-date? It starts with the Welcome screen (refer again to Figure 1-1). Do you have e-mail? What's happening on AOL Today, how's the local weather, and what's the top news story? The Welcome screen has the answers to all these questions.

AOL's newest feature, My Calendar, keeps an electronic appointment book custom-tailored to your needs and interests. My Calendar's Event Directory has lists of online events, concerts, TV shows, and sporting events. Just click the items you want to appear on your calendar, and they are added automatically. You can also schedule events for yourself, your friends, and family. Create recurring entries for birthdays, weekly softball games, or your carpool schedule. Not only will you be kept up-to-date but events can also be shared with anyone else who has My Calendar, and reminders can be sent to anyone with an e-mail address. More details on My Calendar are in Chapter 8.

From the moment you sign on to the moment you sign off, there's a world of news and information swirling around you. Monitor the news ticker at AOL News, keep abreast of the financial markets, and keep your eyes on the sports scoreboard, all at the same time. The current weather report is just a click away. Leave every one of these items up on your screen while you chat online, shop, or plan your next vacation with a click or two of your mouse.

AOL will even send you the information you need, automatically. AOL News Profiles is your own private clipping service. Create a profile outlining your interests, and AOL will send you e-mail containing stories from a wide variety of news organizations whenever that news becomes available.

Contribute Something

The online world is a two-way street where you can share your expertise, interests, and passions with others. Thanks to AOL's connection to the fabled information superhighway, you can contribute your spirit and knowledge to the whole world, or just reach any family and friends who have access to America Online and/or the Internet. Exchange files and pictures in libraries, voice your opinions and experiences on message boards and in newsgroups, organize a chat in the People Connection, and even publish to the World Wide Web — AOL provides the means. Every AOL member (in fact, each one of the seven screen names on a member's account) can create a home page on the Web at no extra cost. And when you have a Web page, you've become a citizen of the world.

Once you learn more (and AOL gives you plenty of ways to learn), your Web page will grow in sophistication. Before you know it, you'll be a regular Webmaster!

About Your Tour Guides

We still have a few minutes before we reach our first destination, so now may be a good time to introduce ourselves and share a bit of our backgrounds on America Online.

Jennifer Watson has been immersed in the world of America Online since 1992. Within a few months, she had graduated from chatter to Chat Host and from there to forum leader for Omni Magazine Online and several other areas. She created the first list of AOL keywords, which eventually grew into an online forum and a series of books (more on that in Chapter 3). On AOL's behalf, she also founded and operated an online training academy dedicated to teaching forum staffs how to build, maintain, and operate online forums. Along the way she became acquainted with Tom Lichty, the original author of *The Official America Online Tour Guide*, and has contributed to every edition of the Tour Guide since. Her keyword list begat the book *AOL Keywords*, one thing lead to another, and today she is the author or co-author of over a dozen books about AOL, Macintosh computers, and her other true love, Walt Disney World.

Dave Marx started on AOL about a year after Jennifer. The first online community he joined was the AOL beta testers' group, AOL members who volunteer to test the newest versions of AOL's software before that software is released to the general membership. By their nature, beta testers learn every in and out of a program, so it was only natural for Dave to share that knowledge with his fellow members as a volunteer in

TechLive (now known as Members Help Interactive Live). During his tenure in TechLive, AOL's membership grew from around one million members to over five million, although he takes no personal credit or blame for that. Along the way he also signed up for a tutorial at Jennifer's training academy, and before long he was an instructor, course developer, and team leader. He also began helping Jennifer with her first book, *AOL Keywords*, and has since contributed to or cowritten over eight books with Jennifer.

Planning Your Journey

Before you embark on your tour, there's one more thing you need to do — select an identity for yourself.

Passports and Identity Papers

You can select up to seven identities for yourself and/or other members of your family. Those identities are called *screen names*, and they may come to mean nearly as much to you and your friends as your real name or your street address. Come to think of it, on America Online screen names *are* your real name and street address.

Note

We wrote this book together, so we use the pronouns *we* and *us* throughout the book. When we talk specifically about one or the other of us, we call ourselves by our first names. Now, of course, we didn't actually sit down at the same desk and type together on the same computer. Instead, we collaborated by each taking specific sections of chapters, working on them at our own computers, sending them back to one another through e-mail, and then melding our words into coherent chapters.

Tom Lichty

Tom Lichty, or "Major Tom" as he's known to countless AOL members is the original author of *The Official America Online Tour Guide and Membership Kit*. Tom's comfortable, humorous writing style has eased millions of new AOL members into the mysteries and wonders of this still-new online world and for that he is due many thanks. He also deserves credit for recognizing Jennifer's budding skills as an author, for bringing her on to the Tour Guide team, and for teaching her so much about the world of writing and publishing. We'd like to thank him for all he's done, and for passing his Official Tour Guide cap over to us. We can all be a bit jealous of Tom, too. He got to spend this past summer on his boat, while we spent *our* summer writing and writing and writing. Tom is a very wise man!

A screen name travels with you wherever you go on AOL, whether you're in a chat room, posting to a message board, or writing e-mail. Your screen name is your chat "handle" (to borrow a term from CB radio) and it's also your e-mail address. If you write e-mail to JenniferAndDave from your AOL account, it'll come straight to us. If a friend on the Internet sends us e-mail, it will be addressed to JenniferAndDave@aol.com. Why the difference? The @aol.com (pronounced "At A O L dot com") part of the second address is like the city, state, and country on a regular postal address. Folks out on the Internet have to specify that our e-mail be sent to AOL instead of some other online service. AOL knows that e-mail lacking the @ symbol gets delivered locally.

Of course, a person with seven names could drive a customs official a bit crazy. It's as if everyone using AOL was a secret agent, donning a disguise and crossing borders undetected. However, in the online world, having all these names affords you some real benefits. They allow you to separate business activities from pleasure. You can have one "regular" name for family and friends to use and one for the personality you present in a favorite chat room. If you join an e-mail discussion group (or two), a different name helps you separate all the discussion group e-mail from the rest of your correspondence.

Every screen name on an account comes with its own rights and privileges. Each screen name has its own Buddy List, Personal Filing Cabinet, Online Mailbox, member profile, News Profile, Interest Profile, Stock Portfolios, e-mail signatures, WWW home page, FTP storage, and online calendar (you'll learn about these features later in the book). AOL recognizes your screen name no matter where you go so that you never have to identify yourself. Any message you send automatically carries your return address, and every line of chat is captioned with your screen name.

The most important benefit of those seven names, though, is that each member of your family can have his or her own name (unless your family is the size of the Brady Bunch). This is more than just convenience, as this allows your family to save the expense of additional AOL accounts for various members of your family. Additionally, AOL's Parental Controls allow you to custom-tailor your family's access to AOL's many features on a screen-name–by–screen-name basis. Thanks to Parental Controls, AOL knows exactly what your children are allowed to do and see online.

For all these reasons (and especially the last), it's important that every member of your family with access to AOL has his or her own screen name, and parents should be sure that junior members of the family only have access to only their own screen name. If screen names are your passport to AOL, your passwords are your identity papers. Each screen name requires a separate password, each password should be unique, and those passwords should all be carefully safeguarded. After all, if someone other than you has your password, they can pose as you, and you will be held responsible for their actions. This is especially important for parents, since your kids could assume your identity and change the Parental Controls on their own screen names. Children should also know to carefully safeguard their own passwords. If one of their "friends" uses that password to borrow your child's identity and violates AOL's rules, AOL can cancel your AOL membership, and the whole family is out of luck.

Cross-Reference

Read more about Parental Controls in Chapter 2.

Note

Never give your password to anyone for any reason, not even to someone claiming to be AOL staff. AOL staff will never ask you for your password online.

Choosing Screen Names

Think about it for a second. AOL may have 20 million members by now, and each of those members may have seven screen names. That's 140 million possible screen names on AOL! Consider that every one of those screen names has to be unique, and the problems become absolutely mind-boggling. After all, there are probably tens of thousands of John Smiths in the United States, but there can be only one John Smith on AOL. And what if you wanted to be known only by your first name? Can you imagine the odds against becoming the only Jennifer on AOL? Suffice it to say, for names like that, you can be sure someone else got there first!

Devising an absolutely unique screen name can be quite a creative challenge, and finding out that the wonderfully imaginative name you cooked up has already been used by someone else can be the height of frustration. It always pays to have one or two names in reserve, just in case your first choice has been taken.

There are also a few tricks you may be tempted to try if your first choice isn't possible, but we don't recommend them. For example, you can use a zero in place of the letter O, or a one in place of the letter l. The problem with this is people will misread your name and send e-mail to the wrong person. Somewhat safer are intentional misspellings, like *Dayve*

Note

Internet e-mail addresses do not permit spaces, so John Doe becomes JohnDoe@aol.com.

Tip

It pays to click the More About Screen Names button when you visit the Screen Name area to read the complete AOL Screen Name Guidelines.

instead of *Dave*. Still, people will forget the misspelled version and send their e-mail to Dave anyway. Additional screen name limitations are as follows:

- ▶ AOL also places some limits on the kinds of names you can create (or continue to use).
- ▶ All screen names can contain up to 16 characters (including spaces).
- ▶ All screen names must begin with a letter, rather than a number. (AOL automatically capitalizes the first letter in the name.)
- ▶ Screen names may be any combination of numbers and letters, but punctuation marks and symbols such as & can't be used.
- ▶ Screen names may contain any combination of upper- and lowercase letters, and AOL will always display your name the way you first typed it. However, screen names are not case sensitive or space sensitive. There's only one John Doe, so whether your friends address their e-mail to John Doe or johndoe, it will still arrive at your doorstep.
- ▶ Screen names are the property of AOL and are only yours to use for so long as you continue to be a member.
- ▶ Some screen names cannot be created. Certain terms such as HOST are reserved for AOL staff. Vulgar terms and terms that may be used in a fraudulent manner may also be recognized and rejected if you use them when you try to create the name.
- ▶ You may not pose as someone else. This goes for AOL staff identities, celebrity names, government officials, private individuals, and company names and trade-marks that do not belong to you.
- ▶ Screen names may not contain sexually explicit, vulgar, suggestive, or racially or ethnically offensive language. They also can't include telephone numbers, include or promote a Web site, include individually identifiable information about a minor (such as full name, home address, Social Security number, telephone number, or name of their school), or advertise products or services.

Now that you've made a short list of screen names you'd like to use, create a good password for your screen name. When you're done with that, we'll show you how to add the screen name to your account.

Setting Passwords

Passwords are the key to your account, so make sure your key is difficult to copy or guess. Longer passwords are more difficult to guess than short ones. Passwords should not contain easy-to-guess information about you or family members (don't use the name of the family dog, for instance). Totally random passwords containing a combination of letters and numbers are much more secure, but much harder to remember. A reasonable substitute is to choose the initials of an easy-to-remember phrase, such as "Four score and seven years ago . . ." (FSASYA) and intersperse it with numbers, such as F4SAS7YA. We don't recommend this particular example, though, as the phrase is much too well known, and the numbers are direct substitutes for the words in the phrase (besides, you should never use passwords you've seen in examples). Choose a line from a favorite poem or song, and make sure the numbers are unrelated to the phrase.

You probably will want to write down your password in case you forget it. If you do, be sure it's in a secure place. People have a way of losing their daily planner, and if you write the password on a sticky note and put it on your computer monitor or hide it under your keyboard, you may as well not use a password at all.

To change a password, sign on to AOL, click the My AOL icon on the AOL toolbar, and select Passwords from the menu; or use Keyword: **Password**. AOL presents some brief advice about choosing passwords, which is always worth reading. Next, click the Change Passwords button (see Figure 1-4).

Note

If you do forget a password, call AOL Member Services at (1-888-265-8004). Once you properly identify yourself as the account holder (have your address and the last four digits of your credit card handy), AOL will give you a new temporary password. Be sure to change the temporary password as soon as you sign back on to AOL.

Tip

Use a different password for every screen name on your account, and don't use those same passwords for other purposes, such as accessing Web sites. If a key is lost or stolen, it's better if it can only open one door.

Figure 1-4. Changing a password requires knowing the old password.

You'll be asked to type in the new password twice, to be sure there are no errors. Each character you type will appear as an asterisk on screen to protect your password from anyone who may be looking over your shoulder. Your new password will go into effect immediately.

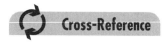

Cross-Reference

Learn how to use keywords in Chapter 3.

Creating, Deleting, and Restoring Screen Names

Once you've selected your name and password, it's time to sign onto AOL and create your additional screen names. Sign on to AOL using the primary screen name (the original name created when you joined AOL). Click the My AOL icon on the AOL toolbar and select Screen Names from the menu, or use Keyword: **Names** (see Figure 1-5).

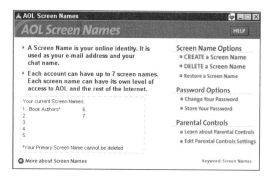

Figure 1-5. Create, delete, and restore screen names here.

The AOL Screen Names window displays all the screen names on your account. You can create, delete, or restore a deleted screen name; change and store passwords; and access Parental Controls, all from the handy Screen Names window. It pays to review all the information provided in this window.

For now, click CREATE a Screen Name. Review the instructions presented and then click the Create Screen Name button. The screen name process takes four steps: choosing a screen name, choosing a password, selecting an access level, and accepting the new screen name and its attributes. Step 1 of 4 asks you to type in the screen name you desire (see Figure 1-6).

AOL will check its records, and if the name you want is available, you'll move on to the next step. If it is already an active screen name or has been used sometime in the recent past, you'll be advised to try a different name. If the next name you try has also been used, AOL will recommend a name that will work (although it probably won't be very appealing to you). You can keep trying until you succeed, though.

Once you have an acceptable name, you are asked to enter a password in Step 2. You remember the password you created in advance, right? (See Figure 1-7.)

Step 1 of 4: Choose a Screen Name

AOL Screen Names

Step 1 of 4: Choose a Screen Name

Screen names can be between 3 to 16 characters and can contain letters, numbers, and spaces. The first character must be a letter and will be capitalized automatically. The rest of the characters will appear just as you enter them.

Reminder: When creating a screen name for a child, we recommend that you do not use the child's full name. A screen name is public and can be viewed by others online.

Examples: Ski Racer, Skatr12345

Please enter the screen name you want to use:

We Love Books

Continue   Cancel

Figure 1-6. Type in your first choice for a screen name.

Cross-Reference

For more information about Parental Controls, see Chapter 2.

Step 2 of 4: Choose a password

AOL Screen Names

Step 2 of 4: Choose a Password

Your password should be easy for you to remember, but not for others to guess. If your AOL password can be easily guessed, your AOL account is not secure.

Reminder: America Online employees will never ask you for your password. If you have children online, tell them that their password is secret and shouldn't be shared with anyone except a parent.

To protect your AOL account, choose a password that incorporates these easy rules:
- Make your password at least 6 characters in length.
- Include a combination of numbers and letters (e.g. 1x556w or bel4jar2 or 12hat93).
- Do NOT use your first name, your screen name, or other obvious words.

Please enter the password you would like twice:

********   ********

Continue   Cancel

Figure 1-7. Type your sufficiently complicated and hard-to-guess password twice.

Once you've typed in your password, AOL asks you to choose a parental control setting for the new name in Step 3. You have four choices: General Access (18+), Mature Teen (16–17), Young Teen (13–15), or Kids Only (12 and under). See Figure 1-8.

Step 3 of 4: Select a Parental Controls setting

AOL Screen Names

Step 3 of 4: Select a Parental Controls Category

Parental Controls let you choose the people and information this screen name can interact with online. Select the appropriate category for the user of this screen name.

⦿ General Access (18+)   Allows full access to all features and content on AOL and the Web.

○ Mature Teen (16-17)   Allows access to most AOL features and content. Web sites and Newsgroups with explicitly mature content and Premium Services are blocked.

○ Young Teen (13-15)   Allows access to age-appropriate features on AOL and the Web. Premium Services, private and member-created chat rooms, and Instant Message™ notes are blocked.

○ Kids Only (12 & Under)   Allows access only to age-appropriate features, chat and content through AOL's Kids Only channel and the Web. Premium Services and Instant Message™ notes are blocked.

Continue

Figure 1-8. Choose the appropriate access level for your new screen name.

Master Rights

If you designate a new screen name as General Access, you can also assign it Master Rights. This is an appropriate setting for you, your spouse, or business partner, but not for most others. When a screen name has Master Rights, it can be used to create and delete screen names, modify Parental Controls restrictions for all other screen names, and change your AOL billing information. That's a lot of power, which shouldn't be given to just anyone, or be allowed to fall into the wrong hands.

Once Parental Controls have been set, you are offered the option to customize the parental control settings (see Figure 1-9).

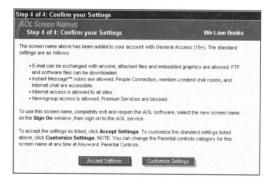

Figure 1-9. Accept the current settings for now, or click Customize Settings if you know how to set Parental Controls.

For now, you'll probably want to pass on this option. After you press the Accept Settings button, the new screen name is ready to use. AOL displays it in the AOL Screen Names window (see Figure 1-10).

If you assigned Parental Controls to the screen name, sign off AOL and exit the AOL software to be sure the Parental Controls are properly established. When you next use AOL, click the arrow button to the right of the Select Screen Name box, and you'll see the new name on the drop-down list.

What happens when you tire of a screen name, or you've used all seven available names and you need to create a new one?

You can delete any screen name on your account with the exception of the name created when you established your account. Just return to the Screen Name area — click the My AOL icon on the AOL toolbar and select Screen Names, or use Keyword: **Names**, and click the DELETE a Screen Name button.

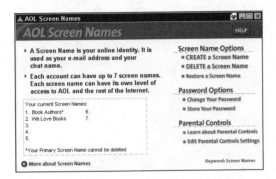

Note

Be sure to write down the password of a screen name before you delete it. That password will still be in effect if you restore that particular screen name.

Figure 1-10. Your new screen name is added to the list in the lower-left corner of the window.

If you delete a screen name by accident (or on purpose), you have a six-month grace period during which you can restore the old name (provided there is an unused screen name slot on your account). All you have to do is return to the Screen Names area and click the Restore a Screen Name button.

Sharing the Computer

Once you have an AOL membership, you may be amazed at how much competition there is to use your computer. Since you probably already know how to resolve battles over the TV remote control, we'll leave it to you to decide how to share the computer. However, you should probably know about some of the AOL features that affect shared accounts.

In the past, AOL's reputation suffered because of the long delays folks could encounter when trying to sign onto the service. Although AOL has made enormous strides toward reducing or eliminating those problems, it can still take a bit of time to sign off and sign back on to AOL when you or a family member wants to use a different screen name. You don't have to wait so long, though. Just use the Switch Screen Name feature. While you're signed on, click Sign Off on the AOL menu bar at the top of your screen and select Switch Screen Name. Then select the desired screen name, enter the password, and start using the other screen name in a matter of seconds (see Figure 1-11).

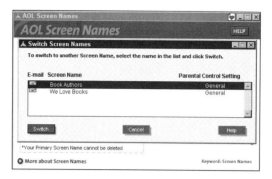

Figure 1-11. The Switch Screen Names window even shows you which screen names have e-mail and what parental control settings are assigned to each name.

Another concern for computer sharing is security. AOL provides a feature called Stored Passwords. Store Passwords lets you store your sign-on password on your computer's hard disk. Once you activate this feature, you or anyone with access to your computer can sign on to AOL without entering a password. You certainly wouldn't want your children or employees signing on in your name. One exception to this rule is with a child's password. If you store a child's password, they don't have to learn their password at all, and that means they can't tell it to anyone else, either. This can be a good thing. With more than one child, this feature again becomes risky, since Tommy could sign on as Patty and do a bit of mischief.

Another aspect of the Store Passwords feature protects your Personal Filing Cabinet (PFC). This feature, which we describe in Chapter 7, can automatically save all your e-mail onto your hard disk. It's a great feature, but unless you add a password for your PFC, anyone with access to your computer can read your stored e-mail. Although we believe in honesty between spouses, there may be things in your e-mail that your children shouldn't be reading.

Independent Explorations

AOL wants to be sure your experience as a new member is satisfying. As you may have already noticed, AOL recommends this book to every new member, and extends an invitation to take a new member tour of AOL and its features. If you haven't already taken the tour, why not check it out? We even guide you through this tour in Chapter 4.

Before we go much further, we'd like to address an important topic: online safety and courtesy. So turn the page and let's get started!

CHAPTER

2

TRAVELING WITH SAFETY
AND COURTESY

Quick Look

▶ **AOL Neighborhood Watch**   **page 27**

Learn how to keep yourself and your family safe at AOL Neighborhood Watch. Advisories, tools, and resources are available to help you safeguard your account and personal information while online. Use Keyword: **Neighborhood Watch** to reach the area quickly.

▶ **Terms of Service**   **page 30**

The AOL Terms of Service, which you agreed to at sign-up, contains your rights and responsibilities as an AOL member. To read the Terms of Service in their entirety, visit Keyword: **TOS**.

▶ **Notify AOL**   **page 31**

When you observe another member violate the Terms of Service, you may report it at Notify AOL. Use Keyword: **Notify AOL** to report inappropriate activity witnessed in chat, e-mail, files, Instant Messages, message boards, Web pages, screen names, or profiles.

▶ **Parental Controls**   **page 33**

Take control of your family's online experience with Parental Controls. You can block e-mail, Instant Messages, chat rooms, file downloads, premium services, and more at Keyword: **Parental Controls**.

Chapter 2

Traveling with Safety and Courtesy

CHAPTER ITINERARY

Protecting your family and personal information

Understanding AOL's community standards, the Terms of Service

Applying Parental Controls to keep kids safe

Respecting others with online etiquette

Whenever you think about visiting strange new destinations, your mind is likely to drift towards safety concerns. Can you drink the water? Is it safe to walk the streets? How can you protect your family? Can you call for help in a foreign language? So before we venture out onto the streets of America Online, let's sit down and talk about your fears, and what the folks at AOL are doing to make sure your visit is safe and enjoyable.

Can You Drink the Water?

Along with the many time- and money-saving benefits of being online come a few drawbacks as well. After all, every new environment poses its own set of cautions and dangers. Do you know if it is safe to give out your personal information? How about buying something online? Or reading e-mail? These are questions many new AOL members ask, which we're happy to answer here in this chapter and throughout the book.

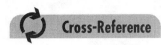

Cross-Reference

Learn how to use keywords in Chapter 3.

2

Traveling with Safety and Courtesy

Online Safety

America Online has over 18 million members, making it the size of a very large metropolis. In fact, according to U.S. Census projections, it is almost as large as the New York–Northern New Jersey metropolitan area! Knowing this, you can probably surmise the importance of safety online. AOL also recognizes the need for community safety and offers the Neighborhood Watch to help safeguard its membership. Use Keyword: **Neighborhood Watch** (see Figure 2-1).

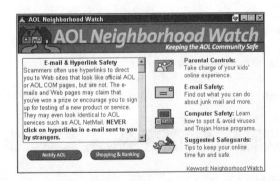

Figure 2-1. Learn how to stay safe at AOL Neighborhood Watch.

Without knowing more about the features and services on AOL (most of which we've yet to cover), many of the topics at Neighborhood Watch simply won't make sense yet. So let's go through each one, introduce it, and explain it or point you to the chapter where you can find more details.

Parental Controls are settings that allow the master account holder to restrict access to potentially dangerous or adult areas on AOL and the Internet. Click the button to go directly to the Parental Controls area, which we discuss in detail later in this chapter.

Although e-mail has various pitfalls to avoid, contracting a virus simply by opening a piece of e-mail is not one of them. You must actually do something, like download an attached file or click a hyperlink, to contract a virus from a piece of e-mail.

AOL staff will never ask you for your password or credit card information.

Don't use the same password for your AOL account that you use with your ATM card, home security alarm, or other Web sites. If a key is lost or stolen, it's better if it can only open one door.

E-mail Safety gives you control over your e-mail, ways to control unsolicited mail, methods of avoiding objectionable or dangerous e-mail, and information on computer viruses. We discuss e-mail in great detail in Chapters 5, 6, and 7.

Computer Safety offers help and information on safeguarding your computer from viruses and Trojan Horses. We discuss viruses and Trojan Horses in detail in Chapter 10.

Suggested Safeguards recommends password protection tips, describes online scams and schemes, details Privacy Preferences settings, and discusses online etiquette, kids' online safety, and Internet safety resources. We discuss password creation and protection in Chapter 1 and Privacy Preferences in Appendix B, and the rest is covered in this chapter.

Along the bottom of the Neighborhood Watch window are two buttons: Notify AOL and Shopping & Banking. Notify AOL is a way to let AOL know when you encounter inappropriate behavior or activities online, and we discuss it in the next section of this chapter. Shopping & Banking offers reassurances on the safety of shopping and banking online, which are covered in Chapter 11.

Are you eager to begin your adventures online now before you continue through the book? If so, online safety is still a concern, so we've prepared a list of top ten "travel advisories" to protect you and safeguard your account (see the "Top Ten Travel Advisories" sidebar). Read them, live them, love them. They will save you, your account, and your sanity.

Top Ten Travel Advisories

1. *Devise complicated passwords for each of your screen names.* Make your password as long as possible (at least six characters, preferably eight), and use a combination of numbers and letters. See Chapter 1 for more password creation tips.

2. *Protect your password like the crown jewels.* Never divulge your password to anyone online, no matter who they claim they are or what disaster they claim just happened. AOL staff will never ask you for your password.

3. *Make quick password recoveries.* If you or a member of your family accidentally gives out a password, change it and all other passwords on your account immediately at Keyword: **Password**.

4. *Keep private information private.* Don't put your street address in member profiles or tell just anyone your phone number. Be on your guard about divulging information in children's member profiles. Be wary of listing geographic locations, school names, or any other identifying information. We discuss member profiles in Chapter 8.

5. *Lock your mailbox with AOL's mail controls* (at Keyword: **Mail Controls**). Use the feature to block all e-mail you or members of your family do not want to receive, such as e-mail from the Internet, e-mail from specific addresses, or e-mail with attached files and pictures. Mail Controls are discussed in Chapter 7.

6. *Never download files attached to e-mail unless you know specifically what it is and trust the person who sent it.* Attached files are discussed in Chapter 6.

7. *Don't believe everything you read in e-mail.* Be skeptical of free offers, wild claims, or anything that seems too good or bad to believe. Online scams and schemes are discussed in more detail in Chapter 5.

8. *Protect your information on the Internet.* Not all Web sites have a commitment to protecting your privacy as AOL does. Look for a privacy policy and read it before divulging any private information. Web sites are discussed in more detail in Chapters 3, 14, and 15.

9. *Talk to your children about what is and isn't okay to talk about online.* Teach them not to give out any personal information or their password, and to come to you if someone does ask for any information that makes them uncomfortable. Kids' safety is discussed in more detail later in this chapter.

10. *Report problems to AOL.* Use Keyword: **Notify AOL** at any time you're online to file a report. Notify AOL is discussed in detail later in this section.

Looking for a specific reference in the Terms of Service? Check the Index to Terms of Service at the top of the Terms of Service window. Click any of the blue, underlined words to jump to that reference.

Terms of Service

AOL is a community, and it has a set of guidelines for what goes on in its community. AOL calls these rules the *Terms of Service*. Each and every member agrees to abide by these terms when they sign up for their accounts with AOL. Do you know what the terms entail? If not, take a moment now to visit Keyword: **TOS** and read the terms in their entirety (see Figure 2-2).

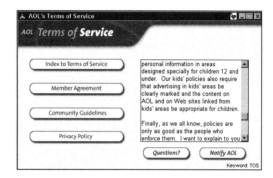

Figure 2-2. America Online's Terms of Service apply to every member online.

AOL's Terms of Service (which most of us shorten to the acronym TOS) contain America Online's commitments to its members as well as our rights and responsibilities as members of the AOL community. AOL organizes its Terms of Service into three sections: the Member Agreement, the Community Guidelines, and the Privacy Policy. AOL prides itself on offering all three in straightforward language, which we can read and understand easily.

Although we don't want to reprint the Terms of Service here in the book (they do change from time to time, after all), we do strongly encourage you to read them. Here are a few highlights and teasers:

▶ You must be at least 18 years of age to be an AOL member (if you are not, a parent or guardian must create and register the account for you).

▶ Posting content on AOL (such as in a message board or your member profile) expressly grants AOL the complete right to use, reproduce, modify, and distribute the content in any form, anywhere.

▶ Chain letters and pyramid schemes in e-mail are not allowed.

▶ AOL does not read your private online communications, nor do they use any information about where you go on AOL or the Web (nor give it out to anyone else).

Note

If you have questions about TOS, click the Questions? button at the bottom of the Terms of Service window. A list of frequently asked questions appears (see Figure 2-3); double-click any one to read its answer. If your question isn't here, click the Ask the Staff button to send your question to AOL's staff.

Don't send replies to unknown screen names to reprimand them for inappropriate behavior. Let AOL handle it.

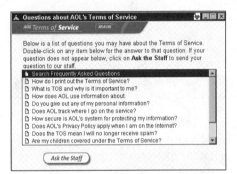

Figure 2-3. Get your TOS questions answered here!

Notify AOL

Once you know what *is* acceptable and unacceptable behavior online, you are in a better position to notice inappropriate behavior by someone else. If you are confronted with such behavior, do what you'd do in your community — notify the authorities. In this case, that's AOL, and you can report a problem at Notify AOL, which is accessible through the button in the bottom-right corner of the Terms of Service window or via Keyword: **Notify AOL** (see Figure 2-4).

Notify AOL lets you report violations that occur in the following: chat, e-mail (and attachments), Instant Messages, message boards, Web pages, and screen names/profiles. Just click the appropriate button on the left-hand side of the screen for the report form. Fill in the information as requested (the more information, the more likely that action can be taken). In most cases, you'll need to demonstrate the problem, and that often requires pasting a copy of the violation into the Notify AOL window. If you're unfamiliar with this technique, read the sidebar "Copying and Pasting," or just click the How to Copy & Paste button in the lower-left corner of the Notify AOL window.

2

Traveling with Safety and Courtesy

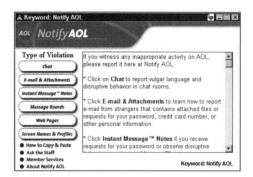

Figure 2-4. File a report with AOL at Notify AOL.

Copying and Pasting

Unlike many altercations that happen in dark alleys, you can record an exact copy of a violation on AOL. If you witness inappropriate behavior in a chat room, Instant Message, or message board, you can *copy* it and *paste* it into your report. Here's how to copy text:

1. Position your mouse pointer at the start of the text you want to copy.

2. Hold down your mouse button and drag your pointer to the end of the text you want to copy. Notice that the text becomes highlighted.

3. Release the mouse button when all the text you want to copy is highlighted.

4. Select Copy from the Edit menu at the top of your screen. Alternatively, you can press Ctrl+C on your keyboard. A copy of the text is saved in your computer's memory.

You should now head directly to the location into which you wish to paste the text you just copied. Here's how to paste text:

1. Move your mouse pointer to the field into which you want a copy of the text pasted and click once.

2. Select Paste from the Edit menu. Alternatively, you can press Ctrl+V.

An exact replica of the text you copied should appear at your pointer.

All reports are sent to AOL's Community Action Team, which reviews the reports and takes appropriate action whenever possible. Members who violate the Terms of Service may receive warnings or even have their account terminated. AOL takes its Terms of Service very seriously. As members, we do not learn what action was taken, but in most cases the Community Action Team will confirm that a report was received and reviewed.

If you receive an e-mail warning that you violated the Terms of Service, yet you feel the warning is in error, read the letter carefully before proceeding. The e-mail should advise you what to do if you feel the warning was unwarranted; do not, however, click any hyperlinks (the blue, underlined words). A recent online scam involved sending fake warnings to members, and the hyperlinks lead to Web pages that asked for personal information. Instead, we recommend you call Ame-rica Online to verify and discuss any warnings you may receive.

Tip

Parental Controls aren't just for setting access levels for kids. You can also use them to tailor an online experience for anyone else who accesses AOL through your account, such as another adult family member, friend, or coworker. You can even use Parental Controls for yourself!

Keeping Your Family Safe

Dave is the proud father of a bright seven-year old who feels at home on computers and it is only a matter of time before she gets online and asks for her own screen name. Dave is concerned about the safety of his daughter. Will she receive inappropriate e-mail? Download files from people she doesn't know? Fall prey to scams in Instant Messages? Or venture into dangers on the Internet? Children are particularly vulnerable online and deserve the care and attention of their parents to protect them.

Parental Controls

Thankfully, AOL recognizes the needs of parents and children. AOL offers what it calls *Parental Controls*, a set of tools that allow or restrict access to various parts of the AOL service. While Parental Controls don't eliminate the need for parents to sit down with their kids and experience AOL together, it does give kids the freedom and security for independent explorations. And it gives parents peace of mind! Parental Controls are accessible by selecting Parental Controls from

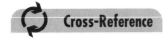

We discuss slideshows in more detail in Chapter 10.

When creating a screen name for a child, keep in mind that screen names are visible to everyone on the AOL service. Thus, we recommend that you do not use the child's full name as their screen name, nor any other information that someone could use to locate your child. More details on creating screen names (and good ones at that) are in Chapter 1.

the My AOL button on the toolbar, or by simply going to Keyword: **Parental Controls** (see Figure 2-5).

Figure 2-5. Parents are empowered with Parental Controls.

Upon opening the Parental Controls window, AOL presents you with an array of choices. We recommend taking a moment to watch the slideshow about the features and benefits of using Parental Controls. The slideshow starts automatically; if you don't want it to play , just click the Pause button.

To get started with Parental Controls, you need a screen name to control. All parental control settings are tied to individual screen names. If your child doesn't yet have a screen name, you can create one using the Create Screen Names button in the lower-left corner of the Parental Controls window. Remember that you need to be on a master screen name to create a new screen name.

As you may recall from Chapter 1, the third step in the screen name creation process is to select a Parental Controls category. Go ahead and set the appropriate level for your child's new screen name. Once you accept the settings and return to the AOL Screen Names window, you can start customizing the Parental Controls by clicking the Edit Parental Controls Settings on the bottom-right side of the window. If there is already a screen name you want to edit controls for, just click the Set Parental Controls button at the bottom of the Parental Controls window. Either method opens the Parental Controls category window (see Figure 2-6).

Begin by choosing the screen name you want to edit. Just click the arrow to the right of the screen name field at the top of the window, move your pointer down to the appropriate screen name on the list, and click it to select it. The small icon of a person next to a screen name denotes that the name is designated as a master screen name. So, as long as you are using a master screen name, you may edit any of the screen names on the account. Once a screen name is selected for editing, the category setting and custom controls update to display the current setting. For example, Dave created the screen name Little Mermaid for his daughter to use when she's ready to begin exploring AOL. When we selected the screen name for editing, the category setting changed to Kids Only (along with a description of what that means), and the custom controls changed to display their current settings (see Figure 2-7).

Tip

To see all eight custom controls, use the down arrow button on the right-hand side of the window.

Cross-Reference

E-mail is discussed in depth in Chapters 5, 6, and 7.

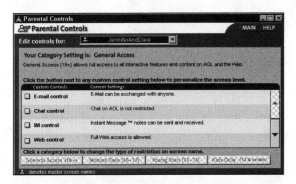

Figure 2-6. Choose a screen name, review settings, and customize categories here.

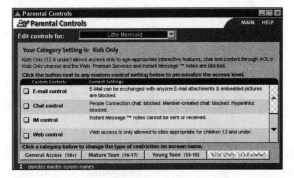

Figure 2-7. Parental Controls offers an overview of the parental control settings for Little Mermaid, Dave's daughter.

If you want to make changes to Parental Controls, you have a variety of options. You can customize any of the eight custom controls in the middle of the window. Just click one of the green buttons next to the custom control to open the customization window. We'll discuss each of the custom controls in turn. Note that our figures depict the default settings for the Kids Only category.

E-Mail Control

Note that AOL displays the screen name you're currently editing in the upper-right corner of the window.

A *domain* is the location of an e-mail address. For example, in the e-mail address jennifer@ passporter.com, the domain is passporter. com. Learn more about domains and e-mail addresses in Chapter 5.

Mail controls let you determine limits on how a screen name can send and receive e-mail, and with whom (see Figure 2-8).

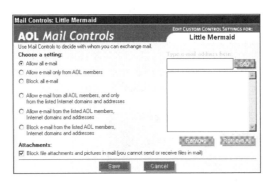

Figure 2-8. Edit custom control settings for e-mail.

The first three settings near the top of the window allow for general, across-the-board control. You can decide whether the screen name can exchange e-mail with all AOL and Internet addresses (Allow all e-mail), exchange e-mail only with other AOL members, or block all e-mail entirely.

The next three settings let you allow (or block) specific e-mail domains and addresses. You can allow e-mail only from AOL members and the specific domains and addresses you select, allow e-mail only from listed AOL and Internet domain and addresses, or block e-mail from listed AOL and Internet domain and addresses. You can list the specific domains and addresses you wish to allow or block by typing them in the top field on the right and clicking the Add button.

At the bottom of the Mail Controls window is the file attach-ments setting. If you don't want the screen name to receive e-mail with attached files or pictures, be sure this setting is enabled. Note that with this setting enabled, any e-mail con-taining file attachments or pictures will be returned to the sender, and the member with that screen name will be unaware that it was sent.

When you've completed making Mail Control changes, click the Save button to keep your settings.

Chat Control

Chat rooms can be a particularly scary place for kids. These real-time conversations are often a little too fast and furious for young readers, and you never know who your kids can meet in them. AOL offers several settings to empower parents to control access to chat rooms (see Figure 2-9).

Cross-Reference

We discuss chat rooms in detail in Chapter 8

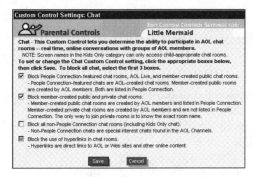

Figure 2-9. Protect your kids from chat rooms with Chat Controls.

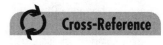

Cross-Reference

Learn how to determine the location of a hyperlink before you click it in Chapter 3.

You can block three kinds of chat rooms. The first setting allows you to block all People Connection chat areas, such as featured chat rooms in People Connection, AOL Live auditorium events, and member-created chats. The second setting allows you to block all non-AOL-sanctioned chat areas, such as member-created chats and private chats. The third setting blocks all the rest of the chat areas, such as conference rooms (found in forums) and Kids Only chats. You can select just one setting, or block all access to chat areas by selecting the top three settings.

The fourth setting at the bottom of the Chat Control windows lets you block hyperlinks in chat rooms. This is strongly recommended for any screen name of a family member who you think may be in danger of clicking a hyperlink without first knowing where it leads. This can result in giving out personal or billing information to the people who will compromise it.

IM Control

Instant Messages are the real-time, one-on-one notes that members can pass back and forth between themselves. The Instant Message controls are simple: You can either allow Instant Messages or block them (see Figure 2-10).

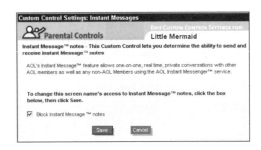

Settings with gray boxes (such as the hyperlink setting in Figure 2-9) indicate they cannot be changed. This may be because of the Parental Controls category chosen (as is the case with the hyperlink setting), or the fact that you may be using a screen name other than the original master name to edit the settings.

We discuss Instant Messages in detail in Chapter 8.

Figure 2-10. Block Instant Messages with a simple click of the mouse.

Web Control

The Internet is a worldwide network of computers, offering rich resources for kids but also inappropriate content intended for adults. Web controls let you restrict access to sites based on age (see Figure 2-11).

The first setting is intended for children 12 and under, and the second setting is best for kids ages 13 through 15. If you'd prefer to give your child access to all Web sites with the exception of those that contain explicitly mature content, choose the third setting (recommended for those aged 16 through 17). The fourth setting allows access to all Web sites, regardless of content.

Recommend a Site

If you know of a good kid-friendly site on the Web that isn't accessible with one of the kid-friendly Web control settings, recommend it! Just return to the main Parental Controls window and click the Recommend or Report Web Sites button in the right-hand corner of the window. Now click the Recommend a Site button, type the address (URL) of the Web site you wish to recommend into the entry box of the Recommend a Site window, select the appropriate category, and press the Send button. Of course, if you discover your child has access to a site you don't feel is appropriate for children, you can report that site as well. Just use the Report a Site button, type the address in the entry box of the Report a Site window, select the category, and click Send. The Learning Company will review your recommendation/report and act accordingly.

Only the original master screen name (the first one you created on your account) can grant or remove the master screen name status to other screen names.

Figure 2-11. Block access to Web sites inappropriate for your child.

Additional Master Screen Names Control

As described in Chapter 1, you can designate other screen names on your account as master screen names. This allows the users associated with those names to create, delete, and restore screen names, change an account's billing options, and edit the majority of parental control settings. Only screen names set for the General Access category can be designated as master screen names. Note the gray box next to the setting at the bottom of Figure 2-12, indicating that this screen name cannot be given master screen name status.

Figure 2-12. Give the privilege of master screen name status to appropriate screen names.

Download Control

Download controls let you block the ability of a user of a particular screen name to download files from AOL software libraries and/or FTP sites (see Figure 2-13).

2

Traveling with Safety and Courtesy

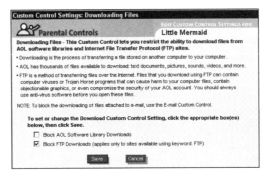

Download from libraries and FTP sites is described in Chapter 10.

Learn more about newsgroups in Chapter 9.

Figure 2-13. Restrict file downloads from libraries and FTP sites.

Newsgroup Control

Newsgroup controls let you restrict access to newsgroups, which are discussion areas on the Internet. They can be adult in nature or contain inappropriate information (see Figure 2-14).

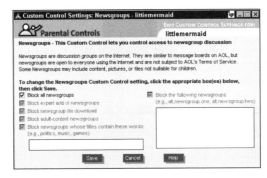

Figure 2-14. Get control of unruly newsgroups with custom controls.

The first setting lets you block any and all newsgroups. If you want to allow some newsgroups, choose instead to block expert add of newsgroups, file downloads in newsgroups, and/or newsgroups with adult content.

The fifth setting in the bottom-left corner lets you block newsgroups with titles containing specific words (for example, you may want to block any newsgroup with the word *sex* in it). Just type the word(s) you want blocked in the field below the setting, separating multiple words with commas. You can also block specific newsgroups with the sixth setting on the right side of the screen. Type the complete newsgroup name, with multiple newsgroup names separated by commas.

Premium Services Controls

Don't want your little angel playing Air Warrior after school? Block premium services and prevent your monthly bill from skyrocketing (see Figure 2-15).

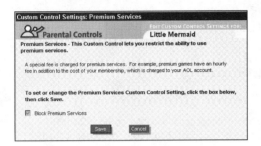

Figure 2-15. Block premium services, which incur hourly fees in addition to the cost of your membership.

Parental Control Categories

If you're in a hurry or don't need such minute control over a screen name's access, you can click one of the general category buttons arrayed along the bottom of the main Parental Controls window. Changing a category resets all custom controls to that category's settings.

To see what settings each category encompasses, just click one of the category buttons. AOL displays a description and the settings of each custom control. You can then choose to accept the new category or cancel.

Are you wondering what members with screen names set to the Kids Only category see when they sign-on? Why not sign on with the screen name yourself and take a look around? We encourage you to do this for all screen names on your account, just to be sure that settings work the way you expect. Kids Only screen names do have their own AOL, so to speak. Let's take a look at the world of AOL through the eyes of Kids Only.

Kids Only

Any screen name set to the Kids Only parental control category is greeted with a unique welcome screen upon signing on to AOL (see Figure 2-16).

Tip

We recommend that you completely exit and restart the AOL software after making changes to Parental Controls if you intend to sign on with the newly edited screen name. If you don't restart the software, other screen names on the account may still be able to edit the Parental Controls (and that's like giving kids the key to the lock).

2

Traveling with Safety and Courtesy

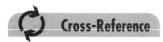

We explore the Kids Only channel in detail in Chapter 13.

Figure 2-16. The pint-size version of the AOL Welcome screen

The Kids Only welcome screen bears some resemblance to the regular version. Weather, e-mail, help are all there, Cool Tips replace the daily features, and a Come On In! button leads to the Kids Only Channel. Wait! Did you set your kid's e-mail controls to block e-mail? Don't worry — if the screen name is blocked from e-mail, clicking the mailbox only results in a note to that effect.

The Kids Help section is a child's version of Neighborhood Watch and Member Services (described in Chapter 4) rolled into one (see Figure 2-17).

Figure 2-17. Kids have their own help!

We strongly recommend that you introduce your child to the Kids Only Help area. Point out the safety tips and discuss each one with them. If you feel your child is old enough, you may also want to show them how they can tell AOL if something bad happens while they are online. The buttons along the right lead to help articles on using various aspects of the AOL software. We also encourage you to show your kids the differences between regular AOL features and advertisements — all ads in Kids Only have the word *Ad* next to them on the left.

When in Rome

Every community has its rules, however defined or loose they may be. AOL is no exception. Indeed, due to the text-based nature of the service, we would suppose there are even more strange customs and traditions on AOL than you've encountered in a while. Even so, many online manners are rooted in common sense and are easy to understand and appreciate. We call our collection of informal rules and customs *netiquette* (as in InterNET + ETIQUETTE).

Netiquette

There's no hard and fast rule to any situation online. But we can give you plenty of guidelines. Keep in mind that many of these guidelines will apply to tools and technologies we've yet to address, so please refer back to this section as you progress through the book.

Live the Golden Rule

As always, treat others the way you'd like to be treated yourself. Be kind, be helpful, and be honest. It is easy to hide behind the computer monitor when you're online, knowing you can sign off whenever you want. Remember that there are real people behind all these screen names online.

Let Your Fingers Do the Talking

Until all our computers have video cameras, microphones, and Internet connections fast enough to handle the load, we still need to rely on text to communicate with one another online. Thus, you should pay as close attention to your typing as you would to your appearance and speech if we really did have audio and video. Use upper- and lowercase letters as appropriate, and watch your spelling and grammar. Avoid the temptation to press your Caps Lock key and type in all uppercase letters to save a bit of time. Typing in all caps makes it look as if you're shouting.

2

Traveling with Safety and Courtesy

You can use AOL's built-in spell checker to double-check your spelling before you expose it to the world. Read more about the spell checker in Chapter 7 and Appendix B.

See our recommendations for good screen names in Chapter 1.

Be careful to send your e-mail to the exact screen name of the individual(s) you want to receive it. Otherwise, someone else may get your e-mail, and if your e-mail contained anything questionable or objectionable, you are responsible for it.

Put Your Best Name Forward

In addition to the way we type, people pay attention to our screen names. Is your screen name the first impression you want to give people? Is it meaningful or obscure? If your screen name contains a lot of numbers, you may want to consider creating a new screen name that better reflects you and your personality.

Respect the Privacy of Others

You should be as concerned about protecting the privacy of people you meet online as you are about protecting your own. If you were privileged enough to learn information about them, don't share that information with others without their expressed permission. Even then, we strongly caution you to not share that information in a public area, such as a chat room or message board.

Put the E(tiquette) in E-Mail

Considering the popularity and scope of e-mail, it's no wonder that e-mail has its own set of netiquette. We discuss e-mail guidelines in detail in Chapters 5, 6, and 7, but allow us to present a few simple guidelines here. First, use descriptive subject lines — no one dislikes subject lines like "letter" or (worse yet) "no subject" more than your readers. Second, when replying to a letter, use the automatic quoting feature built into the AOL software or forward a copy back with your reply — your recipients will appreciate knowing what you're replying to. Third, when sending e-mail to a large group of people, blind carbon copy their names; this protects the privacy of those you're sending the e-mail to and makes the e-mail quicker to open. Fourth, please don't ever send out a chain letter; not only is it against AOL's rules, but it's also very annoying. If we confused you with any of these guidelines, don't worry — we describe subject lines, quoting, blind carbon copies, chain letters, and much more later in the book.

Keep the Bored out of Boards

Message boards (and newsgroups) have similar netiquette to e-mail. Be sure to post a message only when you have something to say. Compose descriptive subject lines and short, snappy messages. Don't write overly long posts that require several trips to the scroll bar. Remember also to quote passages in your replies, just as you should do in e-mail. Keep chain letters and advertisements out of message boards — they are rarely welcome. Finally, avoid personal attacks and emotional responses. If you simply must say something to someone, consider a private e-mail message instead.

Cut the Fat in Chat

Chat and conference rooms offer one of the most interactive experiences online. And as such, it is here that your online manners matter most. We recommend you observe the conversation for a bit before you jump into it. When you do have something to say, make it clear when you are addressing the room or addressing an individual. If you have something private to say to another person, consider opening an Instant Message instead of broadcasting it to the room. Avoid profanity, sexual references, and subtleties; not only don't they work well online as they can warrant TOS violations on your account.

Respect Your Buddies' Space

The Buddy List lets us keep tabs on our friends, family members, and coworkers, and just as easily send them an Instant Message or invite them to join us in a chat room. Remember that not everyone who comes online has the time or inclination to have a conversation, however. Respect their space if they decline an invitation. And if you find yourself the target of buddies' invites too often, remember to use your Privacy Preferences to keep your name out of their Buddy Lists when you're busy.

Mind Your Manners on the Internet

Be particularly careful of what you say and do when on the Internet, such as when visiting Web sites, posting to newsgroups, and so on. Internet citizens are particularly attuned to breaches in netiquette and do not take kindly to crass or inappropriate behavior. Pay attention to your surroundings at all times, seek out and read any posted guidelines, and, when in doubt, ask questions about what is and isn't acceptable behavior.

 Find It Online

Message board etiquette is available at Keyword: **Help**. Just click the Search button at the bottom of the page, type in **Message Board Etiquette**, and voilá!

 Cross-Reference

See Chapter 8 for more on chatting, Buddy Lists, and Instant Messages.

2

Traveling with Safety and Courtesy

Find It Online

Years back Jennifer wrote an article called "Angel's Guide to Communicating Online." It's now considered a classic guide to etiquette and online communication (gee, Jennifer must be getting old). We think it is still good, and encourage you to seek it out if you want to read more. You can find it in the Mac AOL software libraries — search for *Jennifer Watson* (you may be interested in the other results, too).

Independent Explorations

In truth, nothing in this chapter is too strange or overboard; most is simple common sense, which we're sure you have in abundance (you got this book, after all). Now that you've digested the safety guidelines and ground rules, you're ready to start exploring the world of America Online in security and comfort.

The next stop on our tour will get you acquainted with the many navigational tools available online. We'll outfit you with your virtual compass (the AOL toolbar), an online map (the various windows and menus), and even an electronic walking stick (online shortcuts such as keywords and favorite places).

CHAPTER

3

FINDING YOUR WAY

Quick Look

▶ **Keyboard Shortcuts**   **page 51**

Keyboard shortcuts let you speed up common actions, such as opening e-mail or sending an Instant Message. Most keyboard shortcuts are displayed to the right of an item in a menu. We've included a complete list of keyboard shortcuts in this chapter.

▶ **Hyperlinks**   **page 53**

Hyperlinks are the blue, underlined words you see frequently around AOL and the Internet. Clicking a hyperlink takes you somewhere else, such as to a new page or just to new information within the same page. Beware of clicking hyperlinks in e-mail from strangers, however.

▶ **Toolbar**   **page 62**

The bar of menus, icons, and buttons at the top of your AOL window is the toolbar. Use the toolbar to navigate and perform a variety of actions on AOL.

▶ **Keywords**   **page 63**

Keywords are shortcuts to channels, forums, and areas online. Type a keyword into the text entry box at the bottom of the toolbar and press Go to activate it. You must be online to use keywords.

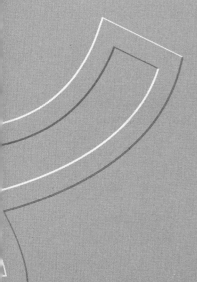

Chapter 3

Finding Your Way

CHAPTER ITINERARY

Mastering windows, buttons, icons, and more!

Touring the AOL main screen

Speeding up your sessions with keywords

Storing favorite places for future reference

Before we board the bus for our tour of America Online, we thought you might like a brief tour of your hotel and your hotel room. Well, maybe we're being a bit silly here, but we're quite serious about showing you how to use the many windows, buttons, icons, and other controls you'll encounter as you use AOL.

Pressing Buttons and Peering into Windows

The keyboard and mouse that are sitting on your desk are very real, but they can be used to click "buttons" and open "windows" on your computer screen that are nothing more than pictures. All these controls are essential to getting maximum enjoyment from the AOL service and software, so without further ado, let's get mousing!

Mouse Clicks and Keyboard Shortcuts

The mouse attached to your computer is an indispensable part of your AOL travels. We hope you're already familiar with how to use it. If not, you can practice by playing the Solitaire card game that comes with nearly every computer.

Now, what about that second button, the one on the right? Every so often, though (mostly when you're working with text or graphics) a click of the right button (*right-click*) opens a small menu, called a *context menu*. Context menus are neat little things, full of just the kinds of options you need at a particular moment.

Now that you know how to use your mouse, we'll mention that many things you can do with your mouse can also be done without your mouse. These things are called *keyboard shortcuts,* and you may find a few that you adopt as your very own. As you open various menus on your menu bar and toolbar, (both of which we discuss later in this chapter), you'll see that certain selections have an extra notation next to the name, such as Ctrl+S or Ctrl+C (you can also use Command+S or Command+C on the Mac). These are shortcuts. Hold down the Ctrl key and press a letter key, such as *S* or *C* (if you're curious, those letters stand for *save* and *copy*). There are many shortcut combinations, and it's unlikely you'll want to memorize them all, but you may find a few of them quite handy at those times when both hands are already on your keyboard. See the sidebar titled "Keyboard Shortcuts" for a complete list.

You can also open and navigate through menus using just your keyboard. Hold down the Alt key and press the key corresponding to the underlined letter in the menu's name. Alt+F opens the File menu, for example. You can also move from menu to menu by using the left and right arrow keys, move within a menu using the up and down arrow keys, and press the Enter key to make a selection. The Esc key closes the menu.

Keyboard Shortcuts

Function	Windows	Macintosh
New	Ctrl+N	Command+N
Open	Ctrl+O	Command+O
Close	Ctrl+F4	Command+W
Save	Ctrl+S	Command+S
Print	Ctrl+P	Command+P
Exit (Quit)	Alt+F4	Command+Q
Undo	Ctrl+Z	Command+Z
Cut	Ctrl+X	Command+X
Copy	Ctrl+C	Command+C
Paste	Ctrl+V	Command+V
Select All	Ctrl+A	Command+A
Spell Check	Ctrl+=	Command+=
Exit Free Area	Ctrl+E	Command+E
Read Mail	Ctrl+R	Command+R
Write Mail	Ctrl+M	Command+M
Send Mail	Ctrl+Enter	Enter
Add to Favorite Places	Ctrl++ (plus sign)	Command++ (plus sign)
Go To Keyword	Ctrl+K	Command+K
New Instant Message	Ctrl+I	Command+I
Send an Instant Message	Ctrl+Enter	Enter

Function	Windows	Macintosh
Locate AOL Member Online	Ctrl+L	Command+L
Get AOL Member Profile	Ctrl+G	Command+G
Find	Alt+D	Command+F
Help	Alt+H	Command+/ (slash)-
Abort Incoming Text	Esc	Command+. (period)

Buttons, Icons, and Hyperlinks

As you navigate through AOL, much of what you do will involve buttons, icons, and hypertext links (or hyperlinks). *Buttons* are on-screen representations of push buttons. In fact, when you click them they'll move, just like a push button would. Buttons are used to perform all sorts of actions — open and close menus and windows, send information to AOL, or take you to another online area. You'll know that an on-screen item is a button if you move your mouse pointer over the item and the mouse pointer turns into a little hand, with one pointing finger (although this isn't true for all buttons). If that test doesn't work, click the suspected button and hold down the mouse button. You'll see the button appear to go in. If you'd rather not perform the action associated with the button, keep holding down the mouse button and slide the mouse pointer to the side, away from the button, before you release the mouse button. The button will bounce back, and nothing will have happened.

Icons are symbols or pictures that represent some important feature or function. If you click or double-click most icons, some action will be performed. For example, a single click of the mailbox icon in the upper left of your AOL screen opens your Online Mailbox. Again, your mouse pointer will usually turn into a pointing hand if it is moved over a functioning icon.

Hypertext links are a wondrous thing, because they're one of the features that made the World Wide Web the wonder that it is today. Hypertext links are words that work like buttons. They can perform actions, such as opening new windows or

Tip

Since hyperlinks can lead almost anywhere (good or bad), it pays to look before you click. To see where a particular hyperlink leads, move the mouse pointer over a hyperlink or button on the Web page. A small caption may appear telling you the destination of the link. If you don't see a caption, look at the bottom border of the page's window. It may display the address or description of that button or hyperlink.

Web pages. You can identify a hyperlink in several ways. First, hyperlinks are almost always colored bright blue, and the text is underlined. You will find some exceptions to this rule. Regardless, if you move the mouse pointer over a suspected hyperlink, it should turn into the familiar pointing hand. One click on a hyperlink will take you wherever the hyperlink leads, and once you've clicked a hyperlink, it changes color to show that you've already clicked it.

Windows and Scroll Bars

Windows are so important that an entire computer operating system was named after them. In fact, one of AOL's old advertising slogans was, "The more windows you open, the cooler it gets!" AOL itself is one large window, within which you can open many other windows. You can have many windows open at one time, some of which you may be reading while you write or chat in others. See Figure 3-1 for an example of a typical window on AOL.

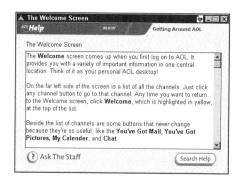

Figure 3-1. AOL Help's article on the Welcome Screen. Note the title bar at the top, with its icons and control boxes, and the scroll bar at the right.

At the top of each window is a *title bar*, which contains text that describes the contents of the window. To the left of that title is a triangular *AOL icon* that hides a control menu. On the right may be a *heart icon* (more about this icon, also known as the *Favorite Places icon*, later in this chapter) and three little square buttons. We describe what each of the three *control boxes* does in just a bit. Each window also has a *frame* around it, a thin border that holds things within the window.

In some cases, the window will also have *scroll bars* — broad gray ribbons running along the right-hand border of the window, and perhaps across the bottom, too. Imagine that there's a broader vista hidden behind the window's frame. The scroll bars let you move that vista up and down, left and right, so that you can see another portion of the view. Each scroll bar has several buttons. There will be a button with an *up arrow* (or *left arrow*), another with a *down arrow* (or *right arrow*), and a square box called a *slider* in the middle. Click the various arrow buttons to scroll the contents of the window. Click once to make a small move, or hold down the mouse button to keep scrolling. The slider has two purposes. It shows which part of the view you're seeing (when it's in the center you're viewing the middle of the window's contents), and you can click and drag the slider box to scroll the contents of the window to a new position. You can also scroll in larger steps by clicking the gray *ribbon* above or below the slider.

The title bar may have a dark background color, such as navy blue, or it may be gray. In fact, that color changes, depending on whether the window is *in front* (or on top). You can have many windows open at one time, but only one window can be in active use. That's the window that's in front, and no other window will obscure your view of that window. To bring a window in front, just click your mouse anywhere within its borders, and note that the title bar changed from gray to blue (or some other color).

Close, Maximize, Restore, Minimize, Resize, and Move

As you move about on AOL, there will be some windows you want to keep around, some you need to move out of the way, and others you'll want to banish immediately.

To close a window, click the *Close Box* — the little button with the X on the far right of the window's title bar (refer again to Figure 3-1).

You can make a window fill the entire AOL window with a click of the *Maximize Box*. That's the button on the right of the title bar labeled with a square. Once a window is maximized, you'll find its control boxes in the upper-right of the main AOL window, right below the main AOL window's own control boxes.

You'll note that after you've maximized a window, the Maximize Box has changed. It now has a symbol that looks

After you resize and/or
move a window, you can
make the change permanent
by selecting Remember
Window Size Only or
Remember Window Size and
Position from the Windows
menu at the top of your AOL
screen.

like two overlapping boxes. It has become a *Restore Box*.
The next time you click this box, the window will be restored
to its original size. You can also shrink most windows down
to an icon. (Click the *Minimize Box* — the one with the minus
sign (–) on it — and the window shrinks down and moves to
the bottom of the AOL window. You can have more than a
dozen minimized windows at the bottom of your screen. If
you look at that little title bar, you'll see the Minimize Box
has been converted to a Restore Box (with the overlapping
squares). To restore a minimized window, you can either
double-click its title bar or click the Restore Box.

Many windows (but not all) can also be *resized*. Resizing is a
great way to make a text easier to read, or to make room on
your screen for more windows. You can make a window wider,
narrower, taller, or shorter. You can even change height and
width at the same time. To resize a window, move your mouse
pointer over one of the borders of that window. If the mouse
pointer changes to a double-headed arrow, you're free to resize
the window. Just click and drag the mouse until the window is
the size you want. If you move the mouse pointer over one of
the corners of the window, you can drag the mouse diagonally
and change width and height at the same time.

You can also *move* a window around on the screen. All you
have to do is a bit of dragging and dropping — click the title
bar, hold down the mouse button, move the mouse (and window) to the desired position, and release the mouse button.

Finally, let's return to that little AOL icon on the left side of the
title bar. A single click opens a small *control menu* that performs many of the tricks we've discussed in this section.

Menus, List Boxes, and Drop-Down Lists

The top of the main AOL window is lined with menus. Each
word — File, Edit, Window, Sign On, and Help — is a menu. Just
click one of these words to open the corresponding menu
(see Figure 3-2). We discuss the function of each of these
menus a little later in this chapter.

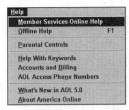

Figure 3-2. Select Members Services Online Help from the Help menu.

Move your mouse pointer down through the menu, and note how each item is highlighted in a contrasting color when the pointer hovers over it. Click the mouse to select the highlighted item. Some menu items are followed by an ellipsis (. . .). If you click such an item, another window will open, offering you a variety of choices. Menu items followed by a little right-pointing triangle lead to additional *submenus*. Just slide your mouse pointer sideways to make selections from the new menu.

List Boxes

Wherever you go on AOL, you'll encounter list boxes. Each list box is another kind of menu that may offer a wide choice of items — forums to visit, articles to read, files to download, message boards and chat rooms to visit, and Web sites to see. Most list boxes come equipped with scroll bars so you can see the entire list. To access a choice, simply double-click the item. See Figure 3-3 for an example of a window with a list box.

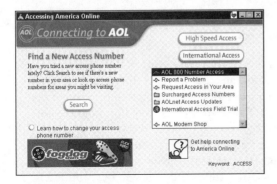

Figure 3-3. The Connecting to AOL window, complete with list box and mini-icons

3

Finding Your Way

Tip

The four arrow keys, usually located between your character keys and the number pad, are useful in moving through lists and menus.

All Grayed Out

As you explore menus, note that some items are in black, and others are merely gray shadows. Such grayed-out selections are choices that aren't working at the moment. For example, you cannot select Member Services Online Help from the Help menu unless you are signed on to AOL. Menu items aren't the only things that may be grayed out. You'll occasionally encounter buttons and icons that are similarly "off duty," waiting for the right conditions before they become useful again.

AOL tries to make your choices easier by providing *mini-icons* to help describe the items being offered in a list box. Text articles are often accompanied by a little sheet-of-paper icon, forums by a file folder, Web sites by a blue globe, and chat rooms by two people in profile. There are many other mini-icons, too.

Drop-Down Menus and Drop-Down Lists

Drop-down menus and drop-down lists are another kind of menu or list box. Typically, you'll see an icon and/or a line of text flanked by a little down-pointing arrow. If you click the arrow, a complete list box or menu appears. The AOL toolbar (described below) has many drop-down menus.

Text Entry Boxes

Whether you're entering your password in the sign-on screen, composing e-mail, looking up a word in the online dictionary, or participating in a freewheeling chat, you'll be using a *text entry box* (or *field*). These are pretty easy to recognize and just as easy to use. If you see an empty white box within a window, you can be fairly sure you've found one. Sometimes the flashing, vertical *text insertion mark* is already waiting for your first word. Other times the box will be completely empty. Just click your mouse anywhere within the box and that flashing insertion mark should appear. If it doesn't, AOL doesn't want your text (for example, you can't type in the AOL toolbar when you're signed off). The Write Mail window has four good examples of text entry boxes (see numbers 1-4 in Figure 3-4).

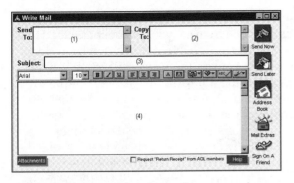

Figure 3-4. The Write Mail window has four text entry boxes. (To see this window, click the Write icon on the toolbar).

Tip

You can move around some windows by pressing the Tab key to hop from field to field. The Write Mail window is a good example of this.

The AOL Window

The AOL window is your home base, and everything you do with AOL occurs within its borders (see Figure 3-5).

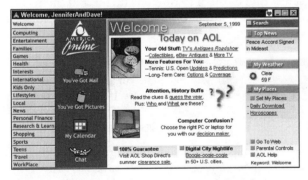

Figure 3-5. The AOL Window in all its glory, with the Welcome screen right in the middle

Welcome Screen

From the moment you sign on to the moment you sign off, AOL's Welcome screen stays with you, in one form or other. By design, it's one window you can never totally banish from your AOL experience. You can minimize it to a small box at the bottom of your AOL window, or you can transform it into a main channel window, but it will never be far from your reach (refer again to Figure 3-5).

3

Finding Your Way

Tip

To customize My Places, click the Set My Places button on the Welcome screen. Now use the drop-down menus to select the five places — such as the Computing Channel's Daily Download or Horoscopes from the Entertainment Channel — you'd like to see on your Welcome screen. Click Save My Changes, and the Welcome screen automatically updates to display your places.

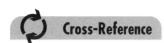

Cross-Reference

Read more about the Welcome screen in Chapter 12.

The Welcome screen offers a wide variety of useful information and services intended to make your AOL experience as enjoyable and productive as possible. Along its left-hand side is an array of buttons that convert the Welcome screen into the channel of your choice. Right next to the channel buttons are a row of large icons for e-mail, You've Got Pictures, My Calendar, and Chat. The center of the Welcome screen is packed with hypertext links and buttons that lead to the day's hot topics and useful features. Finally, down the right-hand side of the screen are buttons that lead to AOL Search, Top News, your local wea-ther report, Parental Controls, the World Wide Web, and AOL Help. My Places, a group of useful AOL and Internet sites you can customize on your own, makes its Welcome screen debut in AOL 5.0 (see the tip for more information).

Menus

Five quiet little phrases stretch across the top of the AOL window: File, Edit, Window, Sign Off, and Help. Each one represents a drop-down menu chock-full of useful functions and features. Click any one of them to open its menu, and then click the desired menu item. Here's what those menus offer (see Figure 3-6).

Figure 3-6. Close-up of the AOL menu bar, toolbar, and navigation bar

File — The File menu has selections familiar to any experienced computer user, including New, Open, Save, Save As, Print Setup, Print, and Exit. New opens a blank text document that you can use for word processing, Open can open many kinds of text, graphic, audio, and HTML documents stored on your hard disk. Open Picture Gallery is a neat feature for anyone who saves a lot of graphics. A Picture Gallery displays the graphics stored in a single folder on your hard disk as a collection of small images, so you can quickly find the image you seek. Save and Save As preserve the e-mail, graphics, and the contents of articles and Web pages you're currently viewing. (The files are saved on your hard disk, of course.) Save to Personal Filing Cabinet comes into play when you're reading e-mail, as the Personal Filing Cabinet is custom-made for storing e-mail. Print Setup and Print are familiar functions to anyone with a printer attached to their computer, and Exit is just one of several ways to close the America Online software.

Edit—The Edit menu is your helper whenever you're writing or viewing text and images on AOL. We cover all these functions in later chapters, but we'd like to note that Find in Top Window is very handy for locating text in a large online document, and Dictionary and Thesaurus are shortcuts to AOL's online versions of these writer's tools. Capture Picture comes into play if you have a scanner connected to your computer.

Window—The Window menu helps you organize, modify and find the windows that tend to fill your AOL screen. Cascade takes all the windows on the screen and arranges them like a stack of playing cards. Tile arranges them side by side, like a mosaic floor. Arrange Icons gathers any windows that have been minimized to icons, and Close All Except Front cleans house by shutting all but one of the windows on your AOL screen. Use Add Top Window to Favorite Places to create a shortcut to whatever the top window happens to be (we discuss this later in the chapter). If you have modified the dimensions of a window and/or moved it to a new position on the screen, you may find Remember Window Size, Remember Window Size and Position, and Forget Window Size and Posi-tion to be quite useful. At the bottom of the Window menu is a listing of all currently open windows. Just click the window's name to bring it to the front, where you can see it.

Sign Off—The Sign Off menu offers two powerful choices. Switch Screen Name lets you switch to another screen name on your account without signing off. This saves time and frustration, as you won't be hanging up and redialing AOL to use the next screen name. Sign Off is a bit different from Exit, as it signs you off from AOL without closing the AOL software. If you sign on and off of AOL very frequently, this is a huge time-saver.

Help—Need we say more? As with most computer programs, Offline Help offers information regardless of whether you're signed on to AOL. Unlike the Help menu for most computer programs, this Help menu also connects you to online resources, such as Member Services Online, Parental Controls, Accounts and Billing, and AOL Access Phone Numbers. What's New in AOL 5.0 is a handy guide to AOL's newest features, and About America Online can provide information about AOL and your computer that the folks at AOL Technical Support may want to know, should you have to call them for assistance.

3

Finding Your Way

The Favorites icon on the toolbar boasts a feature called *My
Shortcuts*, which are do-it-
yourself keyboard shortcuts.
You can customize your shortcuts by selecting the Favorites
button on the toolbar, then My
Shortcuts, and finally Edit
Shortcuts. Type titles in the left
column and keywords/URLs in
the right column (keywords
and URLs are explained later
in this chapter). Click Save
Changes when finished.
Now you can press Com-
mand+0 through 9 to
access your own keyboard
shortcuts.

Toolbar

Right below the AOL menus is the AOL toolbar, a row of
icons that conceal even more drop-down menus (refer again
to Figure 3-6). The toolbar is a very powerful feature of AOL,
and you'll be moving your mouse in its direction throughout
your online travels. At the left you'll find four icons dedicated
(mostly) to e-mail: Read, Write, Mail Center, and Print. Next
come My Files, My AOL, and Favorites. As the names imply,
these menus are the center of your personalized AOL experience. They provide access to information stored on your computer, open AOL features that have been customized to your
needs, and offer shortcuts to your favorite places on AOL and
the Web. Internet is a menu of useful Internet-related features.
Channels is an alternative route to AOL's programming channels. People offers AOL's features for chat and member interaction. Quotes takes stock market fans to Quotes and Portfolios.
Perks goes to the special offers at AOL Member Perks. Calendar
opens My Calendar, your own personal appointment calendar.

Navigation Bar

The navigation bar comes right below the toolbar, and contains
some powerful features for getting around AOL and the Web
(refer again to Figure 3-6). The basic features of the toolbar will
already be familiar to those of you who know how to use a
Web browser, but AOL has gone one step further by extending
its functions to areas within AOL as well as those on the Web.

On the far left, in order from left to right, are the Back,
Forward, Stop, Reload, and Home Page buttons. Back moves
you backwards through AOL windows or Web pages you've
previously viewed (provided those windows are still open).
Once you've gone backwards a bit the Forward button can
take you in the other direction. The Stop button mostly works
on Web pages. If you know that you've gone to the wrong
page, you can stop the loading process, which can be a real
time-saver. The Reload button is used when viewing Web
pages. Sometimes the page gets stuck during the loading
process and never finishes loading. Reload gives you a chance
to try again. Reload will also refresh (retrieve the information
again) the browser window, in case you think something has
changed. The Home Page button takes you to AOL's home
page on the Web, AOL.COM.

Customize the AOL Toolbar

Do you want one-click access to a few of your favorite spots online? You can add their icons to the AOL toolbar! Just open your favorite AOL or Web page, and then drag and drop the heart icon that you find in the upper-right corner of that window onto the toolbar. AOL will then ask you to select an icon for your item and give it a short name. To remove an item from the toolbar, move your mouse pointer over it, click the right-hand mouse button, and select Remove from Toolbar. You'll be asked to confirm your request, after which that icon will be gone. Only the icons in the rightmost section of the toolbar (with the purple background) can be removed, though.

If you want to stop a window while it's still loading, press the Esc (escape) key on your keyboard.

In Appendix B, we show you how to access WWW preferences to replace AOL.COM with a home page of your own choosing.

To receive more search options, don't type your search word in the text box. Click the Search button first to open the AOL Search window.

The wide white box in the center of the Navigation Bar serves a few purposes. As the text in the box indicates, you type search words, keywords or Web addresses within the box, and then either click the Go button, press the Enter key, or click the Search button. AOL will open the desired AOL area or Web page, or perform a search. If you click the little down arrow icon to its immediate right, you'll reveal the History Trail, a list of the last 25 AOL areas or Web pages you visited. To return to any item on the list, just click the item you want.

At the far right of the Navigation Bar are the Search and Keyword buttons, which open the AOL Search window and AOL's Keyword entry window, respectively. The far right-hand side of the AOL toolbar holds one item that couldn't fit on the Navigation Bar — the AOL Progress icon. This is a version of the triangular AOL logo. When you're loading an AOL page or Web page, the icon "swirls" to show you that the requested page is on its way. When the page has finished loading, the icon stops its animated motion.

Keywords and URLs

The shortest route between two points is a straight line, and when you want to go somewhere on AOL, there's no line straighter than a *keyword*. When you know an online area's keyword, you can stop clicking link after link after link in order to get there — just type the keyword. You can type it into the text entry field on the AOL Navigation Bar and press the Enter key. Alternatively, you can press the Keyword button on the Navigation Bar, type the keyword into the Keyword window, and click the Go button (see Figure 3-7).

Figure 3-7. The Keyword window — just type the keyword and click Go.

Your next stop will be your desired destination. Keywords only work on AOL, for areas operated by AOL and its partners, but at last count there were over 15,000 AOL keywords providing shortcuts to everything from AA (American Airlines) to ZOO.

How do you find keywords? When you arrive at an online area you like, look around and see if there's a keyword listed on the window. Another way is to visit Keyword: **Keyword** (or click the Keyword List button on the Keyword window). You can also guess at keywords. Keywords are often easy to guess. If you're wrong, AOL may even suggest keywords that will work for you.

The Queen of Keywords

Jennifer Watson, one of the coauthors of this book, can safely be called the Queen of Keywords. Years ago, before anyone else thought of it, she started distributing free lists of keywords to AOL members and staff. Some years later, she founded the KEYWORD online area, which is now maintained directly by AOL. Finally, she became the author of *AOL Keywords* (MIS:Press), the only book dedicated to that topic. *AOL Keywords* is now in its third edition, so it looks as if Jennifer knows her stuff.

If you try a keyword and a window opens informing you that the keyword was not found, don't worry. If AOL cannot find a keyword, it automatically initiates an AOL Search for you with the results displayed in the window that opened. If you simply misspelled the keyword, AOL provides a hyperlink in the window that lets you enter the keyword again.

URLs are addresses on the World Wide Web. You see them everywhere these days, in advertisements, on business cards, and embroidered on people's shirtsleeves. URL (pronounced "earl") stands for *Universal Resource Locator*, and they look like this: `http://www.aol.com` (which is the URL to AOL's home page on the World Wide Web). You can use an URL just like you use a keyword. Type it into the box on the navigation bar, or enter it into the keyword window. In moments, the corresponding Web page should open right before your eyes.

Favorite Places

The Favorite Places feature can make getting to where you want to go even faster. Each one of your screen names has its own Favorite Places list, which appears when you click the Favorites icon on the toolbar. Once you add a favorite place to your list, all you have to do is click the Favorites icon, select the place from the list, and you're on your way (see Figure 3-8).

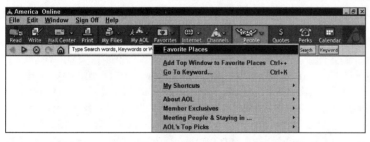

Figure 3-8. Click the Favorites icon on the toolbar to see your Favorites menu.

AOL lets you create a favorite place for nearly any window you can open on AOL, including any place on the Web. Navigate to the place you want to add to the list, and look for the little red-and-white heart icon on the right-hand side of the window's title bar. If it has one, you're in luck. Just click

Cross-Reference

Learn more about AOL Search and how to use its results in Chapter 14.

Tip

Although most World Wide Web URLs officially start with http://www., companies often drop that part and just say Netscape.com or PassPorter.com (for example). You can use that abbreviated name successfully in the text entry box on the navigation bar. If you use the keyword window, you must use the full address.

Find It Online

Our home on the Web is at URL `http://www.jenuine.net`. Stop by and see us sometime!

3

Finding Your Way

Tip

To add a favorite place directly to your list, drag and drop the heart icon onto the Favorites icon on the toolbar.

the icon once, and a small window opens, giving you the following choices: Add to Favorites, Insert in Instant Message, or Insert in Mail. For now you'll just want to add the place to your Favorite Places list, but including favorite places in e-mail and Instant Messages is a great way to share your favorites with your friends. We tell you more about that in upcoming chapters.

Your Favorite Places list can become long and unruly. If it becomes too long, "More Favorites" will appear at the bottom of your Favorite Places list. Select Favorite Places from the Favorites menu to open an editable version of your Favorite Places list (see Figure 3-9).

Figure 3-9. The editable Favorite Places list. Drag and drop the heart icons to reorganize and modify your Favorite Places menu.

You can drag and drop the heart icons to rearrange the items in your list. Click the New icon to create a new subcategory folder, which appears as a submenu on your Favorites menu. Then you can drag existing favorite places into that folder. You can also use the Delete, Edit, and New buttons at the bottom of the window to delete unwanted items, edit the titles (or URLs) of existing favorite places or folders, and even create new favorite places if you happen to know the URL of the Web page. The Save/Replace icon gives you the power to preserve your Favorites list in case of disaster, or to install a copy of that list on another screen name or installation of AOL software on another computer.

Independent Explorations

When it comes to learning how all these features work, there's no substitute for doing it yourself. Go back through the chapter and try every feature you can.

Open a bunch of windows on your screen, and then try reorganizing them. Drag them around the screen, resize some, minimize others, and give your mouse a workout. While you've got all those windows open, experiment with the features offered by the Window menu. Explore every menu and item offered on the menu bar and toolbar.

If you get turned around and lost, don't worry — the next chapter discusses finding and using help on America Online.

C H A P T E R

4

STOPPING TO ASK
FOR DIRECTIONS

Quick Look

▶ **Offline Help**   **page 71**

Your AOL software comes with an entire database of help articles, which you can access while you're offline (disconnected) or online. Just choose Offline Help from your Help menu, or press F1.

▶ **Phone Support**   **page 72**

If you're unable to get online to seek help, give AOL a ring. Member service representatives are on hand to help you with general, technical, and billing questions. Call toll-free 1-800-827-6364.

▶ **QuickStart**   **page 73**

Get off to a great start on AOL with help from QuickStart, an online guide for new members. Use Keyword: **Quickstart** and take a tour, learn AOL facts, get AOL tips, and more!

▶ **Member Services**   **page 75**

The granddaddy of online help is AOL Help, available through Member Services Online Help under the Help menu (or use Keyword: **Help**). Here you can search help articles, get live help, and update your account information.

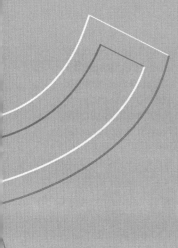

Chapter 4

Stopping to Ask for Directions

CHAPTER ITINERARY

Finding help before you get online

Learning about the new features of AOL 5.0

Getting answers from fellow members and AOL representatives

Registering for a live, interactive class

Searching for the entry ramp to the AOL information superhighway? Pullover and stop for directions! If you're offline (not signed on to America Online) and unable to connect to America Online, we recommend you start with the Offline Help section. If you are able to get online, make a beeline for the Online Help section. Here you'll find directions to the many help resources available online.

Offline Help

We feel that the book you're holding is one of the best offline help sources available. Before you spend valuable time in pursuit of help elsewhere, make sure we haven't already answered your questions in the pages of this book. Use the table of contents, Quick Look pages, Chapter Itinerary introductions, glossary, and index as tools to find what you're seeking.

We don't pretend to have all the answers, or to have had room to include everything we know about AOL in this book. If you don't find what you need here, go to the source — America Online itself.

Software Help

Your AOL software comes complete with a set of help databases that you can access whether you're connected to the service or not. To find them, run your software and select Offline Help from the Help menu or just press the F1 key on your keyboard (see Figure 4-1).

Figure 4-1. The Offline Help database in your AOL software

Three tabs at the top of the Help window offer different ways to find the same information. If you prefer to see the help topics organized by category, view the Contents. If you'd rather see an A to Z list of every help topic, including nested subtopics, click the Index tab. Click the Find tab to search for whatever has you stumped.

The first time you click the Find tab, the Find Setup Wizard appears to create the database from which to search. Just follow the directions on screen.

TTY Service requires TTY-enabled equipment. Callers will be instructed to leave a message for the AOL staff upon calling. A Member Services representative will return the call within 24 hours.

The Offline Help database is similar to help features you may have seen in other programs on your computer. Double-click topics and subtopics to open an article with information and step-by-step descriptions (see Figure 4-2).

Figure 4-2. The Offline Help database has hundreds of help articles.

Watch for words with a dotted line below them — clicking these leads to further clarification or more information. Also note the three buttons arrayed at the top of the help article window. Click Help Topics to return to the database list, click Back to go to the previous help article, or click Print to print a copy of the article.

Phone Support

AOL also provides toll-free telephone support for general and technical questions. Representatives are available from 6 a.m. to 4 a.m. eastern time, seven days a week. Before you call, have the following information handy in case it is needed: your screen name, your account address and phone number, and a detailed description of your problem. The first two items assume you already have an account; if you don't, just be prepared to explain your problem.

Call General Information at (800) 827-6364 or (703)-448-8700 for AOL Support. Upon calling these numbers, listen to the menu choices and choose those that best apply. Hold times are quite reasonable these days. You can also visit Keyword: **Call AOL** once you are able to sign on to AOL — this keyword leads to the current list of AOL telephone support numbers.

More Books

If you're looking for help with a specific topic, you may want to consider other books. For Internet questions, try *Your Official America Online Internet Guide, 3rd Edition,* by David Peal (AOL Press). For e-mail questions, try *AOL E-Mail*

by yours truly, an entire book devoted to making the most of
e-mail on America Online. For navigation questions, try *AOL
Keywords* by Jennifer Watson, with all the keywords and keyboard shortcuts you need to zip around AOL. For a humorous
and irreverent beginner's guide to AOL, try *AOL for Dummies*
by John and Jennifer Kaufeld. For a step-by-step, visually orien-
ted guide, try *Teach Yourself America Online* by Charles Bowen and Jennifer Watson. For a serious, no-nonsense look at
AOL, try *AOL in a Nutshell* by Curt Degenhart and Jen Muehl-
bauer. And finally, for the fun stuff like tips and tricks on using
AOL, try *AOL Companion* by Jennifer Watson. Most of these
titles are available at Keyword: **Bookstore.**

If a call to AOL doesn't solve
your problems, why not ring
a trusted friend, family member, or coworker? AOL is far-
reaching these days, and you
may be surprised at who has
AOL and how much they
know about it.

Online Help

A variety of helpful resources are available on AOL, and they're
all yours for the taking. If you prefer to read, you'll find plenty
of articles and message boards on virtually every AOL topic. If
you benefit more by speaking to someone else, real-time help
is available with member service representatives one-on-one
or in help rooms. If you learn best with a teacher, you can
even take a class on how to use AOL.

Welcome to AOL

The first time you sign on, AOL greets you with a hearty welcome and an offer to learn more about AOL. The Welcome
to AOL 5.0 window is visible to all new members and members with newly upgraded software (see Figure 4-3).

Just click the Tell Me About AOL 5.0 button in the center
of the window to embark on a quick and easy introduction
to AOL 5.0. The button leads to a What's New in AOL 5.0
slideshow. Click the New Features button on the slideshow
window for a quick look at AOL 5.0's newest additions.

QuickStart

New members looking for more depth will appreciate
QuickStart, a guide for new members. QuickStart concentrates
on general features of the AOL service, rather than specific features of the AOL 5.0 software. QuickStart offers five features

of interest to new members: 5 Minute Guide to AOL, FastFacts, Interest Profiles, AOL Tips, and More Help. You'll find it at Keyword: **Quickstart** (see Figure 4-4)

Tip

If you've already dismissed this window in a previous session, don't worry. Just select What's New in AOL 5.0 from the Help window for the same information.

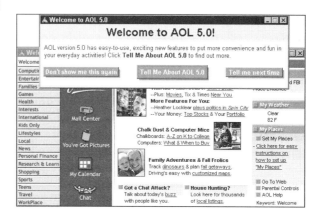

Figure 4-3. Get up to speed on AOL.

Figure 4-4. QuickStart puts you on the fast track to AOL.

The 5 Minute Guide to AOL is a short tutorial on basic AOL features. It helps you learn how to create a screen name and password, send and receive e-mail, get around AOL quickly with keywords and hyperlinks, search AOL, chat with people online, and surf the Web. The second QuickStart feature is FastFacts, a directory of help resources and tools on a variety of topics. This is an excellent resource and one we suggest you set as a favorite place so you can return to it quickly later (or remember the Keyword: **Fast Facts**).

Interest Profiles are almost like a computer matchmaking service for you and AOL. First you create an interest profile, telling AOL about yourself, and then AOL e-mails you recommendations on places that match your interests. AOL will continue to send you e-mail as it finds new forums and services that it thinks may interest you. You can stop it at anytime, and your information is kept private. Complete directions are available in the Interest Profiles area (which is directly accessible with Keyword: **Interest Profiles**).

AOL Tips lead to the AOL Insider Tips collection with friendly, down-to-earth information on getting the most out of AOL. The tips are organized by topic, such as "Using AOL Like a Pro" and "Tips for Making AOL Faster." You can even sign up to have a tip delivered daily to your mailbox. Use Keyword: **AOL Tips** to get to the area directly.

The fifth feature of QuickStart is the More Help button in the lower-right corner of the QuickStart window. If you didn't find the answers to your questions in any of the previous four features, check out More Help. Help resources include a link to AOL Guide Books, information on help buttons around AOL, and a Quick Reference Guide that you can print for offline reading. There's even a link to AOL Help, the next stop on our tour.

Looking for more help using AOL? FastFacts lists five places to look: AOL Help, Members Helping Members, AOL Computing, AOL Basics, and online classrooms. We describe each in this chapter, but the FastFacts list provides hyperlinks to these areas.

AOL Help (Member Services)

AOL Help (also known as Member Services) is the main repository of help information online. In fact, we would go so far as to call it an online guide to AOL, authored by AOL itself. AOL Help is accessible in several ways: Click the AOL Help button in the bottom-right corner of the Welcome screen, select Member Services Online Help from the Help menu, or use Keyword: **Help** (see Figure 4-5).

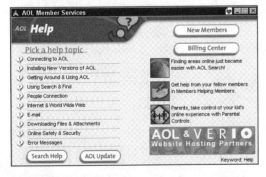

Figure 4-5. AOL Help is always at hand.

Help topics line the left side of the window — click one to go to a list of related subjects, each containing a number of articles. If you're not sure which topic to choose, click the Search Help button at the bottom of the AOL Help window. Now just type in the word that best describes what you need help with and click Search for a list of related articles.

If you don't find the answer to your question within AOL Help, look for the Ask the Staff buttons scattered throughout the area. Ask the Staff lets you, well, ask the AOL staff your question. You can ask via e-mail, in a chat room, in a real-time, one-on-one conversation, or in a post to a message board (see Figure 4-6). Although there is no direct keyword to this area, the quickest path is to click one of the topics at AOL Help and then click the Ask the Staff button in the lower-right corner of the resulting window.

Figure 4-6. Have a question? Ask the staff!

Sending your questions to the staff via e-mail is simple. Just click the E-mail Questions to Our Staff button, decide whether you need general, technical, or billing help, and click the appropriate hyperlink in the box on the right. Now just ask your question in the resulting window, include as many details as possible, and click Send (see Figure 4-7).

Figure 4-7. Type your detailed question in the text box and click Send.

An AOL Member Services representative will reply to your
question via e-mail within 24 hours. If you can't wait that long
for help, we recommend you click the Receive Live One-on-
One Help button on the Ask the Staff window.

Live One-on-One Help

You have two ways of getting live, one-on-one help. One is to
call AOL, as we discussed earlier in this chapter. The other is
to use Live One-on-One Help, an online feature that puts you in
direct contact with someone who can help while you are connected to AOL. Unlike the e-mail–based help, assistance is provided only for technical and billing questions. Just click the
Receive Live One-on-One Help button (as shown in Figure
4-8), click the appropriate hyperlink in the text box on the
right of the resulting window, and then click the Go There button to connect. A new Member Services window appears, cal-
culates the estimated time you will need to wait before help
arrives, and offers a hypertext link in the event you wish to
search the AOL Help database while you're waiting. Feel free
to do other things while you're waiting — you will keep your
place in the virtual queue so long as you stay connected to
AOL. Once your wait is up, a window appears on your screen
along with a greeting from your representative (see Figure 4-8).

Tip

While you're waiting for a
representative, open a new
text window (select New from
the File menu) and type your
detailed question. Now when
the representative appears,
you'll know exactly what you
want to ask. You can even
copy and paste the question
into the window to save some
time and effort.

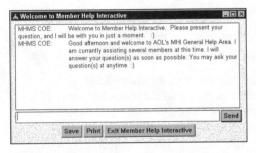

Figure 4-8. Communicate in real-time with your representative through this window.

If one-on-one help is more than you need, or you would feel
more comfortable in a chat room with others, consider a
member help room (discussed next).

Member Help Rooms

You can also get help in chat rooms, which tends to be a bit
more immediate, if a little less orderly. Help with the AOL software (Windows or Mac versions) and general online help and

Learn more about chat rooms in Chapter 8.

If you're familiar with People Connection, you should note that you cannot access the help rooms from People Connection.

tips are available. Links to the chat rooms are only available through the Ask the Staff window by clicking the Get Help sin a Chat Room button.

If you're not in such a hurry or prefer to avoid the real-time aspect of the two previous help resources, try posting a question on a message board through Members Helping Members.

Members Helping Members

In Offline Help, we mentioned that you could ask your friends, family members, and coworkers for help. Now that you're online, you can also ask other AOL members. Members Helping Members is a community of members who gather to exchange and share information on AOL. You can get there directly with Keyword: **MHM** (see Figure 4-9).

Figure 4-9. Members Helping Members is one of the best help resources on AOL.

The Members Helping Members community's main claim to fame is that it offers a network of message boards organized by topic. No AOL employees post in these boards — only members and member volunteers do. To access the message boards, click the Message Board button at the top of the Members Helping Members window (see Figure 4-10).

We recommend you read the topic named Guidelines and Announcements first, which you'll find at the top of the message board. From there, proceed to the topic in which you wish to ask a question or simply learn more. Before you ask your question, glance through the posts to see if it has already been answered. If your question hasn't been asked yet, go ahead and post your question, clearly explaining your situation and giving as many details as possible. Replies are often swift, and you may see an answer as soon as a few minutes later, though in most cases it takes an hour or a day. You may receive a reply to your question in e-mail, though we recommend you revisit the message board itself in the event the reply was only posted and not e-mailed.

Cross-Reference

We introduce member boards in Chapter 9. You'll benefit from reading the section on message boards before you post a question.

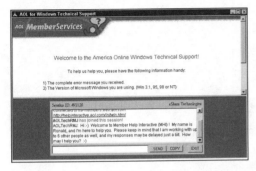

Figure 4-10. Members help members in these popular and active message boards.

Members Helping Members also offers a helpful list of top AOL questions (and their answers). Click the Top AOL Questions button on the Members Helping Members window for the article.

Tip

When you get to the end of this book, you may find that you can answer most of the questions asked by others in Members Helping Members. If you're interested in sharing your expertise with other members, you're free to dive in and start posting replies to posts in the message board. This is also a great way to make friends online!

Help Classes

In addition to the various help resources we've already discussed, AOL has free, interactive classes on a variety of AOL-related topics. At the time of writing, available classes included Basic AOL, Intermediate AOL, Advanced AOL, Basic Internet, and even one on finding help. Classes are taught by member volunteers and are held in chat rooms at specific dates and times. Classes are generally offered several times a day and last roughly two hours, though advanced registration is required.

You can get more information, schedules, and the registration form at Keyword: **Help Class** . Registration is simple and easy — click the Try it Now button at the bottom of the Help Class window, fill out the requested information, and click Submit Registration (see Figure 4-11).

Computing Help

If your help needs run more towards help with your computer than help with AOL, look to the Computing Channel for assistance. Computing offers frequently asked questions (and the answers), how-to articles, live help, a dictionary, and links to other help resources. Topics cover both computing-related

4

Stopping to Ask for Directions

and AOL-related issues. You can get to this help area directly with Keyword: **Get Help Now** (see Figure 4-12).

We recommend you read Chapter 8 before you arrive for your class. It helps to understand how chat rooms work in order to get the most out of your class.

Figure 4-11. Complete the registration form to sign-up for a class. You will receive confirmation via e-mail within 48 hours.

The member volunteers are also called Community Leaders, and this group consists of members from all walks of life. They generously donate their time and effort to helping make your experience on AOL more enjoyable. You can often recognize them by their screen names, which may start with names like Guide, Rngr, and Host. If you're interested in learning more about Community Leaders or becoming one yourself, visit Keyword: **Leaders**. We've both been Community Leaders in the past and found it a rewarding experience.

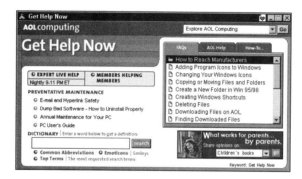

Figure 4-12. Computing offers plenty of assistance . . . now!

We recommend the AOL Computing live help sessions, held every night from 9 p.m. to 11 p.m. eastern time. If you need help outside of those hours, message boards are also available for posting questions. Click the Expert Live Help link near the top of the Get Help Now window to reach both the live help sessions and the message boards.

Another excellent resource is the Help Illustrated diagrams in the How-To section. The Computing Channel prepared over ten figures that show you how to do such things as customize the toolbar and copy and paste (see Figure 4-13).

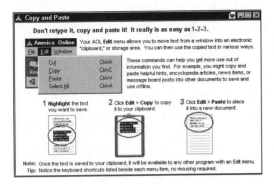

Figure 4-13. Get step-by-step, visual help with Help Illustrated.

Don't overlook the tabs in the top-right corner of the Get Help Now window. Clicking one of these updates the window with new collections of information and resources.

Independent Explorations

AOL has many more help areas. Many channels and forums offer their own help areas — look for a Help button on the main page and click it to learn more.

If you were unable to get your question answered through one of the resources in this chapter, don't lose hope. You can ask us and we'll try to point you in the right direction. To ask us a question, just send us an e-mail at our screen name: JenniferAndDave.

What? You don't know how to send an e-mail yet? It's no coincidence that the next stop on our tour is your Online Mailbox! We'll show you how to read, send, and customize your e-mail in the next three chapters.

Chapter 5
Getting Your Mail

Chapter 6
Sending Your Mail

Chapter 7
Moving Beyond E-Mail Basics

CHAPTER

5

GETTING YOUR MAIL

Quick Look

▶ **Reading Your Mail**   **page 87**

When the AOL guy announces, "You've Got Mail!" it's time to spring into action. There's e-mail in your online mailbox. Don't you just want to rip it open and see what it says?

▶ **Junk Mail**   **page 93**

As exciting as new e-mail can be, it won't be long before junk e-mail starts finding its way to your online doorstep. Here are some tips for recognizing junk when you see it and how to toss it without reading it.

▶ **Address Book**   **page 97**

You've got a "little black book" built right into your AOL software. It's simple to save the e-mail addresses of all your friends and associates, and once they're listed in your address book, you'll be all ready for the day when you start sending them e-mail.

▶ **Mail Center**   **page 99**

You've got an electronic postal clerk sitting at the top of your AOL window. The Mail Center stands ready to help with all your e-mail needs. Although there are other ways to get to some e-mail features, the Mail Center gathers them all up into one handy menu.

Chapter 5

Getting Your Mail

CHAPTER ITINERARY

Discovering the world of electronic mail

Learning how to read your e-mail

Mastering e-mail addresses

Touring the AOL Mail Center

One of the drawbacks of traveling is losing touch with your life back home. You may miss birthdays, important meetings, and the day-to-day news of those you love. Touring AOL may be similar to traveling around the world, but it differs in one significant way: You'll never have a problem keeping in touch when you're on AOL. No, it isn't just because you can access AOL from home or work (though that is part of it). It's because AOL offers *electronic mail* (or *e-mail* for short). E-mail is easy: no paper, no pens, no stamp, no fuss. E-mail is convenient: You can use it wherever you are on AOL. Even better, e-mail costs nothing beyond your normal AOL connect charges.

What Is E-Mail?

E-mail is an electronic, private communication. You will assuredly receive it as an AOL member, and almost definitely send it. Every screen name on your AOL account has an online mailbox, into which e-mail you've received and sent is temporarily held. Thus you can have up to seven mailboxes on your AOL account, which can each hold up to 1,000 pieces of e-mail at a time. That's a *lot* of e-mail, and you're likely never to reach this limit during your AOL travels.

Reading Your First E-Mail

First things first: do you have e-mail to read? You can find out by signing on to AOL and listening for the "You've got mail!" announcement immediately after the "Welcome!" greeting. You'll only hear this if your sound volume is turned up, of course. If you hear the welcome but nothing else, you don't have new mail. Another way to check for new e-mail is to take a look at your mailbox icon at the top left corner of the Welcome screen. If you have new e-mail, the red flag is up on the icon. You can see this same mailbox icon on your toolbar, too (see Figure 5-1).

As you can see, we have new e-mail. We suspect you do also. All new members have e-mail from the moment they sign on. The good folks from America Online, including Steve Case, the CEO, sent you some. To see for yourself, open your mailbox. Just click either of the two mailbox icons or press Ctrl+R (see Figure 5-2).

Scanning Your Online Mailbox

Now that your mailbox is open, let's take a closer look at it. AOL displays all your new e-mail in the list in the center of the window. Each line shows an icon, the date the e-mail was sent, the address (screen name) of the person who sent the e-mail, and the subject line (the topic of the e-mail). Across the top of the window are three tabs: New Mail, Old Mail, and Sent Mail. Clicking each of these tabs in order from left to right would display, respectively, lists of new mail (shown in Figure 5-2), old e-mail (e-mail you read recently), and sent e-mail (e-mail you've sent recently). Across the bottom are five buttons, starting with Read (which opens a piece of e-mail). We'll get to the other four buttons later. For now, let's open the first piece of e-mail in the mailbox.

We created a new account (screen name: Book Authors) for this chapter so we could explain exactly what new members' mailboxes look like. If you don't have the same e-mail as us, don't worry — that either means you or someone else with access to your account already read the e-mail or that AOL themselves changed their e-mail to new members. If you already read the e-mail within the last few days, click the Old Mail tab at the top of the mailbox — you may find the e-mail there.

mailbox

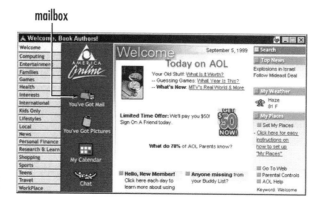

Figure 5-1. The red flag on your mailbox icon means you have new e-mail!

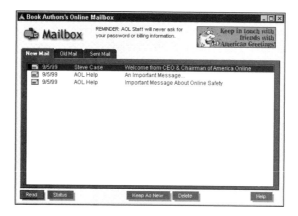

Figure 5-2. Our Online Mailbox, complete with e-mail from AOL

Reading Your New E-Mail

To read a piece of e-mail, first make sure the e-mail you want
to open is selected (highlighted). If it isn't, place your pointer
over it and click. Now click the Read button. Alternatively, just
double-click the e-mail you want to read. Your e-mail opens in
a new window on your screen (see Figure 5-3).

Note

The Reply button automatically fills in the Send To field
and copies the body of the
message you are replying
to, but the Forward button
does not.

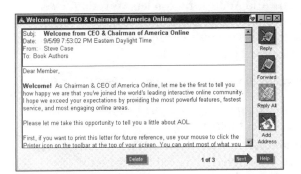

Figure 5-3. Your first e-mail is a welcome message from Steve Case.

The e-mail message itself is in the large box that takes up most
of the window. At the top of the message are the *mail headers*, which essentially display the routing information. Headers
include the subject line (which you already saw in the mailbox), the date and time the message was sent (including the
time zone), the sender's name (Steve Case), and the recipient's
name (Book Authors). The mail headers differ from e-mail to
e-mail, naturally.

The body of the message appears below the mail headers
and the horizontal line. This is actually a long, informative letter from Steve Case. We had to revisit the scroll bar ten times
to read the entire letter. E-mail messages may contain styled
text (**bold**, *italic*, <u>underlined</u>, colored, big, and small), as well
as graphics. The graphics may be within the text, or actually
beneath it as a background.

The e-mail window has a bunch of buttons on it, too. The
Delete button on the bottom does exactly what you would
expect — removes the e-mail from your mailbox. You can
retrieve it by using the Recently Deleted function in the mail
menu, but we don't recommend you use the Delete button
until you feel more comfortable working with e-mail. The
Next button opens the next piece of e-mail in your mailbox,
and the numbers to the left of it tell you how much e-mail you

have in your mailbox. In the upper-right corner of the e-mail window, the Reply button lets you send a response. The Forward button below lets you forward the entire email to another person. The Reply All button below that lets you send a response to all persons who received this e-mail (and as only one person received this particular e-mail, the button is grayed-out). We explain how to use these three buttons in the next chapter. The Add Address button lets you add the sender's address to your Address Book, and we discuss this in more detail later in this chapter. Finally, the Help button at the bottom leads to more help on e-mail.

You can do several things with your e-mail from this point:

> ▶ *Print the e-mail, if you have a printer.* Just click the Print icon on the toolbar.

> ▶ *Save the e-mail to your Personal Filing Cabinet.* Select Save to Personal Filing Cabinet from the File menu and choose Incoming/Saved Mail from the submenu. You don't need to do this if you have your Personal Filing Cabinet Preferences set to automatically save e-mail (see the sidebar titled "Saving E-Mail in the Personal Filing Cabinet"). We discuss the Personal Filing Cabinet again in Chapter 7.

> ▶ *Close the e-mail window without deleting the e-mail.* Click the Close Box in the upper-right corner of the window (the one with X on it).

> ▶ *Delete the e-mail.* Click the Delete button if you have no interest in reading this e-mail again, or if you already saved it.

> ▶ *Open the next piece of e-mail.* Click the Next button. The current piece of e-mail will automatically close (but will not be deleted) when you open the next piece.

Since we have two more pieces of e-mail, we're going to just go on to the next one by clicking the Next button. It turns out that the next two pieces of e-mail are from AOL Help: One offers important tips for getting the most out of AOL, and the other stresses the importance of online safety. All three pieces of e-mail are valuable and worthy of reading. We would even go so far as to recommend you print them out and tuck them in your book for later reference.

When we finish reading the last piece of e-mail in our mailbox, we close the e-mail, and the mailbox window is once again visible on the screen. It looks a little different now, how-ever (see Figure 5-4).

If you look closely at Figure 5-4, you'll see that the e-mail icons on each line have changed. They now have a red checkmark on them. The checkmark indicates that you've read the e-mail already. If you were to now close your mailbox and reopen it, all e-mail with a red checkmark would disappear from the New Mail list and move to the Old Mail list (under the Old Mail tab). If there is a piece of e-mail or two you don't want to move to your Old Mail list quite yet, you can control that. Just select the e-mail and click the Keep As New button at the bottom of the mailbox window. Presto! The red checkmark disappears.

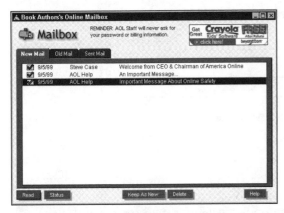

Figure 5-4. Our mailbox indicates which pieces of e-mail we've already read.

Saving E-Mail in the Personal Filing Cabinet

If you want to store your e-mail on your computer perma-nently, we recommend you take a moment now and set your Mail Preferences. Select Preferences from the My AOL button on the toolbar. Now click the Mail icon. In the resulting window, click one or both of the options that read "Retain all mail I send in my Personal Filing Cabinet" and "Retain all mail I read in my Personal Filing Cabinet." We recommend you enable both options for now. Click the OK button when finished. These settings will save all e-mail you open from this point forward. We return to the Personal Filing Cabinet in Chapter 7, and we also cover the Mail Preferences in Appendix B.

Before we peek at the Old Mail list, let's look at the other buttons along the bottom of the mailbox window. The Read button opens an e-mail. Status tells when the e-mail was read and when it was sent (see Figure 5-5). Keep as New keeps the e-mail in your New Mail list. Delete removes the e-mail from your mailbox altogether. Help leads to more e-mail help.

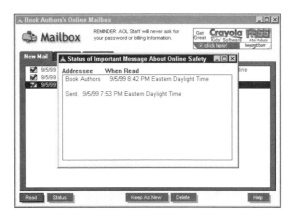

Figure 5-5. The e-mail status window

Old Mail

Click the Old Mail tab at the top of the mailbox window. Any e-mail you've read (and haven't kept as new) appears in the list in reverse chronological order (most recent stuff first). You can see two pieces of e-mail in Figure 5-6, in the opposite order as they appeared in Figure 5-4. The third piece of e-mail isn't listed because we kept it as new.

Figure 5-6. Our Old Mail list

5

E-Mail Expirations

E-mail doesn't stay in your mailbox forever. New e-mail remains in your list for 30 days or until you read it, whichever is shorter. After thirty days, the e-mail expires, disappears from your New Mail list, and cannot be read. Old e-mail in your Old Mail list expires in three days by default. You can extend (or shorten) your old e-mail expiration date in the Mail Preferences window (see Appendix B for a description). E-mail you send, which we discuss in the next chapter, stays in your Sent Mail list for up to 30 days. If you'd like to save your e-mail permanently, see the sidebar titled "Setting Personal Filing Cabinet Preferences."

Note

If you receive more new e-mail while you're signed on, you will hear the "You've got mail!" announcement again (assuming your sounds are turned on) and your red flag will go up on your mailbox icons. (This assumes that your mailbox is empty when the new e-mail arrives.) To see your new e-mail, you must open your mailbox again or refresh it if it is already open; it will not appear in your New Mail list automatically. Just press Ctrl+R, click the mailbox icon on your toolbar (or Welcome screen), or select Read from the Mail Center menu to open or refresh your new e-mail list.

Note that the red checkmark shows up on the e-mail icons in the Old Mail list as well. If you've changed your mind and want to keep an e-mail as new, it isn't too late. Select it and click Keep as New, just as you would do in the New Mail list. The other buttons along the bottom of the Old Mail list are the same as those on the New Mail list, too.

Now that you know how to read e-mail, you may be wondering how you can get more e-mail to read. Relax — you'll have new e-mail in your mailbox before you know it. In fact, some of the e-mail you receive may be unwelcome.

Dealing with Junk Mail

Advertisements for adult sites, offers for questionable businesses, chain letters, and worse are all common in today's world of e-mail. This unwelcome and unsolicited e-mail is known as *junk e-mail*, or *spam*. It's annoying, offensive, and makes a mess of your mailbox. You could just delete it from your mailbox — this is a good use for the Delete button. If you want to help decrease the amount of spam you get in the future, however, we encourage you to take action against junk e-mail at Keyword: **Junk Mail** (see Figure 5-7).

Note

If you do receive junk e-mail, we caution you not to click any hyperlinks in e-mail; they may lead to undesirable places, or infect you with a virus that could compromise your account. Never give your password out to anyone. AOL will never request it in an email!) Remember also that you can check the location of a hyperlink first when in doubt. Just position your pointer over the hyperlink, wait a moment, and the yellow help bubble will appear. If bubble help tells you that the link is on AOL only, you're probably okay. However, it's better to be safe than sorry and simply not click hyperlinks in e-mail sent to you by strangers.

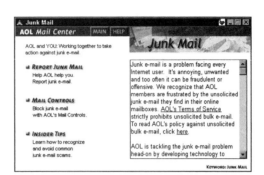

Figure 5-7. Learn how to recognize, report, and block junk mail.

We've been using AOL e-mail for many years and have gotten good at spotting junk e-mail before we ever open it. Here are our tips for recognizing the junk before you click:

▶ *Check the sender's address in the mailbox.* Did the e-mail come from someone you know? If not, you know it is unsolicited and most likely junk mail. Additionally, junk mail often comes from Internet addresses with the @ symbol in them (discussed in detail later in this chapter). This includes addresses that end with @aol.com, as that often indicates Internet e-mail that is disguising itself as AOL e-mail.

▶ *Check the subject lines.* Any subjects with the words *sex, free, giveaway,* or *hot* are almost invariably subject lines of junk e-mail. Subjects that infer familiarity, such as "About last night" or "The picture I promised to send," are probably also junk e-mail when they come from senders you don't know. E-mail subjects that begin with Fwd: are often chain letters.

▶ *Be wary of official-sounding screen names.* Some junk e-mailers will try to trick you into opening e-mail using addresses that sound legitimate, like MailRep57. Exceptions include AOL screen names with AOL, Billing, Help, Guide, or Host in them, unless they have @aol.com at the end of their names.

If you don't recognize junk mail and open it anyway, don't worry — you can't catch a virus or give out your password or credit card information by just reading an e-mail. You have to click a hyperlink or download an attached file for anything to happen.

So what can you do about junk e-mail? Forward it to screen name TOSSpam. We discuss forwarding in more detail in

Chapter 6, but for now, here's how to forward e-mail in three easy steps:

1. Click the Forward button on the opened piece of junk e-mail.
2. Type TOSSpam into the To: box in the upper-left corner of the resulting window.
3. Click the Send Now button.

If you receive an e-mail that violates AOL's Terms of Service (discussed in Chapter 2), forward the e-mail to screen name TOSmail1 instead. If the e-mail had an attached file, forward it to TOS Files.

Another way to stop junk e-mail in its tracks is to make yourself less of a target. Chatting in People Connection is one of the ways that junk e-mailers find your name. If you want to chat, we recommend you create a new screen name and block e-mail entirely (or at least for everyone but those you know) for that particular screen name. Another way junk e-mailers find you is through your member profile. If you don't create a member profile, they can't find your name in the Member Directory. Both chatting and member profiles are discussed in Chapter 8.

Cross-Reference

Attached files are discussed in Chapter 6.

Tip

Consider setting your mail controls to allow or disallow specific kinds or e-mail or e-mail from specific domains. Mail controls are discussed in Chapter 2.

Tip

If you ever forget your screen name(s), check the Screen Name menu in your Sign On screen when you're offline. Alternatively, you can check the name in the title bar of the Welcome screen when you're online. AOL always greets you by screen name when you sign on.

E-Mail Addresses on AOL and the Internet

Just like regular mail, which require names, street addresses, cities, states, zip codes, and sometimes countries to find its recipients, e-mail needs addresses. The great thing about e-mail addresses is that, at only one line, they're much shorter than traditional addresses. On AOL, your screen name is your e-mail address. Thus, our e-mail address is "BookAuthors". We have several other screen names, too, such as "JenniferAndDave." This screen name is also an address, as is every other screen name on AOL. Each unique address leads to its own mailbox. So even though both of these screen names belong to us, we receive the e-mail sent to them separately.

When you give your e-mail address to other AOL members, you can just give them your screen name. In fact, you may not have to give it to them at all; you screen name is automatically attached to every e-mail and Instant Message you send, as well

AOL members can use the Internet e-mail form of your address, too, although they only need your screen name. If someone sends e-mail to jenniferanddave@aol.com, we will receive it in our JenniferAndDave mailbox.

as every message board post you make and chat room you visit. If someone who is not an AOL member but is on the Internet asks for your address, you need to give him or her more information. Just add @aol.com to the end of your screen na-me. For example, we would use bookauthors@aol.com or jenniferanddave@aol.com. When you send e-mail to someone on the Internet or post a message on a newsgroup, AOL automatically attaches this Internet e-mail form of your address. If you want to include your address on business cards, you should use this address. Most people these days have Internet access, but many are not on America Online.

When you read your e-mail, notice the address of the sender in the e-mail headers above the message. If the address is nothing more than a screen name (no @ symbol is included), you know the sender is on America Online. If you see the @ symbol in the address, you can bet that the sender is either elsewhere on the Internet (not on AOL) or used the Internet to send the message (as is the case with some addresses with @aol.com).

As you will undoubtedly receive e-mail from the Internet, it helps to understand how Internet e-mail addresses are constructed. Every address has two components: the name and the domain. The name is similar to an AOL screen name, though it may be a bit longer or contain characters AOL screen names don't have. Everything before the @ symbol is the name. For example, in the address book-authors@jenuine.net, the name is book-authors (see Figure 5-8).

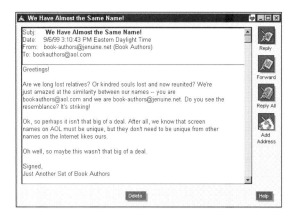

Figure 5-8. A typical piece of e-mail, this one from book-authors@jenuine.net

The domain is everything after the @ symbol. In this case, the domain is jenuine.net. If we compare Internet addresses to traditional mail addresses, the name is similar to the name (or title), whereas the domain is similar to the street address, city, state, and zip code (but much shorter). Because the world is a big place, domains come in many different forms. For example, aol.com (which is AOL's domain), usps.gov (the United States Post Office), aclu.org (the American Civil Liberties Union), umich.edu (the University of Michigan), and so on. The letters after the period at the end of the domain stand for various things: .com (commercial site), .net (network), .gov (government), org (organization), .edu (educational institution), etc. You will also see codes with just two letters; these indicate a country, such as .ca (Canada), .uk (United Kingdom), .de (Germany), and .to (Tonga).

Tip

You may notice that we are putting Internet addresses in all lowercase letters. Not only is this the custom, but it is often necessary — some servers on the Internet are case-sensitive. Always type an e-mail address as you see it — if it has uppercase letters, use uppercase letters as well.

If you think e-mail addresses are hard to decipher, try memorizing them. It really isn't possible. You need some place to store your addresses so you have them when you need them. How about in an address book?

The Address Book

Your AOL software comes with a built-in address book. You can access it online or offline by selecting Address Book from the Mail Center icon on the toolbar (see Figure 5-9).

Figure 5-9. The Address Book stands ready to store e-mail addresses.

The empty Address Book pictured in Figure 5-9 just begs to be used. The easiest way to add an entry to your Address Book is through your e-mail windows. Every piece of e-mail you read has an Add Address button on the right side of the window (refer again to Figure 5-8). Just click that button on a piece of e-mail from an address you want to save, and the window shown in Figure 5-10 appears.

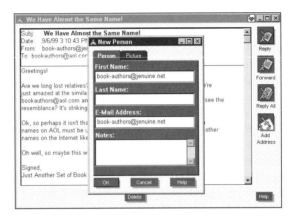

Figure 5-10. Adding a new entry to your Address Book

Did you notice how AOL filled in the First Name and E-Mail Address fields in the window? Of course, you can edit any or all of these fields, though we don't recommend you edit the E-Mail Address field. Use the Notes field to record things you want to remember about the person, such as a birthday, a second e-mail address, and so on. Do you have a picture of this person? Click the Picture tab at the top of the window to add a picture to their address book entry. Click Save when you're finished.

Let's return to the Address Book. If you closed the Address Book window, just select it again from the Mail Center icon on the toolbar. The new entry appears at the top of the Address Book (see Figure 5-11).

Figure 5-11. Our Address Book with its first entry

Now the buttons along the bottom and side make more sense. New Person lets you add a new entry to the Address Book without clicking the Add Address button in an e-mail. New

Group provides a way to add a group of e-mail addresses (separate addresses with commas or the Enter key). The Edit button lets you edit an entry (highlight the entry and then click Edit). Delete removes the entry from the Address Book permanently. Along the right side of the window, the first three buttons are used to send e-mail with the selected address (which we discuss in the next chapter).

The Save/Replace button, a new feature in AOL 5.0, saves a copy of your Address Book to your hard drive. This allows you to later import it to other copies of the AOL software you may have on your laptop or at work. Once you've saved the Address Book, simply transfer the file you saved to the appropriate computer, start AOL on that computer, visit your Address Book again, click Save/Replace, and then choose to replace it with the transferred file. If you have more than one copy of the AOL software on the same computer, you can import it to the second (or third) copy using this feature, too.

Entries in the Address Book are automatically alphabetized, either by e-mail address (if there is no name), by first name (if there is no last name), or by last name. Icons to the right of the entry indicate the type of entry. An individual entry shows an icon of one person waving, whereas a group entry shows an icon of two people waving.

Tip

If you don't like the order of entries in your Address Book, you can force it to order them in the way you prefer. Edit the entry you want to appear at the top of your Address Book and add the number 1 to the start of their last name. Do the same for the other entries using additional numbers in sequential order. Now your Address Book is organized the way you like it!

A Tour of the Mail Center

Now that you're a pro at reading e-mail, let's take a tour of the AOL Mail Center. First, we'd like to clear up some confusion. You really have two things called Mail Center. One is the icon on your toolbar and its menu. The other is a window accessible through the first menu item in your Mail Center menu. Confusing, huh? You can see both the Mail Center menu and Mail Center window in Figure 5-12.

Both the menu and the window deserve closer examination — AOL has filled both with useful e-mail features! Many of the features may not make sense yet as we haven't covered their underlying principles. So we'll just introduce them now and return to them later to discuss in more detail.

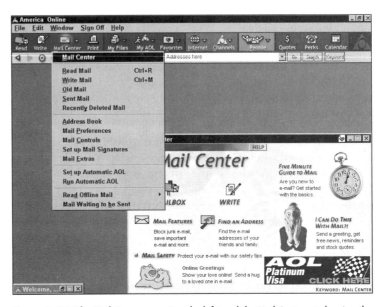

Figure 5-12. The Mail Center menu (on the left) and the Mail Center window (on the right). Use the Mail Center menu item to open the Mail Center window.

The Mail Center menu offers easy access to the most common e-mail features. Mail Center at the top opens the Mail Center window, as we already noted. Read Mail (Ctrl+R) opens or refreshes your mailbox list of new e-mail. Write Mail (Ctrl+M) opens a Write Mail window for composing a new message. Old Mail opens or refreshes your old e-mail list. Sent Mail opens or refreshes your list of sent e-mail. Recently Deleted Mail, a new feature in AOL 5.0, displays all e-mail you deleted in the last 24 hours (see the sidebar titled "The Deleting Dilemma").

Other items accessible through the Mail Center menu include the Address Book (discussed earlier), the Mail Preferences window (discussed in Appendix B), and the Mail Controls window (discussed in Chapter 2). Set up Mail Signatures configures the new AOL 5.0 feature that lets you automatically add signatures to your e-mail (as discussed in the next chapter). Mail Extras brings up a palette of fun and helpful things you can include in the e-mail you send (also discussed in the next chapter).

The Deleting Dilemma

Have you ever accidentally deleted a piece of e-mail?
Recently Deleted Mail (accessible under the Mail Center
button on the toolbar), one of AOL 5.0's new features, lets
you view all e-mail deleted in the past 24 hours. AOL goes
one step further and gives you the option of keeping the
deleted e-mail as new or permanently deleting it (see
Figure 5-13).

Figure 5-13: Our list of recently deleted e-mail (mostly junk e-mail)

This is an obvious benefit to those who accidentally
delete e-mail, or simply change their minds later. If you
delete e-mail to remove it from your mailbox for privacy
or security reasons, however, you must visit your Recently
Deleted Mail list and permanently delete it. If you neglect
to do this, your e-mail may remain accessible to someone
else using your screen name (if they have access to your
password).

The remaining items in the Mail Center window let you set
up and run Auto AOL (discussed in Chapter 7) and read e-mail
you've saved or marked to be sent later. We'll revisit saving
e-mail, but for now you should know that you can choose
Read Offline Mail and then select Incoming/Saved Mail from
the submenu to receive a list of e-mail you've read. This
assumes you turned on the option to retain all e-mail you
read in your Personal Filing Cabinet as we recommended
earlier in the chapter.

The Mail Center window (really an entire area) is an entirely
different beast (refer again to Figure 5-12). Rather than providing access to popular e-mail features, it offers help for getting

the most out of e-mail. Resources include tools for finding e-mail addresses, tips and tricks for protecting your e-mail and yourself, a tutorial on using e-mail, and cool things you can do with your e-mail, such as keep up with the news and track your investments. You can return to the Mail Center window directly with Keyword: **Mail Center**.

Independent Explorations

If you're eager to receive more e-mail and experiment with your e-mail features, we can direct you to a few sources that will send you e-mail before you learn to send it yourself.

Subscribe to a free AOL newsletter at Keyword: **Newsletter**; choose one (or two, or three) you like and follow the subscription directions. Many newsletters will send you a confirmation of your subscription in e-mail, and then follow with periodic e-mails containing the newsletter itself.

Sign up for Interest Profiles (discussed in Chapter 3) at Keyword: **Interest Profiles**. You will receive an e-mail with interests that match your own immediately after you sign up.

Of course, the best way to get more e-mail is to send it yourself. Turn the page and find out how to send e-mail in Chapter 6.

SENDING YOUR MAIL

Quick Look

▶ **Return Receipts**   **page 110**

You can request that AOL inform you when recipient(s) who are AOL members read e-mail you've sent. Just click the Request Return Receipt from AOL members checkbox at the bottom of the Write Mail window. AOL generates automatic e-mail to you as soon as your recipient(s) read your e-mail.

▶ **Courtesy Copies**   **page 111**

If you'd like to send a copy of an e-mail to someone else, just type his or her name in the Copy To field. That person will receive an exact copy of the e-mail. If you'd prefer to send the copy discreetly, put the screen name in parentheses so other recipients don't see that you copied them.

▶ **Status of E-Mail**   **page 116**

Find out if your recipients have or haven't read an e-mail with the Status button, available at the bottom of your Sent Mail window. Status will also tell you when an e-mail was read, and if it was ignored or deleted.

▶ **Attached Files**   **page 117**

You can send a file along with your e-mail messages. Just click the Attachments button, select your file(s), and click OK. AOL will even automatically archive and compress multiple files for speedier upload for you and download for your recipient(s).

Chapter 6

Sending Your Mail

CHAPTER ITINERARY

Mastering the art of sending e-mail

Replying to your e-mail with ease

Staying up-to-date on the status of your e-mail

Sending and receiving files attached to e-mail

O nce you send your first e-mail, you're entitled to call yourself an AOL traveler. A world of possibilities unfolds with the ability to send e-mail, offering adventure, mystery, and perhaps even a bit of romance with each click of your mouse. It is a glorious immersion into one of AOL's greatest features! Maybe we got a little carried away there, but sending e-mail really is something to get excited about.

Sending Your First E-Mail

Before you can send e-mail, you must first compose it. Thankfully, AOL makes it easy to get started. You can click the Write button on the toolbar, choose Write Mail from the Mail Center button on the toolbar, or simply press Ctrl+M. Any of these three methods brings up the Write Mail window, ready to take your e-mail messages (see Figure 6-1).

Tip

You don't have to be signed on to AOL to compose e-mail. The Write Mail button functions whether you're online or offline.

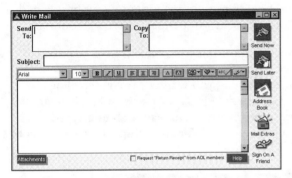

Figure 6-1. The Write Mail window is where you compose your e-mail.

The first field in the Write Mail window, the Send To field, is intended for your recipient's address. As we discussed in the previous chapter, e-mail addresses can simply be an AOL screen name (for sending e-mail to a fellow AOL member) or an Internet address (for sending e-mail to anyone else). For your first e-mail, you can use your *own* screen name to send a practice email to yourself. Type in your exact screen name and press the Tab key on your keyboard.

You can use Tab to move around virtually any window with text fields. Your cursor should now be in the Copy To field. Typing an address in this field sends a courtesy copy to that address. For now, leave it blank and press Tab again.

The Subject field is where you write the topic of your e-mail. Remember, the subject line is all that appears in your recipient's mailbox when sent (other than your address, of course). So it pays to make your subject line as good as it can be, otherwise your recipient may mistake your message for junk e-mail and delete it. Good subject lines are descriptive, short, attention-getting, and relevant. For example, a subject line like

Tip

If you're not sure how to spell your screen name exactly — and it does need to be spelled exactly to work — try this trick: Pull down the Window menu, find the item towards the bottom that begins with Welcome, and note the name after it — this is your screen name. If you find it confusing to spell, you probably need an easier screen name.

6

Sending Your Mail

Note

If you don't type anything in the subject field before sending your email, your recipient sees "(no subject)" as the subject line.

Tip

If you anticipate sending e-mail frequently, we recommend you create a signature that will be automatically attached to your sent e-mail. See Chapter 7 for more details.

Cross-Reference

To learn how to use the formatting buttons arrayed across the top of the message field, see Chapter 7.

"message" isn't going to say much at all, but "My First E-Mail" does. Type in a good subject line and then press Tab again.

The last and largest text field is for your e-mail message. There are no hard and fast rules about what you write in your e-mail message, but we can give you a few pointers. Start with a simple greeting. Follow with your message, keeping it short and to the point unless you know your recipient likes long, newsy messages. Like any other letter you write, remember to whom you're writing and adjust your voice accordingly. A letter to a coworker would be different from a letter to your best friend. When you're finished, "sign" your e-mail by typing your name.

Once you finished composing your e-mail, check your e-mail carefully. Did you type the screen name exactly as it should be? Did you say everything you wanted? Is your spelling correct? Did you remember to sign your name and include any additional contact information you may wish to give? See our composed e-mail in Figure 6-2 for an example of a good piece of test e-mail.

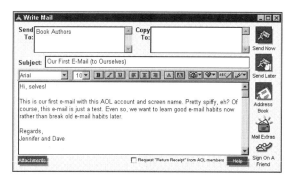

Figure 6-2. Our test e-mail with its address, subject line, and message

When your e-mail is ready to go, click the Send Now button in the upper-right corner of the window. AOL responds by instantly sending your e-mail, closing the e-mail window, and confirming that your e-mail was sent with a dialog box (see Figure 6-3). If you dislike either your e-mail window closing after you send e-mail or the displaying of a dialog box that confirms the e-mail was sent, you can disable these in your Mail Preferences.

Figure 6-3. Your e-mail is now winging its way to your recipient. In fact, it is probably already at its destination by the time you see this window.

Congratulations! You just sent your first piece of e-mail.

If your mailbox was empty at the time you sent it, you should have heard AOL announce "You've got mail!" Even if you don't hear it, the e-mail should be in your mailbox by now. Press Ctrl+M to open or refresh your mailbox (see Figure 6-4).

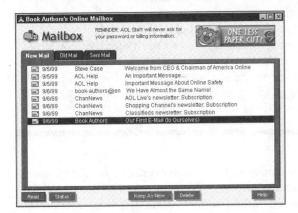

Figure 6-4. Our mailbox, with the e-mail we sent to ourselves at the bottom

When you actually send e-mail to other people, you won't get a copy in your mailbox like this (unless you include your address also). Even so, sending your test e-mail to yourself gives you a chance to see what your recipient would see. Go ahead and open it. You'll notice that the From and To addresses are the same, since you sent yourself the e-mail. Otherwise, everything should look normal.

Now you're ready to send e-mail to others! If you haven't already collected addresses in your Address Book, ask your friends and family for their e-mail addresses. You're also welcome to send e-mail to us at JenniferAndDave.

Note

If you composed your e-mail offline (or wish to send it later for any other reason), click the Send Later button instead of Send Now. This queues the e-mail for later sending. We discuss how to actually tell AOL to send the e-mail you've queued to send later in the next chapter.

Tip

Another place to find e-mail addresses is in the Member Directory. Choose Search AOL Member Directory from the People button on the toolbar, or simply use Keyword: **Members**.

6

Sending Your Mail

Requesting Return Receipts

A return receipt is a notification from AOL that your e-mail was *read* by your recipient(s) on AOL. If you click the option "Request 'Return Receipt' from AOL members" before you send your e-mail, AOL will send you e-mail when your e-mail is actually read. This is very similar to getting a return receipt on a letter or package sent in traditional mail (except the receipt arrives as soon as the recipient reads the e-mail). Frankly, this feature is mostly only useful when you need to be alerted right away that your e-mail was read. Another situation in which you may want to use the return receipt is when sending e-mail to people who don't sign on and check their e-mail often. The return receipt then serves as a reminder that you sent the note and may want to follow up on it. If you only want to know if someone read your e-mail, or if you're sending e-mail to a large group of people, we recommend the Status feature instead (discussed later in this chapter).

Are you curious about all those other buttons we didn't use on the Write Mail window? Send Later queues your e-mail for later, as mentioned earlier. Address Book opens your Address Book so you can find an address if you wish. Mail Extras opens the collection of fun tools for use in e-mail, which we discuss in the next chapter. Sign on a Friend lets you send a sign-on kit to a friend (as discussed in Appendix A). Along the bottom of the Write Mail window, the Attachments button allows you to attach a file (or files) to your e-mail when it is sent — we discuss this in the next chapter also. The Request Return Receipt option is discussed in the sidebar "Requesting Return Receipts," and the Help button leads to help on using e-mail.

We mentioned sending courtesy copies with your e-mail earlier in this chapter. Let's take a closer look at how that is done.

Courtesy Copies

A courtesy copy is identical to a regular piece of e-mail. The only difference is that when your recipient opens the e-mail you copied them on, he or she will see the letters *CC:* in front of his or her screen name (rather than To:). CC stands for courtesy copy, of course. Everything else you send is included: your address, other addresses, subject line, message, and any attached files (discussed later) or embedded images (discussed in the next chapter).

To send a courtesy copy to one address, simply type the address in the Copy To field of your Write Mail window. To send a courtesy copy to more than one address, type a comma or press the Enter key between each address. See Figure 6-5 for an example of an e-mail with multiple courtesy copies.

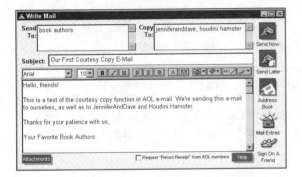

Figure 6-5. This e-mail will be copied to addresses JenniferAndDave and Houdini Hamster, as well as to Book Authors (the primary address).

As you'll recall, all recipients will see to whom your e-mail is addressed and copied. Can you send a copy without anyone else knowing? Yes! Use blind courtesy copies, discussed next.

Blind Courtesy Copies

Blind courtesy copies can be sent along with regular courtesy copies. Just put the parentheses around those addresses you want copied blindly, and leave the parentheses off those you want copied normally. If you have a group of e-mail addresses that all need to be copied blindly, separate each address by commas instead of the Enter key and then put the parentheses around the whole set. If you do send e-mail to a large group of people (large meaning over about five screen names in this case), we recommend you blind courtesy copy the group. Not only does this protect the privacy of everyone, but it also makes it quicker for your recipients to open your e-mail (no waiting for additional addresses to display). See Figure 6-6 for an example.

You will note that the addresses in Figure 6-5 aren't capitalized, even though the screen names themselves have both upper- and lowercase letters in them. When addressing e-mail to other AOL members, capitalization isn't important. Neither is spacing. This contradicts what we told you in Chapter 5 about typing addresses exactly as they appear; this rule *does* apply to Internet addresses, however. So don't worry about case or spaces when addressing e-mail. When your recipients open the e-mail from you, their screen names will be capitalized and spaced correctly (AOL does this for you automatically).

6

Sending Your Mail

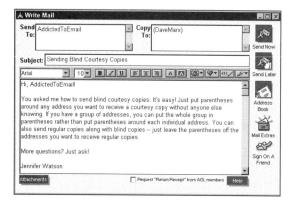

Figure 6-6. Jennifer's e-mail to AddictedToEmail includes a blind courtesy copy to Dave Marx (which happens to be Dave's personal screen name).

The only persons who will know you sent a blind courtesy copy are you and whomever you blind copied. Don't be alarmed if you open the e-mail you sent later and notice the BCC: and the recipient's address that was blind copied. You can see this, and so can your recipient, but no one else can.

Replying to E-Mail

Except for the times you initiate a correspondence, much of the e-mail you send will likely be *replies* to e-mail sent to you. As you'll recall, all the e-mail you read has a Reply button on it. Open the test e-mail you sent to yourself earlier in the chapter. If you already read it and it is no longer in your New Mail list, click the Old Mail tab and open it from there. See Figure 6-7 for the e-mail we sent to ourselves.

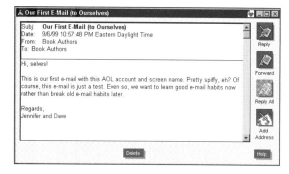

Figure 6-7. Our test e-mail, with the resplendent Reply button

The Reply button appears in the top-right corner of the
e-mail. Click it and a new compose e-mail window appears,
complete with the sender's address in the Send To field and
a subject in the subject field (see Figure 6-8).

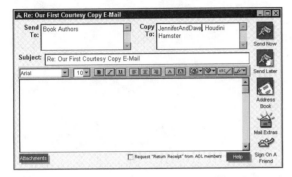

Figure 6-8. The reply e-mail window, with the address and subject line automatically
filled in

To dash off a reply now, you only need to type your message
in the message field and click Send Now as usual. You can,
however, modify any of the fields before you send the reply,
including the Sent To, Copy To, and Subject fields. You'll note
that AOL copies the same subject line to your reply window,
and adds Re: in front of it (which stands for Reply). You can
edit this if you wish.

Reply to All

From time to time, you'll receive e-mail addressed to you as
well as other addresses. For example, the courtesy copy e-mail
we sent in Figure 6-5 went to three addresses. If you reply to a
letter with multiple recipients, you may wish to reply to the
other recipients as well as to your sender. When this option is
available, the Reply to All button becomes active on your
e-mail window. Just click it to create an e-mail reply that will
be sent to all addresses that received the original e-mail (see
Figure 6-9).

Complete your group reply e-mail just as you would for a
regular reply. Again, if your group of addresses is particularly
large, consider sending the e-mail as a blind courtesy copy to
that group.

Tip

Do you want to reply to someone other than the sender? First choose Preferences from the My AOL button on the toolbar, click the Mail button, and enable the "show addresses as hyperlinks" option. Now open your mailbox, read a piece of e-mail (new or old), and click the address you wish to respond to in the headers. Voilá! A new Write Mail window opens, automatically filled in with that particular address.

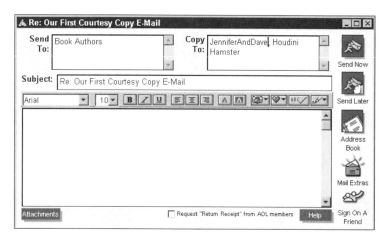

Figure 6-9. Clicking Reply to All on our courtesy copy test e-mail produces this reply window. Note that additional recipients' addresses were automatically added to the Copy To field.

Quoting

When you send a reply, it is considered good netiquette to include references to the original letter Before you click the Reply button in an e-mail, select (highlight) a passage from the letter you'd like to include in your reply. You probably don't need the whole message. Now click the Reply button. Your reply e-mail window appears with the recipient's name, the subject line, *and* the text you selected (see Figure 6-10).

Figure 6-10. Our reply e-mail with quoted text from the original letter

You'll notice in Figure 6-10 that AOL conveniently includes a line of text above your quote, indicating who wrote it at what time on which day. You can edit or remove this attribution text if you wish.

The quote itself is surrounded by carets (<< >) to distinguish it from the rest of the message you will presumably write. If you don't like the style of these carets, you can visit your Mail Preferences and choose Internet style carets instead, which look like this:

```
> Are we long lost relatives?
> Or kindred souls lost and now reunited?
```

If you find yourself quoting the entire e-mail, you may be better off forwarding the e-mail instead. Continue reading to learn how.

Forwarding E-Mail

Forwarding is simply sending an entire copy of the e-mail you received to someone else, which may or may not be the person who sent it to you originally. It is also an alternative to copying an address on an e-mail. Most folks forward e-mail to retain a complete account of the e-mail and create a chain of letters they can refer to during a correspondence. This is fine when sending e-mail between two or three people, but we don't recommend it as a general practice, as it takes more time to read forwarded e-mail and it chews up resources for AOL.

When you come across an e-mail you feel would be best served by forwarding it, just click the Forward button on the right side of the window (below Reply). AOL responds by opening a new e-mail window (see Figure 6-11).

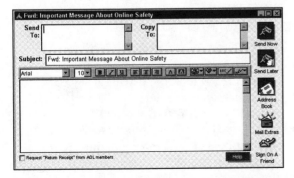

Figure 6-11. Our forwarded e-mail window, complete with subject line

Tip

You can forward e-mail you've sent to others, too. Just click the Sent Mail tab in your mailbox, open the e-mail you want to forward, and click Forward. Note that if you blind copied anyone, their names *will not* be visible to your recipient in the forwarded e-mail (unless, of course, the recipient was one of those who were originally blind copied).

You'll notice that AOL fills in the subject line, but this time prefixes it with Fwd (which stands for <u>Forward</u>). AOL doesn't bother to fill in an address, as it can't assume you want to forward the e-mail back to the person who sent it to you. To complete the forward, type in the appropriate addresses, modify the subject line if you feel it is necessary, and type a note to explain why you're forwarding the letter (again, do this only if you feel it is necessary). Click Send Now, and off it goes! When your recipient opens the forwarded e-mail, they first see your message (if you included one) and then a copy of the forwarded e-mail below that, complete with e-mail headers. You can get an idea of what your recipient sees by choosing Sent Mail from the Mail Center menu, locating the e-mail you just sent, and opening it.

Checking Status of Sent Mail

Did your email reach its destination? To check status of an e-mail you've sent, select Sent Mail from the Mail Center, select the e-mail you want to check, and click the Status button at the bottom of the window (see Figure 6-12).

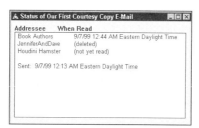

Figure 6-12. The status of our courtesy copy test e-mail

Looking at our status window, we see our three addresses listed in the left column. The status is listed next to each address. Book Authors already read the e-mail (at the date and time noted). JenniferAndDave deleted the e-mail. Hmpf! And Houdini Hamster hasn't yet read the e-mail. Two other status messages you may see are "you cannot check status of Internet mail" (which appears for all Internet addresses), and "ignored." Ignored? Yes, you can ignore e-mail as well as delete it. See the tip in the margin for the details.

Besides keeping tabs on your addresses, checking the status of an e-mail serves another purpose: It enables you to know when someone hasn't yet read your e-mail. Why is this helpful? Because you can unsend any e-mail you sent to another AOL address if it hasn't already been read.

Unsending Mail

Did you send an e-mail before its time? Change your mind about something? You may be able to unsend what you've sent! To unsend an e-mail, choose Sent Mail from your Mail Center menu, select the offending piece of e-mail, and click the Unsend button at the bottom of the window. If your e-mail can be unsent, AOL will ask you if you are sure you want to unsend the message (and notes that no copy will remain in your mailbox). Click Yes to confirm (or No to cancel). If successful, AOL confirms that the message was unsent.

Only e-mail that hasn't yet been read can be unsent. If you send e-mail to more than one recipient, and one reads it but the other hasn't, you can't unsend it. If even one person has read the e-mail, it is off limits. If you send e-mail to two recipients, one an AOL address and the other an Internet address, you can't unsend it either (because AOL can't tell if the person at that Internet address has read the e-mail or not).

Attaching Files

How do you get a spreadsheet into an e-mail? If you try copying and pasting, you'll either get an error or just a bunch of gobbledygook. Instead of copying and pasting, try *attaching* it!

AOL e-mail has a provision for file attachments. Remember that Attachments button at the bottom of a Write Mail window? Clicking it produces the Attachments window through which you can attach (and detach) one or more files (see Figure 6-13).

Tip

To ignore e-mail in your New Mail list, right-click the e-mail in your mailbox and choose Ignore from the context menu. The e-mail icon changes to display a checkmark, indicating it won't be kept as new when you refresh or reopen your mailbox. Ignored e-mail isn't deleted, but it is sent to your Old Mail list. If you later change your mind, display your Old Mail list, select the e-mail, and click Keep As New. Note the other convenient commands in the context menu, such as Read, Status, Keep As New, and Delete.

Note

If you want to unsend an e-mail, we advise you to do it as soon after you send it as possible — you're more likely to catch it before it gets read.

6

Sending Your Mail

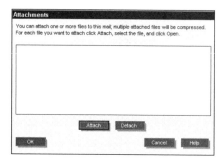

Figure 6-13. The Attachments window. Note the Attach and Detach buttons.

Files are attached one at a time. To attach, click the Attach button, locate the file in the standard find file window, and click Open. Your Attachment window now reflects the attached file, denoted by the file's address and filename on your hard drive. Repeat to add another file. If you accidentally attach the same file twice, don't worry — you won't send the file twice (AOL is smart enough to know that it is the same file). Figure 6-14 shows what an Attachments window with multiple files might look like.

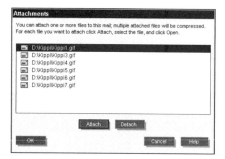

Figure 6-14. Attaching multiple files. Each of these files is a picture of Jennifer's dog, Kippi.

When you're finished attaching files, click the OK button in the lower-left corner of the Attachments window. Your Write Mail window is again visible, but now there is text next to the Attachments window along with a mini-icon of two diskettes (see Figure 6-15). In our case, this text reads "Kippi1.gif, Kippi3.gif, . . ." — the names of the first two attachments. If you need to check your list of attachments before you send it or edit the attachment list itself, click the Attachments button again.

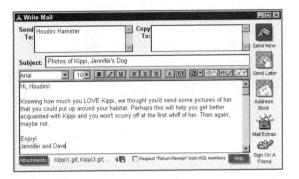

Figure 6-15. Our e-mail with attached files

Complete the e-mail as you normally would, including the address, subject, and message. In your message, we recommend that you reference the attached file(s) for your recipients. Let them know what the files contain, any special software they may need to use or view the files, and so on. When your e-mail is ready, click the Send Now button as usual. AOL responds with a message that it is *compressing* your attachments (which means it is decreasing the size of the files using ZIP file compression techniques and then archiving them into one file for transfer). Immediately after the compression, which usually only takes a second or two, AOL sends your e-mail and your attached files. If the attached files are any larger than a few kilobytes, AOL displays a progress meter window with the progress of the file transfer (see Figure 6-16).

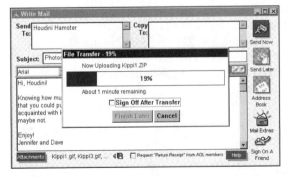

Figure 6-16. AOL is transferring the e-mail and its attached files.

Note the name of the file you're transferring (Kippi1.ZIP in our case), the percentage completed, the time remaining in the transfer, and the Sign Off After Transfer option. If you click Sign Off After Transfer, AOL automatically signs you off when

Note

Although there's no practical limit to the number of files you can add (at least that we found), there is a size limit — you can't attach a file or set of files greater than 16 megabytes total.

6

Sending Your Mail

the thermometer reaches 100 percent. If you click Finish Later, AOL stops the file transfer, queues your e-mail to be sent later, and informs you of this. If you let the file transfer complete on its own, AOL informs you that your file transfer was successfully completed.

Here are a few caveats regarding attached files:

▶ You won't be able to send attached files to everyone. Some members choose to block all e-mail with attached files through their mail controls (discussed in Chapter 2).

▶ Attached file size limits to Internet addresses can be even more restrictive. Some Internet computers only accept files up to 1 or 2 megabytes in size, and some block them completely. It pays to check with an Internet addressee before you send them an attached file.

▶ Be considerate of what files you attach and to whom you send them. Don't send a huge file to someone with a slow connection, or an inappropriate graphic image to a minor. The Terms of Service apply to attached files, too. Additionally, please check your file(s) for viruses before you send them to someone else (see Chapter 10 for details).

▶ AOL compresses file attachments created in Windows AOL into the ZIP compression format, which Mac users may not be familiar with. Conversely, Mac AOL compresses files in the StuffIt file compression format. For utilities that decompress ZIP archives on the Mac and StuffIt (.SIT) archives on the PC, search the AOL software libraries at Keyword: **File Search**. Note that Mac AOL does decompress ZIP files.

Independent Explorations

Now that you've mastered the basics of sending e-mail, why
not send e-mail to all those friends, family members, and
coworkers you know? You may be surprised at how many
people have e-mail addresses these days. Try searching the
Member Directory (described in Chapter 8) for the screen
names of people you know or would like to know better.

Our next whistlestop on the e-mail train is all about getting
more from your e-mail and moving beyond the basics.

Quick Look

▶ **Personal Filing Cabinet**   page 126

Your AOL software comes with a powerful database known as the Personal
Filing Cabinet, which you can use to store and organize e-mail you send and
receive. You can set your AOL software to automatically save copies of your
e-mail in your Personal Filing Cabinet, and then use the built-in find feature to
locate e-mail quickly and efficiently. Your Personal Filing Cabinet is accessible
from the My Files icon on the toolbar.

▶ **Spell Checker**   page 130

You need never worry about sending an e-mail with misspelled words again,
thanks to AOL's built-in spell checker. You can use the spell checker to automatically check every e-mail you send, or just check your text on command.
The Spell Check feature is available under the Edit menu.

▶ **E-Mail Signatures**   page 138

New to AOL version 5.0, you can automatically add your signature to the end
of e-mail you send. You can create and use up to five different signatures, all
stored on AOL's computers so they're always handy. Click the pencil button
on the Write Mail window to set up your signatures.

▶ **Pictures in E-Mail**   page 142

E-mail isn't just for text anymore. You can also add full-color pictures to your
AOL e-mail sent to other AOL members. To add a picture, click the camera
button on the Write Mail window.

Chapter 7

Moving Beyond E-Mail Basics

CHAPTER ITINERARY

Safeguarding your e-mail in the Personal Filing Cabinet

Polishing your e-mail with the spell checker and Mail Extras

Using styled text and signatures in your e-mail

Embedding pictures and graphics in your messages

AOL's e-mail system is loaded with features, yet it still manages to stay easy to use. Within the bounds of this book, we lack the space to tell you everything there is to know about AOL e-mail. Most members get by knowing little more than we covered in the previous two chapters; however, with just a touch more effort, you can raise your e-mail from the gray, drab basics to a colorful and efficient communications tool.

Saving and Organizing Your E-Mail

Don't make the mistake of thinking your e-mail will stay in your Online Mailbox forever. Within a few days, the e-mail you've read will disappear, and the e-mail you've sent will disappear after about a month. Why? AOL is keeping that e-mail on its own computers, and space is at a premium. If you want to keep track of your online correspondence, you're going to have to use space on your own hard disk.

The two best ways to do this are to use your Personal Filing Cabinet, which we discuss in detail in just a bit, or to save your e-mail as individual files on your hard disk.

Saving files on your hard disk seems like the easiest way to go, especially if you're used to saving word processing or spreadsheet files. All you have to do is open the e-mail you want to save and then do one of three things: Select Save from the File menu, press the keyboard shortcut Ctrl+S, or right-click your mouse and select Save from the context menu. After that, you can give the e-mail a useful name, and place it in a convenient folder on your hard disk, such as My Documents (see Figure 7-1).

Figure 7-1. The Save File As dialog box. Name your file, select the destination folder, and then click Save.

You may want to create an entire folder in your hard disk for e-mail, and create individual folders within that one to organize as you see fit. whatever system works for you. There are a couple of drawbacks to saving your e-mail this way. First, it's a lot of bother to save and name every e-mail as an individual file, especially when you get a lot of e-mail. Second, each of those files takes up a lot of hard disk space, sometimes as much as 32K, even when the message is short. -mail itself. After you've spent some time saving e-mail this way, you'll start to wonder if there's another way to do it. Fortunately, there is.

Personal Filing Cabinet

The Personal Filing Cabinet (PFC) is AOL's built-in system for saving, organizing, and searching the e-mail you've read and sent. It's also a part of the Offline Mail system, which we discuss a little later in this chapter, Auto AOL, and Download Manager (both of which are discussed in Chapter 10). If you're beginning to think that your PFC is an important feature, you're right. Each of the screen names on your account has its own PFC, and as we noted in Chapter 1, you can password-protect your PFC to hide its contents from prying eyes.

Although there is a way to save the e-mail to the PFC only on an item-by-item basis, most folks prefer to automatically save to the PFC every piece of e-mail they read and send. To do this, you have to change some of your AOL Mail Preferences. If you didn't do this back when we mentioned it in Chapter 5, now is the time to do it. Click the My AOL icon on the AOL toolbar, select Preferences, select Mail, and enable the options "Retain all mail I send in my Personal Filing Cabinet" and "Retain all mail I read in my Personal Filing Cabinet". These preferences affect all screen names on your account, so you'll only have to do this once. Your PFC will be a bit empty in the beginning. After all, you have to start sending and reading e-mail before any of it can be automatically saved. Eventually, though, there will be something worth seeing, so why don't we take a look?

You can read what's in your Personal Filing Cabinet whether you're online or offline. All you have to do is click the My Files icon on the AOL toolbar, and select Personal Filing Cabinet (see Figure 7-2).

Figure 7-2. The Personal Filing Cabinet. All the folders are closed in this example. Double-click a folder to see what's inside.

For now we'll only be concerned with the folders named Incoming/Saved Mail, Mail Waiting To Be Sent, and Mail You've Sent folders. Double-click the Incoming/Saved Mail folder, and let's see what's inside (see Figure 7-3).

Cross-Reference

We cover Send Later in "Offline Mail," the next section of this chapter.

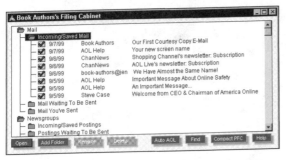

Figure 7-3. The contents of the Incoming/Saved Mail folder

The PFC lists every piece of e-mail by date, the screen name of the sender, and the subject of the e-mail — the same information you saw in your Online Mailbox. The buttons along the bottom of the Personal Filing Cabinet window let you open the selected item of e-mail, add or rename a folder, delete an item, configure Auto AOL, and search (using Find) the PFC for e-mail containing certain names, words, or phrases. Compact PFC is a maintenance feature that we discuss in a little while.

Double-click any item to open it. The e-mail window is just the same here as it is when you read your Online Mailbox. You can use the Reply, Forward, or Reply All options, or add a name to your Address Book, just as always. The only difference may be if you're replying to e-mail while you're offline. In that case, you can only use the Send Later option.

Your PFC can get stuffed with e-mail, so at some point you'll want to clean house and organize it. Start by deleting all the junk mail you've received. You may also want to create one or more folders in order to organize the e-mail by topic or sender. To create a folder in your Incoming/Saved Mail folder, click that folder once to highlight it. Then click the Add Folder button on the Filing Cabinet window, type a name for that folder, and the new folder will appear inside the Incoming/Saved Mail folder. Now you can drag and drop e-mail items into that folder. If you like, create more folders, and place folders inside of other folders, until your PFC is organized to your satisfaction. You can do the same thing with the Mail You've Sent folder.

One of the joys of the PFC, in our opinion, is the Find feature (see Figure 7-4).

Tip

As you're cleaning house, you can save a step or two with a right-click of your mouse button. Right-click any item you want to delete, and a Delete button will appear right under your mouse pointer. All you need to do is left-click to dispatch the file.

Tip

You can add a password to your PFC to protect it from prying eyes. Read how to do so in Appendix B in the section "Password Preferences."

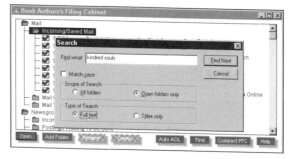

Figure 7-4. Search for an elusive e-mail with your PFC's Find search engine.

PFC Find can be incredibly useful. Type all or part of a screen name or important words or phrases into the Find what: text entry box. The Match case option looks for words with capitalization matching the text you entered. Scope of Search can look through every folder in your PFC, or only search the open folders. If you only want to search the Mail You've Sent folder, close the Incoming/Saved Mail folder and select the Open folders only option. Type of Search can look in the full text of every saved e-mail, or use Titles only option if you're looking for e-mail with a particular subject or sent by a particular person. A full text search can take much longer than a titles only search, but it's a lifesaver if you don't remember much about the e-mail other than the information within it.

Your PFC is a much more efficient way to use hard disk space than saving e-mail as individual files, but it can still get pretty large. Even if you delete lots of e-mail, the PFC won't shrink until you click the Compact PFC button. If you find you're deleting far more e-mail from your PFC than you're keeping, perhaps you should manually save e-mail to your PFC, rather than save it automatically. First, turn off one or both of the preferences we mentioned earlier in this section. Now, when you read and/or write your e-mail, open the AOL File menu, move your mouse down to Save to Personal Filing Cabinet, and select the appropriate folder.

Offline Mail

Offline Mail is one of best ways to avoid toll charges, stay within your AOL budget, and prevent conflicts over telephone usage. You can start by writing your next new e-mail while you're offline. Select the screen name you want to use from the Sign On screen and click the Write icon on the AOL toolbar. Write your e-mail as you always do, and when you're done, sign on to AOL and click Send on the Write Mail window.

The next step is the Send Later button. Compose a new e-mail offline, just as you did in the previous paragraph, but click Send Later when you're finished writing. One of the big benefits of Send Later is that it saves your e-mail on your hard disk. That way it won't be lost if someone shuts down the computer or needs to sign on with another screen name before you can sign on yourself. When you're ready to send that e-mail, sign on, click the Mail Center icon on the AOL toolbar, and select Mail Waiting to be Sent. The Mail Waiting to be Sent window (see Figure 7-5) lists any e-mail that you've chosen to send later. You can open that e-mail for editing or review, delete it altogether, send one item, or send every item on the Mail Waiting to be Sent list.

Figure 7-5. The Mail Waiting to be Sent window saves your works in progress.

Select any one item from the list that you wish to send, and click the Send button, or double-click the item to open the e-mail for review or editing prior to sending. If you wrote and edited everything offline, you can save a bunch of time by simply clicking the Send All button as soon as you open the Mail Waiting to be Sent window.

Next, we'll build on our earlier discussion of the Personal Filing Cabinet. Without the PFC, you'd have a very hard time reading and replying to your e-mail offline. Once you enable

The Mail Waiting to be Sent window is available offline, too. Use it to review and edit your e-mail before you sign on.

You can access all these offline e-mail features by opening your Personal Filing Cabinet. Just click the My AOL icon on the AOL toolbar, select Personal Filing Cabinet, and open the appropriate folder.

You can also select Spell Check from the Edit menu, or open the right-click context menu and choose Spell Check.

the "Save all mail I read to my Personal Filing Cabinet" option (see the section "Personal Filing Cabinet," earlier) you can gather your e-mail very quickly while online, then read and reply to it offline. When you're online, just open the first piece of new e-mail in your Online Mailbox and start clicking the Next button as quickly as you can. Don't bother to stop and read the messages as they flash by. When you sign off, click the Mail Center icon on the AOL toolbar, select Read Offline Mail from the menu, and choose Incoming/Saved Mail from the submenu.

This is only half of the Offline E-Mail picture. Auto AOL can totally automate the process of collecting and sending your e-mail, which minimizes the time you spend online. You can read all about Auto AOL in Chapter 10.

Spell Checking

Not evriwon wood agre, butt spellin and grammer is verry importint two gud komyounicashuns. Fortunately for us, we have a little spelling and grammar helper built right into our AOL software. You can start a spell check in several ways. The most obvious is to click the Spell Check button on the Write Mail window (it's the one that has the letters *ABC* and a check mark on it).

The spell check begins wherever the text insertion mark happens to be, which can just as easily be at the end of a document as at the beginning. The spell checker starts looking for misspelled words, common typographical errors, and common grammatical errors. When it finds one, the Check Spelling window opens to display its findings (see Figure 7-6).

Here's a feature-by-feature description of all the buttons and boxes you'll see:

▶ **Questionable:** The questionable term is highlighted in the text and listed in the Check Spelling window.

▶ **Error message:** The spell checker explains why it found the term questionable and describes your options.

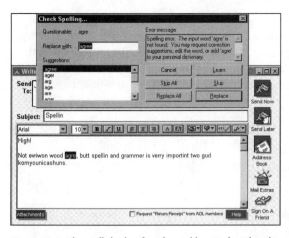

Figure 7-6. The spell checker found a problem. It describes the questionable term, explains why it thinks there's a problem, and proposes a solution.

▶ **Replace with:** The term in this box will replace the questionable term, if you so choose. You can use the solution suggested by the spell checker, select a different term from the Suggestions box, or type in your own replacement text.

▶ **Suggestions:** A list of potential replacements for the questionable term. Click the item of your choice if you disagree with the spell checker's first choice.

▶ **Cancel:** The Cancel button ends the spell check.

▶ **Learn:** The Learn button adds the questionable term to your personal spelling dictionary.

▶ **Skip All:** Skips all instances of a questionable term in the document being checked. This is useful when unusual names or terms are used correctly and appear often in the text.

▶ **Skip:** You may want to allow a questionable term just this once, rather than add it to your personal dictionary.

▶ **Replace All:** Replaces all instances of a questionable term, throughout the document, with the text in the Replace with box. This is especially useful for unusual names.

▶ **Replace:** Replaces the current (highlighted) instance of a questionable term with the text in the Replace with box.

You can spell check a single word. Just highlight the text with your mouse and click the Spell Check button in the Write Mail window. Cancel the spell check when you're finished.

See Appendix B for a detailed description of your Spell Check Preferences.

Spell checking software is never perfect. It will find problems where there are none, and miss other common problems altogether. However, a spell checker will find all sorts of problems you never would have caught yourself. Save yourself some embarrassment and start spell checking your e-mail before you click Send.

Mail Extras

Have you ever wondered what the Mail Extras button on the Write Mail window does? Why not click it and find out? (See Figure 7-7.)

Figure 7-7. Mail Extras — your introduction to dandy ways to jazz-up your e-mail.

The Mail Extras feature is an introduction to some of the ways you can go beyond basic e-mail and add some sparkle to your communications. Two buttons on the Mail Extras screen take you to the American Greetings Online Greetings store. When you buy online greetings for your friends, American Greetings does the e-mailing for you. Since our purpose is to teach you how to do your own e-mail, we're going to move along quickly to the other features.

Colors & Style

Go here to learn a bit about how you can add colors and style (and you'll learn even more later in this chapter). You can also choose from a selection of mail art (also know as ASCII art) that you can use in your own e-mail. You can open a new Write Mail form with the art already copied into it, or copy and paste it yourself, right from the window. Once you've copied it, you can start making modifications of your own.

Smileys

Here's a quick introduction to *smileys* (also known as *emoticons*), the symbols online chatters use to express their emotions. Learn how to smile, wink, kiss, and frown with just a few simple keystrokes. You can discover the "formula" for each smiley and copy a colorful version from the screen to paste into your e-mail. We discuss smileys a bit more in Chapter 8.

Photos

Did you know you can put photos and other graphics right into the e-mail you share with others? We'll be discussing how to do that in just a bit. The information in Mail Extras Photos, on the other hand, is a little different: AOL tells you how to use Favorite Places hearts to add a hyperlink to e-mail so your friends can see the pictures supplied here.

Hyperlinks

Here's a quick lesson in hyperlinks, those blue underlined words you find all over Web pages and all around AOL. AOL shows you how to recognize them and provides a group of popular AOL destinations that you may want to include hyperlinks to in your e-mail.

Stationery

Why send a plain e-mail when you can use colored letterhead? AOL supplies eight predesigned letterheads. Choose the one you like, fill in the blanks on the form AOL supplies, and AOL will open a new Write Mail form with the letterhead already added. Save the results to your hard disk and read the next section in this chapter to discover how to modify AOL's design to your taste.

Mail Controls

Cross-Reference

You can find more information on using and designating master screen names in Chapter 3.

Are you getting too much junk e-mail? Take control of your online mailbox with Mail Controls! This group of e-mail settings enable you to block (or allow) a wide range of e-mail. You can access your mail controls at Keyword: **Mail Controls** while signed on with a master screen name (see Figure 7-8).

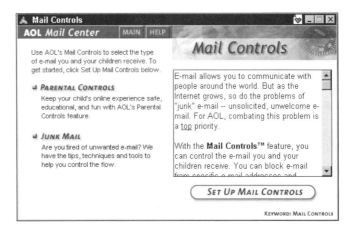

Figure 7-8. Mail Controls are within reach whenever you're online with a master screen name.

To access your Mail Controls, click the Set Up Mail Controls button in the lower-right corner of the window. Assuming you're signed on with a master screen name, AOL will ask you the screen name for which you want to edit mail controls (see Figure 7-9).

To select a name, click the radio button to the left of the screen name and click the Edit button at the bottom. The Mail Controls window for the screen name you chose appears (see Figure 7-10).

To get the most out of your AOL e-mail, we recommend these Mail Control settings:

▶ When you receive junk e-mail, copy the address, visit your Mail Controls, add the address to your list, and be sure you've chosen "Block e-mail from the listed AOL members, Internet domains and addresses." Doing this means you cannot receive junk e-mail from those addresses ever again.

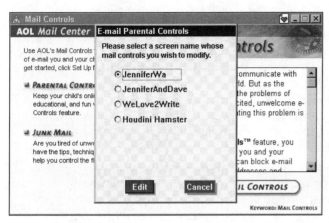

Figure 7-9. Choose the screen name you want to modify.

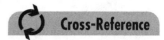

Cross-Reference

If you're not yet familiar with Mail Controls, you can learn the basics back in Chapter 3.

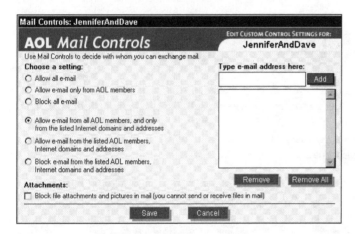

Figure 7-10. The Mail Controls window

▶ If you continue to receive junk e-mail from different addresses at the same domain, such as makemoney @junk.com and freeoffer@junk.com, you can block the entire domain. Just type the domain (such as junk.com) into your list. Once you do this (and set your controls to block e-mail from the listed addresses), you won't ever receive e-mail from this address again.

▶ If most of your junk e-mail is from Internet addresses, consider choosing "All e-mail from AOL members only." This will block all Internet e-mail. If you do occasionally get Internet e-mail that you want to continue receiving, choose the "All e-mail from AOL members, and only from the listed Internet domains and addresses" settings and then add the domains and/or addresses you want to get Internet e-mail from to your list.

7

Moving Beyond E-Mail Basics

Note

AOL's styled text features can only be seen by fellow AOL members. AOL removes all styled text features before e-mail to be sent to Internet addresses leaves AOL.

▶ If you enjoy chat rooms but hate all the junk e-mail you get as a result, we recommend you create another screen name just for chatting. Once your new screen name is created, use Mail Controls to block all e-mail on that name. Once you begin using your new screen name and making friends, you may want to change your setting to "allow e-mail from the listed AOL members, Internet domains and address" and then add your friends' screen names to your list.

▶ If you're concerned about security, seriously consider using the "block file attachments and pictures in e-mail" setting at the bottom of the Mail Controls window. If no one is able to send you attached files, there is no risk of downloading a Trojan Horse or virus.

Styled Text

Styled text is just another way to say *formatting*, a concept that is very familiar to anyone who uses a word processor. The truth is, AOL's e-mail system includes a built-in word processor, so if you've never processed a single word before, here's your chance.

The AOL Write Mail window includes a formatting bar, which makes all this styling possible (see Figure 7-11).

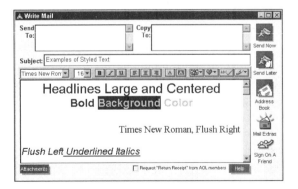

Figure 7-11. The formatting bar on the Write Mail window — choose fonts, text formatting, colors, and more.

As we describe the features in the text that follows, why not experiment as you read along? Open a Write Mail window and type a few sentences of sample text. Highlight a bit of the text and start experimenting.

We're really concerned with the features on the left and center of the formatting bar. The buttons on the far right are discussed in other sections.

- ▶ **Font selection:** Select a font (or typeface) from the drop-down list. You can choose from every font installed on your computer. Unfortunately, if the recipients of your e-mail don't have the same font(s) on their computer, all they'll see is their default font (usually Arial).

- ▶ **Text Size:** Make the text larger or smaller. The bigger the number, the bigger the text.

- ▶ **Bold:** Make a **bold** statement.

- ▶ **Italics:** Use *italics* for emphasis.

- ▶ **Underline:** <u>Underline</u> important concepts.

- ▶ **Align Left:** Straight margins on the left, ragged text on the right

- ▶ **Align Center:** Text is centered on the page, both margins are ragged.

- ▶ **Align Right:** Straight margins on the right, ragged text on the left (which is backwards from what is usually seen).

- ▶ **Text Color:** Change the color of your text for extra impact.

- ▶ **Background Color:** Put a block of color behind your text for extra contrast.

Now that you've experimented a bit with all these features, start thinking about good taste. Learn to use these effects with subtlety. A little bit of formatting brings clarity and emphasis, whereas a lot simply distracts from your message.

7

Moving Beyond E-Mail Basics

You can change the default font and many other aspects of your e-mail. Check Appendix B for a discussion of the fonts preference settings.

Adding Hyperlinks

The Insert Favorite Place button on the formatting bar is the first and easiest step towards adding hyperlinks to your e-mail. Click the button, select the desired favorite place, and the hyperlink is inserted wherever the text insertion mark happens to be. You have another choice, though, which creates the kind of hyperlinks you see on Web pages. You know, the kind that say, "If you want to see my home page, click <u>here</u>." How can you do this? To start, all you have to do is know the URL of the Web page to which you want to hyperlink. Type the text in the Write Mail window, and highlight the word or words you want to turn into a hyperlink. Right-click your mouse to open a context menu, and select Insert Hyperlink from that menu. Then you can type (or paste) the URL into the Edit Hyperlink window. It's a good idea to test the URL before you send it to someone else, which is why there's a Launch button. Once you're satisfied with your hyperlink, click OK.

Signatures

E-mail users have their version of pen and ink, called a *sig* (or *signature file*). A sig is more like letterhead than an actual signature. Sigs usually include a person's full name, e-mail address, and Web page address. After that, some folks go on to add telephone numbers, street addresses, favorite slogans, or a quote of the day. You can also create signatures from the toolbar in the compose mail form. See Figure 7-12 for a tasteful sig.

Sigs can be very plain or very fancy. There's even netiquette for sigs. Quite simply, when communicating with friends or folks who already know you, keep your sig simple and avoid advertisements. If it's pertinent to the conversation, include your professional credentials but don't beat people over the head with them. Unless it's absolutely necessary, do not create a sig that requires folks to scroll the text.

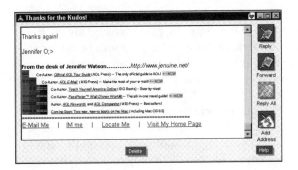

Figure 7-12. One of Jennifer's colorful signatures

Every screen name on your AOL account can have up to five signature files, which are stored on your hard disk. To install the same sigs on another screen name or another computer, send yourself e-mail containing the sig(s) you need, and paste it into the Set up Signatures window.

To create your sigs, click the Mail Center icon on the AOL toolbar, select Set up Signatures, and click the Create button (see Figure 7-13).

Figure 7-13. The Create Signature window

The Create Signature window helps build elegant signatures. Give your signature a name that distinguishes it from the other signatures you may create later, and go to work on the signature itself. The window comes equipped with all of the styled text capabilities we discussed earlier, plus the spell checker and the Insert Favorite Place button, which is handy for sharing your favorite URL. When your sig is done, click OK.

7

Moving Beyond E-Mail Basics

While the Set up Signatures window is open, you have the choice to edit or delete the sig(s) that you created, or declare one of your sigs as a default. Your default sig will be automatically added to every piece of e-mail you create with this screen name. Now it's time to use your sig. Open a Write Mail window, and write your e-mail. When you're done, click the Insert Signature File button on the far right of the formatting bar and select the sig you'd like to insert. Of course, if you've already chosen one of your sigs as a default, you don't even have to do this, because your e-mail already includes that sig. You'll also note that you can select Set up Signatures when you click that Insert Signature File button.

Inserting Pictures and Graphics

Why not send illustrated e-mail that includes a picture? AOL gives you the creative power to exchange fully illustrated e-mail with all your friends and family who use AOL. Build a family photo album or just a snapshot. You can even make greeting cards that rival Hallmark!

To begin, you need images work with. You can use photos downloaded from You've Got Pictures (use those with low resolution), or other images in GIF, JPG, or BMP format stored on your hard disk.

Open a Write Mail form, click the Insert a Picture button on the formatting bar (it's the one with the camera on it), choose Insert a Picture and browse to find the file you're looking for, and click OK. The photo will be added to your e-mail (see Figure 7-14).

If the image happens to be large, AOL may ask if you want to resize the image. In most cases, you'll want to choose Yes, but if you don't like the results, you can go back and do it again, without resizing.

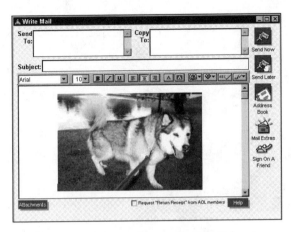

Note

If you insert images into your e-mails, other AOL members receiving the e-mail will see them, but recipients on the Internet will not see the images.

Figure 7-14. A simple e-mail starring Kippi the Malamute

Once the picture has been inserted in your e-mail, you can move it around as if it were a block of text. Highlight the picture with your mouse and try the Center text alignment option. Insert text before or after the picture. Change the background color. Have a blast! Is this easy, or what?

Why not add more pictures? You can use the Insert a Picture button again, or try something different. Select the AOL File menu, select Open, and open another graphic file. The picture will open in another window. Just drag and drop the graphic into the Write Mail window! Do you want to remove that graphic from the e-mail? Just highlight it with your mouse and press the Delete key.

Here's how to create a greeting card: Click the camera button in the formatting toolbar of a Write Mail window, select Background Picture, and choose a graphic file from your hard disk. The graphic will completely fill the Write Mail window through a technique called *tiling*. That means the picture is repeated over and over, like a floor tile. Obviously, this is not the best effect possible. However, if your background graphic is a simple colored pattern like the kind created for the backgrounds of Web pages, you're in great shape. You can then insert other pictures over that background, add text in a contrasting color, and before long you'll have something that looks like Figure 7-15.

7

Moving Beyond E-Mail Basics

Note

E-mail with inserted graphics cannot be sent to Internet addresses. If you want to send pictures to your friends on the Internet, send them as attached files instead.

Note

Graphics can take a long time to transfer via e-mail. An e-mail with a dozen pictures could take ten minutes or more to download, and if the original graphics were high resolution, the e-mail could exceed the maximum allowable size.

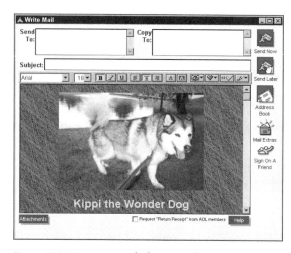

Figure 7-15. Doesn't Kippi look great in this greeting card?

Picture Gallery

Picture Gallery is yet another way to find pictures on your hard disk that you can insert into e-mail. Click the File menu, select Open Picture Gallery, and select a folder on your hard disk that contains the pictures you're interested in. A Picture Gallery window opens, displaying a small *thumbnail image* of every picture in the folder (see Figure 7-16).

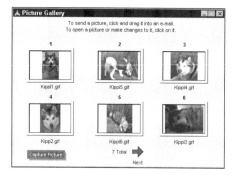

Figure 7-16. The Picture Gallery shows Kippi grinning for the camera.

You can drag an image directly into e-mail from the Picture Gallery, or you can view it full size and/or edit it by clicking once on the picture. The picture opens in an editing window. You can rotate, flip, resize, crop, modify the contrast and brightness, and even turn the picture from negative to positive and from color to black and white. When you're done, you can drag the results into e-mail, or open a new e-mail with the edited image already inserted.

Picture Gallery is also a wonderful tool for searching for lost images or cataloging the contents of your hard disk. It's a very nice feature, indeed!

AOL NetMail

AOL NetMail gives you the power to access your e-mail from almost any computer connected to the Internet. You could be visiting a public library in Peoria, an Internet café in Istanbul or a college dorm in Cambridge. If you can browse the Web, you can read your e-mail. This is the perfect solution if your company won't let you install AOL on your Internet-connected office computer. All you have to do is access the NetMail Web page, sign on with your regular AOL screen name and password, and start reading your e-mail (see Figure 7-17).

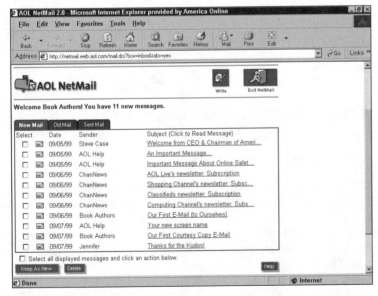

Figure 7-17. AOL NetMail's version of your Online Mailbox, including the New Mail, Old Mail and Sent Mail tabs

If you want to check for newly arrived e-mail while you're signed on to NetMail, just click the Sent Mail or Old Mail tabs, and then return to New Mail. If you received additional e-mail, it will have been added to the list.

To sign in to NetMail, go to `http://www.aol.com/netmail` or visit the AOL.com home page at `http://www.aol.com` and click the link for NetMail. What you'll see is very much like the regular AOL Online mailbox. You can view New Mail, Old Mail, and Sent Mail. Each e-mail item is listed, as usual, but note that the subject of each e-mail item is a hyperlink Click the hyperlink to open the e-mail item.

Your e-mail looks remarkably similar to the way it does on AOL. You'll find the familiar AOL e-mail icon and the Close, Keep As New, Delete, Reply, Reply All, and Forward buttons, and you can step through your e-mail by clicking the same Prev and Next buttons you're accustomed to using (see Figure 7-18).

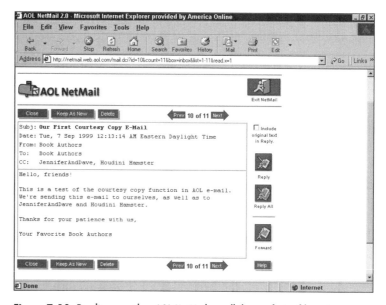

Figure 7-18. Reading e-mail on AOL NetMail — all the comforts of home!

The Write Mail page (as well as Reply and Forward) is a bit simpler than the one you're used to. Although the Send To:, Copy To:, and Subject: boxes are the same, you don't have the styled text buttons or other features, such as the Address Book, Insert Picture, Insert Favorite Place, Spell Check, and Insert Signature File (see Figure 7-19).

Because you're away from your regular computer, you won't be able to save e-mail you've read to your Personal Filing Cabinet or hard disk unless you indicate to keep the e-mail as new and read it again when you return home. You can click the Keep As New button as you read each e-mail, or return to the New Mail screen, click the Select checkbox next to every item you want to preserve, and click Keep As New. The same is true of e-mail you compose and send from Net Mail. Your best bet in this case is to include yourself in the distribution list of the e-mail you've sent.

Caution

NetMail doesn't look for the Reply to: address in Internet e-mail headers, so your reply may be addressed to the wrong recipient. Be sure to double-check.

Note

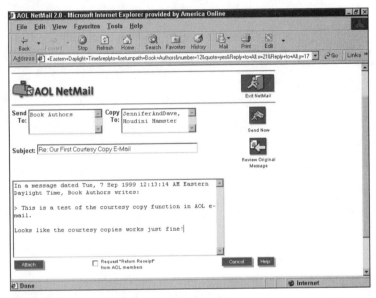

Figure 7-19. Write e-mail on AOL NetMail — all the basic features you need.

Although NetMail doesn't come with all the bells and whistles you're accustomed to, it covers the basics and a bit more with ease, and that's really just what you need when you're on the road.

NetMail should work on nearly any computer with an Internet connection and a Web browser, but it is optimized for Microsoft Internet Explorer versions 3.0 and higher and Netscape Navigator 3.02 and higher.

Independent Explorations

There's so much you can do with e-mail. We've just barely scratched the surface. We encourage you to use AOL's e-mail features to enhance your communications, but be careful not to let them overpower your message. If your bells and whistles draw more attention than your letter itself, it's time to tone them down a bit.

If you enjoy the interactive aspect of e-mail, you're going to love the next stop on our tour: People Connection. This is where people gather to chat in real-time with one another.

7

Moving Beyond E-Mail Basics

Chapter 8
Staying in Touch with Friends and Family

Chapter 9
Making New Friends

Quick Look

▶ **Sending and Receiving Instant Messages**　　　**page 152**

Chat one-on-one with friends, family, and colleagues with Instant Messages.
Each totally private conversation occupies a compact window, so you can
exchange comments no matter what else you may be doing online at the
time. Even your friends on the Internet can chat with you!

▶ **Buddy Lists**　　　**page 157**

How would you like to know which of your friends and colleagues are online at
the moment? Once you've set up your Buddy Lists, you can do just that. Buddy
Lists keeps track of who just came online, who just left, and who's just hanging
around. It also makes sending Instant Messages a piece of cake!

▶ **AOL Instant Messenger**　　　**page 156**

Instant Messages and your Buddy List can reach far beyond the borders of
America Online when your friends on the Internet use AOL Instant Messenger.
Instant Messenger is totally free and connects nearly 50 million people on the
Internet, AOL, and Compuserve.

▶ **Member Profiles**　　　**page 153**

You can be much more than just a screen name, thanks to member profiles.
List your hobbies and interests and any other information you care to share.
A profile will help new friends find you, and make introductions a good deal
easier when you walk into a chat room.

My Calendar　　　**page 171**

Keep track of all your personal and business interactions with My Calendar,
AOL's interactive appointment book. My Calendar can send e-mail reminders
to all participants, and the Event Calendar makes it easy to add TV shows,
movies, sports, and cultural events to your calendar!

Chapter 8

Staying in Touch with Friends and Family

CHAPTER ITINERARY

Sending Instant Messages to family and friends

Keeping tabs on important people with your Buddy List

Getting together in chats and conferences

Hobnobbing with celebrities in auditoriums

Organizing your activities with My Calendar

Do you see your friends and family as often as you'd like? Our busy schedules don't allow for much leisure time, so we don't see the important people in our lives as frequently as we'd prefer. We even find it hard to talk on the phone, as we keep late hours, and calls to all those people could break the bank. Even letter writing is out for us — we never seem to have the time to put a pen to paper, and there are never stamps around when we need them.

With all this in mind, you may be surprised to learn that we communicate with our friends and family on a daily or weekly basis. How do we manage this if we don't get together, talk on the phone, or send them mail? One word: AOL.

With AOL, we can chat with them in real-time and at no additional cost. It's easy, quick, and simple . . . and it makes a real difference in our lives. We can show you how to do the same through the use of Instant Messages, Buddy Lists, chat and conference rooms, and auditoriums.

Instant Messages

An Instant Message is a live, totally private, one-on-one chat session between two people who are currently online. The Instant Message (or IM) window doesn't take up a lot of space on your screen and doesn't interfere with any of your other online activities (although the conversation itself may be a distraction). If you're in a chat room, you can chat with other people in the chat room through IMs, and nobody else will know it. If you're browsing AOL or the Web, you can share the experience with a friend. Although keeping track of 15 conversations is difficult, we've known people who have kept 15 different Instant Messages going at the same time (we haven't done it ourselves, but we've come awfully close at times).

Some people start Instant Messages with their friends as soon as they sign on to AOL, and exchange occasional comments for the entire time they're online. Instant Messages can even be a valuable collaboration tool for coworkers. In fact, we've written several books while in entirely different states (Michigan and New Jersey) with the help of Instant Messages. As we wrote, we could pass information back and forth and coordinate our efforts.

Instant Messages may also be used to meet new people. It's very common to receive an IM after you enter a chat room from someone who wants to get to know you a bit better. If you've created a listing in AOL's Member Directory, folks can find your listing, see if you're online, and send you an IM. Their messages may or may not be welcome, of course.

Note

By default, Instant Messages are turned off for screen names for which Parental Controls have been set to Kids Only or Young Teens. This helps protect young people from unsavory adults. Parents, be sure to learn about Parental Controls and apply them appropriately to your children's screen names.

Tip

The easiest way to deal with an unwanted Instant Message is to totally ignore it or to click Cancel without saying a word in reply. If you're silent, the person on the other end will get the message soon enough, and skulk off in search of another conversation.

Note

If an IM can't go through because someone isn't signed on or because their IMs are blocked through Buddy List Preferences, a dialog box appears and states that "[*screen name*] is not signed on." If a person has used the $im_off command to turn off Instant Messages, AOL displays a dialog box with this message: "[*screen name*] cannot currently receive Instant Messages."

Instant Con Artists

Unfortunately, not everyone who sends you an Instant Message is a friend. People who discover your screen name, or simply guess it at random, may use an IM to try to fool you into giving them important personal information, such as a credit card number or your AOL password. Nobody from AOL will ever ask you for your password or billing information online, and you should never share that information with anyone, no matter how official they may seem or what threats they make. If you receive such a message don't close it — click the Notify AOL button and follow the instructions. If you or another family member did divulge a password, immediately change the password for that screen name at Keyword: **Password**. If your credit card number was divulged, contact your credit card company immediately. Be sure everyone in your household knows this.

Sending and Receiving Instant Messages

It doesn't take much to start an Instant Message (IM) conversation. To open an IM window, click the People icon on the AOL toolbar, and select Instant Message from the menu. The keyboard shortcut is even faster. Just type Ctrl+I. A window titled Send Instant Message opens (see Figure 8-1). Type your friend's screen name into the To box, type a greeting into the message box below it, and click Send.

Figure 8-1. The Send Instant Message window — just add a name, a greeting, and click Send.

Not every IM goes through. If your friend is not online, or has chosen to not receive Instant Messages, AOL will tell you the "call" cannot be completed. If your IM does go through, your friend will hear a chime, and a small window will open on his or her screen, displaying your screen name and greeting (see Figure 8-2). Your friend can respond to your message, ignore you altogether, check your AOL member profile, or, if your behavior is out of line, report your misdeed to AOL.

Member Profiles

Would you like to know more about someone you just met online? Perhaps he or she created a member profile in AOL's Member Directory. To view a profile, click the People icon on the AOL toolbar, select Get a Member Profile, type the person's screen name, and press the Enter key (you can also open the Get a Member's Profile window by pressing Ctrl+G). Don't be surprised if AOL tells you that there is no profile for that member. Listings in the Member Directory are completely voluntary. (Later in the chapter when we discuss chat rooms and auditoriums, we'll show you other ways to get a member's profile.)

Would you like to tell your fellow AOL members a bit about yourself and your interests? Member Directory listings provide space for your name, city and state, birth date, sex, age, marital status, hobbies, computers used, occupation, and a personal quote. You can provide as much or as little information as you please, but please be careful. The Member Directory is very easy to search, and unsavory individuals are very adept at playing detective. A first name, last name, and city are all that's needed to bring an unwelcome telephone call, or worse. Fortunately for concerned parents, children whose parental control settings are Kids Only and Young Teen cannot create member profiles (but Mature Teens can). To create a member profile, click the My AOL icon on the AOL toolbar, select My Member Profile, and start filling in the blanks.

Would you prefer your privacy? A listing in the member directory can draw undesired attention in the form of unsolicited e-mail and Instant Message. Fortunately, a listing in the member directory is completely voluntary — until and unless you create a listing you'll be completely unlisted. Profiles are also simple to edit or delete, if you decide your profile is drawing too much negative attention. Just click the My AOL icon on the AOL toolbar, select My Member Profile, make the desired changes, or click the Delete button at the bottom of the Edit Your Online Profile window.

If you're looking for AOL
members with common
interests, a search through
the Member Directory may
be just what you need. We
discuss how to do this in
Chapter 15.

When you have two or
more Instant Messages
open, it can become hard to
tell when someone made a
new comment. You will hear
the familiar chime, but which
person sent the message?
Look at the title bar of each
IM window, where it says
Instant Message From: If
there's a > preceding that
phrase, it means your
friend has responded to
your previous comment.
You may need to move
the windows as they
appear on top of one
another.

Figure 8-2. Receiving an Instant Message — Respond, Cancel, Get AOL Profile, or Notify AOL's Community Action Team? Tough choice, this one.

Since we are talking about your *friend*, we'll assume he or she clicked the Respond button. Immediately, the window on his or her screen changed. Your greeting is now displayed in a box at the top of the window, and there's a text entry box below it, waiting for your friend's reply (see Figure 8-3). Your friend will tap, tap, tap on the keyboard and click the Send button; you'll hear a chime, and your friend's greeting will join yours at the top of your Instant Message window.

Figure 8-3. Replying to an Instant Message — a click of the Send button, and the reply is on its way!

As the conversation continues, you'll see that everything you've said is preceded by your screen name, and likewise for your friend's responses. Your names are even in contrasting colors, so it's easy to see who said what. The conversation will quickly fill the upper window and scroll up out of sight. Just use the scroll bars on the side of the window to review what was said earlier in the conversation.

Once the conversation is rolling, your IM can be used in many ways. You can send short excerpts of text with a simple copy and paste (or drag and drop). Drag the Favorite Places heart icon from whatever you're viewing into the IM to create a hypertext link you can share with your friend. If plain text can't quite express your feelings, the IM window comes equipped with styled text buttons so you can use color and change font styles and sizes. The one thing you can't do is invite other friends into the IM to share in the conversation. For that, you'll have to open a private room, which we discuss later in this chapter.

Turning Off Instant Messages

You may want to exercise control over who can and can't send you an Instant Message. Fortunately, AOL gives you a few tools that put you in the driver's seat.

The simplest thing to do when you want to be alone is to turn the Instant Message feature off altogether (see Figure 8-4). Just open a new Instant Message window, type **$im_off** into the To: box, and click the Available? Button. You'll get a message from AOL acknowledging that you've turned IMs off. Your IMs will stay turned off for the length of your online session, or until you turn them on again, whichever comes first. The next time you sign on, your IMs will be turned on again.

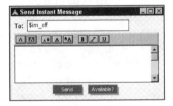

Figure 8-4. Preparing to turn off your Instant Messages — all you have to do now is click Send.

To turn IMs back on during an online session, follow the same procedure, except this time, type **$im_on** in the To: box of that IM.

Do you want more and permanent control over your Instant Messages? AOL has created privacy preferences just for you (see Figure 8-5). Just click the My AOL button on the AOL toolbar, select Preferences, and click the Privacy button on the Preferences window.

You can add flair to your Instant Messages by changing the font at My AOL ⇨ Preferences.

Would you like to create a hypertext link or perform a spell check on your IM text? Just right-click your mouse button. The context menu that appears includes those two options, and several others.

You can also turn IMs off for just an individual, so you can keep talking to everyone else. Just type **$im_off**, press the spacebar, type his or her exact screen name, and then click the Available? button. You can turn IMs back on for that individual using the $im_on code.

8

Tip

You can use AOL Instant Messenger at the same time you're signed on to AOL with your own account. This way, you can send IMs from Instant Messenger using one screen name while you're signed on to AOL with a different screen name.

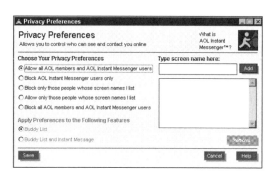

Figure 8-5. Privacy preferences help keep all your Instant Messages friendly.

Privacy Preferences were added to AOL after the introduction of the Buddy List, which we discuss a bit later in the chapter. Whether you use a Buddy List or not, others can use Buddy Lists, the Locate a Member Online feature, or even the Member Directory to see if you're currently online. Privacy Preferences give you the freedom to conceal yourself in the way that suits you best. See Appendix B for details on Privacy Preferences.

AOL Instant Messenger

AOL introduced AOL Instant Messenger to help bring other Internet users into the AOL community. Instant Messenger is a free service that allows AOL members to exchange Instant Messages with friends who are not using AOL, and allows any Instant Messenger user to exchange messages with any other Instant Messenger user. It's also handy for AOL members who may be at an Internet-connected computer that doesn't have AOL software installed on it. Just think about it. You can send IMs to your daughter via her college's computer network, or send an IM to your husband at home from your office's computer network. Instant Messenger is also part of the Buddy List system, so you can see when your Internet friends are online, and they can see you!

To use AOL Instant Messenger (AIM), folks have to download and install a bit of software from the AOL.com Web site, and register for the service. You can make things easier for them by visiting Keyword: **Instant Messenger**, where you can fill in an e-mail invitation with all the details, which AOL will then send to your friends. Every AIM user has his or her own screen name, just like an AOL screen name, and if you're already an AOL member, you can use your regular screen name with AIM, too.

There's only one real difference between receiving Instant Messages from those on AOL and those using AOL Instant Messenger. The first time you receive an Instant Message from someone using AOL Instant Messenger during an online session, you must specifically accept the message — it doesn't just pop up on your screen. This is done to protect AOL members from unwanted messages originating on the Internet.

Buddy List

When you board the AOL virtual tour bus, it's very hard to tell which of your friends are already seated on the bus, and it's nearly impossible to know when they board or exit the bus. Unless, of course, you have added your friend's screen names to your Buddy List (see Figure 8-6).

Figure 8-6. The Buddy List window takes attendance, but takes up very little space.

The Buddy List is an essential tool for anyone who uses Instant Messages or chats online. You'll see a list of which friends and associates are currently online, and you'll see when they've signed on or signed off. If you see a friend's name, you can send him or her an Instant Message with the click of your mouse. Click a different button to locate that friend online (and if your friend is in a chat room, join him or her in that room), or invite a bunch of friends to view a Favorite Place or visit a private room for a group discussion. Since privacy is important, you can also use Buddy Lists to control who does and doesn't know you are online.

 **Note**

Your friends and family members may already have AOL Instant Messenger software, as it is included with the Netscape Navigator browser and comes preinstalled on many new computers.

 **Find It Online**

To learn more about AOL Instant Messenger, visit the AIM Web site at `http://www.aol.com/aim`.

8

Staying in Touch

Who Are Your Buddies?

Your buddies are anyone you want them to be, provided they are AOL members or use AOL Instant Messenger (discussed earlier). If you know a person's screen name(s) or AIM name, you can add it to your Buddy List. You can also create separate lists for special groups of people, such as family members online, or members of your favorite online communities.

Setting Up Your Buddy List

To view your Buddy List Setup window, click the My AOL icon on the AOL toolbar and select Buddy List (or go to Keyword: **Buddy List**). If your Buddy List window is already open, click the Setup button. Once you've set up your Buddy List, it can appear automatically every time you sign on to AOL.

Your Buddy List actually starts with three empty lists (or *groups*) called Buddies, Family, and Co-Workers. You can immediately begin adding screen names to one of these three lists: just select a list and click Edit on the Setup window (see Figure 8-7).

Figure 8-7. The Buddy List Setup window

You can change the name of the group, add screen names to the list, or remove names from the list. You can have around 200 buddies in your Buddy List, though this is the total for your entire AOL account, so you'll probably want to limit yourself to 50 per screen name at most. When you're finished editing the group, click the Save button; otherwise, your changes will not take place (see Figure 8-8).

Returning to the Setup window, you can create a new Buddy List group with the Create button. To delete an entire Buddy List group, select the group name in the list, and click the Delete button. You'll be asked to confirm that you want to delete that list. The View button opens the Buddy List window on your screen (entering Keyword: **Buddy View** does the same thing). A click of the Privacy Preferences button opens the same Privacy Preferences window we discussed earlier in the chapter.

Cross-Reference

Learn all about your privacy preferences in Appendix B, "Setting Your Preferences."

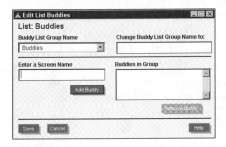

Figure 8-8. The Edit List window helps you manage your Buddy List.

Buddy List Preferences (on the right side of the window) affect "cosmetic" aspects of your Buddy List (see Figure 8-9). Buddy List Preferences are also detailed in Appendix B.

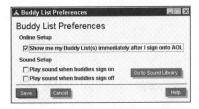

Figure 8-9. Use these preferences to control your Buddy window and include sign-off and sign-on sounds — and visit the Sound Library for fun, new sounds!

Using Your Buddy List

Once your Buddy List is up and running, it's very easy to use. All you have to do is keep your eyes (and ears) open to know when your friends, family members, and/or coworkers arrive and depart. Here are some tips to keep you and your buddies happy:

▶ Do you want to send one of your friends an Instant Message? Just double-click his or her screen name in your Buddy List window, and you'll receive a pread-dressed Instant Message window.

▶ To locate a friend online, click his or her name once and then click the Locate button. If your friend is in a chat room, you can click the Go button to join him or her in that room.

8

Staying in Touch

Tip

If you suspect a friend is online, but you can't see him or her in your Buddy List, send an e-mail to see whether he or she wants to talk.

▶ Buddy Chat (see Figure 8-10) lets you invite your friends to share a hyperlink (such as the cool new forum you found) or invite them all to a private chat room (chat rooms are discussed in the next section). First, click the name of the buddy or the entire Buddy Group you wish to invite, and then click the Buddy Chat button. You can edit the list of buddies to invite, type a message they all will receive, drag a Favorite Place heart to the location box, or type in the name of a private room you want them to visit. When you're done, click Send, and each friend on your list will receive an invitation, which they may accept or decline at their option.

Figure 8-10. The Buddy Chat window helps you keep your friends and family in touch.

Your Buddy List has a bit more to tell you, if you look closely. If a name on your Buddy List has an asterisk (*) next to it, that person just signed on to AOL. If his or her screen name is in parentheses, he or she just signed off. The numbers next to a group name tell you how many group members are currently signed on and how many names are in that group. If you double-click a group name, the names on the list are hidden and a +plus symbol appears next to it, so that you know the names have been hidden. Another double-click reveals the full list.

Chats and Conferences

Our virtual tour bus's next stop is a bit roomier than a telephone booth. We're now going to visit the cafes and meeting rooms known as chat rooms and conferences, and what better place to learn about them than in People Connection, AOL's teeming metropolis of online talk? (See Figure 8-11.)

Figure 8-11. People Connection — AOL's chat headquarters

People come to People Connection with all sorts of interests, from purely social to purely professional, and everything in between. Although you can pop into a chat lobby and meet whoever pops up, with just a bit of effort you can find a room filled with people who share your interests. You can meet others with a love for the arts, news, sports, or romance, or even meet an AOL member from overseas. If you can't find the kind of company you desire in a People Connection room, you're free to create a member room or a private room. Member rooms are listed right alongside People Connection rooms in People Connection's Find a Chat listings, so any AOL member can find your room and join the conversation. If you'd rather limit the party to your own friends and family, create a private room, which is unlisted (details later, in the section "Creating Your Own Chat Room").

Because you can create your own chat rooms, why not organize a regularly scheduled chat on a topic near and dear to your heart? Perhaps your cousins club is free to meet every fourth Thursday of the month at 9 p.m. eastern time, or members of your local hiking club can meet every Wednesday to plan the weekend's activities. Private rooms are great for this kind of discussion. If you're more interested in gathering alumni from your old alma mater, a member room makes sense, since long-lost friends may stumble across it in a chat room search.

8

Staying in Touch

I Need Help!

There's also a dark side to the world of online chat. You can run into people who are rude, offensive, or downright abusive. They may be looking for "cyber" (cyber sex), use language that's far outside your comfort zone, or offer you goodies that turn out to be far from wholesome. Some may be trying to hijack your AOL account, others want your credit card number, and still others may just want to rattle you. Not every kind of behavior that's offensive to you may be a violation of AOL's Terms of Service (TOS), but when it is, AOL makes it very easy to fight back. Just click the handy Notify AOL button in the chat room, and fill in the form. AOL must have a sample of the objectionable behavior. All you need to do is highlight the offensive behavior on the chat screen and drag and drop (or copy and paste) it into the box in the Notify AOL window. To learn more about AOL's Terms of Service and how you can better protect yourself, visit Keyword: **I Need Help**. For advice on many aspects of online safety, visit Keyword: **Neighborhood Watch**.

Finding Communities

Chatting is the essence of online community, since chat rooms are the place for live group interaction on AOL. Very few online areas lack some sort of chat. If you don't believe us, start visiting forums and see for yourself! Some areas host chats around the clock, whereas others present a schedule of chats, classes, or presentations.

Although People Connection is the Times Square of the chat world, if your interests are specific, you'll often find a better community in the online area(s) that directly serves that interest. The best communities offer a combination of online information, newsletters, and human interaction and take great pride in tying all those pieces together for the members of their community.

For now, though, we're going to head back to People Connection, since there's always something going on. Which chat should you choose? No matter what your choice, AOL makes it easy!

To start chatting in a chat lobby, click the People icon on your AOL toolbar, and select Chat Now, or click Chat Now! on the People Connection main screen. Lobbies aren't the best place to make lasting friends, but they're a quick way to get your feet wet. Just don't be surprised if you feel like you're standing in the middle of downtown traffic.

The chat can be better in a room that is organized around a theme or topic. Click the People icon on your AOL toolbar, and select Find a Chat, or click Find a Chat on the People Connection main screen. On the left-hand side of the Find a Chat window is a scroll box with about a dozen different categories, including Town Square, Arts and Entertainment, Friends, Places, Romance, and Special Interests (see Figure 8-12). At the top of that scroll box you'll find two tabs. Click the first tab to select from chats created and operated by People Connection. The other tab lists chats created by AOL members like yourself. In both cases, you'll see the same list of categories.

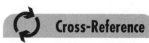

Cross-Reference

We have more to say about finding an online community in Chapter 9. Chapter 14 is filled with tips on how to find information, which, as we've mentioned, often leads you to community. Because Netiquette is so important to good community relations, a review of Chapter 2 is also a great idea.

Figure 8-12. The Find a Chat window, in People Connection. Select a category on the left, and pick a chat on the right.

For now, we recommend rooms created by People Connection, as hosts who can give you a hand and keep the chat running smoothly may be present. Highlight the category you wish to explore, click the View Chats button in the middle of the window, and start scrolling through the list of available chat rooms in the right-hand scroll box. There may be over 100 rooms listed, and the List More button at the bottom of the scroll box may reveal even more rooms. Select a room with an appealing title, and click the Go Chat button at the bottom of the window. If the room is already filled to capacity, you may be given the choice to go to another chat like it, since in some cases AOL automatically creates

8

Staying in Touch

The surest way to find a hosted chat is to use People Connection's Chat Schedule. Click the AOL Chat Schedule button on the People Connection main screen.

To the left of every chat room name is a number. If that number is 23, that chat room has already filled to capacity. You may try to enter that room (as people are coming and going all the time), or you can look down the list for a room that has some space available.

additional chat rooms with the same name. So if there's no room for you in Best Lil Chathouse, perhaps there will be room for you in Best Lil Chathouse 2, or Best Lil Chathouse 22.

Hosts and Other Friendly Helpers

AOL's chat hosts are people who volunteer to help make the online chat experience rewarding for everyone involved. Like any good host, they welcome you to their chat room, make a few introductions, and explain the ins and outs of that particular room. They also work hard to make their room a pleasant and rewarding place to visit. Hosts receive extensive training before they get a chat room of their own, and they know how to deal with the ruffians who like to prey on innocent newcomers.

People Connection hosts have screen names that begin with *Host*, such as HOSTLeff, a friend of ours who was honored some years ago for his contribution to the AOL community. Jennifer herself was a host in People Connection many years ago near the start of her AOL adventure. Chat Hosts in other online areas will have names related to their forum, such as FamCL, the volunteer Community Leaders for the Family Channel.

Anatomy of a Chat

Now that you've found a chat room, you may be wondering what's going on (see Figure 8-13).

Figure 8-13. An AOL chat room has a lot in common with an Instant Message.

The chat box dominates the chat room window. When you first enter a chat room, you'll receive an announcement from OnlineHost identifying the chat room you've entered. There's no point trying to chat with OnlineHost — she's a computer. Unless the chat room is empty, you'll begin seeing comments from other people in the room in short order. Each person's comment automatically includes his or her screen name, so everyone knows who said what. Once the window fills with chat, the text starts scrolling up, like the credits at the end of a movie. Unlike a movie theater, though, you can use the scroll bar on the right-hand side of the chat box to scroll back and review earlier comments.

At the very bottom of the chat window is the text entry box. This is where you type your comments. There's room for about one long sentence in that box. This encourages you to write short comments and send them right to the chat, rather than write the next Great American Novel. Look at your text, make sure it's what you want to say, and click Send (or press the Enter key). Now you should see your own screen name and comment up in lights!

When you go out on the town, you dress to express your individuality, so when you chat, why should your text look like everyone else's? Right between the chat and text boxes are a font selection drop-down list and a few styled text buttons. Dress-up your words with a distinctive font and maybe a dash of color!

Who is in the chat room with you? If they're lurking, the only way you'll know is to scroll through the people list on the right-hand side of the window. If you double-click a name on that list, you can ignore that member, send him or her an IM, or check his or her member profile.

About the only thing left to describe are the buttons in the lower-right of the window, which may come in handy. Find a Chat, Private Chat, and AOL Live are there to make moving from chat to chat a bit easier, and Member Directory will help if you're searching for new (and old) friends. Chat Preferences enables you to change the way chat is displayed in your chat window, and whether you'll be able to hear chat sounds. Notify AOL stands at the ready, in case barbarians from the North invade your chat room. If you must notify AOL, be sure to copy the offending chat into the appropriate field in the Notify AOL window (see Figure 8-14).

Note

Only those who have the same font installed on their computer will see the font you've chosen, so try not to use an unusual or exotic font. Use a common font, and make it more distinctive with color, bold, or italics.

Tip

If someone in the room is behaving badly, you can banish him or her from your sight by using the Ignore feature. Just double-click his or her name in the people list and select Ignore. The neat part is that he or she doesn't know he or she's is being ignored. However, if the person leaves the chat room and returns, you will have to repeat the steps for ignoring him or her.

8

Staying in Touch

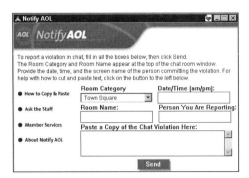

Figure 8-14. The Notify AOL window for chat rooms. Be sure to supply all the information, especially a copy of the chat violation.

What's a Conference Room?

So far, we've been discussing chat rooms, which are the most common group discussion areas online. The biggest difference between a chat room and conference room is capacity; chat rooms hold 23 visitors, whereas conference rooms hold up to 48. Why don't all chat rooms hold 48 people? The simplest reason is it's far too confusing to have 48 people chatting at the same time, and the text in the chat window moves by too quickly. Forums use conference rooms when their events need a bit more space, but people won't be chatting much amongst themselves. Events in conference rooms generally follow protocol — folks are asked to speak only when called on. This makes sense when someone is leading a class, or the room is hosting a panel discussion or an interview with an interesting guest.

Chatting

There's nothing difficult about chatting, but as with any new social situation, you may feel better taking things slow and easy. A chat room can be a busy place, with people coming and going and many conversations happening at once. It pays to sit quietly for a while until you can catch on to the personalities and conversations around you.

Of course, folks may greet you, and it would be rude not to reply, "Hi, Jennifer! I'm new here. I'm just going to lurk a bit."

Whenever you speak, address the person(s) by his or her screen name (or an obvious nickname). With all those conversations going on, it's hard to know who is speaking to whom.

Even the language may be strange. Chatters use all sorts of abbreviations and symbols, such as LTNS, ROFL, {{{{Dave}}}} and :-). To translate, that's "long time no see," "rolling on floor, laughing," enthusiastic hugs for Dave (in this case), and a warm smile (lean your head to the left to see two eyes, a nose and a smiling mouth). The abbreviations are called *shorthands* and the symbols are *smileys*, and when you get to know them, you'll be chatting with the best of 'em.

Chat Sounds and Hypertext Links

Chat room fans have a few extra tricks up their sleeves. They can play sounds in the chat room and exchange hypertext links to Favorite Places online.

Playing chat sounds is simple. A person in the chat room sends a special phrase to the chat, which looks like this: {S *filename*. For example, {S welcome will play the "Welcome" you hear when you sign on to AOL. The only way the people in the room can hear the chat sound is if the same sound file is on their computer's hard disk. That's why {S welcome, {S goodbye, and {S gotmail are so popular. All three of those sounds are included in your AOL software.

If you can't even hear "Welcome" when someone sends {S welcome to the screen, check your chat preferences (there's a button for that right on the chat room window). Be sure Enable Chat Room Sounds has a checkmark beside it.

You can also exchange Favorite Places in a chat room, but only if your Parental Controls settings have been adjusted to permit it. Since hypertext links can take you to some dangerous places, AOL has decided to make viewing hypertext links a conscious decision on your part. If you want to use them, first access Parental Controls from a master screen name, select Custom Controls, and select Chat controls. Now remove the checkmark for Block Hyperlinks in Chat for those screen names that can be allowed this convenient, if sometimes risky, feature.

 Definition

Lurking is not a bad thing in the online world. In fact, it can be downright courteous. It means you've chosen to observe the personalities and customs of the community you're visiting so that when you do start chatting, you'll fit right in.

 Find It Online

The folks at AOL Canada have prepared a delightful introduction to shorthands and smileys, but it's deeply buried. Click the Mail Center icon on the AOL toolbar, select Mail Extras, select Smileys, open any one of the smileys in the list box, and click the Try This! button.

8

Staying in Touch

Creating Your Own Chat Room

Cross-Reference

You can also create a private chat room using your Buddy List's Buddy Chat feature, which we described earlier in this chapter.

As we mentioned earlier, you are free to create your own chat room. You can make either a member room, which any visitor to People Connection may find and enter, or a private room, which is open only to those who know (or can guess) the name of the room. The easiest way to create either kind of room is to click the People button on the AOL toolbar, and select Start Your Own Chat. You can then select whether you want a member chat or private chat (see Figure 8-15).

Figure 8-15. Start your own chat — just follow the simple instructions.

If you click Member Chat, you can choose the People Connection category in which you want your room to be listed. If you select Private Chat, you can create a new private chat, or go to an existing private chat if the name you typed is already in use. As you can see, your room name can be very important. Member chats are listed in People Connection, so it pays to make the name simple and descriptive — "U of M Alumni," for example. To be sure private chats stay private, private chat names should be a bit more complex.

There's one important difference between private rooms and all other kinds of chat rooms. Private rooms are really private. Only you and invited guests should be in it, so no Notify AOL button appears on the Private room window, and in this case AOL does not get involved in policing violations of the Terms of Service.

A member chat or private chat exists only for as long as the corresponding room is occupied. When the last person exits a room, it disappears, but you can always create the room again some other day.

Logging a Chat

Has your memory been slipping lately? Why try remembering what happened in your online party, meeting, or class when you can record the entire thing for posterity with a chat log? Chat logs save every word displayed in a chat room to a file on your computer's hard disk so you can refer to it later.

You can start logging a chat at any time. Click the My Files icon on the AOL toolbar, and select Log Manager. The Logging window that appears (see Figure 8-16) has two sections. Let's concentrate on the Chat Log section.

Figure 8-16. The Log Manager. The Chat Log section lists the chat room you're visiting.

Click the Open Log button to start a brand new log. AOL automatically names the log for the chat room you're visiting, but you can change that if you wish. The Append Log button will add the latest chat to an existing log file. This is especially useful if your online session was interrupted, and you had to sign back on to resume your chat. The Close Log button stops logging cold, which is something you may want to do when your online meeting adjourns and folks hang around to shoot the breeze.

To view your log, open the AOL File menu, select Open, and use the Open a File dialog box to find and open the file. Log files can become very long, especially when you keep appending chat to the same log file. When log files grow to be over 30K in size, you can no longer open a log file with AOL's software. At that point, you'll have to use a word processing program to open the log.

Tip

If you want to use the same private room on a regular basis, add it to your Favorite Places list. That makes a return trip very simple, and you can use the Favorite Places list to add a hypertext link to e-mailed meeting notices.

Tip

Sometimes you're just too busy to sit and watch a discussion or meeting in a chat room. With the capability to log a chat, you don't have to. Just enter the chat room, start your log rolling, and go about your business. As long as you don't close the chat window, the log will keep rolling, and you can read it later when you have more time.

8

Staying in Touch

Auditoriums

You and your friends can meet in a particular auditorium row by exchanging Instant Messages and moving to the row of your choice.

Ladies and gentlemen, step along now, we're about to visit the auditoriums of AOL Live! When major celebrities and noteworthy experts come to AOL to chat with the members, this is usually where you'll find them. Why? The auditoriums at AOL Live can hold thousands of AOL members at one time, not just the 23 that fit into a chat room or the 48 that can squeeze into a conference room. In fact, the current attendance record at an AOL Live event is nearly 400,000 members!

AOL Live typically hosts several events every day, and since the guests are so popular and the topics so hot, AOL promotes them heavily on the AOL Welcome screen and when you enter People Connection. If you'd like to pop in to AOL Live, click the People icon on the AOL toolbar and select AOL Live, or use Keyword: **Live**.

An AOL auditorium is like no auditorium you can visit in the physical world. Sure, it has a stage, like any other auditorium. The acoustics in this auditorium are better than most, though. Anything that is said (written) on stage can be heard (read) by everyone in the audience, but what's more, no matter how raucous some members of the audience may become, it can't disturb the people on stage or, for that matter, most of the people in the audience.

Each auditorium is made up of rows that can hold from four to sixteen AOL members. When you enter an auditorium, you're automatically assigned to a row, but you can switch chat rows at will, with the help of the Chat Rows button on the auditorium screen.

Each row looks a lot like a regular chat room, but there are a few differences (see Figure 8-17).

To chat with other people in your row, type in the box at the bottom of the auditorium window and click Send. The large chat box displays chat between people in your own row, plus everything said by the people on stage. Use the scroll bar on the right-hand side of the screen to review earlier comments. You won't see comments by people in other rows, and the people on stage won't see your chat.

Figure 8-17. A chat row in an AOL auditorium. Every seat in the house is good!

The list in the upper-right of the window shows the screen names of the people up on stage — the host and his or her guest(s). The People button opens a list of those in your chat row, as many as 16 people. Double-click a name to send the person an IM or get his or her member profile. The Interact button is used to send your comments or questions to the folks on stage. There are also vote and bid options for some kinds of special events. The host will tell you whether to comment, send a question, vote, or bid. The Chat Rows button lets you search other auditorium rows for your friends or move to another row if yours is too crowded or lonely.

My Calendar

So much to do, so little time! Now that you've added AOL to your social life, how can you keep track of all the online chats, meetings, TV shows, play dates, ball games, and cultural events that fill your days (and nights)? Take advantage of the latest addition to AOL's lineup of cool features, My Calendar.

To get started with My Calendar, just click the My Calendar icon on either the AOL Welcome screen or the AOL toolbar, or use Keyword: **Calendar**. As a first-time visitor you'll be asked to supply your time zone, zip code (so My Calendar can suggest events happening in your area), and birth date (if you want a daily horoscope). If you wish, AOL will add five-day weather forecasts, too. You can always change any of these settings by clicking the Options button at the bottom of the main calendar window (see Figure 8-18).

Caution

Don't get upset at the people on stage if they seem to be ignoring you. They're not being rude. They can't see you, even though you can see them. Click the Interact button to send your question or comment to the people on stage.

Tip

How do you know whether a comment is being made in your row, or by someone on stage? Everything said by someone in your row will have the row number listed alongside his or her screen name, whereas those on stage will only have their screen names listed.

8

Staying in Touch

Add holidays to your calendar with ease! Click the Event Directory tab at the top of the calendar and click Holidays in the Reference section. You'll find a wide variety of holiday listings, and you can pick and choose holidays from all of those lists.

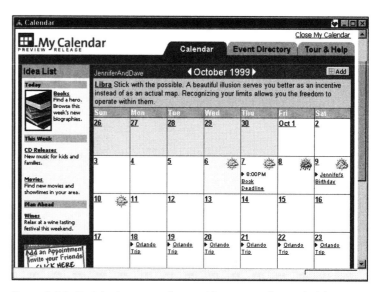

Figure 8-18. My Calendar opens with a monthly overview of your schedule

My Calendar is a good bit more than an old-fashioned appointment book. Thanks to its online connections, every appointment you set up can be shared with anyone you please, via e-mail. My Calendar also includes an Idea List and Event Calendar that list online chats, TV programs, movies, sports, and cultural events that you can add to your calendar with just a click or two of your mouse. Customize your calendar by selecting a one-day or one-week calendar view, and add local weather forecasts, your daily horoscope and your choice of national and religious holidays. Once you get started with My Calendar you'll be amazed by just how much you can do with it.

Each item you add to your calendar has a brief description right on the calendar, and if you click that listing you can view or edit all the details and reschedule or delete the listing. If you chose the weather forecast option the calendar will display icons representing that day's weather conditions. Click the icon to view a more detailed report.

Flipping the "pages" of your calendar is very simple. To move from month to month in your calendar just click the left or right arrows that flank the date at the top of the calendar. To check next year's schedule: enter the date you wish to view in the Jump To box at the bottom of the calendar, and click the Go button.

If you have a jam-packed schedule you may prefer to view a daily or weekly calendar, rather than the default full-month view. Click the Day or Week tabs at the bottom of the calendar when you need to zoom in. You can even change the default setting so that your calendar always opens in Day or Week view. Click the Options button at the bottom of the calendar to change the default view.

Creating an appointment item couldn't be simpler. Click the handy Add buttons at the top or bottom of the calendar, or click the desired date and/or time on the calendar display — all dates and times are hypertext links. My Calendar automatically opens the Appointment Details display (see Figure 8-19).

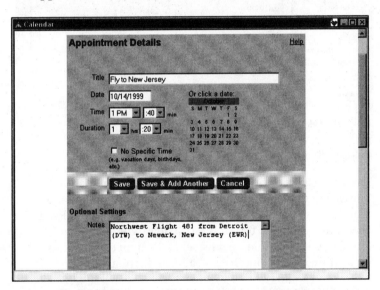

Figure 8-19. The Appointment Details window makes scheduling easy

Use the text entry fields and drop-down lists of the Appointment Details window to give your appointment a title, select (or modify) the date, choose a duration, and click Save or Save & Add Another. Before you click Save, perhaps you want to add notes to the appointment, or send a meeting notice to friends or colleagues. Just type their screen names or e-mail addresses in the Email Attendees field, separating each name with a comma. AOL will send them e-mail in your name. You can also set repeat options. Just enter the information once and My Calendar will take care of the rest.

You can do far more than create your own appointments. My Calendar's Idea List and Event Directory open the door to thousands of events that you can add to your calendar with just a few clicks of your mouse (see Figure 8-20).

Click the date or time hyperlinks on a calendar view to automatically set the date and/or time of your appointment.

If you modify an appointment My Calendar will notify the people on the Email Attendees list.

Before you start sharing events with your friends why not share an event with yourself, so you see how it works? Just view an event, click the Tell a Friend button and supply your own screen name instead of a friend's.

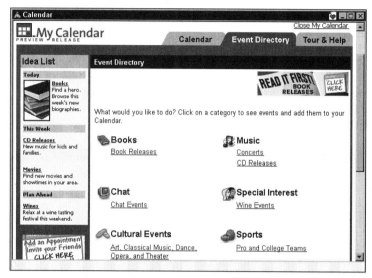

Figure 8-20. My Calendar's Event Directory and Idea List

The Idea List is always visible on your calendar, suggesting things you can do today, this week, and in the weeks and months to come. For a far greater selection, click the Event Directory tab at the top of the calendar window. If you're interested in any item on a list, click its hypertext link to view more details, purchase it, and/or share it with a friend.

If you choose, your friend(s) can receive e-mail sent from your screen name that includes a hypertext link to the event page you selected and any comments you choose to include. What's more, if your friend can add the event to his or her own calendar!

You should also keep your eyes open for the My Calendar icon wherever you travel on AOL and the World Wide Web. The My Calendar icon looks like the one shown in the upper left corner of Figure 8-20. If you see it, click it to add that item to your calendar.

Travelers and business people can access My Calendar from any computer with Internet access, even if AOL software hasn't been installed. Just visit the AOL.com home page (`http://www.aol.com`) and follow the links to My Calendar.

If you think My Calendar is exciting now, just wait. All sorts of plans are in the works! It's very likely that by the time you read this book, My Calendar will be better than ever!

Independent Explorations

One of the most amazing things about AOL is its people. You may be sitting alone at your computer, but when you're on AOL, people surround you. And unlike being alone in a crowd of people in a mall or at a stadium, you can reach out and connect with people online. The term *global village* was never truer than with AOL.

Now that you know where to find people and how to connect with them, we heartily recommend you take advantage of your power. Invite your friends to a virtual party or your family to an online reunion. If your friends and family aren't on AOL, invite them over with Keyword: **Friend** or Keyword: **Instant Messenger**.

Of course, meeting new friends is one of AOL's advantages, too. The two of us met on AOL over four years ago and just look at us now! Many of our friends and family members report similar experiences, and there are legendary tales of grand friendships and romances that started on AOL.

How do you make friends online? Beyond the resources we listed in this chapter, two more AOL features can help you meet and make new friends: message boards and newsgroups. So hop back on the virtual bus and we'll head on over for a tour of those busy discussion areas!

8

Staying in Touch

Quick Look

▶ **Message Boards**   **page 179**

> Message boards are collections of messages, available on virtually every topic.
> All members are welcome to read the messages and add their own if they wish.

▶ **Finding Messages**   **page 183**

> AOL provides a handy search function in every message board. You can search
> by date, word or phrase, or construct a custom search. Look for the Find By
> menu in the bottom right corner of your favorite message board.

▶ **Newsgroups**   **page 190**

> Newsgroups are the Internet-wide version of AOL message boards, offering
> diverse communities and topics. Newsgroups are accessible at Keyword:
> **Newsgroups**.

▶ **Offline Newsgroup Browsing**   **page 197**

> You can download the most recent posts on your favorite message boards and
> newsgroups using the Auto AOL feature. Once downloaded, posts are available
> in your Personal Filing Cabinet. Choose Set up Automatic AOL from your Mail
> Center window to get started.

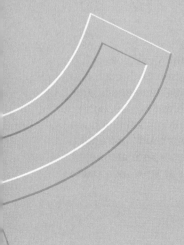

Chapter 9

Making New Friends

IN THIS CHAPTER

Learning where to find message boards

Setting your Message Board Preferences

Discovering how to post a message

Broadening your reach with Internet newsgroups

After the heady rush of Instant Messages and chats, you may be ready for something a bit more down to earth. We have just the thing: message boards and newsgroups. If you're unfamiliar with the names, don't let them worry you. These are centers of community fellowship, information exchange, and shared interests. And unlike Instant Messages and chats, which take place in real-time, these message centers let you take things at your own pace.

Message Boards

Message boards are a cornerstone of community on AOL. You'd be hard-pressed to find an online area that lacks a message board. Message boards turn a one-sided presentation of information into a lively give-and-take among people with common interests.

What precisely is a message board? Imagine a large cork bulletin board. Along the top of the corkboard you'll find a row of labels, identifying a variety of topics. Perhaps one of those topics is reserved for official announcements. Beneath each of the other topics people can post written comments, questions, and replies. As folks reply to a particular message, they pin their responses right on top of the original message. When the board gets too cluttered with messages, the oldest messages are removed. Inappropriate messages are removed by the person tending the bulletin board, or moved to a more appropriate place. When things get out of hand, that same person may remind everyone to tone things down.

Now imagine our bulletin board in an electronic format. Instead of a cork board and push pins, we have a computer screen and icons. Better yet, we have all the power and convenience you'd normally expect online. This is what we call a message board (see Figure 9-1).

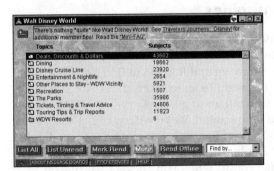

Figure 9-1. A typical message board located at Keyword: **Traveler**. Look at all those topics and subjects!

AOL's message boards follow our bulletin board model very closely, but thanks to technology they make it easier to find and participate in this kind of discussion and also keep things neat and tidy. A message board keeps track of which posts and subjects you have read and hides those that you've already seen. The message board also tells you how many topics, subjects, or posts you'll find as you dig down into the contents of the board. You can set your preferences for reading a board, including how you want the messages sorted, whether you only want to see posts on certain topics, or how far back you can look through the messages. When you open a post, the fun really begins. You can check to see if the author of the post is online. If you reply to the post, you can send your reply via e-mail to the person who made the post and/or post publicly on the board. As with e-mail, you can select text you wish to quote in your reply, and include a prewritten signature line. And that's not the half of it.

Unlike a live chat, where you have to be in the right place at the right time to join a conversation, message boards follow a slower, more civilized pace. A person may post a question in the morning, someone else may read it an hour later and post an answer, the original questioner may ask a follow-up question the next day, and other people may chime in on the conversation for weeks to come. Anyone coming late to the discussion can read the whole thing from beginning to end, and if they have a comment, they'll know if someone has already made a similar point.

Finding Communities

Finding communities is easy. Finding the right community is a bit harder. Not finding any communities at all is very hard indeed. Pick a forum, any forum! It helps to find one on a topic you're interested in or want to learn more about. Are you there yet? (If you're not sure where to go, try Keyword: **MHM**.) Take a second or two to look around. We're willing to bet you've found a Message Boards or Boards button or link. If you didn't, maybe you saw a Chat button. Very often you'll find both message boards and chat rooms when you click a Chat button. For that matter, we've found that almost any button or link that suggests discussion of some sort can lead to a message board. If you can't even find that much, perhaps there's an index of the online area. If you have a choice of areas catering to your topic of interest, try the one with "forum" in its title first, as it's likely to be focused on community interaction.

There's a bit of a difference between finding *any* community and finding a *good* community. What is a good community? Consider what *you* think makes a good community. Do people drop by frequently to see what's happening and contribute their own two cents? Are they courteous, friendly to newcomers, patient with beginners, and generous with their expertise? Is it free of crass commercialism, nastiness, or other inappropriate behavior? Do people take an active interest in maintaining and improving their community? Well, then, we're all in agreement! What's true in your offline community is just as true online.

Once you find a promising community, spend a few minutes peeking through the cracks in the fence to see if it's really what you want. As soon as the message board opens on screen you begin to get an idea. How many topics do you see? Are there many subjects in each topic? If you open a topic, do you see more subtopics? If you open a topic, do the individual subjects each have two or more posts? If your answer is yes, you've found a thriving community. When it comes to good community, the more messages the merrier!

If you like what you've seen so far, wade in and start reading the messages (we explain just how in the next section). Don't think about adding your own comments, though. If you decide to join the community, there'll be plenty of time for that later. For now, concentrate on getting a feel for how the community operates — see how the conversation ebbs and flows, the kinds of things folks discuss, the ways they discuss them. Try to become familiar with some of the personalities who make their home there.

Look for the community's message board guidelines, and be sure you understand them. Although AOL's Terms of Service always are in force, many communities post additional guidelines to address issues unique to their community. And, of course, the rules of netiquette are always in force.

Definition

There are several definitions of *forum*. According to the dictionary, it's a place people meet for free discussion. A forum can also be any online area dedicated to a topic or interest, such as the AOL Families Channel or the Grandstand Soccer Forum (Keyword: **GS Soccer**). To some people, forum means message board or its equivalents elsewhere in the online world (such as newsgroups).

Tip

Many communities exist on AOL, each dedicated to a particular interest. Don't try to make one community serve all your varied interests. Find different communities to serve each of your interests, and keep each community's discussions on topic.

Reading Messages

Reading is easy, and making your way through a message board is only slightly harder.

Message boards are organized by topic, subject, and post. Only forum staff can create a topic (see Figure 9-2), and each topic can be looked upon as a separate message board.

Tip

When you've found a message board you want to call home, add it to your Favorite Places list. Not only can you set an entire message board as a favorite place but you can also make favorite places out of individual topics or even messages. See Chapter 3 for more details on adding favorite places.

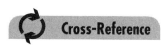

Cross-Reference

You can read more about netiquette in Chapter 2.

Cross-Reference

Learn how to use Auto AOL in Chapter 10.

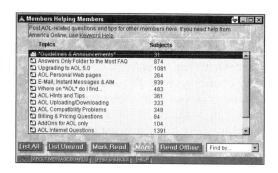

Figure 9-2. The top level of the Members Helping Members message board center at Keyword: **MHM.** Each topic is a message board in its own right.

Let's look at the buttons on a top-level board, as shown in Figure 9-2. Click List All to see every subject within a selected topic, even those you've already read. List Unread, as you'd guess, is a bit more selective. Mark Read will hide every subject in that topic on your next visit, just as if you'd read each one. Read Offline selects that topic so its posts can be saved to your Personal Filing Cabinet during an Auto AOL session (discussed at the end of the chapter). The Find by button helps you search for posts containing specific information.

To browse a topic, select it and press the List All or List Unread button. Double-clicking a topic is the same as clicking the List Unread button. The topic opens in a new window, displaying a listing of the subjects within it (see Figure 9-3).

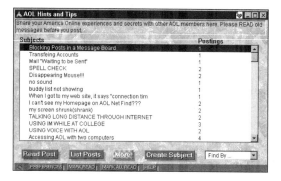

Figure 9-3. A listing of subjects available in the AOL Hints and Tips topic in the Members Helping Members message board

You can just start double-clicking to read subjects that interest you, or select a topic and click the List Unread button. Alternatively, click List Posts to see a list of posts and their authors prior to reading a single post.

Posts look similar to e-mail (see Figure 9-4). They have a subject, a date, and identify the person who made the post by screen name.

Note that the screen name is also a hypertext link. If you click the name, AOL checks to see if the person is online.

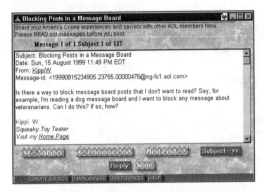

Figure 9-4. A post from the Members Helping Members message board. Note the header information and the signature at the bottom of the post.

Use the buttons at the bottom of the post to move from post to post within a subject, and then move on to the next subject. The More button is available when a post is very long. Click Mark Unread if you want to come back to this post later. The Reply and Create Subject buttons belong in our discussion of posting messages, a little later in this chapter.

Once you've read a post, the message board hides it from your view on the next visit so you don't reread it again, thinking it is a new message. If you want to find the post again, click the Mark Unread button at the bottom of a post's window or click the List All button when you revisit the message board. If, on the other hand, you want to banish posts without reading them at all, select the topic or post and click the Mark Read button at the bottom of the topic window.

If you select a topic and click List All, you'll see every subject in that board. Logically, List Unread will show you only those subjects you haven't read.

Finding Messages

To search message boards, select the Find By drop-down menu in the lower-right corner of a message board on either the topic or subject level (refer back to Figure 9-3). You have three main searching options: Custom Search, Word or Phrase, and Date.

We prefer to use Custom Search (see Figure 9-5), as it provides a more flexible search, though a word or phrase search works well for fast-and-simple searches.

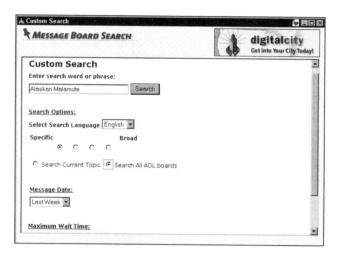

Figure 9-5. The Custom Search window lets you fine-tune your message board search.

Type your search word(s) or phrase in the top field of the search window. For best results you should be as specific as possible. Also indicate whether you'd like to search the current topic or all AOL boards. Use the latter option with caution, as it can take some time and return lots of results.

If you're performing a custom search, you also have the option of making your search specific (exact spelling and/or word order), or broad (close or similar spelling and/or word order), or somewhere in between. Again, use this option with caution. If you're looking for Alaskan Malamutes and don't want results with just Alaska in it, click the radio button on the Specific end. Another Custom Search option is the message date. Choose Last Week (default) or Past Month to find results in either date range. Finally, choose your maximum wait time from the menu at the bottom. If it is important to find good (and numerous) results, increase the wait time. Otherwise, keep it as is, or even decrease it.

When you're ready, click the Search button next to the word or phrase field at the top of the window. After a few moments, AOL displays any results found (see Figure 9-6).

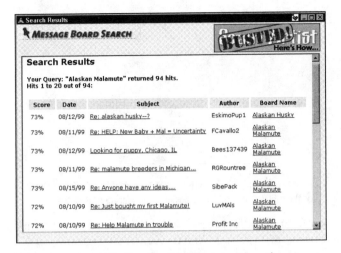

Figure 9-6. The AOL Message Board displays its search results.

AOL lists your results by how closely they matched your search word(s) or phrase. Also included is the date of the post, the subject line, the author's screen name, and the message board where the post was found. To read a post, just click the subject line (which is a hyperlink). The message board name is also a hyperlink.

If you prefer to search for posts by date, drop-down the Find By menu and choose Date on the message board you wish to search. You can search for new posts only (since your last visit), posts in the last *x* number of days (you specify the number of days), or posts between specific dates. Note that the Date search only works for the current message board or topic; it cannot search all AOL message boards.

Setting Message Board Preferences

One button we haven't discussed yet is the Preferences button found at the bottom of every message board window. Clicking Preferences leads to the Global Message Board Preferences window. Preferences you select in this window affect every board you visit. AOL organizes your Message Board Preferences into three categories: viewing, posting, and filtering (see Figure 9-7).

Tip

If you'd like to find all the messages you posted recently, do a search on your own screen name. Unless you have a very common screen name (like Jennifer does), this works like a charm!

Definition

Threading connects all the posts for a single subject, like beads on a necklace. This makes it easy to follow the thread of the conversation.

Tip

If you select a board for Offline Reading, go through that board and mark all undesired topics and subjects as read, so you won't clutter your Personal Filing Cabinet.

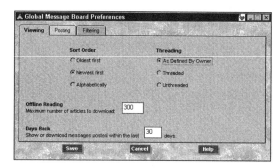

Figure 9-7. The Global Message Boards Preferences window displays your viewing preferences. Click the tabs at the top to view posting and filtering preferences.

Viewing preferences affect the order and accessibility of your message boards. Most people like to see the newest subjects and posts at the top of their windows, but you may prefer to choose Oldest first or Alphabetically if you're having trouble finding a subject or post.

Threading refers to the way subjects are organized. The option As Defined By Owner accepts the forum staff's recommendation regarding threading. Threaded and Unthreaded give you the choice to overrule the forum staff's judgement and see the message board in your own way. There can be a benefit to selecting Unthreaded and Newest first, which brings all the newest posts right to the top of board, regardless of which subject they reside in. However, this could present too many posts to wade through in a busy board. Feel free to experiment.

Offline Reading is a setting for Auto AOL. If you've selected one or more message boards for offline reading using Auto AOL, this preference sets limits on how many posts you'll receive. This prevents the unfortunate accident of downloading thousands of posts from a message board you've yet to read.

You can also use viewing preferences to hide or reveal posts based on their age. You can enter a number as high as 9999, which means you'll see all posts available on the board. If a board is very busy, you may prefer to hide posts after seven days or less.

Click the Posting tab at the top of the Preferences window to access your posting preferences, which holds your signature (or *sig*) for your message board posts. You may type whatever you'd like added to the end of your posts in the signature box.

Feel free to use the format toolbar to spiff up your signature. If you want to add a hyperlink, as we have in Figure 9-8, right-click in the signature box and choose Insert a Hyperlink from the drop-down menu.

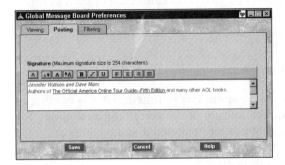

Figure 9-8. Our message board signature

The Filtering Preferences option lets you hide posts you don't want to see and/or read. You can filter out posts with subjects containing certain words or phrases, or posts written by individuals you find objectionable (see Figure 9-9).

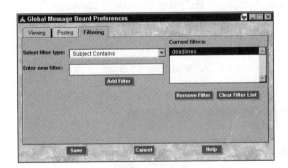

Figure 9-9. Filtering preferences displayed in the Global Message Board Preferences window

To create a filter, just choose a filter type from the first drop-down menu (Subject Contains, Subject Matches, or Author Is), type in the word(s) or screen name you wish to filter in the field below, and click Add Filter. AOL adds your filter to the list on the right. You can add up to 25 filters. To remove a filter, select it from the list on the right and click the Remove Filter button. Or click Clear Filter List to remove all filters.

Note

Signatures can contain up to 245 characters of visible text. An additional 217 characters is available to accommodate nonvisible characters, such as formatting (colors, styles, and so on) and hyperlink addresses.

Tip

Your message board signature is different than the one(s) you may have created for your e-mail, so if you'd like to have a message board signature, you'll have to create one in the Message Board Preferences window. If you already have an e-mail signature you like, consider copying it to your Message Board Preferences. Open a Write Mail window, click the Insert Signature File button, and then select the signature of your choice. After that, you can drag and drop (or copy and paste) the signature from the e-mail window into the Message Board Preferences window.

See our signature suggestions in Chapter 6, which apply to message board signatures as well as e-mail signatures.

When you are finished setting your preferences, click the Save button to preserve your settings. Any change that you make to your Message Board Preferences goes into effect the next time you open a message board. To see how they affect the current board, you'll have to close that board and then open it again. Feel free to try out new settings and see how they affect a board. You can always change them back afterwards.

Posting Messages

By now we trust you've spent lots of time lurking — reading posts and learning the culture of the communities you've visited. We wouldn't be at all surprised if you wanted to respond to something you read or post a message of your own. Well, here's your chance!

Just as with e-mail, you have two basic choices. You can reply to the post you're currently reading, or create the first post of a new subject. The steps and options for creating a new subject are almost too simple, so we'll start with that.

Let's go back to the Members Helping Members message boards (Keyword: **MHM**). We're sure you must have some sort of question about AOL. Just find the topic that suits your question, open that topic, and click the Create Subject button in the lower-right corner of the window to open a Post New Message window (see Figure 9-10).

Figure 9-10. The Post New Message window looks a lot like a Write Mail window, doesn't it?

Each Post New Message window lists the name of the message board in which the subject will be posted and has text entry fields for a subject and the message. You'll also find a format

bar with styled text buttons of the same sort found in a Write Mail window. Instead of the Insert Signature File button you'd find in an e-mail window, you'll find the option Use signature (set in Preferences) in the lower-left of the window. If you included a signature in your Message Board Preferences (discussed in the previous section) and you'd like to use your signature in your post, be sure the box is checked.

Every post must have a subject. Be sure that folks reading the subject will understand your question or comment without having to read the post itself.

When you've finished writing your post, reread it. You cannot unsend a message board post, so be sure you've said what you mean and that it's in line with AOL netiquette, AOL's Terms of Service, and the guidelines for that board. We also recommend you check the spelling by choosing Check Spelling from the Edit menu (or just press Control+=).

Once you've double-checked and spell-checked your post, click the Send button in the lower-right corner of the window. AOL confirms that your message has been sent to the message board with a dialog box — click OK (or press Enter) to dismiss it (see Figure 9-11).

Note

If you have set a signature in your Message Board Preferences, the Use signature (set in Preferences) checkbox should always be checked by default. Thus, if you don't want to use your signature, be sure to uncheck it.

Cross-Reference

Read more about Netiquette in Chapter 2 and subject lines in Chapter 5.

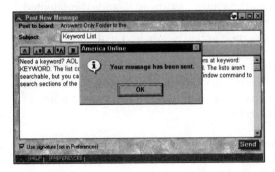

Figure 9-11. Posts away!

To see the post you've just made, close the message board and reopen it. Your new subject should be there for all to see!

Now that you know how to create your own subject, replying to someone else's post should be even easier, right? Well, replying is definitely easy, but you're faced with a few new options when you click the Reply button on a post (see Figure 9-12).

If you select the Send via e-mail option, your post will be sent to the screen name in the adjacent field. You can, however, edit the screen name if you prefer to send the e-mail to another member or even to yourself for your records.

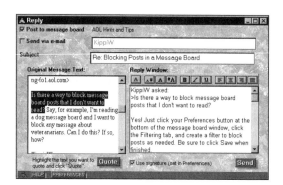

Figure 9-12. The Message Board Reply window offers all kinds of options.

Replies can be posted on the message board and/or sent via e-mail to the person who wrote the post using the options in the upper-left corner of the reply window. After all, some responses should be shared with everyone, and some things are best said privately. Just click one or both of the check-boxes to turn those options on or off.

It's always helpful to include quotations from the post(s) you're replying to, and AOL makes quoting very easy. The origi-nal message is displayed in a field on the left-hand side of the Reply window. Just highlight the text you want to quote with your mouse, and click the Quote button. AOL adds the selected text to the text entry box on the right. You can even continue typing below the quotation and add an additional quote later on.

Finally, to round out your reply, you can choose whether or not to use the signature you created. Remember, if you created a signature it will be used by default, and you must uncheck the Use signature checkbox.

When finished writing your reply, double-check and spell-check it, and then click Send just as you do when creating new subjects. That's all there is to it!

Newsgroups

If you enjoy message boards but hunger for discussions with a wider range of participants, you're ready to step up to news-groups. Thanks to the fact that newsgroups originated years ago on the Internet, more people (and a more diverse group of people at that) frequent newsgroups in general. Newsgroups also offer more control over posting your own messages and reading others' posts. On the downside, Internet newsgroups are usually unmonitored, meaning you're more likely to find objectionable material and advertising on them. Even so, if you can navigate the obstacles, you're likely to find strong communities and fascinating conversations.

Finding Communities

Speaking of finding things, how do you find newsgroups in the first place? Unlike message boards, which are more often than not scattered throughout the AOL service, newsgroups are mostly clustered in one area on AOL. You have a couple of paths to get to the newsgroup area. Use Keyword: **Newsgroups**, or choose the Internet icon on the toolbar and select Newsgroups from the drop-down menu. Regardless of the path, the Internet Newsgroups window opens on your screen (see Figure 9-13).

Figure 9-13. AOL offers a convenient and friendly gateway to Internet newsgroups.

If you get a message from America Online about selecting the Preferences button, just click OK. We'll get to the preferences later in this chapter. For now, make a beeline for the Search All Newsgroups button on the right side of the window. Click the icon and type your search word(s) into the resulting Search window for a list of newsgroups that match your interest. Double-click any listed newsgroup to receive a description of the newsgroup and hypertext links that you can use to preview the newsgroup's contents or subscribe to the news-group. If you don't get any valid results, modify your search word(s) and search again.

Another good place to look for newsgroups is at AOL NetFind. Use the Keyword: **Netfind** to open the NetFind window, and then click the Search Newsgroups hyperlink (or just use Keyword: **Newsgroup Scoop** to go there directly). In the resulting window, click the "descriptions" radio button, type in your search word(s), and click Find. NetFind lists results, if any, by how closely it "thinks" it matches what you were seeking (see Figure 9-14). NetFind offers no descriptions of the newsgroups, however.

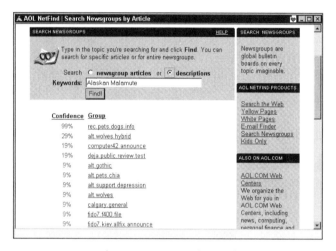

Figure 9-14. NetFind returns newsgroups that match your search criteria.

Once you find a newsgroup, your next step is to take a closer look. The best way to do this is to open it and read a sampling of its messages, just as you would on a message board. You can learn more about reading newsgroup posts later in this section.

Subscribing to Newsgroups

Although a subscription seems like a major commitment, all it really means is that the newsgroups of your choice are added to your personal list of newsgroups, which AOL maintains for you. Nobody is actually notified of your subscription, so you can read the newsgroups of your choice, and nobody will be the wiser.

AOL automatically subscribes you to a handful of useful newsgroups, through which you can learn more about newsgroups and practice your newsgroup skills. Just open the AOL newsgroups area (Keyword: **Newsgroups**) and click the Read My Newsgroups button to view the list.

There are three ways to add newsgroups to that list:

▶ Use Search All Newsgroups to find a newsgroup by topic. Open the newsgroup's description, and click the "Subscribe to newsgroup" hypertext link.

▶ The Expert Add button can be used when you already know the name of the group you want to join. If you found the name of a newsgroup using AOL NetFind, this is where you'd type in the name, such as rec.collecting.sport.baseball, which is a haven for baseball card collectors.

▶ The Add Newsgroups button opens a list of newsgroup categories. Each category hosts newsgroups of a particular type, or sponsored by a particular organization. When you find the newsgroup you want, click the handy Subscribe button.

Tip

If you are having troubles finding or subscribing to newsgroups, you may want to check your Parental Controls settings. Some types of newsgroups are blocked by default. Then again, maybe Mom and Dad have your best interests at heart.

Reading Messages

Reading newsgroups is very similar to reading message boards, which we described earlier in this chapter. Begin by opening the Internet Newsgroups window and clicking the Read My Newsgroups button. Your list of subscribed newsgroups appears in alphabetical order (see Figure 9-15).

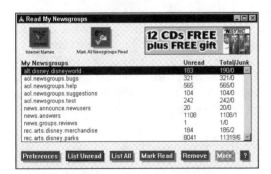

Figure 9-15. Our list of subscribed newsgroups. We have alot of messages to catch up on!

The newsgroup address is listed on the far left, followed by the number of unread posts, the total number of posts, and the number of posts AOL guesses to be junk (such as advertisements). The buttons along the bottom of the window work just as they do in a message board. The Remove button allows you to unsubscribe a newsgroup. At the top of the window, you'll find two more unfamiliar buttons: Internet Names and Mark All Newsgroups Read. Internet Names displays descriptions of your newsgroups. Use Mark All Newsgroups Read to hide all current posts — this is useful for seeing only the new posts since your last visit.

To open a newsgroup, simply select it and click List Unread or List All. Double-clicking the newsgroup also works (which is the same as clicking List Unread). A newsgroup's list of subjects is pretty straightforward, with subjects on the left and number of posts in the thread on the right (see Figure 9-16).

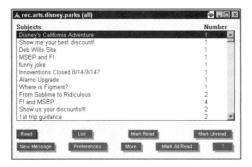

Figure 9-16. The rec.arts.disney.parks newsgroup for Walt Disney World and Disneyland enthusiasts

Reading newsgroups works the same as it does on a message board. Double-click a subject to read the first post in the thread, or click the List button for a list of all posts in a given thread. Use the Mark Read and Mark Unread buttons as needed. Do note that you may need to click the More button to see all subjects in a newsgroup, particularly those that are very active (such as rec.arts.disney.parks).

Setting Newsgroup Preferences

Unlike message boards, you can choose to apply Newsgroup Preferences globally (that is, your settings affect all newsgroups) or only to a specific newsgroup or set of newsgroups. Your global Newsgroup Preferences are accessible by clicking the Set Preferences button on the Internet Newsgroups window. Global Newsgroup Preferences look very similar to global Message Board Preferences, with Viewing, Posting, and Filtering categories (see Figure 9-17).

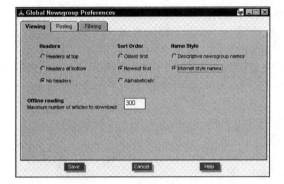

Figure 9-17. Set your global Newsgroup Preferences. Don't overlook the Posting and Filtering tabs at the top, which lead to more sets of preferences.

Rather than go through each setting, we'll just detail those preferences that differ from your global Message Board Preferences:

▶ Viewing preferences:

■ Headers — A newsgroup header comprises a set of technical information about how the newsgroup was posted. You can choose to view newsgroup headers at the top of a post, at the bottom, or not at all (default).

■ Name Style — Choose between descriptive newsgroup names (simple English) or the Internet-style names (technically correct but often obtuse).

▶ Posting preferences:

■ Real Name — Use this option to display your real name in posts, if you wish others to know it. Anything you type in the Real Name field appears in parentheses after your screen name in all your posts (considered polite in newsgroups). For example, when we make newsgroup posts, readers see jenniferanddave@aol.com (Jennifer Watson and Dave Marx).

■ Junk Block — Specify a phrase that will appear after your screen name to thwart junk mailers from harvesting your name in newsgroups. For example, if we type *nojunk* in the field, our name appears as jenniferanddave@aol.comnojunk.

■ Signature — This option allows you to include a signature with your post. You set a newsgroup signature as you would a message board signature, except you cannot format the signature or include hyperlinks.

▶ Filtering preferences:

  ■ Excessively cross-posted or repeated messages —
    Turn on this option to hide posts that meet this
    description, which are also known as *spam*.

  ■ Make Money Fast and similar messages — Select this
    option to hide posts that meet this description.

  ■ Messages longer than *x* characters — Hides
    long posts.

  ■ Forged messages — Hide posts that AOL determines
    to be falsified.

  ■ Binaries posted to nonbinary newsgroups — Check
    this box to hide posts with binary information
    (usually graphics or programs).

Newsgroup-specific preferences are accessible via the
Preferences button at the bottom of any newsgroup
window (see Figure 9-18).

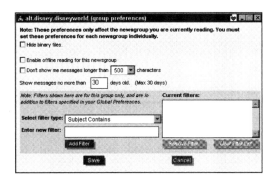

Figure 9-18. Get down to the nitty-gritty with your Newsgroup Preferences.

Use these Newsgroup Preferences to fine-tune your settings.
New options include the following:

▶ **Enable offline reading for this newsgroup** — Check this
  box if you want to use Auto AOL to download posts.

▶ **Show messages no more than** *x* **days old** — Decrease this
  number if you want to see only the most recent posts.

▶ Additionally, you can add filters that affect only that
  specific newsgroup.

Finding Messages

While there is no nifty Find button or menu in the newsgroup window, you can still search newsgroups. Here are two ways:

▶ To search just the subject lines in a newsgroup, begin by opening the newsgroup you wish to search and list all the subjects (you may need to click More a few times). Now use the Find in Top Window command under the Edit menu to search for words or phrases in the subjects.

▶ To search the contents of newsgroup messages, use Keyword: **Newsgroup Scoop**. Enter your search word(s) or phrase, click the "newsgroup articles" radio button, and click Find!

Posting Messages

Posting to a newsgroup is also similar to message board posting. The biggest differences aren't technical, but cultural. Each newsgroup has its own culture, social rules, and quirks; we strongly recommend that you get to know a newsgroup by reading it first before you post in it. Read the Newsgroup Etiquette article at the top of the Internet Newsgroups window for a general set of guidelines to follow when posting to newsgroups.

Once you're ready to contribute something of your own, you can start a new thread with the New Message button at the bottom of a newsgroup window. It works almost exactly the same as the Create Subject button does in a message board. To see your post, close the newsgroup and reopen it — you may need to give it a few minutes to show up.

You can also reply to posts. Just click the Reply button on a post you'd like to respond to and fill it out. The newsgroup reply window is identical to the message board reply window (but without the format toolbar).

Find It Online

Another place to search for newsgroups is at `http://www.deja.com`. This community-oriented service offers lots of searching and reading options, including ways to find all posts made by individuals.

Tip

If the poster is using a junk block in his or her address (it's usually obvious) and you want to send him or her e-mail, you'll need to remove the junk block in the screen name field before you click the Send button. If you're not sure what is and isn't a junk block, check the original post — often posters specify what words and/or letters to remove from their address in order to send them e-mail.

Note

If clicking Reply results in a note that reads "Follow-up to newsgroups is allowed via posting only," this simply means that the poster cannot receive e-mail. You can reply to his or her post in the newsgroup as normal, however.

Downloading Messages

Love to read messages but just can't keep up with everything? Or do you wish you could keep records of your messages to read later at your leisure? Both wishes are possible with AOL's Offline Reading feature. Posts on message boards and newsgroups can be downloaded, organized in your Personal Filing Cabinet, and read whenever you like (online or offline). This also means you can search them easily with the Find feature in your Personal Filing Cabinet.

To mark a message board for offline reading, open the message board, select the topic you want to download, and click the Read Offline button at the bottom. We recommend you try only one message board your first time out. Next, make a beeline for your Preferences button. Indicate the maximum number of articles to download. You may want to decrease this number to something reasonable if the message board you marked for offline reading is particularly active. Click Save to keep your changes.

To mark a newsgroup for offline reading, open the newsgroup, click Preferences at the bottom of the window, and click the Enable offline reading for this newsgroup checkbox. Also, set the number of days for which you want to see messages. Again, you may want to decrease this number if the newsgroup has a lot of posts.

To actually download the messages in the boards or newsgroups you've marked for offline reading you use Auto AOL. We explain how Auto AOL works in Chapter 10.

Independent Explorations

Alas, we really didn't have the opportunity to explore the most fascinating aspect of message boards and newsgroups: community! It's time to find your own community. We recommend you drop by Keyword: **AOL Search**, enter your hobby or interest, and explore the results. We recommend you stick with the resources under the On AOL tab, as AOL's community is one of the strongest anywhere on the Internet, but feel free to venture out if you find something intriguing.

We also recommend one community that we think you may find helpful as an AOL member. It is Members Helping Members, which we hinted at earlier in this chapter (and discussed in Chapter 4). This is a full-fledged community in addition to being a help center, and you'll find it a welcome respite.

Beyond message boards, many communities offer libraries for their members to contribute and share files. The next stop on our tour explores these rich repositories of information.

PART

IV

SITE-SEEING
AND SOUVENIRS

Chapter 10
Unearthing Treasures

Chapter 11
Shopping the Electronic Bazaar

Chapter 12
Seeing the Sites: Business

Chapter 13
Seeing the Sites: Pleasure

Chapter 14
Finding Places and Things

Chapter 15
Finding People

Quick Look

▶ **Downloading Files**   **page 205**

AOL has thousands and thousands of files available online. These files can be downloaded (saved to your computer) using your AOL software to transfer them. Visit Keyword: **Download Center** for libraries of files you can download.

▶ **Download Manager**   **page 214**

Your AOL software comes with a tool to organize and control the files you want to download (or already downloaded). This tool is called the Download Manager, and you can access it under the My Files icon on the toolbar.

▶ **You've Got Pictures**   **page 219**

AOL and Kodak have teamed up to offer a new alternative to photo developing: electronic pictures. If you sign up for this option when you drop off (or send in) your roll of film, your pictures will appear online and AOL will announce that "You've Got Pictures." Visit Keyword: **Pictures** for details.

▶ **File Transfer Protocol**   **page 225**

AOL gives all its members access to File Transfer Protocol (FTP), which allows you to download files from the Internet. FTP also lets you upload files and make them accessible to others on the Internet. Use Keyword: **FTP** to get started.

Chapter 10

Unearthing Treasures

CHAPTER ITINERARY

Learning how to download and upload files

Protecting yourself from viruses

Using Download Manager

Managing your files with Automatic AOL

Reliving memories with You've Got Pictures

Finding files on the Internet through FTP

AOL is truly a goldmine of free and low-cost treasure. The newly acquainted often overlook it, or worse yet, don't realize it even exists. We have the treasure map to the goodies, and we'll show you the way. Before we embark on our quest, let's get a handle on two important concepts: *files* and *downloading*.

What Are Files?

Did you hear about the prisoner whose mother baked a file into a chocolate cake? If you have, forget about it. The files we're talking about have nothing to do with escaping from jail. When we refer to files, we are talking about information stored in a computer or transported between computers.

A word processing document is a file, and so is a picture viewed on a computer screen. Computer programs such as America Online 5.0 are made up of many files, each of which fulfills a certain purpose. Some of those files contain program instructions so that you can view Web pages, visit chat rooms, and receive e-mail. Other files contain information, such as the contents of your Personal Filing Cabinet, a photo of your sister Sara, or the voice of the "You've Got Mail!" guy. Some files store special program settings so you can customize AOL to your own tastes. Of course, some files are games, utilities, and business applications.

Many types of files are associated with AOL, but those of most interest in this chapter are those you can download. If you don't yet know how to download files, AOL offers a useful area filled with help and tips with this process, as described next.

Definition

Downloading is the act of transferring something from someone else's computer (such as AOL's) to your own computer. You can *download* files, whereby you get *downloads*. Thus, this term functions as both a verb and a noun.

10

Unearthing Treasures

How to Download

The folks at the Computing Channel are downloading maniacs. Well, actually, they'll download just about anything, not just maniacs — computer programs, sound files, videos, graphics, the works! The Computing Channel has prepared an entire area to teach you how to download called, appropriately enough, How to Download. You can find it quickly at Keyword: **How to Download** (see Figure 10-1).

See Chapter 9 for more information about using and participating in message boards on AOL.

You can use the new find files feature in AOL 5.0. Go to My Files ⇨ Download Manager ⇨ Show Files Downloaded ⇨ Locate. This feature shows the location of all the files you've recently downloaded.

Figure 10-1. How to Download teaches you the art and science of downloading.

To get started, click the blue How to Download hyperlink on the bottom of the How to Download window. If you find you have more questions, click the Take a Class link on the right side of the How to Download window (see Figure 10-2). AOL 101 Downloading Files is a free online course designed to help you learn about downloading files from live instructors. A link to the classroom, transcript, and a new user computer guide are available here also.

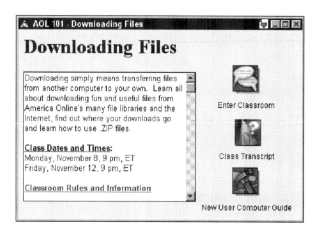

Figure 10-2. Get help downloading at the AOL 101 Downloading Files class.

If you're in a hurry to learn how to download, follow these easy steps:

1. Locate a file to download. Tips on how to do this are found throughout this chapter, but if you need a file to download now, use Keyword: **Daily Download** and

click the Download it Now button on the left side of the resulting window.

2. Choose a location on your hard drive for your new file in the resulting window. Make a note of the filename and the location so you can find your file later. Click the Save button.

3. Wait as AOL transfers the file from its computers to your hard drive, displaying a progress meter as it goes. If you need to cancel the download process, click the Cancel button. Click the Finish Later button if you want to complete the download later (see "Download Manager" later in this chapter for details).

4. Click the OK button when AOL informs you that your file has been transferred.

5. Locate your new file on your hard drive. Unless you changed the default location, your file is probably located in the Download folder within your America Online folder on your hard drive. You may now open or run your file if you wish. If the filename ends in .zip, this means it was compressed, and you will need to decompress it before you can use it. AOL will automatically decompress it when you sign off from the service (unless you disabled this setting in the Download Preferences dialog box). If you need to decompress the file before you sign off, Download Manager has an option for this — see "Download Manager" later in this chapter for details.

Tip

Don't confuse the name of the file saving window (which is called Download Manager) with the Download Manager feature found under the My Files icon on the toolbar, which we describe in detail later in this chapter.

Definition

File compression is common with files found on AOL and the Internet. Files are compressed so they are smaller and thus faster to download. A compressed file may also be called a *zipped* file due to the .zip extension at the end of its filename.

10

Unearthing Treasures

Once you understand how the download process works, you're likely to be eager to download a file or two (or three or thirty). Where do you actually find files? You will encounter them throughout your AOL travels: attached to e-mail, under icons and hyperlinks, in lists, and on the Web. The greatest concentration of files is found in file libraries, of which there are hundreds (if not thousands) on AOL.

File Libraries

If the term *file library* conjures up thoughts of hushed tones and towering stacks of floppy disks, you're in for a treat. AOL's

Definition

To *upload* means to send a file from one computer to another, usually a personal computer to AOL's computers. Upload is the opposite of download.

file libraries are nothing so inconvenient. File libraries are collections of related files, which you can browse, sort, and/or search. Virtually every forum online has a file library (usually several), though the greatest concentration of file libraries are in the Computing Channel. File libraries are usually identified by name, but you may also recognize them by their distinctive appearance (see Figure 10-3).

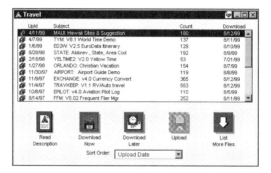

Figure 10-3. A typical file library, listing filenames and relevant information

On opening a file library, AOL lists the files in the order they were uploaded to the library. To change this order, click the Sort Order drop-down menu at the bottom of the window and choose a new order; you can sort the list by subject (alphabetically), download count, or download date. *Download count* is an indicator of a file's popularity. A file's download count is listed beside the file's subject, along with the date last downloaded (on the far right) and the date uploaded (on the far left).

Use the buttons arrayed along the bottom of a file library to gain more information. First select a file in the list above (highlight it), and then click Read Description for a file description containing detailed information (see Figure 10-4).

If you want to bypass the file description and download the file immediately, click Download Now in the file library window. You may instead decide to click Download Later to add it to a list of files to be retrieved later (see "Download Manager" later in this chapter).

The Upload button lets you send your own file to the library. The List More Files button shows the next 20 files in the library; if you're looking for something but can't find it, click this button to see more files.

```
┌─────────────────────────────────────────────────────────┐
│ ⚠ MAUI: Hawaii Sites & Suggestions          💙 ▭ □ ✕    │
├─────────────────────────────────────────────────────────┤
│ Subject:  MAUI: Hawaii Sites & Suggestions            ▲  │
│ Author:  Jon Blum                                        │
│ Uploaded By:  Derm1                                      │
│ Date:  4/11/99                                           │
│                                                          │
│ File:  MAUI99.TXT (90098 bytes)                          │
│ Estimated Download Time (28800 baud):  < 1 minute        │
│ Download Count:  180                                     │
│                                                          │
│ Needs:  Text File Reader                                 │
│                                                          │
│ Keywords:  Blum, DERM1, Hawaii, Island, Hotel, Restaurant, Phone, Information, Sights │
│                                                          │
│ Type:     Freely Distributed                             │
│                                                          │
│ Version Date: 4/9/99                                     │
│                                                          │
│ Uploaded by the author.                                  │
│                                                          │
│ A text file describing things to see and do, sights, restaurants, hotels, phone numbers and │
│ other helpful information, for anyone planning a trip to Maui, Hawaii.  Written by an America │
│ Online member who has been to Maui many times, and loves it. This file can be read or printed │
│ out by any word processing program that can read text files.  Send any comments via e-mail to │
│ Derm1.                                                ▼  │
├─────────────────────────────────────────────────────────┤
│  [ Download Now ] [ Download Later ] [ Ask The Staff ] [ Related Files ] │
└─────────────────────────────────────────────────────────┘
```

Figure 10-4. Every file in a library has a description similar to this one.

We recommend you read file descriptions carefully before downloading a file. Descriptions list the subject, author, screen name of the person who uploaded the file, date uploaded, filename, estimated download time, and download count. More importantly, descriptions tell you what you need to have to use the file and how the file itself works. You may wish to save this file description to your hard drive so you can refer to it at a later time (just press Ctrl+S when the description window is open). Note that you can download directly from the file description window with the Download Now button at the bottom. Click the Ask The Staff button if you have a question about a file or the Related Files button to return to the library itself.

We've discussed browsing and sorting libraries, but how about searching them? You'll need to visit the Download Center for a more comprehensive search, which just happens to be next on our tour!

Download Center

Now that you're a pro at downloading, where can you find more files to download? The Download Center is AOL's central treasure chamber (see Figure 10-5). Here you'll find thousands of files, including vibrant graphics, rich sounds, and

Cross-Reference

Before you download any file, read the section titled "Viruses and Trojan Horses" later in this chapter.

10

Unearthing Treasures

valuable programs that can make you as powerful as a genie
or as rich as King Midas (well, almost). You don't need a magic
lamp to find this treasure, either. Just type Keyword: **Download Center**, press Enter, and hold on to your magic carpet.

Figure 10-5. Dive into the downloads at the Download Center.

You can find files in two different ways at the Download
Center: by searching or by browsing. We recommend searching for a file if you know what you're seeking. Browsing, on
the other hand, works best when you know what *kind* of file
you want, such as a game or utility, but not the specifics of it.
Let's take a closer look at both searching and browsing
through the Download Center.

Searching for Files

If you're seeking shareware files, click the Shareware button
under Search for Software in the Download Center window.
This brings up the Software Search window (see Figure 10-6),
in which you can choose your search parameters.

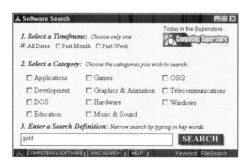

Figure 10-6. Use the Software Search window to find shareware files.

Choose a time frame if you're looking for a recent file; otherwise, you can leave it set to All Dates. Select a category to narrow down your search. Most importantly, type your search word(s) in the text box at the bottom of the window. You can use Boolean operators such as AND, OR, and NOT to fine-tune your search. When you're ready, click the Search button (or just press Enter) to start your search. (see Figure 10-7).

Note

The Download Center search encompasses almost all Computing Channel libraries, but very few libraries in other channels on AOL.

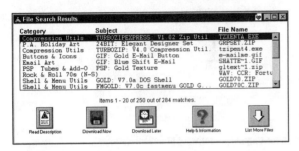

Figure 10-7. AOL displays your search results in a new window.

AOL displays the first 20 results in the window. If there are more than 20 results, the List More Files button at the bottom of the window will be active; click it to display the next 20 matches. You can get a closer look at your search results by double-clicking the file in the Search Results window. This produces a description of the file, which we explained in more detail in "File Libraries," earlier in this chapter.

If you're in the market for commercial software, click the Buy Software link below Search for Software in the Download Center. This leads you to Beyond.com, which you can access directly with Keyword: **Beyond**. Beyond.com offers a large selection of commercial software, some of which you can download immediately. Begin a search for commercial software by typing your search word(s) into the Search field and clicking Go (see Figure 10-8).

Software titles display in order of relevancy, along with their availability (downloadable now or shipping time), and price. If you're interested in something, click the Add to Cart button to place the software in your "shopping cart."

If a simple search in Beyond.com doesn't yield results, you may want to try an advanced search. Just click the Advanced Search hyperlink in the results window (or the "no results found" window, as the case may be). You can now specify the

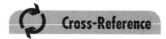

Read more about online
shopping and shopping
carts in Chapter 11.

Another treasure trove of files
is the Weekly New Files
area, at Keyword: **New
Files**.

product name, supplier, category, SKU (product ID number)
and/or supplier part number, as well as your operating system,
and media type (for example, electronic download, CD-ROM,
3.5" disk, and so on).

Figure 10-8. Search for commercial software at Beyond.com.

Browsing Files

If you're the type who likes to just stroll through the aisles,
make a beeline for the Download Catalogue in the Download
Center. Here you'll find collections of libraries organized by
topic, category, and subcategory. First choose a topic from the
list in the Download Center and click the Go Button; this
opens a topic window (see Figure 10-9).

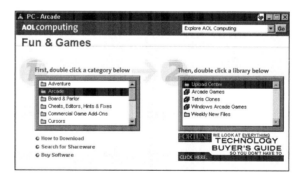

Figure 10-9. A download category window containing collections of libraries

Double-click a category in the list box on the left. This produces a list of libraries in the list box on the right. Double-
click any of the libraries to open it and begin browsing. Be
sure to use the scroll bar to see all categories and libraries
available.

If you'd like to browse commercial software, click the Buy Software tab above the list box in the Download Center window. This displays a new list of commercial software categories. Double-click one to open a Web page with related software.

Those of you who love to browse but don't know where to start may enjoy the Top Ten Picks, available from the Down-load Center window. Just choose one of the topics from the drop-down menu and click Go to get a list of recommended files.

Viruses and Trojan Horses

Along with the benefits of downloading files, we must also accept the risks involved — namely, contracting viruses or encountering Trojan Horses. *Viruses* are specific kinds of files designed by their programmers to cause damage. Viruses generally damage the files on your computer's hard drive. *Trojan Horses*, on the other hand, are dangerous files disguised as useful or desirable programs. Trojan Horses generally contain objectionable or inappropriate images, conceal viruses, or even compromise your AOL account or credit card information. Thankfully, most files available in file libraries have been carefully scanned for viruses and Trojan Horses before they were released to the public. However, due to the proliferation of viruses, not to mention their tenacity, AOL cannot guarantee that all files available on AOL are safe. Even so, it isn't difficult to avoid viruses and Trojan Horses with some prevention and a lot of common sense.

Your first line of defense against viruses and Trojan Horses is knowledge. For this, we direct you to the Anti-Virus Center at Keyword: **Virus**. Here you will find plenty of information about what is a virus, a Trojan Horse, or just a hoax. You can also download demo versions of antivirus programs or purchase commercial software.

Keep your antivirus program up-to-date by checking for virus definition updates on a regular basis. Depending on which antivirus program you go with, you can find these updates in AOL's file libraries or on the program's Web site.

Cross-Reference

You may also find files in your e-mail! To learn more about downloading files from e-mail, see Chapter 6.

Definition

An *antivirus program*, properly installed and updated, can scan your computer and all files you download to it for possible viruses. We strongly recommend that everyone who intends to download files from AOL and/or the Internet, or even simply receive files from friends or coworkers, use an antivirus program.

10

Unearthing Treasures

Find It Online

Visit http://www.drsolomon.com/ for information and updates on Dr. Solomon's antivirus programs. Visit http://www.mcafee.com for McAfee's antivirus programs. Or visit http://www.symantec.com/ for Symantec's antivirus programs.

Note

Just because your computer acts funny or strange doesn't mean it contracted a virus. You may have a hardware problem instead (in which case you may wish to visit Keyword: **Hardware**).

Find It Online

For more information on viruses and what to do if you think you've been infected with one, visit the Computer Protection Center at Keyword: **Virus Info**.

In addition to an antivirus program, it helps to use your common sense before you click that Download button. Download files from people and sources you feel you can trust, and avoid strangers and disreputable Web sites. If something sounds too good to be true (such as a free, full-featured word processor or adult software), it is probably a Trojan Horse — resist the temptation to check. If you must download a file and you aren't sure of its contents, first make sure your antivirus program is up-to-date and functioning. You can then download the file to a floppy disk and scan the file on the disk. If the file is infected, you may safely delete it without worrying that any harm was done to your computer; the simple act of downloading a file is not dangerous in itself. In order to do damage, a virus or Trojan Horse must be executed (run) or loaded into software that can run it. It is always a wise precaution to keep a full backup of your data in the event that your computer becomes infected with a virus.

If you think your computer is infected with a virus or has encountered a Trojan Horse, stay calm. Immediately stop what you're doing, exit your programs, and turn off your computer. Restart your computer, open your antivirus program, and scan your computer. If you don't find anything, visit your antivirus program's Web site, download the latest file descriptions, and scan again. You may also wish to scan your computer with another antivirus program. If your antivirus program finds a virus, it can usually eliminate it. Do not upload any files, attach any files to e-mail, or exchange floppies with anyone until you are sure you've eradicated the virus — otherwise you will spread the virus to others.

Download Manager

Download Manager keeps track of the files you've downloaded and those you choose to download later, and it knows where on your hard disk those files have been stored. If you've selected several files to be downloaded later, one click of Download Manager's Download button will collect the entire list of files. You can also use download manager to decompress zipped files, access your download preference settings, and decide where the file will be stored on your hard disk.

You can reach Download Manager by clicking the My Files button on the AOL toolbar or via Keyword: **Download Manager** (see Figure 10-10).

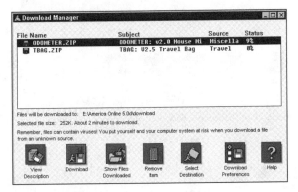

Figure 10-10. Download Manager displays files waiting to be downloaded.

Buttons along the bottom of the Download Manager window give you access to your downloads. Click View Description to read the file description. Click Download to retrieve the file right then and there. Click Show Files Downloaded to view a list of files you've already downloaded. Click Remove Item to delete a file from the download list (but not actually delete the download if you've already downloaded it). Click Select Destination to change the default download folder. Click Download Preferences to make changes to your download-related settings. Click Help for more assistance.

When you're trying to figure out what you've downloaded and where you put it, click the Show Files Downloaded button on the main Download Manager screen. By default, the Files You've Downloaded screen (see Figure 10-11) lists the past 100 files you've downloaded (click the Download Preferences button to adjust the number of files listed).

If you can't remember what the file is, click View Description. The Locate button will find the folder on your hard disk that contains the, and the Decompress button will unzip zipped files on command. Altogether, Download Manager is a handy manager to have around.

Download Manager only lists files that have been attached and downloaded from e-mail or from AOL file libraries. If you download files from an FTP or Web site, they won't be listed here.

If an interruption occurs during a download from e-mail or an AOL file library, you can visit Download Manager to resume that download. AOL displays the filename in Download Manager, along with the percentage of the file that has already been downloaded.

10

Unearthing Treasures

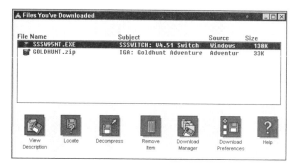

Many people depend on AOL's software to automatically decompress files when they sign off AOL. If you downloaded a zip file and would rather not sign off before using it, the Decompress button on the Files You've Downloaded screen is a very handy thing to have around.

Figure 10-11. Files You've Downloaded is your downloading Lost and Found.

Automatic AOL

Your computer must be turned on and your AOL software must be running, or Automatic AOL won't work.

If you've always wanted your very own robot, Automatic AOL may be the robot for you! Automatic AOL can run down to your AOL e-mail box to send and collect your e-mail, download your files, and collect and send message board and newsgroup postings. All this fetching, sending, and saving can be done automatically — while you sleep or even while you're on vacation. When you return home, just open your Personal Filing Cabinet and everything is there, waiting for you.

Automatic AOL is easy to set up. Just choose the Set up Automatic AOL command from the Mail Center icon on the toolbar. The setup process asks you to answer a series of simple questions, and once completed, your little robot is ready to go! You may change your settings at any time by returning to the Automatic AOL preferences window (see Figure 10-12).

Alternatively, you can click the My AOL button on the AOL toolbar, select Preferences, select Auto AOL, and click the Walk Me Through button.

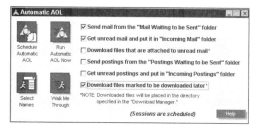

Figure 10-12. Select your Automatic AOL options in the Automatic AOL preferences window.

Automatic AOL sessions can be set to take place as often
as every half-hour, seven days a week, regardless of whether
you're around. Just click the Schedule Automatic AOL button
in your Automatic AOL preferences window to see scheduling
options (see Figure 10-13). You can also use Automatic AOL
to "make the rounds" whenever you like, even if you never
schedule an unattended session. Just click the Mail Center
icon on the AOL toolbar, select Run Automatic AOL, and head
to the kitchen for a snack.

Figure 10-13. The Schedule Automatic AOL window, the autopilot for your
online world

File downloads expose you
to the risk of receiving a
computer virus or offensive
image. Since you're not present to decide whether a file
seems risky or not, it may be
best to avoid the "Download
files that are attached to
unread mail" feature. You
can usually download the file
later, if you want it, by signing on and reading your
old mail.

If you're a fan of message boards and newsgroups, you have
one more thing to do. Go to your favorite message boards and
newsgroups, and set them up to be read offline. For message
boards, this means you have to visit the board(s) of your
choice, select the topic(s) or subject(s) you want to read
offline, and click the Read Offline button. For newsgroups, go
to Keyword: **Newsgroups** and click the Read Offline button.
You can then select which newsgroup(s) you wish to read
offline. Later, after your Automatic AOL session, you can visit
your Personal Filing Cabinet — or click My Files, and then
click Offline Newsgroups — to read the postings. Just as with
e-mail, you can compose your replies and new subjects offline
and have them posted automatically during the following
Automatic AOL session.

If your computer will be left
unattended in a place where
others can access it, you may
want to add passwords to
your Personal Filing Cabinet
so that your e-mail and
postings stay private. See
Chapter 7 for instructions
on setting Personal Filing
Cabinet passwords.

Uploading Files

Uploading to a library is very similar to sending an attached
file in e-mail. In both cases you are sending a copy of a file

located on your hard disk to AOL's computers. Some of the steps are different, but the idea is still the same.

Uploading to a file library also has a lot in common with posting to message boards or participating in chat sessions. The public will see your file, so the rules of netiquette and AOL's Terms of Service are in full force. Libraries have firm policies about whether they accept uploads, and the type of files they do upload, in order to keep the contents of the file library on topic. Look for an upload policies statement when you visit a file library.

Files you upload will be reviewed for their content, function, and suitability, and tested for viruses. This process will take several days, and there's a chance the file librarians will decide that your file doesn't belong in that library.

To submit a file for consideration, visit the library of your choice and click the Upload button. A form will open on screen, which you should fill out to the best of your ability (see Figure 10-14).

Be sure you have the legal right to share your files with others. Just about anything you can upload, including photographs, sounds, music, and computer programs, are covered by copyright law, and unless you created the contents of the file yourself, you may be violating someone else's copyright.

A good description is an important part of a successful downloadable file. The library may have posted pointers on how to write a good description. Also take a look at the descriptions of other files in the library before you upload, as they can help you make your file description the best it can be.

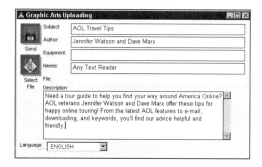

Figure 10-14. Fill in the Uploading form to the best of your ability. The more detail, the better!

Once you've completed the form, click the Select File button on the Uploading window and select the file using the Select File dialog box. Now double-check the Uploading window to be sure you selected the correct file and described it adequately. Click the Send button, and your file is on its way! If your file is acceptable to the librarians, your file will be "up in lights" in a matter of days.

You've Got Pictures

Have you been hungry to share your snapshots with family and friends online, but lacked a scanner? Kodak and AOL are changing that with You've Got Pictures, a new service that combines conventional photo processing and online delivery of scanned images. Bring or mail your film in to a participating photo developer (40,000 stores plan to participate) and check off the option for You've Got Pictures. For an extra fee (between five and nine dollars), you will get not only the prints you would normally receive, but digital versions of your photos as well. Within one to three days after the film reaches the lab, you'll sign on to AOL and hear a familiar voice announcing, "You've got pictures!" (see Figure 10-15).

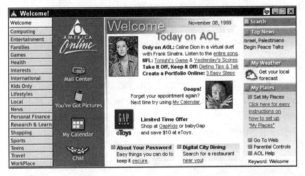

Figure 10-15. You've Got Pictures, right on the AOL Welcome screen

Whenever you want to view your pictures, go to Keyword: **Pictures**. When you've got your pictures, you can arrange them into online photo albums to be shared with whomever you please, just so long as they have Internet access.

Your newly processed photos will be stored online for 30 days, after which they will be deleted, much like unsaved e-mail. Before they disappear, you can save them online, or download them to your hard drive. You get free online storage of 50 pictures per screen name (up to 350 images per account, spread among the seven screen names). Additional online storage is rented in blocks of 30 images for $1.49 per month, which will be added to your AOL bill. Storage space can be added in blocks of 30 and decreased by the same amount, too.

Note

During a file upload, your AOL software puts everything it has into the process of uploading. Some people refer to this as being *locked out*, since you can't do anything else on AOL during the course of an upload. If you're sending a very large file, you may want to go to dinner while the file is uploading.

Note

The "You've Got Pictures!" voice announcement and new roll icon (shown in Figure 10-15) will remain for 30 days from the day your pictures are available online. Unlike the new e-mail announcement, which goes away when you've read all your e-mail, this announcement plays as long as you have rolls available.

10

Unearthing Treasures

Note

Photo developing prices may be different, as the various photo developers participating in You've Got Pictures can charge different rates. Thirty days after your pictures appear online (regardless of when you save your roll), the pricing reverts to the official You've Got Picture rates.

Protecting Your Good Name

When you bring your film into a participating store, you are asked to supply an AOL screen name, plus your real name and phone number with your roll. If you want to keep a particular screen name private, you don't need to give it out. Instead, give a screen name that you don't mind sharing, or don't provide a screen name at all. Then when you get notification that your pictures are ready, sign on with the screen name with which you'd rather retrieve the pictures, go to Keyword: **Pictures**, and click the Don't See Your Rolls? button. Type in the Roll ID and Owners Key # listed on the claim card enclosed with your prints. Do note that if you access a roll using the ID a second time, using a different screen name or account, that roll will disappear from the account in which it had been residing.

If you click the You've Got Pictures icon on the Welcome Screen (or use Keyword: **Pictures**) before you receive a roll of pictures or are sent a Buddy Album, you will see the You've Got Pictures Quick Start screen (see Figure 10-16).

Figure 10-16. Quick Start offers an introduction to You've Got Pictures.

The Quick Start window offers a brief introduction to You've Got Pictures. Feel free to view the slide show, browse a sample album, or request a list of participating dealers in your area. Click the Go to You've Got Pictures NOW! button if you want to see the real thing. Once you've got pictures you'll automatically bypass the Quick Start window in favor of the regular You've Got Pictures window.

The You've Got Pictures window (see Figure 10-17) gives you a choice of four views that can be selected by clicking the tabs near the top of the window.

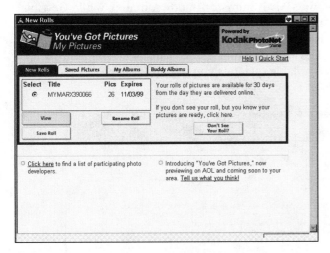

Figure 10-17. The Roll Viewer catalogs every picture available to you.

Here's what the four buttons do:

▶ New Rolls gives you access to newly developed rolls of film.

▶ Saved Pictures displays all the pictures saved in your online storage area.

▶ My Albums gives you access to the Albums you have created from your own saved pictures and/or from pictures you received in Buddy Albums.

▶ Buddy Albums accesses Albums that you received from others.

When you get a new roll you can immediately create an album from those pictures, and share that album with friends, even if you don't intend to save the pictures yourself. For the first 30 days you can view all your new pictures using the New Rolls section. If you save any of those pictures online they can be viewed by clicking the Saved Pictures tab. You can also create an album in Saved Pictures. Once an album has been created it will be accessible in the My Albums area, which is also the place to go if you want to share an album with others. Select My Albums if you want to create a new album incorporating any combination of pictures you've saved and pictures found in your albums and your Buddy Albums (described later).

10

Unearthing Treasures

Tip

The easiest way to view the downloaded pictures is with AOL's picture gallery feature. Pull down the AOL File menu, choose Open Picture Gallery, navigate to the folder containing the downloaded pictures, and click Open Gallery.

If you want to edit or manipulate your pictures you must download them. Pictures stored online can't be modified. To download pictures, first view your pictures (in New Rolls, Saved Pictures, My Albums, or Buddy Albums). While viewing your pictures, click the checkbox next to the picture(s) you want to download (shown in Figure 10-17), and click Download Pictures at the bottom of the page. Now choose which of the three available qualities you would for like your picture(s), as shown in Figure 10-18.

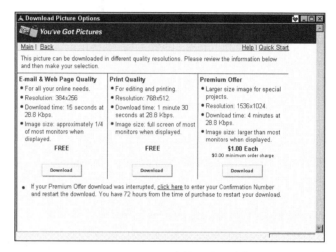

Figure 10-18. Your pictures are available in three different qualities (resolutions).

The lowest quality (E-mail & Web Page Quality) downloads quickly, and will be adequate for casual use online, such as sharing the images with your friends and family. The middle quality (Print Quality) is suitable when you want a better version for printing at home. The highest quality (Premium Offer) will probably appeal only to professionals (especially since there's a $1.00 surcharge for each high-quality image downloaded, and a minimum charge of $3.00 per transaction). Click the Download button underneath the quality level you prefer to initiate your download.

Your pictures are downloaded as an executable zip file, with an .*exe* file extension. It's most efficient to select all the various pictures you wish to download prior to requesting the download. That way all the pictures you selected will be added to the same download file. After you download the file, you have to "run" it in order to view the picture(s). To do this, open your Windows Start menu, choose Run, click the Browse button, navigate to the folder containing the downloaded file, and click the Open button. A small "DOS" window opens on screen to report on the extraction of your pictures. You'll probably want to rename the newly-extracted picture files, as You've Got Pictures automatically gives them a file name consisting of an 8-digit number, even if you gave the file a different name when you downloaded it.

You've Got Pictures' Albums feature is a great way to organize your pictures for your own enjoyment, or to share your pictures with friends and relations. Albums are especially convenient, because you don't have to download the pictures. The pictures you save online are simply incorporated into a Web page by You've Got Pictures. This makes it easy to share your album with anyone with Internet access.

To create an album, begin by viewing your pictures. Click the checkbox(es) next to those picture(s) you'd like to place in an album and click the Create New Album button towards the bottom. Your pictures are displayed in a new window, where you are given a variety of options, including the ability save your album (see Figure 10-19).

Tip

If all 50 of your online photo storage spaces are full, why not save photos on another screen name, or have someone else (like a doting grandparent) save the photos on *their* account? Create a Buddy Album using photos from the New Rolls area and share the album with one of your other screen names, or with anyone else willing to store them. Once the Buddy Album has been received, those photos can be permanently saved on that other screen name. Then create a new Buddy Album on that screen name and share it with yourself.

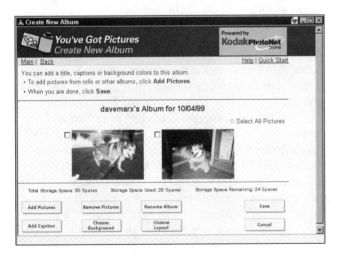

Figure 10-19. Albums of pictures are easy to create.

Albums can contain up to 100 photos. You can add captions for each photo (limited to 32 characters per caption), give each album page a name, add a brief description, and change the background color and the layout of the page. You can also

Note

Once you send someone a Buddy Album, that person is free to do anything at all with your pictures. They can save or download the pictures, use them to create Buddy Albums of their own, and send them to anyone they please (and who knows what *those* people may do with your pictures). Although copyright law says you still own them (and AOL makes it clear that they must have your expressed permission before your pictures can be used for any purpose), it's best to be cautious about whom you share your pictures with.

Tip

The same photo can be included in dozens of different albums, but it only has to be saved online once. Every album that includes the photo is linked back to the same saved image, no matter who is viewing it, and no matter who created that album. This saves a lot of precious online storage space. If you delete a picture from Saved Pictures it disappears from all those albums, which may or may not be a good idea.

make changes to the album at any time, which will affect everyone who has access to that album.

Albums are automatically private, but you can share them with friends and family with AOL accounts or other Internet access. Just add their names to that album's distribution list. They'll receive e-mail telling them how they can view the album, and if they use AOL they'll also get the "you've got pictures" message when they sign on.

Albums can be made from photos in the New Rolls, Saved Pictures, My Albums, and Buddy Albums areas, so your friends can include your pictures in their albums, too. Anyone receiving a Buddy Album can also order conventional prints and picture CDs, and buy gifts such as mugs and T-shirts featuring those images. This means grandma and grandpa can cover their coffee table with framed enlargements without needing the original negatives. (This also means you shouldn't share any photos that you wouldn't want the world to see). The recipient of a Buddy Album can also save that album to his or her own Saved Pictures space. So now grandma and grandpa can build their own permanent album of their favorite grandkids and share it with the rest of the family.

For those concerned with online safety, you'll be pleased to know that Kids Only and Young Teens accounts cannot send or receive Buddy Albums or share pictures online. You can access Parental Controls to customize a screen name's access to these pictures. To do this, go to Keyword: **Parental Controls** on a master screen name, click the Set Parental Controls, and select Web controls from the Parental Controls Custom Controls list. Now choose from either "Access sites appropriate for ages 12 and under" or "Access sites appropriate for ages 13 to 15" if you want to restrict access. Among other things, this prevents the sending and/or receiving of Buddy Albums. Also, people receiving notification of a Buddy Album are given the choice whether or not to view it, and are warned to be cautious when viewing Buddy Albums from strangers.

Terms of Service

AOL has instituted a set of You've Got Pictures guidelines that apply the Terms of Service to the unique issues faced by You've Got Pictures. The guidelines address issues such as illegal images, copyright infringement, solicitation of business, and the like. We highly recommend you refer to these guidelines in the You've Got Pictures Help area before using this feature. If you need additional assistance with You've Got Pictures, we recommend you try Keyword: **Picture Help** for plenty of instructions, tips, and answers to frequently asked questions. You may also call You've Got Pictures technical support directly at 1-800-YGP-3883.

Note

Did you not receive your pictures at your screen name? First, be sure you're using the screen name you supplied to the photo dealer. If that's okay, make sure the address and phone number you gave the photo lab match the address and phone number of your AOL account (go to Keyword: **Billing** to check). If the screen name you supply does not match your billing info, AOL will not deliver the photos to that screen name. This prevents accidental delivery to the wrong person. Use the Roll ID and Owners Key # that came with your prints to access your photos online.

10

Unearthing Treasures

FTP

FTP, or *File Transfer Protocol*, is a system used to transfer entire files across the Internet. FTP is a much more efficient and reliable way to exchange files than e-mail, but not everyone has the software needed to use it. Luckily for you, FTP is built into your AOL software. In fact, downloading files from FTP is very much like downloading files from an AOL file library. To use FTP, click the Internet icon on the AOL toolbar and select FTP from the drop-down menu, or use Keyword: **FTP** (see Figure 10-20).

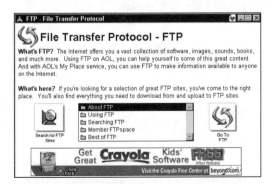

Figure 10-20. Use AOL's main FTP screen to learn how to use FTP, to search for FTP sites, and to access FTP Space.

Many companies and organizations maintain FTP sites, although you may need a username and password to gain access. Other FTP sites may be accessed by anyone at all. AOL supplies a list of useful public FTP sites you can visit, but you're also free to search for and visit other sites. To use FTP, browse the Best of FTP folder in the main window and open one of the recommended FTP sites. Alternatively, you can click the Go To FTP button on the right side of the window and choose one of the favorite sites listed there. If you prefer to go directly to another site for which you have the address, click the Other Site button at the bottom of the window (see Figure 10-21) and type in the requested information.

Figure 10-21. Connect to FTP sites around the world through this window.

FTP space is organized like a computer's hard disk, with directories (folders) that hold files. It's not always easy to know what information is stored where, so most public sites include easy-to-find text documents to help you find your way around their site (see Figure 10-22).

Figure 10-22. The PC Games FTP site at mirrors.aol.com/pub/pc_games. Open the README file to learn how to use the site.

What's not so well known is that every AOL account comes with up to 14MB of FTP storage space, 2MB for each screen name on the account. (To get the full 14MB, you need to use AOL 5.0.) This space is most commonly used for Web publishing. If you create a home page on AOL, this is where your pages are stored. It can also be used to share files of nearly any kind with friends or business associates. The easiest way to get to your personal FTP space is via Keyword: **My FTP Space** (see Figure 10-23), but you can also reach it by entering FTP and going to members.aol.com.

Tip

To learn more about making the most of your FTP storage space, we recommend *Your Official America Online Internet Guide* by David Peal (AOL Press, 1999). This guide offers plenty of details on the wonders and workings of the Internet on America Online.

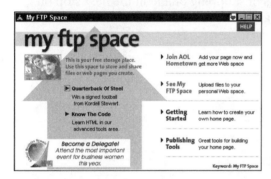

Figure 10-23. My FTP Space, the quickest way to access your personal FTP space on AOL

Independent Explorations

An entire world of software awaits you on America Online and the Internet. At one point — many, many years ago — we had a good handle on the scope of files you could expect to find online. No longer. The availability of files for download has grown in such scope and magnitude that it is almost overwhelming. Suffice it to say if you're looking for something, you can probably find it somewhere online.

If you're reading between the lines, you may wonder if we're hinting that commercial software is available for free online. The answer is yes, though only in the back alleys and black markets of the Internet. You download any such software at your own risk, and we do mean risk — viruses, Trojan Horses, and other dangers run rampant in such places. You get what you pay for, after all. Enough said.

10

Unearthing Treasures

So where do you go to find quality software on your own? Beyond your favorite forum's libraries and the Download Center, we recommend `http://www.shareware.com` for a large collection of valuable downloads. C|net's `http://www.download.com` is also an excellent resource.

If you're looking for commercial software, you can also find plenty of it available online. In fact, like any tourist destination worth its salt, you can scarcely avoid shopping opportunities. Thankfully, there's not a tourist trap in sight. Let's take a closer look at the benefits of shopping online in the next stop on our tour, "Shopping the Electronic Bazaar."

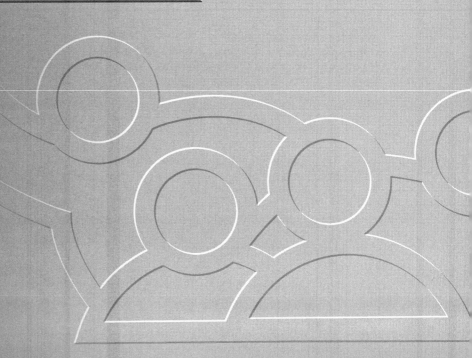

Quick Look

▶ **Shop @ AOL**   **page 233**

AOL offers an entire channel devoted to shopping online: Shop @ AOL. The channel offers online retailers, organized by category, as well as a way to search for brands and products. You can reach the Shopping Channel with Keyword: **Shopping**.

▶ **AOL Shopping Guarantee**   **page 237**

Worried about shopping online? Thanks to the AOL Shopping Guarantee, you can relax while shopping through AOL Certified Merchants, which all meet or exceed AOL's standards of customer service. Learn more at Keyword: **Guarantee**.

▶ **AOL Quick Checkout**   **page 239**

Zip through the online express lane with AOL Quick Checkout. With Quick Checkout, you can tell AOL to store your billing and shipping information on its secured computers, making checkout smoother and faster. Learn more at Keyword: **Quick Checkout**.

▶ **ClassifiedPlus**   **page 243**

Reach the world with ClassifiedPlus, AOL's own classified section. You can browse or search for items (or people) listed in ClassifiedPlus, or place your own ad for a reasonable price. You'll find ClassifiedPlus at Keyword: **Classifieds**.

Chapter 11

Shopping the Electronic Bazaar

CHAPTER ITINERARY

Finding the stores and shops

Using Customer Service

Staying safe with the AOL Shopping Guarantee

Remembering birthdays with Gift Reminder Service

Shopping from the world through the Classifieds

Shopping on America Online is even better than shopping on Rodeo Drive or in the streets of Paris. Not only do you find a wide variety of items within every price range on AOL, but you can shop from the comfort of your desk — no sore feet, no overflowing bags, and no parking problems. So grab your shopping lists and come with us as we explore the electronic bazaar of America Online.

Shopping Online

If you enjoy mail-order catalogs, shopping online should come as second nature to you. You're free to browse, and browse, and browse at any time of the day or night, with no salespeople to pressure or intimidate you. Price comparisons are easy, because you can open windows into as many stores as you like at the same time.

Although you'll find shopping opportunities in many of AOL's channels and forums, AOL's Shopping Channel (also known as Shop @ AOL) is the best place to start. Click the Shopping button on the left side of your Welcome screen or use the Keyword: **Shopping** (see Figure 11-1).

Figure 11-1. Shop@AOL is an electronic bazaar of goods and services.

The Shopping Channel offers more than 200 retailers displaying their wares in over 16 categories, from some of America's oldest household names to the hottest "dot coms." Shop@AOL is the place you can come to find all the great brands you know and trust, and browse or shop in a safe and secure environment (see Figure 11-2). Just click the A-Z Listing of Stores to find a comprehensive list of merchants. You can also find what you're looking for by typing in a product in the Shopping Search field.

Use the Search Shop@AOL feature at the top of each category window to hone in on the product you're seeking. Results are ranked by relevancy and include hyperlinks to go directly to the stores that carry the matching products.

Figure 11-2. AOL Shopping's Kids & Babies department

When you think about AOL's Shopping Channel, think shopping mall. Think really, really *big* shopping mall. Many of the retailers in the Shopping Channel's categories are familiar shopping mall names, from big department stores such as J.C. Penney and Macy's to specialty shops such as Godiva Chocolates, the Gap, Victoria's Secret, and Eddie Bauer. Mail-order favorites L.L. Bean, Lands' End, Spiegel, Lillian Vernon, and Chef's Catalog, among others, have also set up shop. Door-to-door specialist Avon comes calling, you can "call" 1-800 Flowers, and even cable TV's QVC shows up on this channel as iQVC. Just about the only thing you can't get at this shopping mall is a burger and a hair cut (although you *can* buy a frozen steak from Omaha Steaks).

Although the procedures vary a bit from store to store, making purchases is very straightforward. As you browse through a store and find something you like, "toss" it in your "shopping basket" — choose the item you're interested in and click the Order, Purchase, Add, or OK button with your mouse. You may be asked questions about size, color, and similar options. See Figure 11-3 for an example.

The stores maintain an electronic shopping cart that holds all the items you select until you're ready to check out. You're free to check the contents of your shopping cart, add or remove items from your cart, or quit shopping altogether without spending a cent or divulging your personal information. Many stores are able to retain the contents of your shopping cart, even if you leave the store, though this isn't true of all stores. When you're finished in a store, click the Check Out button (see Figure 11-4). During the checkout process, you are asked for payment and shipping information, and you're done!

Find It Online

Click Quick Tips on the bottom of the Shop@AOL screen to learn more about finding what you want, using your shopping cart, and checking out at 1-2-3 Shop. You'll also find special bargains for first-time shoppers at 1-2-3 Shop.

Figure 11-3. Click the Add to Shopping Cart button when you see something you like, such as these way cool sunglasses from shades.com.

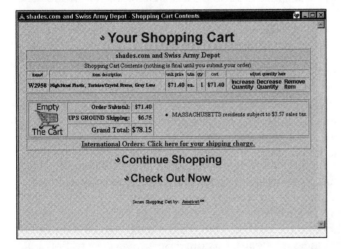

Figure 11-4. Click the Check Out Now button when you're ready to purchase your items.

Chic Simple

Do you ever go shopping with a friend whose taste, shopping savvy, and sense of style is "to die for"? AOL figures everyone can use the kind of advice that leaves you looking outrageous for far less than you thought you'd pay, so Kim Johnson and Jeff Stone of Chic Simple are now fixtures at Shop@AOL. Chic Simple puts together seasonal wardrobes with items selected from merchants throughout Shop@AOL. Everything from tops and bottoms to undies and accessories are selected with an eye for comfort, value, and style. If you're really stumped, you can even ask Kim for a bit of help. You can find links to Chic Simple right on the Shopping Channel's front page and in many other departments around the Shopping Channel, or use Keyword: **Chic Simple**.

Customer Service

Have you ever noticed that the customer service department in a large retail store is tucked away in a far corner of the basement, and none of the salespeople know where it is? Well, it's not like that at AOL. AOL goes out of its way to be sure you have a happy AOL shopping experience.

If you do have a problem with a merchant, your first stop should be its own customer service department. AOL's Certified Merchants Program requires merchants to provide a high level of customer service, so most problems should be resolved without AOL's help. If you can't work things out with the merchant, though, AOL is ready to back you up.

AOL's customer service representatives are on duty from 8 a.m. to 2 a.m. eastern time to help with any of your shopping questions or problems. You can chat with them online, speak with them on the phone, send them e-mail, or post your question on a message board. Customer Service is easy to find; all you have to do is click the Customer Service button on the Shopping Channel main screen, or use Keyword: **Shopping Customer Service** (see Figure 11-5).

Figure 11-5. Find answers to your shopping questions at Shopping Customer Service.

If you do have a problem with a merchant, the more information you have for AOL's customer service representatives, the better. Be prepared with a written description containing the name of the merchant, the date of purchase, the price you paid, and describe what you've done to resolve the problem and how the merchant responded.

AOL Shopping Guarantee

AOL carefully selects, evaluates, and tests merchants before they sell merchandise on AOL. All merchants must meet or exceed a certain level of service, which includes processing orders promptly, conducting transactions securely, shipping the product professionally, responding to customer questions quickly, and adopting policies to ensure customer privacy. Those merchants that meet these standards become certified and are entitled to display the AOL Certified Merchant Guarantee seal of approval (see Figure 11-6).

Now what about this guarantee? AOL backs up every purchase made through its Certified Merchants Program. Here's how it works: If you have a problem with a merchant, first contact the merchant in question. Should the merchant refuse to provide a satisfactory resolution, you can contact AOL to intervene on your behalf. If the merchant still does not comply with its return policy, AOL will refund the full purchase

Note

Send Customer Service e-mail to screen name ShopHelp. You can also phone 1-800-349-1945 any time between 8 a.m. and 2 a.m. eastern time.

Tip

AOL Shopping Channel Customer Service provides more than help with problems. They'll help you with just about any online shopping-related question, including where to find the most unusual kinds of merchandise.

11

Shopping the Electronic Bazaar

Note

AOL may use information about the kinds of products that you buy online to make other marketing offers to you. If you prefer that they do not, indicate so in your marketing preference settings at Keyword: **Marketing Prefs** (detailed in Appendix B).

price — guaranteed. Do remember to read each merchant's return policy before you make purchases; not all merchants will refund purchase prices if you have a problem. You can usually find refund policies in a merchant's customer service area. AOL maintains a complete list of certified merchants online at Keyword: **Guarantee**, where you can also read more about the AOL Shopping Guarantee itself (see Figure 11-7).

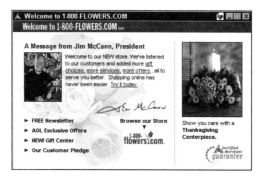

Figure 11-6. The America Online Seal of Approval at 1-800-FLOWERS

Figure 11-7. AOL's 100% Shopping Guarantee

Safety

Did you know that shopping on AOL is statistically safer than shopping at your local mall? Besides avoiding the obvious safety considerations such as potential accidents while driving to and from the mall, the dangers lurking in parking lots, purse and wallet snatchers, and those over-the-top impulse items at the checkout counter, your credit cards are also more secure on AOL than in a mall. AOL hasn't received even one report of a compromised credit card since the Shopping Channel opened its doors in 1996. How does AOL do it? They provide a secure environment for credit card transactions by encrypting all data sent and received during the purchase. This means that even if someone intercepted the transmission (very, very unlikely, but still a remote possibility), that person wouldn't be able to make heads or tails of the information.

AOL only guarantees this secure environment with its certified merchants, however, so your safety is also your responsibility. Be careful not to give your credit card information or any other personal information to an unauthorized party. If you receive an unsolicited e-mail or Instant Message requesting your credit card information, you can be pretty sure the message is fraudulent. The only times you will be asked for your credit card number are during the initial AOL registration or when making a purchase online. If you receive what you believe is a fraudulent credit card request, notify AOL immediately at keyword: TOS. You can also send e-mail to screen name MarketMail.

AOL Quick Checkout

Welcome to the Express Checkout lane! With a little help from AOL Quick Checkout, you can fly through the online stores in record time. Sign up for Quick Checkout by visiting Keyword: **Quick Checkout** (see Figure 11-8), or click Set up Quick Checkout Now when you checkout the normal way at any merchant who accepts Quick Checkout.

Once you've become a frequent online shopper, you'll wish there was much less typing when making a purchase. Every time you enter a merchant's checkout process, you have to enter your credit card and shipping information all over again. AOL Quick Checkout saves you some of that time and trouble and helps you avoid typing errors. It saves information on up

Cross-Reference

See Chapter 2 for more information on security and creating good passwords, and refer to the section titled "Safety" elsewhere in this chapter.

to 10 of your credit/debit cards and the shipping addresses of up to 50 of your friends and relatives on AOL's carefully secured computers so you can finish paying for things and get back to the fun of shopping.

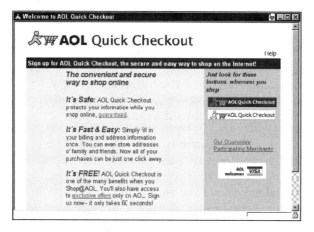

Figure 11-8. Quick Checkout, where the express lane is always open

Whenever you reach the checkout at a participating AOL merchant, Quick Checkout will automatically supply your default information (your preferred credit card and regular shipping address). If you want to use a different card or ship the goods to someone else listed in your Quick Checkout address book, just click Edit and select the desired changes. Of course, you can also replace the information supplied by Quick Checkout — just type in something completely different.

Quick Checkout is also the place to go if you want to add, delete, or modify credit card and address information, or to get in-depth information on how Quick Checkout works. There's also a special Quick Checkout Customer Service number at 877-385-2330 if you have problems or questions regarding your Quick Checkout account.

There's a lot of trust involved in any relationship in which you provide such sensitive financial information, and AOL goes to great lengths to earn that trust:

▶ Your Quick Checkout account is protected by a separate password. The first time you use Quick Checkout during an online session you'll be asked for that password.

▶ To make changes to your Quick Checkout information, you are also asked a security question, the answer for which you provided when you set up your Quick Checkout account.

▶ Your information is protected from prying eyes. Once it has been entered into the system, your credit card numbers will not be displayed on screen. Only the last four digits of your card number will be shown, so you can recognize the card.

▶ Your information is stored at AOL on computers that are not accessible via the Internet.

▶ The highest level of SSL encryption available with your browser protects credit card information as it flows between your computer and AOL (128 bit with Internet Explorer 5.0, which is the browser supplied with AOL 5.0).

▶ Only screen names with Parental Controls set to 18+ may create Quick Checkout accounts.

▶ You are free to delete information or your account at any time, and AOL erases that information immediately.

Of course, computer security becomes even more important once you set up a Quick Checkout account. Be sure your passwords are unique, hard to guess, and hard to find (if you wrote them down). Don't use the Stored Passwords feature of AOL, as that removes one of the two locks on your Quick Checkout access, and don't use the same password for your AOL account and Quick Checkout.

Money

To shop online, you're going to need a credit card (or a bank/debit card with the Visa or MasterCard symbol on it). All stores we surveyed take credit cards, specifically Visa, MasterCard, and American Express. Some stores accept Discover, including all Quick Checkout stores. Some stores, such as BarnesAndNoble.com, also accept Diners Club, JCB, and corporate purchasing cards. Some (but not many) AOL stores accept checks and money orders, and some of the stores also issue and/or accept gift certificates.

 Note

Give your credit card information only to established and trusted retailers. Beware of any individuals asking for your information, or anything suspicious during transactions. No AOL employee will ever ask you for your credit card information online (though you may be required to give it if you call AOL regarding a billing issue).

11

Shopping the Electronic Bazaar

Gift Reminder Service

Has all this talk of shopping reminded you of anything? Like an upcoming birthday or holiday, perhaps? If you're still drawing a blank, you may need a reminder — Keyword: **Reminder**, to be specific. The AOL Reminder Service (see Figure 11-9) is a free tool that lets you save dates of birthdays, holidays, and so on, and then reminds you beforehand so you don't miss them.

Figure 11-9. Never forget a date with the AOL Reminder Service.

Reminders come in the form of e-mail messages two weeks before your important date — you can also opt to have a second reminder sent four days beforehand, too. It's a simple but very effective tool. Click the Create Your Reminder button to begin the registration process (see Figure 11-10).

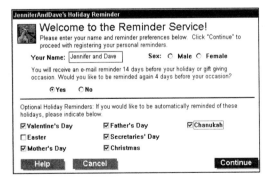

Figure 11-10. Registration for the service is free and easy.

In the registration window, type in your name (your first or full name), and then indicate your gender (optional) and

whether you'd like the 4-day reminder in addition to the
14-day reminder. You can also choose to be automatically
reminded of up to seven major holidays — just click the boxes
to the left of the name to select them. When you are done,
click the Continue button. Once you've registered, AOL shows
you your reminder list (see Figure 11-11).

Tip

Use the reminder service to
help you remember events
besides gift-giving occasions.
Just type in the occasion
(meeting, bill payment due,
and so on) in the Other field
under Occasion when creating a reminder.

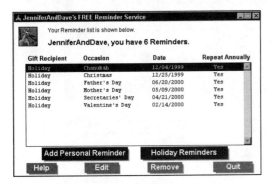

Figure 11-11. Our new reminder list

Any holidays you chose when you registered appear here,
organized alphabetically by occasion. Note the columns, indicating recipient, occasion, date, and repeat rate. To create a new
reminder, click the Add Personal Reminder button near the bottom. Fill out the reminder form as requested. Note that only the
gift recipient's name and the date are required. When finished,
click the Save button to create your reminder. The new reminder
now appears in your reminder list. Reminders are easy to edit.
Just select a reminder in your reminder list, click the Edit button,
make your changes, and click Save again. If you'd rather just
delete a reminder, simply select it in the reminder list and click
Remove. Use the Holiday Reminders button to add or remove
the automatic holiday reminders in your list.

Shopping Through the Classifieds

Is your attic overflowing with really great stuff, or do you need
a bunch of really great stuff so you can fill your attic? Either
way, AOL's ClassifiedPlus is a great place to start (and finish).
Over 55 million AOL and Internet users have access to the
ClassifiedPlus listings. That's a lot of people, and a lot of stuff!

11

Shopping the Electronic Bazaar

You can access ClassifiedPlus by choosing Classifieds from the AOL Top Pick's submenu under the Favorites menu, or just use Keyword: **Classifieds** (see Figure 11-12).

Figure 11-12. Choose a category or place an ad on the ClassifiedPlus main page

The ClassifiedPlus main page is clean and easy to use. You can place an ad (and change or delete it if you wish), subscribe to the ClassifiedPlus newsletter, access extensive customer service information, and jump into any of the ten main classifieds categories. ClassifiedPlus offers classified listings in ten broad categories — Employment, Personals, Computing, Auctions, Vehicles, General, Business, Real Estate, Antiques & Collectibles, and Travel & Travel Tickets.

Once you've selected a category you can select from a variety of sub categories. For example, the Vehicles department (see Figure 11-13) has sections devoted to used autos, boats/marine, parts/service, motorcycles, aircraft, commercial vehicles and RVs.

One of the most powerful features of online classifieds is the power to search for advertisements matching your needs, rather than simply browse through column after column of small print. Your search options vary, depending on which category you're visiting. In the Employment section you can choose job categories from a drop-down list, type in a useful word or phrase, and select whether that search will look for at least one word, all words, or the exact phrase you're looking for. You can further refine the search by typing the name of a company, choosing in which region (including *Outside USA*), state, city or ZIP code you'd like to focus your search, or even decide whether to restrict a search to the city limits or cover its entire metropolitan area.

Learn about the finer points of the classifieds with the ClassifiedPlus Newsletter. You can read it online while you're visiting ClassifiedPlus, or sign up for their mailing list and receive a copy in your e-mail. Just click the Newsletter link on the ClassifiedPlus main page.

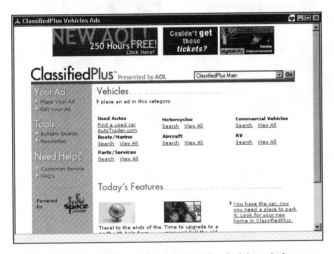

Figure 11-13. Pick a car, any car, from the ClassifiedPlus Vehicles section.

ClassifiedPlus and Safe Shopping

"May the buyer beware!" These words are seldom more important than in the world of classified advertising (online or offline). As buyers may never meet sellers face-to-face, or see the merchandise (or payment) before delivery, buyers and sellers have to be triply cautious about everything they do. The customer service area at ClassifiedPlus supplies a generous helping of advice on how to protect yourself during buy-sell transactions, and we strongly suggest you read everything there before you place or respond to that first ad. Also note that due to the nature of classified ads, AOL and ClassifiedPlus will not intervene in disputes between parties bought together by a classified listing.

If you're interested in placing an ad the entire process takes place online. First, click the Place Your Ad link on the far-left

The folks at ClassifiedPlus want your ad to shine. Visit the ClassifiedPlus Help area for lots of tips for creating and placing your ad, or click the handy hyperlinks to those tips that you'll find at the bottom of the window as you create your ad.

side of the window, and then select the category in which you want to place the ad. Then you fill in a series of forms that contain the contact information for the ad and the ad itself (see Figure 11-14).

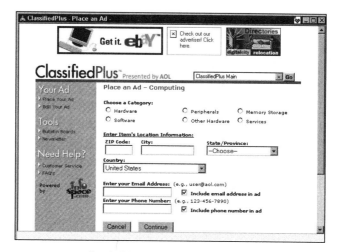

Figure 11-14. ClassifiedPlus makes it easy to sell your computer.

ClassifiedPlus then displays the text of your ad and gives you the opportunity to go back and edit it. When you're satisfied with the ad you'll either be asked for your ClassifiedPlus password (if you already have a ClassifiedPlus account) or you'll be asked to provide a password and the information required for creating an account. The next step is for existing account holders and beginners alike — you'll have to pay for the ad. Once you've provided the billing information your ad will be online in about 24 hours.

At the specially-discounted AOL member rates (you must be using your AOL account and its built-in browser to qualify for the rates) you pay from around $2 to $25 for a two-week listing, depending on what you're advertising. The romantically inclined get the very best price — Love@AOL's personal ads are free!

A Picture's Worth . . .

ClassifiedPlus gives you something you'll never get from your local gazette — an option to include a color photo along with your ad, at no extra charge. GIF or JPG graphics may be uploaded when you create your ad. Of course, the images must be consistent with the ClassifiedPlus Terms of Service and it's best if the file is smaller than 150K, so it will download quickly.

AOL Shop Direct

AOL Shop Direct (Keyword: **Shop Direct**) is America Online's very own store, offering just the kind of merchandise you need for a great online (and offline) experience. Everything from computers, modems, and digital cameras to software, books, and logo merchandise has been selected and pre-tested for value, ease of use, and suitability to an AOL member's needs. Shop Direct turns up some great bargains and its Outlet center is a fun place to look for close-out merchandise, so it pays to pay a visit to AOL Shop Direct.

Shopping Outside of AOL

Many shopping opportunities exist outside of AOL. AOL's Shopping Guarantee does not extend to Internet merchants that are not certified, however, and it is certainly a "buyer beware" situation. If you venture into the unknown in search of great deals, keep these tips for safe shopping in mind:

▶ *Secure your Web browser.* AOL's built-in Web browser offers a variety of security features, which you should use when shopping online. These features include Secure Sockets Layer (SSL), variable user-defined security levels, and lists of trusted/restricted sites. You can learn more about setting these security preferences in Appendix B.

11

Shopping the Electronic Bazaar

More consumer tips on shopping online are available on the Web from the Federal Trade Commission. Visit `http://www.ftc.gov/ bcp/menu-internet. htm`.

▶ *Pay by credit.* Purchases made with credit (or charge) cards are protected by the Fair Credit Billing Act, which gives you the right to dispute charges under certain circumstances. You are generally liable for only the first $50 in charges. Inquire with your credit card company for additional warranty or purchase protection benefits.

▶ *Shop familiar or established companies.* Virtually anyone can open an online shop these days. If you're not familiar with a particular company, get specific information on their refund and return policies. Also get details on the company itself by requesting a catalog, brochure, or sample.

▶ *Protect your passwords.* Some stores require that you sign up and establish a user account before you can make purchases. If required to enter a password, do not use your AOL password. Rather, choose a unique (and equally complex) password.

▶ *Keep records.* Save and/or print all order information, confirmation numbers, purchase orders, and anything else offered during the transaction process. If the ordered goods or services are not fulfilled within 30 days, the company is required by law (unless otherwise stated) to notify you first.

Independent Explorations

Our brief tour of AOL's shopping district barely skims the surface of what awaits you at AOL Shopping, in other areas on AOL, and out on the wider Internet. If you're half the shopper we think you are, you'll have to come back some other time to shop in earnest. When you do, keep some of these tips in mind:

▶ Be the same careful consumer you'd be anywhere else. Visit the shops' customer service areas, read the fine print, and be sure you understand all the ins and outs before you commit real cash.

▶ If you're a serious wheeler-dealer and bargain hunter, you may want to check out an online auction. There are several examples of this hot new way to buy and sell merchandise at AOL Shopping Channel — just click the Auctions & Outlets button.

▶ Some apparel shops let you build an electronic mannequin so you can see how their clothes will look on someone who looks like you. Mix, match, and see how an ensemble will look on you. Pretty neat!

Now that you know how to spend your money on AOL, we're going to show you where you can earn more of it. At the next stop on our tour you get a chance to explore the business-related channels and forums on AOL.

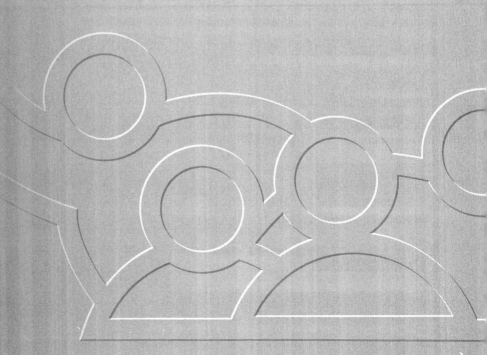

CHAPTER

12

SEEING THE SITES:

BUSINESS

Quick Look

▶ **Today on AOL**   **page 253**

AOL highlights the top headlines of the day as well as the interesting programs
and happenings offered on AOL in the Today on AOL section of the Welcome
screen. These frequently updated teasers are links to the areas on AOL where
you will find more information on the topic that caught your eye.

▶ **Search & Explore**   **page 264**

Every channel offers a Search & Explore button, somewhere on its main window, which leads to tools and resources to help you find what you seek. You
can browse a list of a channel's forums, search for something specific, read a
channel overview, or take a tour. Look for Search & Explore near the bottom
of a channel's window.

▶ **Investment Portfolios**   **page 266**

Track your investments with AOL's online portfolio system, free to AOL members. The system is powerful and easy, offering customization features, detailed
reports, and an "investment snapshot" with charts, news, and quotes. Visit
Keyword: **My Portfolios** to set up and access your own portfolios.

▶ **Ask-a-Teacher**   **page 274**

When you need help with a homework assignment, just ask a teacher . . .
on AOL! At Keyword: **Ask a Teacher**, you can look up answers to previously
asked questions, post your question on a message board, get live help from a
teacher, or e-mail your question to a teacher. This free service is available
for students in elementary school, middle school, high school, college, and
beyond.

Chapter 12

Seeing the Sites: Business

CHAPTER ITINERARY

Surfing the AOL Channels

Staying informed at News and Influence

Going around the world at International

Making money at Personal Finance and WorkPlace

Learning more at Computing and Research & Learn

Visiting the neighbors at Local

Good morning, everyone! We hope you've had a full, satisfying breakfast. Now, please walk this way — it's time to board the virtual tour bus and begin our exploration of the channels, the main thoroughfares and byways of America Online.

Today's route will take us among the towering skyscrapers of AOL's business and financial districts, up the broad steps of its great research libraries, past Embassy Row, and down Main Street. Along the way, we'll stop at one of the world's most remarkable newsstands, and hang out on a virtual street corner where you can get the inside buzz on what's really happening, and spread a little "dish" yourself. Of course, AOL could never have gotten down to business without computers, so we'll also pay a visit to the Computing Channel.

Although today's tour is supposed to be all business, life is rarely all business at all. Like any bustling metropolis, America Online thrives on its diversity.

Welcome

We're starting our tour with a quick visit back to the Welcome screen, which we described in Chapter 3. It's fully integrated into the button bar you'll find at the left of the main screen of every channel (and on the Welcome screen itself). AOL designed the Welcome screen (see Figure 12-1) to be the perfect jumping-off spot for your daily online travels.

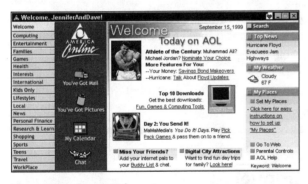

Figure 12-1. The AOL Welcome Screen

The Welcome screen greets you with top news stories, important search and help resources, and the enticing Today on AOL section, featuring all sorts of juicy information, contests, and merchandise. You could even consider the Welcome screen to be a personalized "My Channel," thanks to the inclusion of your Mailbox, You've Got Pictures, My Calendar, My Weather, and My Places features. Of course, it's also something of a TV remote control, since every channel on AOL is only a button-click away.

Tip

Not every selection on the Welcome screen is obvious. There's a little surprise lurking behind that big AOL logo in the upper-left of the screen (maybe you already found it when your mouse pointer's arrow changed into a hand). Click and you'll discover What's New on AOL!

Tip

Unlike most windows on AOL, you cannot completely close a channel window. If you click the close box in the upper-right corner of the channel window, the window is minimized instead. You can reopen the window by double-clicking the title bar of the minimized window, clicking the resize button on that title bar, selecting a channel from the AOL toolbar, or using its keyword.

Traveling from Channel to Channel

Flipping the channels at AOL is nearly as simple as changing channels on your television. Each and every main channel screen comes equipped with a *remote control* — an identical set of buttons, arrayed down the left-hand side of the window like the push buttons on some television sets. Click once and the screen is instantly converted to the desired channel.

If you don't flip for that method, AOL offers several more:

▶ Click the Channels icon on the AOL toolbar and then select the desired channel from the menu.

▶ Use keywords. Every channel name is also a keyword. Just type the channel name into the text entry box at the top of the AOL screen and click Go (or press Enter).

▶ Use Keyword: **Channels**. The Channels window has a large, colorful button for every channel.

We're probably forgetting one or two methods, but this should be enough to get you started. The next time someone loses the remote control, you'll still be able to switch channels.

News Channel

It's huge! If you had to carry it in from the front stoop, you'd need a forklift, but fortunately, all you need is your mouse and all the time in the world. This is AOL News, your route to what's happening now throughout the world at Keyword: **News** (see Figure 12-2). Please be sure to stay with our tour group. News fans may become so engrossed that they may never want to leave.

The News Channel gathers news from many of the top sources online, in print, and on the air. Among AOL's news gathering partners are CBS News, National Public Radio, TIME magazine, The New York Times, the Associated Press, Reuters, and Bloomberg.

Figure 12-2. AOL's News Channel. All the news that fits, and then some!

The AOL News Channel screen is packed tightly with news headlines and features. If you click any one selection, you'll be swept deeper and deeper into the news. If the headline leads to a news story, there's a good chance the story will be accompanied by a photograph and/or collection of additional stories on the same topic. Other buttons lead to entire news departments, such as Business News or U.S. and World News, and still others lead to news-gathering organizations such as CBS News. The News Search feature can find hundreds of articles on a given topic, and there are always several surveys or quizzes for those who want to lend their voice or test their knowledge.

Here's a rundown of what you can expect to find on the front screen of AOL News:

News Search

Type in your search phrase and be prepared to dive into an ocean of search results. There's more here than ever makes it to the front page. Use Keyword: **News Search**.

CBS News

See slideshows of CBS news reports, prepared especially for AOL. Hear the reports and see an ever-changing series of still photos. You'll also find links to CBS News top stories and On Air, featuring transcripts and reports from CBS News magazines such as 48 Hours, 60 Minutes, and the CBS Evening News. Use Keyword: **CBS News**.

Tip

How fresh are the headlines at the News Channel? A quick glance at the top of the News Channel screen, where AOL posts the time of the last update, will tell you. If the headlines don't seem quite fresh enough, close and reopen the window. If there's been another update, you'll receive it! No matter what happens, the headlines on the news ticker (discussed later) in the upper-right of the screen are constantly changing.

12

Seeing the Sites: Business

Speak Out

AOL News collects editorials and commentaries from its diverse partners, including The New York Times and National Public Radio (see Figure 12-3). You can also make yourself heard at the many chats, message boards, and surveys offered at the bottom of the Speak Out window. Use Keyword: **Speak Out**.

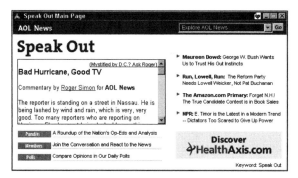

Figure 12-3. Express yourself at AOL News's Speak Out.

U.S. and World

Here's all the news you'd expect to find, and a good bit more. Search around a bit (hint: click the More Stories button) for collections of world news organized by region and by nation, and news from Washington, DC. Use Keyword: **US World**.

Business News

Track the course of commerce and finance at AOL Business News. The AOL Business News Center is shared by AOL's News, Personal Finance, and WorkPlace Channels, and features stories from Bloomberg News, AP, and Reuters. A stock ticker highlights top financial averages and provides links to AOL Personal Finance's Market News Center (MNC). Top Stories, Business News Search, Overseas Markets, News Summary, Technology, Economy, International, Industry, and Consumer Briefs all have a home here. And what about AOL Business Newsstand? It has links to the business sections of more than a dozen online news sources, including Business Week, Nightly Business Report, Financial Times, The New York Times, and TIME magazine. Use Keyword: **Business News**.

Tip

For even more international news, visit AOL International Channel's News department, at Keyword: **INTL News**. Among its fascinating resources are links to hundreds of online newspapers throughout the world, many in their native languages. We discuss this channel later in the chapter.

Health News

Today in Health offers news and articles of interest from AOL's Health Channel. Use Keyword: **Today in Health**

Entertainment News

Show biz news from AOL's Entertainment Channel. Read the hot news and find links to the entertainment news sections of PEOPLE Online, E! Online, Entertainment Asylum, and SonicNet. Use Keyword: **Ent News**.

Life

This is the human-interest side of life with late-breaking stories, today's Features, and a news ticker all its own. PEOPLE magazine, Weird News, and AOL's Buzzsaw round out the offerings. Use Keyword: **Life News**.

Politics

Learn more than you wanted to know about politicians, lawmakers, and elections from the major news organizations. Of course, what's politics without a link to NewsTalk, where the soapbox is king (or president)? Use Keyword: **Politics**.

Newsstand

The AOL News Newsstand provides links to newsstands at other AOL channels. This includes more than dozen major online news publications including Business Week, the Columbia Journalism Review, National Review, National Public Radio, The New York Times, CBS News, and TIME magazine. Use Keyword: **Newsstand**.

Weather

Visit AOL Weather Central for the national weather map, local weather conditions, and torrents of useful news at Keyword: **Weather**. Just enter an area code, ZIP code, city, or state into the Search box to get a detailed forecast for your hometown, or anyplace else in the U.S. (see Figure 12-4).

Tip

Add an icon for your local weather forecast to your AOL toolbar for one-click access to your local weather forecast. Call up your local forecast at the AOL Weather Center, drag its Favorite Place heart to the toolbar, select an icon (the sun-and-clouds icon works well), and add a caption (see Chapter 3 for more details on Favorite Places). You'll never have to look out your windows again!

Cross-Reference

Delve into ClassifiedsPlus in Chapter 11.

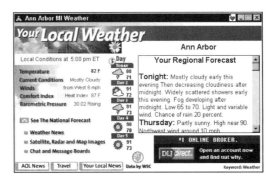

Figure 12-4. Local conditions in Ann Arbor, Michigan (Go, Blue!) from AOL Weather Central

Local

AOL News and Digital City have teamed up with local news organizations across the country to bring a local slant to the AOL experience. Get local news, sports, and weather from your old hometown, from just around the block, or for the city you'll be visiting tomorrow. Use Keyword: **Local News**. See also the Local Channel, described at the end of this chapter.

Classifieds

What's a newspaper without classifieds? Thanks to ClassifiedsPlus, this question is moot. Use Keyword: **Classifieds**.

News Ticker

Up-to-the-moment headlines flash across the top of the News Channel window, just the way they do in New York City's Times Square. The similarity ends there, though. Just one click on the headline brings you the stories behind the headlines from the U.S. and World News Summary.

Does access to all this news seem just a wee bit overwhelming? The news can be like that, as anyone who has hefted the Sunday edition of *The New York Times* can tell you. At least at AOL your mouse can do all the heavy lifting!

International Channel

When you signed-up for our little AOL tour, did you think you'd be traveling the world? Thanks to our virtual tour bus and AOL's International Channel (see Figure 12-5), the entire world is only seconds away. The folks at AOL International have prepared a warm welcome for travelers from every modem on the globe (at Keyword: **INTL**).

Figure 12-5. AOL's International Channel — an entire globe to explore!

Despite its name, America Online is a worldwide phenomenon. There are AOL services in Canada, the U.K., France, Germany, Sweden, Austria, Switzerland, Japan, Hong Kong and Australia — all in the native languages. Services for Brazil and other Latin American countries are also in development. AOL International gives you a chance to sample some of those services and to interact with fellow AOL members around the globe.

AOL International ranges far beyond the boundaries of those ten national services. World travelers, students of foreign cultures, and just plain folks will find information on more than 200 countries and political subdivisions. The folks at AOL International have knit together in-depth guides to each of these places, combining travel, economic, cultural, and political information in an easy-to-use format that is consistently applied from country to country.

International Channel hides a wealth of information and community activities behind its uncluttered main screen.

> **Tip**
>
> Whichever headline is visible when you click the News Ticker will be the first story to be displayed when the summary appears. Wait for the ticker to come back around to your story, click, and that item will be right at the top of your summary. Or, just click the News Ticker and scroll down to that story. Pretty slick, huh?

What does AOL U.K. have that AOL U.S. does not? How about BBC News Online? For a taste of Great Britain's legendary news source, head for AOL International News, select AOL's Foreign News Sources from the list, and then select AOL UK News. The "Beeb" should be right there on the AOL UK News front screen.

News

What does International Channel News have that AOL News doesn't? How about the entire AOL Canada, AOL U.K., AOL Australia, AOL France, and AOL Germany news departments? How about world news organized country by country, overseas weather forecasts, links to hundreds of newspapers around the world, and TIME magazine's Asia edition? Does that sound like a good reason to visit Keyword: **INTL News**? We certainly hope so!

Business

The global economy is never at rest, but the resources of AOL International Business, at Keyword: **INTL Business**, can help you rest a bit easier. Research world market conditions with the Financial Times. Dig deeply into global economic conditions with the Economist Intelligence Unit. If you're considering investments in overseas businesses, a visit to Worldlyinvestor.com (Keyword: **Worldly Investor**) focuses on the needs of mutual fund and stock traders like yourself (see Figure 12-6).

Figure 12-6. Worldlyinvestor.com helps you take stock of world financial conditions.

AOL International Business also delivers Business Week International, information for those working abroad, exchange rates, and a currency conversion calculator. Finally, consider the riches buried in the AOL Foreign Services, (located in the Business section of the International Channel), including AOL UK Finance (see Figure 12-7), The Economist, Far Eastern Economic Review, and Emergea, an English-language emerging markets forum at AOL France.

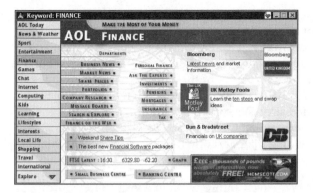

Figure 12-7. AOL UK Finance opens the door to the London markets.

Cultures

Whether you're headed for Korea or the kitchen, International Cultures has the recipe for greater understanding of people, their languages, and cultures at Keyword: **INTL Cultures**.

Jane Lasky's International Etiquette Guide at Keyword: **Global Citizen** delivers business-oriented etiquette and travel tips for over 30 nations. Even if your interest is pleasure, there's a lot to be learned here.

Planning a dinner at home or boning up on what you can expect to eat while abroad? Visit The Global Gourmet (Keyword: **GG**). They serve up a huge menu of authentic recipes and delightful, food-oriented destination guides for 40 countries and regions (see Figure 12-8).

Figure 12-8. The Global Gourmet's pantry is stock-full of International cuisine.

One of the less-heralded gems of International Channel is its collection of language dictionaries and resources (Keyword: **Foreign Dictionary**). From Afrikaans to Zulu, you'll find dictionaries and language aids by the dozen. Raise Your Cultural IQ pulls together a number of these resources and includes Cultural Differences, a collection of multicultural tips prepared by Jane Lasky, the person behind International Etiquette. International Culture also gives you the chance to play Name That Flag, and download the national anthems of nearly any country you can think of.

Finally, we can't leave Culture without a visit to Keyword: **Royalty**. The folks at the Royalty Forum are fascinated by the world's monarchies, past and (especially) present. This is *the* place to visit if you're intent on keeping up with the Windsors.

Fun & Games

AOL International's Fun and Games forum crosses oceans and continents to gather games, quizzes, contests, and entertainment news that help us learn a bit more about the world and the people in it.

Travel

When you've finished your virtual world tour on America Online, AOL International Travel stands ready to help you travel the globe at Keyword: **INTL Travel**. Preparing for vacation and business travel has never been easier, thanks to the many resources gathered here.

Country Information

AOL International maintains profiles on over 200 countries around the globe (see Figure 12-9) at Keyword: **Countries**. Whether you're planning a visit, researching a school project, or looking for new friends from your old homeland, you'll find everything you need in rich detail.

Figure 12-9. Bhutan, sandwiched between China and India, and located at Keyword: *Bhutan*

Global Meeting Place

If you'd like to teach the world to sing in perfect harmony, there are few better places to start than AOL International Channel's Global Meeting Place (Keyword: **Global Meeting**). You can visit chat rooms in France, Britain, Germany, Canada, and Australia, search for a pen pal (although perhaps "keyboard pal" would be the better term), and find romance in Passport to Love. Perhaps AOL is the true international language! Be sure to also stop in The Bistro, which offers live chat in over 30 foreign (or native) languages (see Figure 12-10) at Keyword: **Bistro**.

Figure 12-10. Bridge the cultural gap in 30 languages at The Bistro.

Search & Explore

Buried beneath the deceptively simple list of AOL channels is a mother lode of information, entertainment, and online resources. To help you mine these riches, AOL includes a Search & Explore feature for nearly every channel.

A typical Search & Explore window (this one is from International)

Depending on the channel, you may find the following:

- ▶ A–Z Guides listing every department and forum in the channel

- ▶ Search tool to help you dig for gold

- ▶ Channel guides that deliver an overview of what the channel has to offer

- ▶ Slideshow tours of the channel

- ▶ Essential information about the channel, its policies, and tips for making the most of your experiences online and at the channel

- ▶ Lists of the best resources in the channel

If you want to know our opinion, we'd tell you to seek out and pay a visit to Search & Explore soon after you pay your first visit to a channel. You'll be far richer for the experience.

Personal Finance Channel

We're about to drive among the towers and spires of America Online's Financial District. Please stay in your seats, and don't strain your necks. AOL has managed to pack every financial service from Wall Street to Main Street into one little channel, so although it's easy to drive right through it, a proper tour could take several days. We don't have much time now, but feel free to come back and explore in your spare time.

AOL Personal Finance is for the homeowner, the stockholder, and the just-plain-everyday person who strives to put his or her life and finances in order and make the most of their economic resources. Although the main screen looks like something created for stock market fanatics, there's far more lurking beneath the surface. See what it has to offer at Keyword: **PF** (see Figure 12-11).

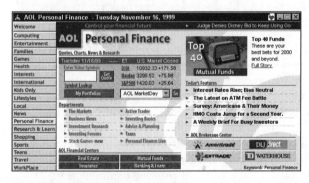

Figure 12-11. AOL Personal Finance is a rich resource.

Quotes, Charts, News & Research

AOL packs just about everything an investor needs to track the stock market, individual stocks, and their personal portfolio in one small, unassuming box at Keyword: **Quotes**. Type in the stock ticker symbol for nearly any stock, mutual fund, or stock index on U.S. and other major International exchanges, and you'll receive a snapshot with all the key trading statistics, pertinent news articles, and charts of historic performance for that stock, fund, or index. Access your online portfolios (you can have up to 20 portfolios per screen name), keep an eye on the major market averages, and pull up news reports on a wide variety of key indicators.

Tip

You can track nearly 200 stock indices and other measures of market and investment performance in your portfolio. For a complete listing of the indices and their symbols, click the Help button on either the My Portfolios screen or one of your personal Portfolio windows, select Index Quotes, and click the hypertext link for the "complete and printable list of Indices."

Online Stock Portfolios

Whether you're an active investor or an armchair capitalist, AOL makes it simple to track your investments and test investment strategies at Keyword: **My Portfolios**. Every screen name on an AOL account can maintain up to 20 online portfolios, each of which can contain up to 100 stocks, mutual funds, money market funds, and financial indices.

Online Stock Portfolios track your financial realities or fondest fantasies.

You can track the value of those portfolios throughout the day and get a detailed report on each item in your portfolio with just a quick double-click of your mouse. Each portfolio displays seven columns of information, including such things as number of shares, current price, change up/down, purchase price, current value, and percentage gain/loss. AOL lets you customize those columns with your choice of more than 25 different measures of performance. You can look up stocks, add them to your portfolio with a few clicks, keep track of purchase information, adjust for splits, and transfer an item to another of your portfolios. You can even download your portfolio for import into spreadsheets, databases, and Quicken. Once you have your portfolio up and running, add it to your AOL toolbar for easy access.

Departments

Whether you're a buy-and-hold investor, a day trader, or someone who's just beginning to explore your financial options, the departments of Personal Finance stand ready to serve your needs. Here are a few choice stops.

The Market News Center (Keyword: **MNC**) is a one-stop shop for current events in the major financial markets, with charts, news headlines, and detailed reports of every description (see Figure 12-12). With a few clicks, the Market News Center can go from a general overview of the major markets to specialized views of stocks and mutual funds, bonds, currencies, the U.S. economy, international markets, and futures trading.

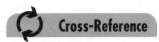

Cross-Reference

The extensive news resources of AOL Business News (Keyword: **Business News**) are discussed earlier in this chapter, in the News Channel section.

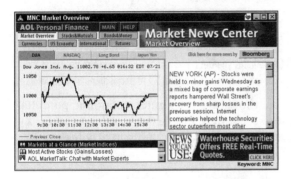

Figure 12-12. Track the markets with a few quick clicks at the Market News Center.

Investing Basics (Keyword: **Investing Basics**) is ready to school you in all the ins and outs of investing. Take an eight-step course in how to become an investor. Sample Investing Basic's full portfolio of forums and tutorials. Or visit The Motley Fool (Keyword: **Fools**) to learn the Fools' not-so-foolish approach to investing. The wisdom you can learn here is priceless.

Financial and Brokerage Centers

The AOL Financial Centers — Real Estate, Insurance, Mutual Funds, and Banking & Loans — are a gold mine of information, advice, and services. With a little help from AOL's partners and experts, you can calculate the what-ifs of almost any real estate transaction and search for a new home (see Figure 12-13) at Keyword: **Real Estate**.

You can also comparison shop for all sorts of insurance coverage, research mutual funds, and discover the joys of online banking. The Brokerage Center is a gateway into the world of online investing, where you can learn about investing through discount brokers and engage the services of some of the best-known online brokers in the business.

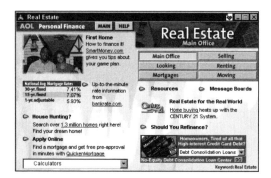

Figure 12-13. Real Estate helps you get a piece of the American Dream. Open the drop-down list in the lower left to access more than 20 financial planning calculators.

Whew! Who'd have thought that so much economic potential lurked within those seemingly simple surroundings? Invest a bit of your time here sometime soon, and you may reap rich rewards later on.

WorkPlace Channel

We're now leaving the downtown Financial District and are headed to the offices, lofts, and storefronts of the WorkPlace Channel. On its narrow side streets, energetic entrepreneurs are founding small businesses, while career-minded workers, striving to get ahead, fill the big businesses of its main streets. The sidewalks are full of hopeful job seekers looking for the next step on the path to success. The WorkPlace Channel is a great place to turn, no matter which career path you're on. The first rung on the ladder begins at Keyword: **Workplace** (see Figure 12-14).

Start-Up Businesses

Running your own small business is a constant challenge. Turn to WorkPlace Channel's Start-Up Businesses department (Keyword: **Startup**) for an array of resources that will keep you one step ahead of the pack. Find advice and resources on sales and marketing, finance, getting started, doing business online, business travel, and a wide array of informational tools and reference materials. Find and network with your peers at one of dozens of Professional Forums. Visit Entrepreneur Magazine's Startup Channel for another slant on start-ups, and dig deeply into the Business Know-How forum (see Figure 12-15), which seems to have the answers to nearly any new (and veteran) businessperson's questions.

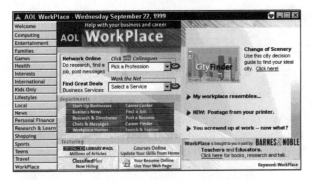

Figure 12-14. Get ahead with AOL's WorkPlace Channel.

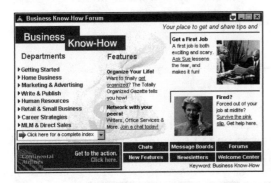

Figure 12-15. Business Know-How helps you build a successful business.

Career Center

For those on the corporate career path, Keyword: **Career Center** is the route to the next step up (see Figure 12-16).

The AOL Career Center challenges you to "map your career in five simple steps!" Just open the drop-down menu in the Career Center window to get started. If your career is already firmly established, the WorkPlace Channel stands ready to help you update your skills, network with your peers, and enjoy a knowing laugh with a daily dose of Dilbert.

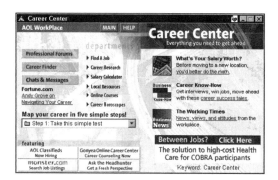

Figure 12-16. This isn't your father's Career Center.

We also can't leave the WorkPlace Channel without mentioning the fabulous online job listings at Keyword: **Find a Job**. Here, you'll find more than two dozen sites where you can search for openings, leave a résumé, or post a listing of your own. When you include the 60-plus city-by-city listings available from Digital City, that adds up to a whole lot of opportunity!

Computing Channel

Is anyone on the bus carrying a laptop computer? Great! You'll love the next stop on our tour, the Computing Channel (see Figure 12-17), at Keyword: **Computing**.

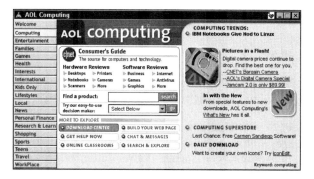

Figure 12-17. Learn to make the most of your computer at the Computing Channel.

Whether you have a laptop or not, this is a channel for you! AOL's Computing Channel (Keyword: **Computing**) is founded on a very basic truth: If you're using AOL, you're using a computer, and the more you know about your computer, the more you'll get out of your AOL experience.

c|net

A recent addition to AOL Computing is c|net (or CNET), known for its computer-oriented television programming and extensive Web sites dedicated to (you'll never guess in a million years, will you?) . . . computers! C|net's Consumer Guide (available by clicking the c|net icon in the opening screen of the Computer Channel, shown in Figure 12.22) supplies computer hardware and software reviews, an interactive guide to buying the right computer, and a search engine to reach deep into CNET's archives. C|net contributes its articles and expertise throughout the Computing Channel, including the Get Help Now department (which we take you to next). If you want to visit c|net's home page, Keyword: **cnet** will take you right there.

Help and Education

Whether you just bought your first PC or have already worn out your fifth computer, the Computing Channel's help desk (Keyword: **Get Help Now**) and online classrooms have a lot to offer.

Keyword: **Online Classrooms** offers courses in everything from AOL basics to Microsoft advanced networking system certification. Many courses are free, taught by volunteer community leaders, whereas others are provided for a fee by organizations such as tutorials.com. You can study desktop computing, computer graphics and computer programming, or become a Webmaster.

Go to Keyword: **Get Help Now** (see Figure 12-18) to get help with computer software and hardware problems and access links to AOL's Member Help area for problems relating to AOL's own software and service. Here you'll find answers to frequently asked questions about using your computer and how-to guides to computing and AOL. Among the how-to guides is Help Illustrated, a very visual guide to using dozens of AOL's features. And from 9 p.m. to 11 p.m. eastern time every night, Computing Channel volunteers are on hand live to answer your questions about PC and Mac computing.

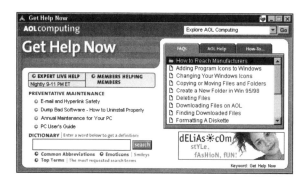

Figure 12-18. Get Help Now at the Computing Help Desk, open 24 hours a day.

Communities

Tucked quietly away behind the Chats & Messages button on the AOL Computing screen are dozens of vibrant areas dedicated to all aspects of computers and computer use. These are home to the AOL Computing Anti-Virus Center (Keyword: **Virus**), the Desktop Publishing Community, PDAs & Palmtops, the Windows Community, and many more groups with a passion for their topic. You'll find answers, wisdom, and a whole lot of good people at Keyword: **Computing Communities** (see Figure 12-19).

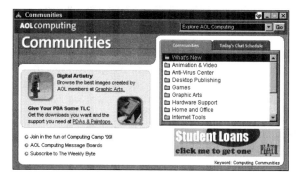

Figure 12-19. AOL Computing Communities — people sharing their passion for computing

Download Center

It's about time to wrap up our tour of Computing. But before we go, we really ought to mention that AOL Computing is also home to the Download Center, where you can find computer software of nearly every description. When you use Keyword: **File Search** (as we discuss in Chapter 10), you are searching the contents of the Download Center. Whether you're looking for freeware, shareware, or shrink-wrapped applications, this is the first place to turn.

Research & Learn Channel

Folks, as you can see from your windows, we've arrived at the Research & Learn Channel (see Figure 12-20). We'd like to remind you to please be quiet when you enter the building — there are people studying!

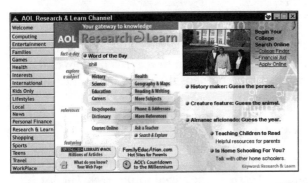

Figure 12-20. Learn something new at the Research & Learn Channel.

Whether you need general reference resources or help with schoolwork, college admissions, enhancing your child's education, or furthering your own professional education, AOL's Research & Learn is a great place to turn.

References

Research & Learn offers a handy collection of desktop references. Take your pick of two general-purpose online encyclopedias: Compton's Encyclopedia Online and The Concise Columbia Electronic Encyclopedia, plus a handful of specialized encyclopedias on topics such as baseball, chemistry, and mythology. The business-minded will appreciate the collection of telephone and address listings, including the Chamber of Commerce Directory. Electronic Library@AOL is a commercial reference service that offers access to articles on a wide range

The online dictionary is sur-
prisingly powerful. If you
don't know the spelling of a
word, you can replace the
letter(s) you're unsure of with
an asterisk. For example,
*n*bor* will fetch *neighbor*. If
you're looking for synonyms
or alternate spellings, you
can search the full text of the
dictionary's definitions, too.

of topics. You can try the Electronic Library for a free trial
period and, if you like, subscribe to the service on a monthly
basis. Research & Learn is also home base to Keyword:
Dictionary, the Merriam-Webster Collegiate Dictionary
online (see Figure 12-21). This is the kind of resource worth
adding to your AOL toolbar.

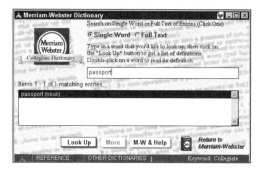

Figure 12-21. The online dictionary places thousands of words at your fingertips.

Look for the Other Dictionaries button at the bottom of the
Dictionary window, which opens the pages of another dozen
specialized dictionaries.

Explore a Subject

When general references only manage to skim the surface, try
one of Research & Learn's specialized topic areas. The list
looks like a school curriculum: History, Science, Education,
Careers, Health, Geography & Maps, and Reading & Writing.
The More Subjects area covers the Arts, Business Research,
Consumer & Money Matters, and Law & Government, among
other topics.

Ask-a-Teacher

Although we've all been told to look it up, Research & Learn
is also home to Ask-A-Teacher, AOL's Academic Assistance
Center at Keyword: **AAC** (see Figure 12-22). The thousands of
volunteer teachers of the AAC provide targeted assistance for
every age group from elementary school through college.
Okay, so one of the first things you'll see at Ask-A-Teacher *is* a
link to the Look Up Answers area — which features thousands
of answers prepared by the AAC staff to commonly asked

questions. If you don't find your answer there, you can post a question on one of hundreds of topic-specific message boards. Or if your need is more urgent, send e-mail to a teacher or get direct help from live teachers during the evening (check the daily schedule for times and subject matter).

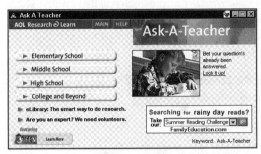

Figure 12-22. Ask-A-Teacher offers personal help with schoolwork for students of all pages.

Education and Courses

The Education Resources department covers every education-related topic, from Study Skills and Resources for Parents K-12 through College Prep, Financial Aid, and Resources for Educators. Featured in this area is the Family Education Network, a must-visit for any parent.

If you're interested in furthering your own education, check the offerings in Courses Online. The Online Campus (Keyword: **Courses**) offers hundreds of enrichment courses in a wide range of topics for fees typically in the $25 to $50 range. The University of California Extension Online at Keyword: **UCAOL** (get it?) offers college-level instruction, and grants course credits that are accepted at the University of California and other degree-granting institutions. Peterson's LifeLongLearning.com (Keyword: **Petersons**) is a database that lists distance learning offerings from colleges and universities throughout the U.S., including Regents College, a degree-granting virtual university.

Well, we hope you all took good notes. You'll be quizzed! (Just kidding.) Please, let's board the tour bus for our final stop of the day, the local neighborhoods of the Local Channel.

Local Channel

Ladies and gentlemen, it's time for the final stop of our business tour — the quaint, ethnic neighborhoods of America Online. Well, in this case *quaint* and *ethnic* really refer to the more than 65 cities of Digital City, from Milwaukee to Miami, Seattle to San Diego, and many places in between (see Figure 12-23) at Keyword: **Local**.

Figure 12-23. The Digital City map of the U.S. boasts 65 Digital Cities, and growing.

Digital City operates local city guides, delivering everything from local news, traffic, movie listings, and dining out guides to personal ads, job listings, and a real estate section (see Figure 12-24). If this sounds like your local newspaper, you're right. Many Digital City guides are produced in cooperation with local newspapers, magazines, or TV stations — organizations that know their towns very well.

You can go directly to the Digital City for your city — the city's name is also its keyword — or you can use Keyword: **Digital City** to access the Digital City map. Click the city of your choice, or access the City Index to find the complete listings. The map also displays a list of the departments of Digital City, which you can also use as a jumping-off point for your travels.

So, what are the departments of Digital City? Entertainment (Dining, Movies, Nightlife, and so on), People & Personals, Live Chat, Sports, News & Issues, Autos, Real Estate, Jobs & Careers, Health, Travel, Money, Shopping, Auctions, and Classifieds. Every Digital City also includes Maps & Directions, Yellow Pages, White Pages, and a collection of links to the Web sites of local governments, civic organizations, and businesses.

Figure 12-24. Read the "front page" of Digital City Dallas-Fort Worth.

Digital City is currently the largest service of its type in the U.S. (although competition is fierce). If it isn't in a city near you yet, there's a reasonable chance that it will be soon.

Tip

You can use a keyword to jump to Digital City departments for many cities. Just use this pattern: *CITY + DEPARTMENT*. For example, Keyword: **Detroit Movies** takes you to the Movies department of Digital City Detroit. Although it doesn't work for every department in every Digital City, it's sure convenient when it works.

Independent Explorations

Well, that concludes our business tour. We're sure you'll agree that we've seen a lot today, but it's really only a fraction of what AOL's business channels have to offer. We hope you've taken lots of notes because we're sure you'll want to go back during your free time and continue your explorations.

Although today's tour hasn't all been business, there haven't been many opportunities for fun and frolic either — but tomorrow, as Scarlet O'Hara said, is another day. Be sure to wear something nice tomorrow when we see the pleasure sites of AOL.

12

Seeing the Sites: Business

CHAPTER

13

SEEING THE SITES:
PLEASURE

Quick Look

▶ **Travel Reservations** page 286

You can research and book flights, hotels, and rental cars without ever leaving your computer or picking up a phone. Use Keyword: **Preview Travel** to access AOL's virtual travel agency and sign up for your free membership.

▶ **Interactive Games** page 289

Computer game enthusiasts will love the interactive games available online in the Games Channel at Keyword: **Games**. Play against a friend or find a new opponent in one of the many games available. Gameplay is free or fee-based, depending on the complexity and nature of the game itself.

▶ **Communities** page 295

AOL plays host to many thriving communities online. There's a community for virtually every interest, lifestyle, and hobby. Find your place by visiting either Keyword: **Interests** or Keyword: **Lifestyles**.

▶ **Kids Only** page 303

Kids can have their own version of AOL, complete with a kid-style Welcome screen and kid-appropriate content. Visit Keyword: **Kids Only** for a look through kids' eyes and learn more about configuring AOL for your child.

Chapter 13

Seeing the Sites: Pleasure

CHAPTER ITINERARY

Getting involved with Sports and Travel

Having fun with Entertainment and Games

Exploring new and familiar Interests and Lifestyles

Enriching your life with Shopping and Health

Getting in touch with Families and Kids Only

As they say, "All work and no play makes for a dull day." Now that you've toured the business district of America Online, let's paint the town red! Pleasure-seekers will find much to do on America Online, whether their interest is in travel, entertainment, or shopping.

So don your swankiest jackets and snazziest dresses . . . we're going out on the town!

Sports Channel

If you're into sports, you'll want to get into the Sports Channel. Virtually everything related to sports, for both spectators and participants, is available here. It's like a huge sports complex, complete with stadium, arena, track, field, and, of course, a pro shop. We just happen to have the ticket to get into the Sports Channel (see Figure 13-1) — just type Keyword: **Sports** into your toolbar and click the Go button.

Figure 13-1. The Sports Channel provides 'round-the-clock sports coverage for fans of all games.

Scoreboard

Have you ever tried following scores of several games at once on the TV or radio? You end up doing a lot of channel flipping just to keep up with two or three games. If this sounds familiar, you're going to flip for the Scoreboard at AOL Sports (use Keyword: **Scoreboard** to go directly there). Virtually every major and minor league game score is available, up-to-date, and accurate. Better yet, the scores don't disappear after the post-game wrap-up — results are kept online for you to check at your own convenience. Just choose a league (click its name), and the scores are displayed (see Figure 13-2).

Figure 13-2. Scoreboard for the American League shows game recaps and box scores.

Grandstand

If you love to talk sports, we have to talk … about the Grandstand. This forum's main events are the message board and chat rooms, in which discussions between sports fans take the field. The Grandstand has a community for almost every sport, from baseball to women's sports. The Grandstand even hosts fantasy leagues to put you in the middle of the action. You can get to the Grandstand directly using Keyword: **GS** (see Figure 13-3).

Figure 13-3. The Grandstand's focus is on community among fans, players, and experts.

We think a visit to AOL Sports is the ultimate spectator-sporting event. It's like having a virtual VIP box seat to monitor your favorite teams and games. There are no lines, no bad seats, and no sunburns or rain-outs. Of course, if you get a hankering to watch the real game up-close-and-personal, AOL can help you plan a trip to any stadium or arena in the world. Come with us as we explore the Travel Channel.

Travel Channel

If our virtual travels throughout America Online have piqued your wanderlust, you're going to love the Travel Channel. It's a destination designed for travelers, whether their trips are for pleasure or business. Even armchair travelers (or should we say "desktop travelers"?) will find a home here. Everything you need to daydream and plan the perfect trip is gathered together in the Travel Channel, from information on vacation resorts and exotic ports to traveler reports and news of all sorts. To reach the Travel Channel, choose Travel from the Channels icon on the toolbar or simply use Keyword: **Travel** (see Figure 13-4).

Figure 13-4. The Travel Channel is a complete travel service, offering information, resources, traveler exchanges, and a full-service travel agency.

From the Travel Channel window, you can explore destinations, find bargains, make reservations (including air, car, hotel, and cruise reservations), get the latest travel news, and much more. It's a bit like standing at a crossroads with signs going off in all directions: "Amazing Travel Bargains — Next Stop on the Left" or "World Famous Travel News Served 24 Hours a Day — Turn Right Here!" Where do you want to go? If you're not sure, click the Destinations button (or use Keyword: **Destinations**) to orient yourself and hone in on just what you need (see Figure 13-5).

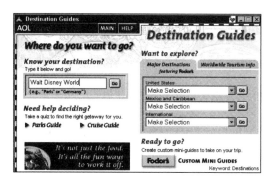

Figure 13-5. Destination Guides from the Travel Channel let you discover and explore destinations within the U.S. and around the world.

Once you've narrowed it down to a handful of potential destinations, we recommend you gather opinions from other travelers before you make a final decision. This is where America Online and the Internet really shine for travel planners. Nowhere else will you find such easy access to thousands of first-hand experiences, and opinions from folks who've really been there. Try Keyword: **Member Opinions** for a collection of message boards, chats, polls, and newsletters (you may also find this area by returning to the main Travel Channel window and clicking the Member Opinions button). Another excellent place to visit for traveler exchanges is The Independent Traveler, our next stop in the Travel Channel.

The Independent Traveler

Imagine a club of travelers who congregate to swap stories of their journeys, exchange tips and tricks, and plan their next adventures. You might call it an adventurer's club, though on America Online this traveler community goes by the name of The Independent Traveler (at Keyword: **Traveler**). It's one of the few forums that has been around since the early days of AOL, meaning its collection of articles, photos, tips, reports, and discussions is truly phenomenal! The Independent Traveler offers very active message boards, regular chats, trip reports, article and photo libraries, travel book reviews — the list goes on and on (see Figure 13-6)

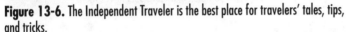

Figure 13-6. The Independent Traveler is the best place for travelers' tales, tips, and tricks.

See Chapter 9 for more details on using and searching the message boards.

Within The Independent Traveler, we feel that one resource in particular stands out: the Travel Boards. Whether your interest is in cross-country road trips or around-the-world journeys, you'll find a message board that suits you. Every state and country is represented, as well as places like Walt Disney World (our personal favorite). Also of interest is a Travel Issues message board, covering topics from aerophobia (fear of flying) and airfare secrets to volunteer vacations and youth hostels. We estimate there are over 300 message boards with hundreds of thousands of posts just in The Independent Traveler. Use the topics and subjects to focus in on your interest. Alternatively, you may want to search the boards using the Find by drop-down menu in the bottom-right corner of the message board window.

Cruise Critic

Cruise on over to the Cruise Critic for everything related to cruise ships. The forum offers cruise news, ship reviews, bargains, tips, and much more. Of special interest is the Cruise Selector, which helps make it easy to find the right cruise for you and your family based on region, price, and interests. If you've never cruised before, the First-Time Cruisers section offers a boatload of articles written for new cruisers. New and experienced cruisers alike frequent the message boards and nightly chats, exchanging tips and adventures. Use Keyword: **Cruise Critic** to reach the forum directly (see Figure 13-7) or click Cruise on the main Travel Channel window and then Cruise Critic in the resulting window.

Figure 13-7. Cruise Critic helps you plan a smooth-sailing vacation.

Preview Travel

Once you've decided where you want to go, make your reservations at Preview Travel. This online travel agency lets you search and book flights, rental cars, hotel rooms, and packages — right from your computer. To begin, use Keyword: **Preview Travel** (see Figure 13-8) and click Air, Car, & Hotel Reservations (or Vacation & Cruise Packages, if that is your interest).

Figure 13-8. Book your next trip at Preview Travel.

Before you can begin browsing available air, car, and hotel reservations, you need to sign in. If you don't have an account already, don't worry — just click the Sign In button and look for the New User section. Preview Travel walks you through the free sign-up process. Be sure to save your user ID and password in a safe place for future visits. If you just want a look around Preview Travel, click the Trial Run button to see how it works first.

The Preview Travel system gives you many of the same tools that travel agents use to make reservations. You can search by destination, travel dates, and a whole slew of other preferences. Help is always at hand (look for the "help with this page" hyperlink), and the process is quite simple. If you find something you'd like to reserve, just click the Reserve Now button and answer the questions.

Entertainment Channel

The Entertainment Channel really speaks for itself. And sings, and dances, and performs up a storm! Show times, movie reviews, concert dates, or celebrity news — you name it, the Entertainment Channel has it. Use the Keyword: **Entertainment** (or **ENT** for short) to reach the Entertainment Channel (see Figure 13-9).

Figure 13-9. Entertainment Channel, the Hollywood-and-Vine of America Online

Movies, music, and TV are in the spotlight at the Entertainment Channel. Click Movies (or use Keyword: **Movies**) for a list of what's playing in the theaters, show times (more on this later), movie reviews, moviegoer opinions, behind-the-scenes glimpses, and movie news. Click a movie name for fact sheets, related reviews, trailers, photos, interviews, and discussion boards. This is also the place to find out what movies are coming out on video.

Music covers the stage from rock to jazz to classical. Click a category for reviews and clips of the latest releases. Use the

You may need to download a music clip before you hear it. For help on downloading and playing sound files, see Chapter 10.

Music Index drop-down menu to get concert tour dates, online events with artists, information on record labels, and the latest charts. Rolling Stone Online is also here, along with SPIN Online and MTV.

Speaking of MTV, the Entertainment Channel TV also offers the scoop on the tube with featured shows, local listings, ratings, news, and reviews. TV Quest provides personalized TV listings.

AOL MovieFone

When was the last time you wondered what was playing at the movie theaters? If your town is anything like ours, there are only a few good theaters, and you have to phone each one to listen to their barely audible recorded listings. Or you may buy the local paper just to get the list of movies and times. If this seems familiar, you're going to love MovieFone. To use it, just go to MovieFone (Keyword: **Moviefone**), type in your zip code and any other search criteria, and click Go (see Figure 13-10).

Figure 13-10. Our local theaters, movies, and show times at MovieFone

Your local movies and show times pop up on the screen, based on your search criteria (by theater, by movie, by actor/actress, by time, and so on). One of the nifty features is that MovieFone is smart enough to show only the *remaining* show times, rather than simply all show times for the day. It can even indicate which show times are sold out. And if you click the movie name's hyperlink, you can get more information about the movie — a synopsis, cast list, and so on. It's wonderfully convenient, fast, and easy. You may never have to call the theater again! But should you want to, MovieFone also displays the theater's phone number. Can you tell we love it?

Entertainment Asylum

Are you an entertainment nut? Check yourself into the Entertainment Asylum for coverage of movies, TV, music, and celebrities. The forum is known for its movie reviews, but it's also a great source for movie trailers, interviews, profiles, and links to Web sites. Entertainment Asylum also offers contests, live events, and interactive games. We particularly like how it invites fellow basket cases to vote, and then displays the votes. Check in quickly with Keyword: **EA** (see Figure 13-11).

If you're a frequent movie-goer, look up your theater express code from the list so you can zip right to your local theater. Also, create a favorite place for MovieFone (see Chapter 3 for details on creating favorite places).

Figure 13-11. Don't be afraid to go nuts at Entertainment Asylum.

Games Channel

Warning! This channel contains highly addictive, interactive games that can cause a sudden drop in boredom levels. Members should be free of finger injuries, mouse problems, and time constraints. You must be as least as tall as your computer to enter the Games Channel. Keep your arms inside the room at all times.

Well, that last rule bends a bit if you're using a laptop on the beach, but that's part of the fun and excitement of the Games Channel. It's total fun and games, 24 hours a day, 7 days a week, 365 days a year — and it goes anywhere your computer goes. If you think you can handle it, use Keyword: **Games** to enter the Games Channel (see Figure 13-12).

Figure 13-12. The Games Channel offers 100 percent pure recreation.

The Game Parlor

Tired of playing solitaire? Step up to classic parlor games you can play online, such as backgammon, bridge, cribbage, hearts, and poker. What makes these games any better than solitaire? Simple — you can play these games head-to-head with other players like yourself! All this fun does come at a price, however — games at The Game Parlor are 99 cents an hour (at the time of writing). To see the list of available games and get more information on pricing, visit Keyword: **Parlor** (see Figure 13-13).

Figure 13-13. Sit in on a game in The Game Parlor.

To play a game, begin by choosing a game from the list and click the Play button in the resulting window. If you agree to the game charges, click Agree and then download the game (which requires its own software). Downloads can take a while, so you may want to use this opportunity to take a break. Oh, and don't worry — you won't be racking up game charges during the download.

Game play is generally intuitive. Tips and game help are offered within each game, and if that isn't enough, you can often ask hosts and other players for assistance. We particularly enjoyed Tetris, which was a new game at the time of writing. If you enjoy these premium games, keep an eye on your bill at Keyword: **Billing**.

Xtreme Games

If you prefer action and adventure games, make Xtreme Games your Holy Grail. They offer such games as Air Warrior III (aerial shoot 'em up game), Dragon's Gate (text-based adventure game), and Warcraft II (graphic-based strategy game). Like The Game Parlor, Xtreme Games are a premium service, though these are a bit more expensive at $1.99 per hour. Again, these are addictive games — be sure you've got plenty of time and money before you get hooked! But what fun they are! The action begins at Keyword: **Xtreme** (see Figure 13-14), which you may also reach by clicking the Xtreme Games link at either the bottom of the Games Parlor window or on the main Games Channel window.

Note

If you get a message stating that your screen name is blocked from playing games, your Parental Controls are set to prevent premium game play (and associated charges). In our experience, AOL blocks premium services on secondary screen names by default. The master account holder can change this setting at Keyword: **Parental Controls**. Refer to Chapter 2 for more information on setting Parental Controls.

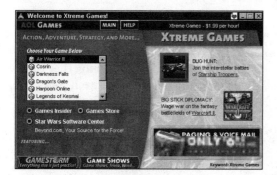

Figure 13-14. Put yourself in the middle of the action at Xtreme Games.

Game Shows Online

If you love games, but don't have the money for the premium games, head for Game Shows Online. Here you'll find a collection of no-charge games, such as NTN Studio (trivia), Puzzle Zone (word puzzles), and Slingo (a cross between bingo and a

Note

Mac users just don't have the same access to the games as PC users. At the time of writing, only Online Casino (in The Game Parlor), Air Warrior, Cosrin, Dragon's Gate (in Xtreme Games), Games Paradise, and NTN Trivia were accessible to Mac AOL users. Many Web-based games are available to Mac users, however. You can find a good selection under the Games Links button within Game Shows Online.

word game). Don't be fooled by their low, low price tag — these games are first-rate and fun! Like The Game Parlor, many of the games on Game Shows Online require that you download software in order to play, but the download times are generally much shorter. NTN Trivia is the notable exception — there's nothing to download! Come on down to Game Shows Online with Keyword: **Game Shows** (see Figure 13-15), or click Games Shows either at the bottom of the Xtreme Games window or on the main Games Channel window.

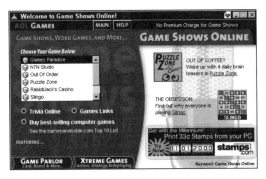

Figure 13-15. Play to your heart's content with Game Shows Online.

Interests Channel

If nothing in this chapter has tickled your fancy yet, odds are you'll find *something* to fancy in the Interests Channel. This is the catch-all channel, covering virtually every hobby that isn't already represented by a dedicated channel. To reach the Interests channel, use Keyword: **Interests** (see Figure 13-16).

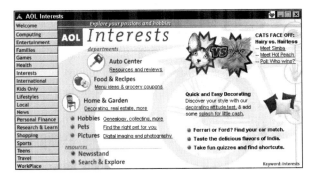

Figure 13-16. Find a new hobby or resume an old one in the Interests Channel.

Auto Center

Don't worry — we aren't taking a tour of Pop's Garage, and you won't get grease on your clothes. In fact, the Auto Center bears more resemblance to one of those new, gleaming auto malls than some old garage. No matter what your interest in cars, there's a department for it: new cars, old cars, enthusiasts, car care, and so on. You'll find articles, message boards, libraries, and guides on how to jumpstart a car, change a flat, and even parallel park. You can even *buy* a car here with the Web links to places such as AOL AutoVantage, Cars.com, and AutoWeb.com. If you can buy a car online, what's next? Traffic citations for speeding along the information superhighway? Use Keyword: **Auto** and observe posted limits (see Figure 13-17).

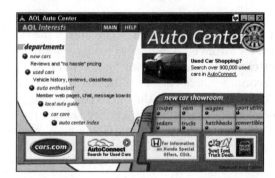

Figure 13-17. Auto Center puts you in the driver's seat.

Home & Garden

When you're traveling, nothing seems better than your own home and bed. Make the most of it at the Home & Garden forum, which offers tips, advice, and information on gardening, home improvement, and decorating. The forum can help you add style and comfort to any home, however modest or grand. We found the information on Feng Shui, the ancient (and trendy) Chinese art of harmony in the home, of particular interest. The key to a comfortable, relaxing home is under the doormat at Keyword: **Home** (see Figure 13-18).

Figure 13-18. Everything for the home front is available at the Home & Garden forum.

Pets

Whether you're just thinking about getting a pet or already madly in love with one, the Pets forum is an invaluable resource for pet lovers. Get assistance choosing, naming, caring for, and training your pet here. Our favorite feature? The Pet of the Day picture on the main window. Pet lovers can send in their pet's picture and see Rover's or Fluffie's name in lights! Kippi, Jennifer's Alaskan Malamute dog, hasn't made it as Pet of the Day yet, but we're sure that's only because we haven't sent in her picture! Use Keyword: **Pets** and bring your best friend along (see Figure 13-19).

Figure 13-19. All pets allowed in the Pets forum

Food

If you're running out of answers to the eternal question, "What's for dinner?" take a trip to the Food forum. You'll find thousands of recipes, guides to healthy living, and information on local dining. You can even share your own recipes and browse other member-contributed dishes. Be sure to save room for dessert with the Dictionary of Desserts and a monthly column called "I Love Chocolate" (so do we). Visit this smorgasbord of information at Keyword: **Food** (see Figure 13-20), or click the Food icon on the Interests Channel window.

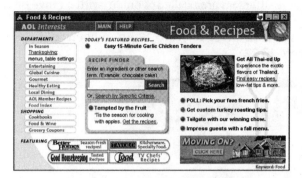

Figure 13-20. Feed your mind as well as your body at Food.

Lifestyles Channel

The Lifestyles Channel is all about identity. If you know yourself, you'll know exactly where you want to be in the Lifestyles Channel, and you probably don't need our help. The channel offers departments dedicated to virtually every imaginable lifestyle, including those focused on gender, age, religion, ethnicity, and sexual orientation. If, on the other hand, you're still searching for your niche in life, this channel may also be just what you need. Use the Keyword: **Lifestyles** to enter the Lifestyles Channel (see Figure 13-21).

Figure 13-21. Meet kindred souls in the Lifestyles Channel.

Women

Back when we started on America Online, women made up only a small percentage of the AOL population. We're happy to report that women now make up 51% of AOL's members. Accordingly, AOL offers an area called Women, with a range of helpful resources and unique forums to help women manage their increasingly busy lives. Keyword: **Women** opens the door (see Figure 13-22).

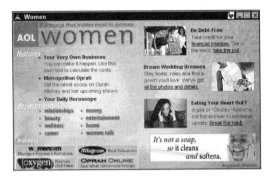

Figure 13-22. Women have their own space in cyberspace.

Notable within Women is Oxygen, a new umbrella forum for several familiar faces including Thrive Online, Moms Online, Electra, and more. Their goal is to incorporate humor, honesty and heart into the relationship between women and the media. You can visit their site directly at Keyword: **Oxygen**.

Ages & Stages

Whether you're 19 or 90, you'll find a home at Ages & Stages. Virtually every age and generation is covered here, from Generation X to the "Third Age." Click the Ages & Stages Communities button for a list of all available communities. Check out the Nerve Center if you're college-bound or college-stuck. If you've successfully made it out of college, visit Alumni Hall to find old college buddies. The Thirties Forum welcomes thirty-somethings. Baby Boomers is a gathering place for those born in the '50s and '60s. Folks 45 and up have a home at ThirdAge. And those in or approaching retirement age will appreciate the AARP (American Association of Retired Persons) forum. Use Keyword: **Ages** to go directly to the Ages & Stages forum (see Figure 13-23), or simply click the Ages & Stages link on the main Lifestyles Channel window.

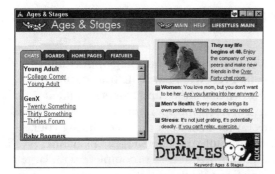

Figure 13-23. There's no need to hide your age at Ages & Stages.

Gay & Lesbian

The Gay & Lesbian scene online is not only a blessing for those who aren't yet "out," but also an incredibly rich and diverse resource for anyone searching for camaraderie or understanding of a loved one's lifestyle. The area encompasses several huge forums, including PlanetOut and onQ. Both offer active communities with message boards, chats, news, advice, experts, and articles. Use Keyword: **Gay** (or **Lesbian** if you prefer) to get there quickly (see Figure 13-24), or click the Gay & Lesbian link on the main Lifestyles Channel window.

Figure 13-24. Come out online at Gay & Lesbian.

Oh, and if you haven't yet "come out," you'll find an entire area of support, information, and resources to help you take the step (Keyword: **Out OnQ**).

Shopping Channel

Cross-Reference

If you played hooky during our Shopping Channel tour in Chapter 11, flip back in the book for a detailed discussion and description of shopping on America Online.

Like most major travel destinations, shopping opportunities are available practically everywhere at AOL. Tour virtually any channel and you'll find virtual shops and stores sprinkled throughout. If you're a serious shopper, you may prefer to go directly to the stores rather than hunt for them during your travels. AOL won't disappoint you. The Shopping Channel is AOL's equivalent of a major marketplace, complete with large department stores, specialty shops, outlet stores, and even grocery stores. Best of all, they are available from your desktop, 24 hours a day, 7 days a week. To reach the Shopping Channel, use Keyword: **Shopping** (see Figure 13-25).

Figure 13-25. Shop 'til your modem drops at the Shopping Channel.

After you've given your wallet a workout in the Shopping Channel, get a real workout at the Health Channel. Ok, so only your fingers will get a workout on the keyboard, but you will learn how to stay fit, healthy, and happy in the Health Channel. Shall we jog over?

Health Channel

The virtual road to wellness begins at the Health Channel. The channel offers healthy coverage of conditions and their treatments, as well as nutrition, fitness, health care, and alternative medicine. This is a haven for all, healthy and hope-to-be-healthy alike, offering support groups and experts in the many topics that are covered here. If you're ready to take your health seriously, use Keyword: **Health** to enter the Health Channel (see Figure 13-26).

Figure 13-26. Stay healthy and happy with the Health Channel.

allHealth.com

Information and community are the cornerstones of allHealth.com. Beyond the articles, resources, and "Experts" features are heart-warming and handholding chats, message boards, and support groups. Click the Resources drop-down menu for a listing of major centers within the forum, covering topics such as Alternative Health, Cancer Center, Emotional Health, Living with HIV, and Senior Health. Use Keyword: **AH** to get to allHealth.com (see Figure 13-27) or find it by clicking the allHealth.com icon below the Other Useful Sites section on the main Health Channel window.

Figure 13-27. allHealth.com offers information and community.

Thrive Online

Thrive Online is a hip, straight-to-the-point wellness forum offering resources on physical, emotional, and sexual health. If that last item got your attention, you won't be disappointed by Thrive Online's Sexuality area — it's honest and, best of all, comprehensive. It offers tips on staying healthy and happy, having fun in bed (or out of it, as the case may be), and learning more about your own sexuality. Each of the Thrive Online areas offers a similar scope, along with community features like chats and message boards. Start thriving at Keyword: **Thrive** (see Figure 13-28), which you can also find by clicking the Thrive Online icon on the main Health Channel window.

Figure 13-28. Thrive Online offers high-energy health.

Families Channel

If family ties are tying you down, the Families Channel may have the solution. The channel provides resources, support, and access to experts on the topic of family, all from the comfort of your family nest. Keyword: **Family** takes you to the Family Channel (see Figure 13-29).

Figure 13-29. Families Channel is the ultimate family room with something for everyone.

Parent Soup

Parent Soup is a heart-warming forum for parents, whether
they are parents-to-be or parents of teens. Even those who
hope to be parents will find a place here. Resources include
news, articles, tips, databases, newsletters, message boards,
chats — you name it, they probably have it. Visit the Pre-
Pregnancy Community to learn how to predict ovulation.
Expectant parents have an interactive pregnancy calendar.
Parents of newborns can find names for their babies online.
Parents of toddlers and preschoolers can commiserate
together over potty-training troubles. Class is in session for
parents of school-agers on summer break. Parents of teens can
learn about adolescent sleep cycles and setting allowances.
This is just a taste of Parent Soup — learn more by visiting the
area yourself at Keyword: **PS** (see Figure 13-30).

Figure 13-30. Parent Soup is m-m-m good for parents.

Moms Online

Mom, mother, mama, or ma ... whatever we call her, she still
has one of the most important jobs in the world. Support is
near at hand with Moms Online, a community for moms-to-be,
working moms, stay-at-home moms, and even Mr. Mom. This
forum has rich, active message boards and ten different chat
rooms offering regular chats on everything from differently-
abled children to second marriages. We're particularly
impressed with their Hot Tips, a huge collection of parenting
tips in over 60 categories. Moms and honorary moms can visit
at Keyword: **MO** (see Figure 13-31).

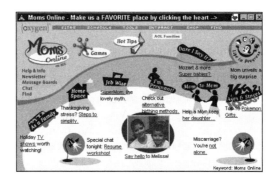

Figure 13-31. Network with other mothers at Moms Online.

The Genealogy Forum

We've met genealogists who became so bogged down in research that they either gave up the whole thing or ignored their living family. You can avoid both pitfalls with The Genealogy Forum, an incredible resource of helpful guides, surname and family history files and databases, and a supportive community of fellow genealogists. The forum has been around for a long time on AOL, so it's gathered an impressive collection of information and garnered a loyal following of family researchers. In fact, the forum itself has become a family of sorts, helping one another track down long lost relatives and forgotten family branches. If the genealogy bug hasn't yet bitten you, wear your bug repellent when you visit Keyword: **Roots** (see Figure 13-32). You can also click the Family Life & Genealogy link on the main Families Channel window, click the Genealogy tab, and then click the Genealogy Forum link.

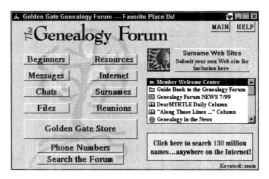

Figure 13-32. Trace your family tree at The Genealogy Forum.

Kids Only Channel

As the sign says, this is a channel for kids only. Technically, parents and adults can sneak in while the kids aren't looking (more on that later), but the entire channel is really geared for the young ones. The magic word to get in is Keyword: **Kids Only** or simply **KO** for short (see Figure 13-33).

Note

Have you noticed that the Kids Only channel is almost like a children's version of the entire AOL service? That's no accident. When parents set their kids' accounts to "kids only" in Parental Controls, kids see the Kids Only channel and nothing else. To learn more about Parental Controls, see Chapter 2.

Figure 13-33. Climb up to the Kids Only tree house.

When you open the Kids Only channel, move your mouse over each of the six big buttons (News+Sports, Art Studio, Clubs, TV-Movies-Music, Games, and Homework Help) for a peek at what you'll find under the button. News+Sports offers kid-oriented features and weather, just as up-to-date as the big kids' news. The Art Studio gives kids cool activity projects, drawing software, and a place to show off their creations. Clubs is really a kids' clubhouse with clubs for cartoons, jokes, recipes, stories, and more. TV, Movies, & Music covers the hottest movies, videos, shows, and celebrities. Games offers a treasure chest of kid-oriented games like trivia, Donkey Boing (keyboard coordination), and MapIt ZapIt (geography game). Homework Help leads kids in finding solutions and researching issues for school with the help of experienced teachers and community leaders.

Adults in Kids Only?

Adults can enter Kids Only and participate and interact with the kids; however, Kids Only is intended for kids. The staff and community leaders work hard to make this a safe and comfortable place for kids, but parents also need to monitor their children's activities online. Encourage your kids to read the Safety Tips (at Keyword: **KO Help**) and discuss them together. If you have a concern about anything in the Kids Only Channel, visit Keyword: **KO Parent** to send feedback to the AOL staff. We also recommend you visit the Parental Control message boards (at Keyword: **Parental Controls**).

Teens Channel

Teenagers have their own hangout at the Teens Channel, a collection of news, entertainment, fashion, and friends. Features include Teen People (an online version of the magazine), AOgirl ("an AOL just for the girls"), and links to teen-related areas throughout AOL. Of particular interest are the collection of teen chat rooms and message boards. Catch a wave to the Teens Channel at Keyword: **Teens**.

Figure 13-34. Teens Channel is *the* place for teens online.

Independent Explorations

What a whirlwind tour of America Online's channels! We've only scratched the surface of the content available on AOL. Many more forums and areas are available in each of the channels we visited, and new content is being added daily. In fact, you can find out what's new at each channel by visiting Keyword: **New**.

We encourage you to return to those spots that intrigue you the most and start exploring! Use the Search & Explore feature in each channel to hone in on exactly what you want. We're always amazed at the depth of information we find online.

Can't find what you what? Our next chapter gives you all the tips and tools you need to find things on AOL and the Internet. Come along with us, and we'll get you pointed in the right direction.

Quick Look

▶ **AOL Search**   **page 311**

Looking for something but don't know where to start looking? Use AOL
Search, which can search both AOL and the Web. You can even narrow your
search to only news articles, posts on message boards, and so on. Use
Keyword: **AOL Search** to jumpstart your search.

▶ **Channel and Local Searches**   **page 313**

Go straight to the source to find something specific using channel and local
searches. Channel-level searches can be initiated at Keyword: **channels**; local
searches are found on the area or forum level.

▶ **Keyword Search**   **page 316**

Keywords can also be search words. If you don't know the keyword to an
area, enter a search word that seems close in the entry field on the toolbar or
in the keyword window (Ctrl+K). If that doesn't lead to an area, AOL gives you
the option to search on your word anyway!

▶ **Netcenter**   **page 318**

Another way to find information online is by browsing through directories
such as Netscape Netcenter. Use the hierarchical list of categories to hone in
on your topic. Enter **http://www.netscape.com** in the text entry field on
your toolbar to go to this Web resource.

Chapter 14

Finding Places and Things

CHAPTER ITINERARY

Exploring with AOL Search

Honing in with Channel Searches

Going to the source with Local Searches

Mining with Keyword Searches

Setting off on your own with search engines

You've nearly reached the final steps of the journey. Even so, your America Online adventure has only just begun. This is the point where you get to explore the online world on your own, setting off in new directions. You're no longer a tourist on a tour. You're now a local, ready to "surf the Net" with the best of them.

Searching and Browsing for Information

In the hunt for great information, picture AOL as a whopping, big-city main branch library. The librarians maintain numerous indexes and catalogs, and many methods of searching those catalogs for just the information you need. When you know how to use all these search methods, the information you seek tumbles onto your computer screen.

Now, if that's America Online, just begin to imagine the Internet, an international network that connects you to countless information resources — venerable universities and museums, governments big and small, corporations, foundations, clubs, non-profit organizations, and passionate, amateur hobbyists. Although nearly all these millions of resources have local indexes, no single organization offers a master catalog of the Internet. In fact, the task is so huge and the information lying beyond so valuable, that indexing, cataloging, and searching the Internet has become a multibillion-dollar industry.

Some of the best-known names on the Internet are companies dedicated to this task, including Yahoo, Lycos, About.com, and InfoSeek. Others, including AOL and Netscape (also owned by America Online), offer those services as an outgrowth of their main business. Some have expert staffs who build catalogs that rate, review, and organize the Web's information so your search will be as fruitful as possible, offering only the best of the best. Others use powerful computer programs that constantly probe the Internet in search of key words and concepts, and return the results of their efforts as a list of available information, tailored to your request. These *search engines* have to be much more than mindless robots — there's just too much information out there. The major search engines have the "intelligence" to rate the information they find by relevancy to your needs, provided you describe your needs accurately.

Both of these approaches have their weaknesses. The amount of information added daily to the Internet dwarfs the ability of mere mortals to review and classify it, so catalogs of the "best of the best" will never be complete. Humans, being what we are, also carry biases and opinions that color our judgement.

Choosing Your Words Carefully

Like volunteering and voting, searching is also a matter of "getting out of it what you put into it." If you want to really hone in on what you seek through a search, you need to choose your search words and phrases carefully. Here are our best tips and techniques to help you craft good search words and phrases:

▶ **Be specific.** If you're looking for information about your new dog, type the dog's breed such as *Alaskan Malamute* rather than simply *dog*. Alternately, try phrases like *dog groom* or *dog train*. If you're looking for an exact phrase (such as *dog bark*), put quotes around it, or you may end up with articles on the bark of the dogwood tree.

▶ **Use boolean operators.** Which is just a fancy way to say, "Use AND, OR, and NOT in your searches." Including these words limits your search and generally produces better results. For example, type *malamute or husky* to find all articles matching either breed of sled dog (and an occasional article about burly football players), but not both. You can also type an asterisk as a wildcard, which is useful when you want to find everything that contains a word or set of characters. For example, searching on *dog*** will find *doghouse*, *dogma*, *dogwood*, and so on. If you're not sure how to spell a word, type it as best you can and then add the tilde (~) character — this finds results with similar spellings.

▶ **Don't worry about case.** Capitalization rarely matters. We recommend you just type in all lowercase — it's faster.

▶ **Don't worry about suffixes either.** Most search engines will treat the words *bark*, *barks*, *barked*, and *barking* as the same word.

The computer-run search engines have the benefit of impartiality, but they can be too literal-minded. Their careful methods miss countless gems that human intelligence can unearth, while they present lists with millions of selections that are barely relevant to your needs. All too often, the best resource on the Internet for your needs will be item number 1,574 on a list of 11,933.

Cross-Reference

Learn more about hypertext and hyperlinks in Chapter 3.

AOL's Search Tools

AOL provides users with a variety of tools for searching both within AOL and outside on the World Wide Web.

AOL Search

AOL Search does something no other search tool can do. It searches both AOL and the Web in one easy step. You can reach AOL Search by clicking the Search button on the AOL toolbar. Alternately, choose AOL Search from the Favorites icon on the AOL toolbar or use the Keyword: **Search**

The AOL Search window is fast and easy to use. Just type a word or phrase that best describes what you are seeking into the entry field at the top of the window and click Search! (see Figure 14-1).

Figure 14-1. AOL Search stands ready to search for you.

Note

If a box pops up and informs you that you are about to send information to the Internet zone, go ahead and click Yes.(You can learn more about this setting in Appendix B.)

AOL Search opens a new window and immediately begins looking for areas that match your word or phrase, displaying the results once located (see Figure 14-2).

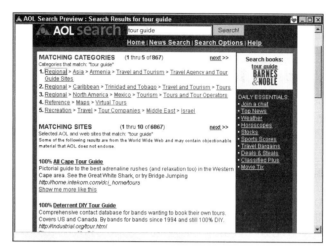

Figure 14-2. AOL Search displays the top matching categories and sites.

Let's take a closer look at the AOL Search results window. Near the top of the window is a search field, available to perform another search when you're ready. Below this are hyperlinks that lead back to the main AOL Search page (Home), the news search page, more options for searching, and help. In the main section of the window are the main matching categories, followed by the matching sites.

Let's look at the matching categories first. If AOL Search finds entire categories that match your search word or phrase, it displays the results near the top of the window. Click one of these to see a list of sites within a given category, which may or may not offer what you need. Note that AOL Search displays the entire path of the matching categories — this means you must click the last item in the path (the word at the end of the line) to go to the matching category. If you click anywhere else in the matching category's line, you may go to another section within AOL Search's hierarchy. If this is your intent, go for it!

Matching sites link you directly to areas or forums that usually contain information and/or articles with information matching your word or phrase. Note that the matching sites are displayed in order of relevancy (the percentage indicates how

You Can't Search AOL from There

It is important to note that if you're seeking information specifically on the AOL service, you need to use an AOL search tool. An Internet-only search tool such as those we describe later in the chapter cannot search AOL, because AOL's online areas are exclusively available to AOL members through AOL software. The only exception is the information AOL posts at its own Web site, AOL.com.

Tip

If you're looking for news articles, click the News Search hypertext link near the top of the window for a list of matching news articles. You can do the same thing with any of the hypertext links near the bottom of the page (prefixed by "Also search in"), such as AOL Articles, Personal Home pages, and Message Boards.

14

Finding Places and Things

closely a page matches your word or phrase). If AOL Search found more results than it was capable of displaying in the initial window, the Next hyperlink is active at the right side of the window — click it to see more matches. You may also wish to click the "Show me more like this" link to see other pages that are similar.

Arrayed beneath the entry field in the main AOL Search window is a group of very handy hypertext links to other search tools, including Yellow Pages, White Pages, Message Board search, and Shopping Channel search.

Browsing is also possible at AOL Search. You may also use the hypertext links in the main portion of the AOL Search window to browse categories, subjects, and topics. You'll also notice more hyperlinks for things such as White Pages and E-Mail Finder — we discuss these later in the next chapter!

Still no luck with your search? Click the Search Options link to narrow your search and hone in on exactly what you seek.

Channel Searches

Another way to search for content on America Online is to go to the source. In this case, that means searching on the channel level. This is most useful when you know generally where to find something, but not specifically. For example, you may know that gymnastics would be somewhere in the Sports channel, so a channel search would likely be fruitful. To do a channel search, go directly to the channel most likely to house what you're seeking. The quickest way to get to a channel is via keyword (and all channel names are also keywords). If you're not sure which channel you need, use the buttons on the left-hand side of the Welcome screen (or the main screen for any Channel) or the Channels icon on the toolbar, or go to Keyword: **Channels** to select one. Once the channel of choice is open on your screen, look for an option called Search & Explore or simply Search — it is usually near the bottom of the channel window. Alternatively, use Keyword: **Channel Guide**, choose a channel, and look for the Search option. Regardless of how you find it, click the channel's Search option to open it (see Figure 14-3).

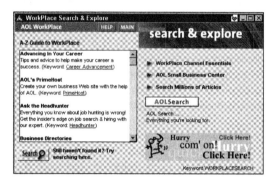

Figure 14-3. Exploring the AOL WorkPlace channel

A channel's search and explore window generally offers an A–Z guide of all forums in the channel, as well as links to popular or helpful features. If you don't find what you seek in the text, click the Search button below it to open the channel's dedicated search page (see Figure 14-4).

Figure 14-4. Digging deeper in the AOL WorkPlace channel

To use a channel search page, begin by typing your search word or phrase into the top field. You could click the Start Searching button now, but it pays to spend a few extra minutes refining your search. You can select the type of results you're seeking (for example, all articles or only those that are new in the last 24 hours). Consider indicating how detailed the search should be — choose "specific" if you want only results that match your search word or phrase exactly, or choose "broad" for as many results as possible. The maximum time you want to wait is useful when you're in a hurry (choose 10 seconds) or are interested in finding the best results possible (choose 5 minutes). When you're ready, click the Start Searching! button (or just press the Enter key). Results are displayed in the same window (see Figure 14-5).

Figure 14-5. The search page lists results in the order of relevancy.

To open the window wider and see more of the results list at one time, position your pointer over the lower right-hand corner of the window until it changes to a double-headed arrow. Now just press and drag the mouse to expand the window to a new size. You can click the blue hyperlinks to view matching pages. If you don't see good matches, scroll to the bottom of the results window and click the hyperlink near the bottom to return to the search page. Try a new search with different parameters.

Local Searches

Sometimes there's just no substitute for being there. In the same way you'd head to your local library to search through the local papers, it often pays to head directly to a forum to search through its content. You often get more detailed, specific results with a local search on the forum level. The downside is that you're only searching one forum's content and thus won't find anything that isn't available in the forum.

To perform a local search, go directly to the forum in question using its keyword. Alternatively, use Keyword: **Channel Guide** (see Figure 14-6) to browse the forums available in each channel and choose one.

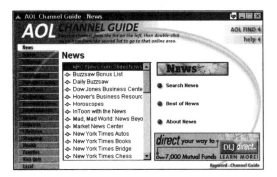

Figure 14-6. Channel Guide can be your virtual compass.

Finding a search option in a forum is more hit-or-miss than in a channel — not every forum can be searched. If you see a Search or a Find link, click it. Otherwise, your best bet is to look for a Help or a Site Map link. Search pages will differ from forum to forum, but all should offer a text entry field for your search word or phrase and a Search or Find button to initiate the search. If you get lost, look about for a Help button — they're often treasure troves of information.

Keyword Search

Believe it or not, keywords are another useful tool for finding information on America Online. Although you may mostly use keywords to reach areas you're already familiar with, you can also use them to explore for new areas. One way you can do this is to simply *guess* a keyword. Type in a keyword the way you would type in a search word (use the text entry field in the toolbar or Ctrl+K). Chances are good your search word is a keyword and may lead to the exact information you seek. This technique works best when you use general search words rather than specific.

If your search word isn't a keyword, one of two things will happen: AOL suggests alternate keyword(s) or offers the option to search on your word. If you get an alternate keyword that looks promising, select it in the list (see Figure 14-7) and click Open (or press Enter).

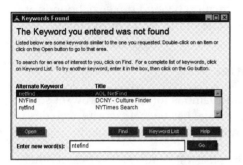

If you're searching for the latest additions to the AOL service, pay a visit to Keyword: **New**. Although What's New on AOL doesn't include a search engine, you may find things listed here that haven't been added to the official search engines yet.

Figure 14-7. America Online often suggests alternate keywords for similar or misspelled words.

If no alternate keywords are suggested, AOL offers the opportunity to search on your word. You can even modify the word before you search on it, if you wish.

Another technique for locating information with keywords is via the keyword list. search the keyword list online at Keyword: **Keyword**. Alas, the online keyword list has no built-in search option, but you can still search it. Open a keyword list and use the Find In Top Window command under the Edit menu (press Ctrl+F).

Keywords

Another route to keywords is to buy Jennifer's book, *AOL Keywords*, available at Keyword **Aol Bookstore** Currently in its third edition, *AOL Keywords* contains a master list of keywords, additional lists of keywords presented in a variety of manners, and reviews of over 100 AOL areas that can be reached by keyword.

14

Finding Places and Things

Searching Outside of AOL

If you're looking for information beyond the cozy bounds of AOL, you can also turn to one of the Web's most famous names: Netscape.

Netscape Netcenter

Although Netscape is most famous for its Web browser software, the Netscape home page has been a favorite Web destination for years and continues to grow in popularity.

Netscape Netcenter offers lists of useful Web sites and other Internet resources, such as Usenet Newsgroups and Gopher sites. These lists are quick and easy routes to scads of helpful information. Just find your topic, read the brief Web site descriptions, and start clicking hypertext links. Human beings have created the lists, so there's very little "trash" to wade through. Netscape Netcenter also offers a wide variety of other useful services, including links to major search engines and news and articles related to your topic of interest.

To reach Netscape Netcenter, type its URL (`http://www.netscape.com`) into the text entry field on the AOL toolbar, and click Go (or press Enter). You'll probably want to create a Favorite Place for this site, once you get there. When you arrive, you'll notice that the site has a familiar organization (see Figure 14-8).

Figure 14-8. Netscape Netcenter is a good jumping-off point.

Favorite Place Lists on Steroids

At its core, Netscape's Netcenter offers much the same service — lists of useful Internet sites. It sounds so simple, but favorites lists, whether prepared by devoted individuals or large organizations, have been a critical part of the growth of the World Wide Web. There are real people behind these sites who separate the good from the bad, and the useful from the useless. Because even a carefully worded search at a search engine can generate thousands of matches, the judgement of the real people at Netcenter can be a huge time-saver. The only problem is that these people are, of course, human; they can't possibly know every good site, especially with the Web changing as rapidly as it does.

In Netscape Netcenter, you'll find a list of around 15 major topics much like AOL's own Channels. As you click the hyperlinks in a topic, you can "drill down" level by level to find the subtopic that interests you. Each also offers a search tool, so you can type an appropriate search phrase, such as *Ancient Japanese Architecture*, and get links to appropriate lists.

Search Engines

Search engines are the detectives of the Internet. Using automated programs called *bots* and *spiders*, search engines probe the contents of every Web site they can find. Visitors to a search engine (such as AOL Search and AOL NetFind, which we've already discussed) type in a search word or phrase and initiate a search. The search program (or *engine*) goes to work, combing its files for every Web site that even remotely matches the search phrase.

Search results are scored, so Web sites that seem to most closely fit your needs will be at the top of the resulting list. This doesn't mean that what the computer "thinks" are the best sites for your needs are actually the ones that suit you best. As we've noted, a search is only as good as your search word or phrase, and the nature of a search can bury you in useless Web sites while the best information lies tantalizingly out of reach.

The companies in the search engine business (and it *is* a business) know this all too well, and take pains to make their search results as useful as they can possibly be. Many include convenient features such as a More Like This link so that when you do find a perfect match the search engine can find more of a good thing.

A visit to various search engine home pages may leave you wondering what makes each one unique, as all of them now offer directories like Yahoo's, current news, weather, telephone listings, and the like. It's still what's "under the hood" that matters in the search engine business, so why not take all these search tools for a test drive?

Independent Explorations

Probably the most fruitful exploration you can pursue following this chapter is the search for an eloquent search phrase. As you've probably already noted, a search engine can produce radically different results based on a very small change in a search phrase. Why not focus your energy on creating the best possible search phrase for one particular search, on one particular search engine? Don't make the topic too broad, or you may never get the results down to a manageable size. Be sure to find that search engine's search tips or help area, and learn more about how to get the most out of that search engine.

A bit of time and effort put into mastering search engines will result in major time-savings over the years to come.

CHAPTER

15

FINDING PEOPLE

Quick Look

▶ **Member Directory** page 325

Search for fellow AOL members in the Member Directory. All members with
profiles can be searched by name, location, sex, hobbies, and so on. Go to
Keyword: **Members** to do a Quick Search (or click the Advanced Search tab
for a more in-depth search).

▶ **Yellow Pages** page 327

Forget calling information — look up the number of virtually any business in
the Yellow Pages. Just use Keyword: **Yellow Pages**, enter a business category
or business name, city and state, and click Find! Results include the business
name, address, phone numbers, and e-mail address whenever possible, as well
as maps, driving directions, and related categories.

▶ **White Pages** page 329

You can find phone numbers and addresses of individuals online, too! Use
Keyword: **White Pages** to search for a long-lost family member or even your
neighbors. Use links on the results window to search for an e-mail address,
save the address, send a greeting, and find services in an individual's
neighborhood.

▶ **E-Mail Finder** page 330

If you're looking for e-mail addresses of individuals who aren't AOL members,
make Keyword: **Email Finder** your first stop. Enter the last name, plus first
name, city, state, and country, if known. Results won't show the exact e-mail
address, but they will let you send an e-mail directly to the address(es) found.

Chapter 15

Finding People

CHAPTER ITINERARY

Searching the Member Directory

Browsing the Yellow and White Pages

Using E-Mail Finder

AOL and the Internet are great places to find information. And what better information can you find than the e-mail address of a long-lost friend or relative? Your search can start right in AOL's own Member Directory and spread outward from there. Searching for friends and relatives isn't quite as straightforward as browsing through a telephone book. For a variety of good reasons, people online are hard to find unless they *want* to be found. Still, searches like these can be far more fruitful than flipping through a telephone book or dialing directory assistance, since you don't need to know city or state.

Member Directory

Are you looking for a fellow AOL member? Head for the AOL
Member Directory. Everyone on AOL with a member profile is
in the Member Directory, and it's completely searchable. You
can find someone by name, location, or just about any criteria.
The catch is that the information must be in a profile or you
won't find it. If a member only lists a first name in a profile
and you search on a first and last name, you won't find them.
This is the exception, however — we've found many long-lost
friends and elusive colleagues by searching the Member
Directory.

To do a Quick Search of the Member Directory, begin by
opening the Member Directory — choose Search AOL
Member Directory from the People icon on the toolbar
or use Keyword: **Members** (see Figure 15-1).

Figure 15-1. Performing a quick search of the Member Directory

Type in a search word or phrase in the first field of the resulting window. Alternatively, you can type a name (first, last, or
both) in the Member Name field and/or a location (city, state,
country, and so on) in the Location field to refine your search.
You do not need to have information in every field, but you do
need something in at least one field. Click Search (or press
Enter) to begin your search. AOL displays the Member Directory search results in a new window (see Figure 15-2).

The results window lists the first 20 profiles that match
your search word or phrase. You can scan through the screen
names (and corresponding member names and locations) of
each matching profile. If more than 20 matches were found,
the More button at the bottom of the window becomes
active — just click it to view the next 20 matches. The results

Tip

If a member is online at the time of the search, a red arrow appears next to their listing in the results window.

Note

In addition to the screen name, a profile lists all information volunteered by a member. This may include member name, location, birth date, gender, marital status, hobbies, computers, occupation, and a personal quote. If all this information isn't listed in a profile, it simply means that the member left the associated field blank when filling out the profile form.

aren't listed in any logical order, so you may need to browse through them to find what you're seeking. Double-click a screen name to view the complete member profile (see Figure 15-3).

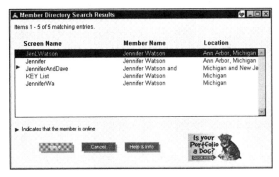

Figure 15-2. Results of a Member Directory search

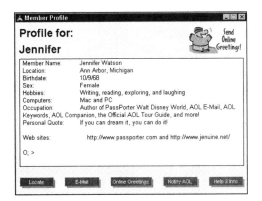

Figure 15-3. Jennifer's AOL member profile

Use the first two buttons along the bottom of the member profile window to locate or e-mail a member. Use the Online Greeting button to send a message to an AOL Member. Use the Notify AOL button to report inappropriate information (refer to AOL's Terms of Service described in Chapter 1). Use the Help & Info button for more searching tips and assistance.

If your search returns many results, you may discover that one search is limited to finding 100 matches. This can be a real problem if your friend turns out to be number 101. Besides,

while you could browse 100 member profiles, who wants
to? Instead, get fewer (and better) results with an advanced
search. Click the Advanced Search tab in the Member Directory search window to get more search fields. Now you can
further define a search by birthdate, gender, marital status,
hobbies, occupation, computers, and quote (see Figure 15-4).

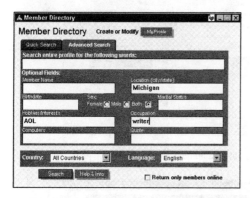

Figure 15-4. Digging deeper with the Advanced Search feature

Yellow Pages

When you need to find a business, its address, and phone number, where better to turn than the Yellow Pages? To go the old-
fashioned yellow pages one (or two) better, an AOL Yellow
Pages listing includes a map, driving instructions, and (sometimes) fax numbers and e-mail addresses! AOL's Yellow Pages
are part of AOL Search and AOL Find. It can be reached
through Keyword: **Yellow Pages**. Alternately, choose Yellow
Pages from the Internet button on the toolbar.

You can search for businesses by either business category or
business name, and you must narrow the search by selecting
which state to search (see Figure 15-5).

If you know which city to search, so much the better!
Category searches are most accurate if you select a category
from the Yellow Pages' Category list (see Figure 15-6).

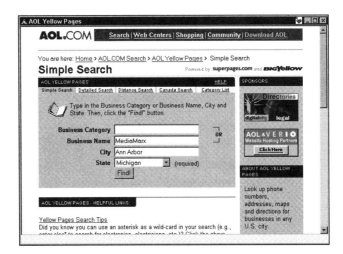

Figure 15-5. Searching for a business name in the AOL Yellow Pages

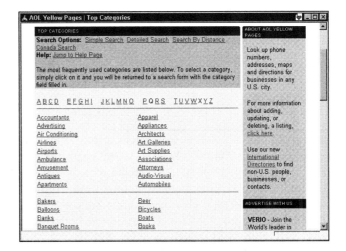

Figure 15-6. Choosing categories in the AOL Yellow Pages

Other types of searches can be made using the Search By Distance option (which helps you find businesses within five miles of home) and the Detailed Search option (which lets you search by useful keywords, such as *free delivery*). You can also use the detailed search to get a business's address, map, and driving instructions (see Figure 15.7)!

Figure 15-7. Search results in the AOL Yellow Pages

Like any telephone directory, the AOL Yellow Pages listings
can be a bit out of date, but unlike the paper-and-ink version, a
business can create or update its own listing using the handy
hyperlink right on the search page. One thing's for sure: You'll
always know where to find your copy of AOL's Yellow Pages.

White Pages

Not everyone has an e-mail address yet. AOL recognizes this
and makes an international, fully searchable White Pages available. It can virtually eliminate the need to call directory assistance! Best of all, it contains more information than your
run-of-the-mill directory assistance offers. In addition to phone
numbers, the AOL White Pages offers e-mail addresses, street
mailing addresses, neighborhood maps, driving directions, lists
of nearby businesses, and more. You can reach the AOL White
Pages with Keyword: **White Pages**. Alternately, choose White
Pages from the Internet button on the toolbar.

The White Pages search window asks for much the same
information as the E-Mail Finder. The biggest difference is
the Metro Search checkbox, which searches an entire area
when enabled.

15

Finding People

Updating Your Listing

While you're in the White Pages, do a search on yourself. Did you find a listing (or two)? Chances are you will, but the information may be too specific or inaccurate. If you'd like to change the information displayed by the White Pages, click the update hyperlink to the right of your listing. You will need to provide your e-mail address and your updated information. Note that even if your information is correct, you can use the Update feature to add more information. Alternatively, you can click the delete hyperlink to remove your listing entirely.

E-Mail Finder

The AOL Member Directory is a powerful tool for finding people on AOL, but what about people who aren't on AOL? The AOL E-Mail Finder can help you locate virtually anyone with an e-mail address, whether they're on AOL or not. Use Keyword: **Email Finder** to go directly to the Web-based search page (see Figure 15-8).

Figure 15-8. The AOL E-Mail Finder searches a vast database of e-mail addresses.

Because of the sheer number of people and e-mail addresses, E-Mail Finder works best when you give as much information as possible. Type in a last name (required), followed by a first name (or initial), city, state, and country. Check that your spelling is as accurate as possible and click Find! AOL displays the results in the same page (see Figure 15-9).

Note

A search is limited to 250 results — if you reach this limit, refine your search for fewer results.

Figure 15-9. E-Mail Finder's search results

E-Mail Finder lists results in alphabetical order by name. The window only displays five records at a time, so you'll need to click the "next" hyperlink to view the next five matches.

Each record includes any other available information, such as an address, city, state, or country. What isn't included is the e-mail address itself — only the words *Send Email* and the domain name are given (for example, "Send Email@aol.com" or "Send Email@netscape.net"). To actually send e-mail, you click the blue Send E-mail hyperlink and fill out the e-mail message form. This may seem odd, until you realize that AOL is protecting each indi- vidual's privacy by not revealing their actual e-mail address. You can obtain the actual e-mail address when your recipient replies to your message — just be sure you type your own e-mail address correctly in the Web e-mail message window.

15

Finding People

Independent Explorations

Congratulations! You've reached the end of the tour. We hope you aren't too road-weary — you have an entire world ahead of you to explore on your own, after all. We're confident you'll find what you're seeking, too. If you reach a dead end, be persistent. Sometimes you need to come at it from several directions. Your reward is finding that elusive bit of information that can help you finish the paper, seal the deal, or find that long-lost friend.

If what you're seeking is us, we won't make you search. While we can be found in any of the places we've told you about (it seems we're everywhere these days), we're happy to give you our information right here. Feel free to visit our Web site at `http://www.jenuine.net` and/or e-mail us at jenniferand-dave@aol.com! We love to get e-mail and always try to send a reply. Send us a "virtual postcard" along your AOL travels to let us know how you're doing!

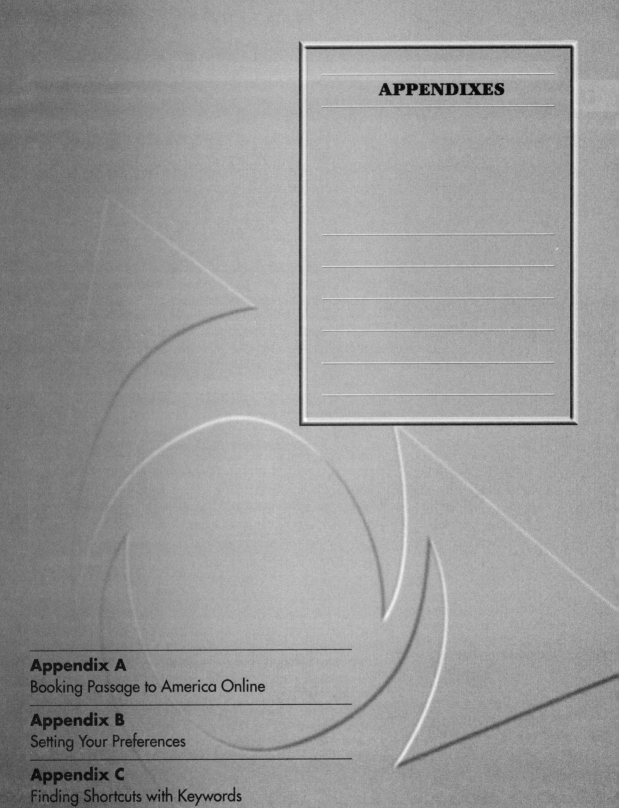

APPENDIXES

Appendix A
Booking Passage to America Online

Appendix B
Setting Your Preferences

Appendix C
Finding Shortcuts with Keywords

Glossary

Appendix A

Booking Passage to America Online

Getting online with AOL is fairly simple, and this appendix will guide you through the process so that you can begin your grand adventures with AOL. We show you how to gather what you need, install the AOL software, and survive your first online session. For those of you who are already on an older version of the AOL software, we explain how to upgrade your software to AOL version 5.0. Finally, we show all our travelers how to get online remotely and as a guest with the AOL software.

Gathering What You Need

Definition

A sign-on kit is the free software, registration codes, and directions for creating a new America Online account. A sign-on kit generally comes on a CD and is packaged in a cardboard CD sleeve with printed codes and directions.

Before you embark on your AOL adventures, you need a few travel essentials. Namely, you need a computer capable of running the AOL software, a copy of the AOL software itself, a way to pay for the AOL service, and some ideas for screen names. Below we explain what each of these items entails (and how to go about getting them if you don't already have them).

The Computer

AOL software version 5.0 (for Windows) requires a Pentium-class PC. Your computer should have at least 16 megabytes of RAM, 30 megabytes of available hard disk space, a monitor capable of displaying at least 256 colors at 640×480 resolution, and a 14,400 bps or faster modem. Also required is Windows 95 or Windows 98.

The Software

The latest version of AOL software is version 5.0, which is included on the CD-ROM bundled with this book. If you lost your bundled CD-ROM disc, don't worry — AOL distributes many CDs bearing the software. You may have gotten it in the mail. If not, the software may be installed (or ready to install) on your computer (if it is new); search your hard drive for *AOL*.

If you don't have the software handy, we've seen free copies of AOL sign-on kits at bookstores, video stores, and even grocery stores. You may also find it in magazines (though you'll need to purchase the magazine to get the software, naturally).

If you're unable to find the AOL software locally, you have several options. We recommend you call AOL at 1-800-827-6364 and request a sign-on kit. Delivery takes about a week. An even better solution may be to ask a friend who is already on AOL to go to Keyword: **Friend** and request that a sign-on kit be sent to you in the mail. If you use the sign-on kit they ordered for you and stay online for at least 90 days, your friend will earn $20 (or even $50, depending on the current promotion). Better yet, you may get more free time to use AOL in your first month if your friend orders a sign-on kit for you (more on this later). Alternatively, if you are already on the Internet with another online service or ISP, point your Web browser to `http://www.aol.com`, and download the software from AOL's Web site.

If you have an older version of AOL, you can use it to get the latest version. If the older software is already installed on your computer, skip to the section "Upgrading Your Software" later in this appendix. If you simply have an older version of the AOL software on a CD that hasn't yet been installed, it may be easiest to find the disk that came with this book or order a CD with the latest version. If you can't wait that long, go ahead and install the older version (using the section "Installing the Software" as a general reference — there will be differences). Once you're online, refer to "Upgrading Your Software" later in this appendix.

 Note

None of the pricing plans include free use of premium areas (such as certain games), which carry additional charges.

The Money

Of course, you'll have to pay for using AOL. Thankfully, it doesn't cost too much. At the time of writing, AOL offers five different pricing plans. The Standard Unlimited Monthly plan costs $21.95 a month and gives you unlimited usage of AOL. The One Year Plan gives you the same benefits as the Standard Unlimited Monthly, but is a bit cheaper because you pay a lump sum for the year upfront ($239.40, which is a savings of $24 over the monthly plan). If you plan to use AOL less frequently, the Limited Plan is $9.95 a month and includes five hours; additional hours of usage are $2.95. If you really don't expect to use AOL often, try the Limited Plan — $3.95 a month for three hours, with additional hours at $2.50. Finally, the Bring Your Own Access plan is for those of you who already have an Internet service provider (ISP) or other network connection that you can use to access AOL. This plan is $9.95 a month and includes unlimited usage. Please note that the pricing plans are subject to change — use Keyword: **Pricing Plans** once you're online to double-check the rates.

Once you decide on the plan that's right for you and your family, you need to figure out how to pay for it. AOL accepts credit cards (VISA, MasterCard, American Express, Discover/ Novus, and Diners Club). Automatic withdrawals from checking accounts are also accepted, though this carries an additional handling fee of $5 each month. Whichever method you opt to use, get the information ready and have it at hand during installation.

The Screen Name

AOL (and the rest of the world) needs to know how to address you while you're online. Thus, you should brainstorm several possible screen names *before* you actually begin the installation process. We recommend you come up with at least a handful of possibilities — jot them down on a piece of paper. If you're not sure what makes a good screen name, refer to Chapter 1 (see the section "Planning Your Journey").

While it isn't crucial that you have your screen name picked out before you begin installing the software, it is certainly less stressful. It is also likely that you'll come up with better screen name ideas if you brainstorm ahead of time.

Installing the Software

Once you've gathered everything you need, you're ready to begin the AOL software installation process. If your software came on your computer or you downloaded it to your hard drive, locate the installation file and run it. If your software came on a CD, insert the CD into your computer — it should begin the installation process automatically upon loading. Either way you initiate the process, you should arrive at the Welcome to America Online screen shown in Figure A-1.

If you do not already have an America Online account, click the circle next to New Member and then click the Next button (or just press Enter). If you already have an America Online account, choose Current Member instead (and jump to "Upgrading Your Software" later in this appendix).

Upon clicking Next, AOL checks to see if you have a previous version of America Online already installed on your computer. When the check is complete, AOL recommends a directory for the installation of the software (see Figure A-2).

Figure A-1. America Online welcomes you and begins the installation process.

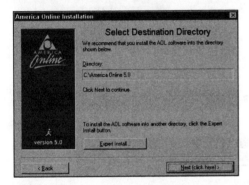

Figure A-2. Confirm your installation directory, or choose another.

AOL displays the directory in which your new software will be installed at the top of the window. If this isn't where you'd like the software to reside on your computer, click the Expert Install button and select a new location. When you're ready, click Next to begin the actual installation of the software to your computer (see Figure A-3).

AOL keeps you informed of the installation progress with the thermometer in the lower-right corner of the installation screen. While you're waiting, you can read about the new features in your software as they pop up on the screen. You may be asked to reboot your computer during the installation process. Once the installation is complete, your computer automatically runs the AOL software and begins the connection process (see Figure A-4).

Note

If at anytime you need to cancel the signup process, just click the Cancel button. If the Cancel button isn't available, press the Esc key.

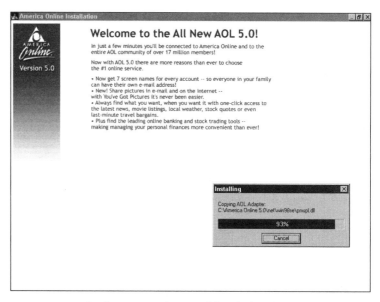

Figure A-3. AOL briefs you on new features while it displays the progress of your installation.

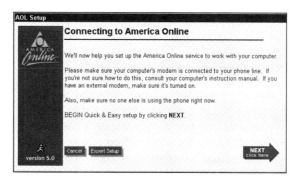

Figure A-4. AOL is ready to connect with just a bit more information from you.

You're now in the AOL software itself, which is evident by the name "America Online" across the top of the screen and the toolbar below it. Read the AOL Setup window (and subsequent windows) carefully, as important notes appear here. For example, before you click the Next button, you must be sure your computer's modem is connected to your phone line and turned on. You'll also need to make sure no one else is currently using that phone line. When you're ready, click the Next button (pressing Enter works in these windows, too). AOL promptly searches for a way to connect you and then displays your available connections (see Figure A-5).

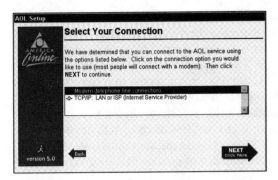

Figure A-5. Select your connection to AOL from the available options.

To select a connection option from the list, simply position your pointer over it and click once. You can also use the down and up arrow keys on your keyboard to move down and up the list, if you prefer. Which connection option is best? If you intend to use your modem to dial AOL directly, choose Modem. If you intend to connect to your ISP or local area network (LAN) first, and then connect to AOL through it, choose TCP/IP. If you have only one option available, simply click Next to continue.

If you choose a TCP/IP connection, you're ready to sign on to AOL. Just choose the TCP/IP option shown in Figure A-5 and follow the onscreen directions. LAN users may need to enter their server's proxy information (if you're not sure what this is, see your LAN administrator). Follow the directions on screen for more information.

If you selected the Modem connection option, AOL displays the Search for AOL Access Numbers window (see Figure A-6).

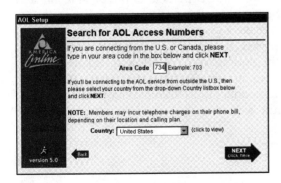

Figure A-6. AOL prepares to search for access numbers.

Cross-Reference

If AOL has included a copy of the access number database with the installation software, skip to Figure A-8.

Enter your area code and, if you're outside the United States, select your country from the drop-down list at the bottom (just position your pointer over the Country box, click once, and click on your country). When ready, click Next. Depending on the source of your AOL software, an access number database may be built-in or you may need to go online to access the database. AOL determines this automatically for you and presents the appropriate windows. In our case, AOL needed to go online to search the access phone number database, and thus needs to ask some preliminary questions first (see Figure A-7).

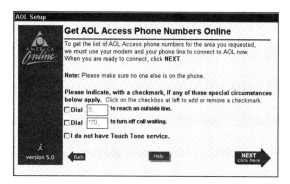

Figure A-7. Configure your phone dialing requirements.

If you need to dial a number to reach an outside line (such as in a business environment or hotel), click the first checkbox. If the number needed is something other than a 9, change it by selecting it, deleting it, and typing the appropriate number. Call waiting works in a similar fashion. If you have call waiting on your phone line, click the second checkbox. If the code to turn off call waiting is something other than *70, change it as needed. You should keep the comma after the outside line and call waiting numbers — this serves as a pause in dialing and is often necessary to make a proper connection. If you do not have touch-tone service, be sure to indicate this by clicking the checkbox at the bottom of the window. If you do have touch-tone service, do nothing — this is the default. When ready, click Next to connect to AOL and select your access numbers (see Figure A-8).

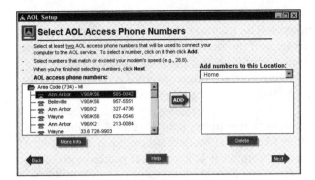

Figure A-8. Choose as many access numbers as you can.

AOL displays all available access numbers in your area code (or near to your area code). Your task now is to select as many access numbers (preferably at least two) that are as close as possible to you. The goal is to find local numbers. If you have to go outside your local calling area for an access number, you'll be responsible for any long distance charges that you incur. If you aren't sure whether a phone number is long distance or not, consult your phone book for details. If you cannot find any local numbers, you can decide to choose nonlocal numbers or explore other options detailed in the sidebar "Access Alternatives."

Access Alternatives

Local numbers aren't the only way to connect to AOL without incurring long distance fees. Consider establishing an account with an Internet service provider (ISP) in your area that provides one of its own local access numbers. Through it, you can then use the TCP/IP connection option to access AOL (and sign up for the Bring Your Own Access pricing plan, too). If an ISP isn't an option, AOL offers toll-free numbers that can be dialed anywhere within the U.S., Puerto Rico, and the U.S. Virgin Islands for 10 cents a minute. If you wish to use this surcharged number now, click the Back button on the Select AOL Access Phone Numbers window. Now enter 800 or 888 as the area code, click Next to sign on to AOL again, and select the appropriate number(s).

Note

You have 30 minutes from the time you connect to complete your account setup. If you take longer than this, you will be disconnected. This is another reason why it pays to be prepared ahead of time with your payment information and screen names.

Other factors to keep in mind when choosing access numbers are speed and type. The middle column (between the city/community name and the number itself) displays this information. 28.8 means the number supports connections up to 28,800 bps. 33.6 means the number supports connections up to 33,600 bps. V90 means the number supports connections up to 53,000 bps. If you have a high-speed modem, be sure to choose numbers that support your speeds. Additionally, those with older, high-speed modems should pay attention to whether an access number is K56 or X2. If you have an older modem that uses X2 or K56flex protocols, you should use a local access number that supports the V.90 standard *and* your modem's protocol. Check your modem's documentation if you are unsure of the protocol your modem uses.

While searching for possible access numbers, you can select them and then click the More Info button for additional details. AOL displays the number's city, state, digits, maximum speed, network, and area code, which may or may not be useful in determining if a number will work for you. When you're ready to select a number, you can highlight its name in the list on the left and click the Add button. Alternatively, you can just double-click the number in the list on the left. Both methods display the access number again and give you the option to edit it if you wish. Click the Next button to complete the selection. Once you've selected your access numbers, click Next to connect to AOL again using one of your chosen access numbers (see Figure A-9).

Figure A-9. Your software connects to the AOL system.

As your AOL software connects, it displays its progress. Pay close attention to this screen, as it can forewarn you of connection problems. Each of the three boxes changes as the connection progresses; if you need to stop it at any time, just press the Cancel button. Once your software successfully connects, AOL prompts you to create your America Online account (see Figure A-10).

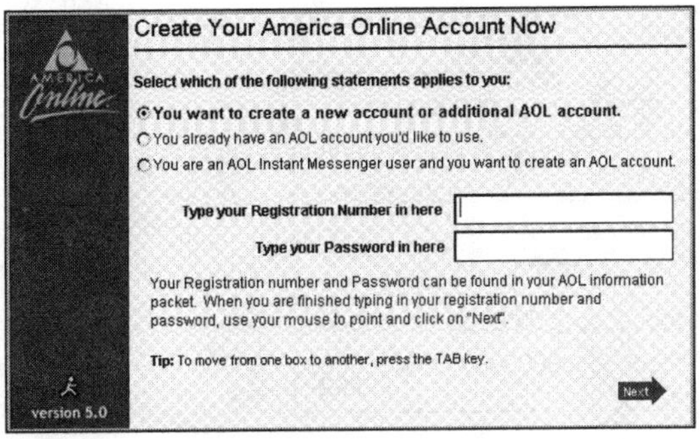

Create Your America Online Account Now

Select which of the following statements applies to you:

⊙ You want to create a new account or additional AOL account.
○ You already have an AOL account you'd like to use.
○ You are an AOL Instant Messenger user and you want to create an AOL account.

Type your Registration Number in here ▢
Type your Password in here ▢

Your Registration number and Password can be found in your AOL information packet. When you are finished typing in your registration number and password, use your mouse to point and click on "Next".

Tip: To move from one box to another, press the TAB key.

version 5.0   Next ▶

Figure A-10. Creating your AOL account

Begin by letting AOL know if you already have a relationship with AOL. If you are new or simply want to create a brand new account, do nothing — this is the default. If you already have an AOL account you want to use (that is, if you are upgrading to the new software), click the circle next to that option. If you have an AOL Instant Messenger account through the Internet, click the circle next to that option. The two fields in the middle of the window will change appropriately based on the option you chose. We'll assume for now that you're a new member.

Before you can continue, you'll probably need to type in your registration number and password as a new member. Where can you find these? If your AOL software came on a CD-ROM, check the disc sleeve. If it came with your computer, check your computer box for an AOL brochure or flyer. If you can't find your registration number and password, call AOL at 1-800-827-6364 to request new ones. Once you have them, be sure to type them in exactly as they are shown, and then click Next. The following window asks for your information (see Figure A-11).

AOL needs your full name, address, and phone numbers to properly identify you in its database. If you do not want AOL to give out your mailing address, you can visit Keyword: **Marketing Prefs** after your account is established and request that they not do so (see Appendix B for more details on Marketing Preferences). Once your information is typed in, press Next to learn more about how your AOL membership works, such as the number of free hours to which you're entitled in your first month online. Clicking Next again produces the billing method selection window (see Figure A-12).

Note

If you downloaded the AOL software from the Internet, you may not need to enter a registration number and password, as these may have been automatically included with your specific download. Just follow the directions on the screen if they differ from those in this appendix.

A

Booking Passage on America Online

Note

If you choose to pay with your checking account, the next screen asks you to type in your bank name, state, transit number, and account number. Your transit number and account number can be found at the bottom of one of your checks.

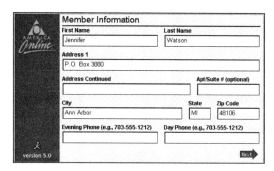

Figure A-11. Enter your name, address, and phone numbers as requested.

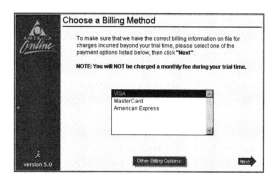

Figure A-12. Select a billing method for your AOL account payments.

As you can see, AOL lists VISA, MasterCard, and American Express as billing methods. If you prefer to use one of these, select it and press the Next button. Otherwise, click the Other Billing Options button at the bottom of the window to expand the list to include Discover/Novus, Diners Card, and Checking options. Make your choice and click Next (see Figure A-13).

Figure A-13. Type your billing information exactly as it appears on your card.

AOL prompts credit card users to enter their card numbers, expiration dates, and names as they appear on the card. Follow the directions on the screen to type the information exactly as requested. Click Next to have AOL verify your credit card number; if AOL informs you the number is invalid, double-check the number, make any necessary corrections, and try again. If successful, AOL asks you to verify your billing information — change the address if it doesn't match the address on your billing statement, otherwise leave it as it is.

When ready, click Next to carefully read AOL's membership agreement. Once you agree to the member agreement, AOL prompts you to choose your screen name (see Figure A-14).

Note

If AOL tells you your credit card number is already on record and does not accept it, this may be because you are a current or previous AOL member and used that credit card number before. AOL will allow you to use the number again if you call and request so at 1-800-827-6364.

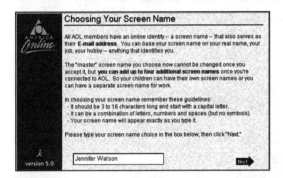

Figure A-14. Finally! It's time to choose your screen name.

Read the screen name information carefully, noting that screen names must be at least three characters and no more than sixteen characters long. You may use a combination of letters and numbers (though your name cannot start with a number), but symbols are not allowed. Spaces are allowed and count as one character each. Most importantly, note that your screen name will appear virtually exactly as you type it. Capitalize the letters you want in uppercase, add spaces where appropriate, and so on. The only thing you can't control is the first character — AOL automatically capitalizes it for you.

Type in your first screen name choice (you did brainstorm some ideas already, right?) and click the Next button. If the screen name is already taken, AOL lets you know and gives you the choice to choose the screen name they recommend (usually something unintelligible) or try another screen name of your choice. We suggest you keep trying your own screen names ideas; if successful, you're much likely to be happier with it in the long run. Also note that while you can add up to

More password creation tips are available in Chapter 1.

To get more help with using the AOL software, see Chapter 4.

six more screen names to your account later, you can never delete this initial screen name (unless you cancel your entire account).

Once you find a screen name that isn't already taken, AOL asks you to select a password. Choose as long a password as possible, incorporating both numbers and letters. The harder to guess, the better. Click Next to complete the creation of your account and sign on with your new name (see Figure A-15). Congratulations!

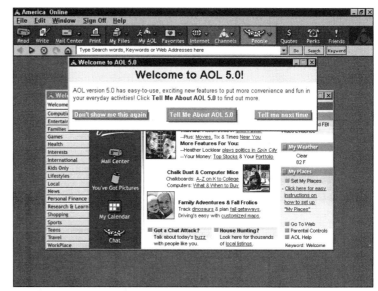

Figure A-15. Your first online session might look something like this.

Upon signing on for the first time, AOL welcomes you and offers to show you around AOL 5.0 (see the top window in Figure A-15). Click the Tell Me More About AOL 5.0 button to learn more about the new and improved features of the software. This window will come up each time you sign on unless you specifically dismiss it. You can revisit the introduction to AOL 5.0 at anytime in the future by choosing What's New in 5.0 under the Help menu.

Upgrading Your Software

Are you still using that old version of the AOL software? While many of the older versions can continue to connect to AOL, they don't give you access to all the bells and whistles that AOL version 5.0 offers (and which this book is based upon). Upgrading to AOL 5.0 is free of charge and easy to do. Here's how it works:

Find or Download the Software

If you have an AOL 5.0 CD-ROM, you're home free! If not, sign on with your older AOL software and go to Keyword: **Upgrade**. The Upgrade Center not only lets you download the most recent version of AOL software, but also gives you a peek at the new features and get help installing and troubleshooting the software itself. If your computer isn't quite up to speed for AOL 5.0, the Upgrade Center even offers resources to upgrade your computer as well.

Install the Upgrade

Whether you have the installation disc or download the software, the AOL upgrade installation process begins automatically, just as it does for a new installation (which you can see in Figure A-1 earlier in this appendix). For an upgrade, however, you want to indicate that you are a current member rather than a new member (see Figure A-16).

Figure A-16. Let AOL know that you are a current member if you wish to upgrade your existing software rather than create a new account.

Note

If for some reason you want to start with a clean slate, or do not want your settings and e-mail copied, you're better off not doing an upgrade. Instead, click the Back button, choose the "Adding your existing AOL account to this computer" option, and continue with the installation process.

Upon clicking Next, AOL asks you to indicate whether you are upgrading to a new version of AOL, adding an existing AOL account to this particular computer, or creating a new AOL account on your computer (see Figure A-17). In most cases, you should do nothing; the default setting is to upgrade to a new version of AOL. Otherwise, click the appropriate circle, then click Next to continue.

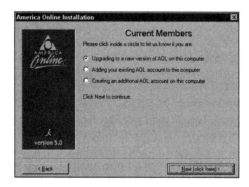

Figure A-17. Let AOL know whether you want to upgrade, add your existing AOL account, or create a new AOL account.

Upon clicking Next, AOL begins to search your computer for previous versions of AOL. Assuming you indicated that you wish to upgrade to a new version, this is a crucial step in the installation process. Note that the search may take a while if you have a particularly large hard drive or many copies of AOL installed. If AOL finds that you've already installed this version of AOL, it will notify you of this and confirm that you really do wish to install it again. Otherwise, AOL displays all versions of the AOL software found on your computer and asks you to choose the one you want to upgrade (see Figure A-18).

AOL suggests, and so do we, that you upgrade the version you've been using most recently. This is important because it has your most recent settings and e-mail (if you save e-mail in your Personal Filing Cabinet), and you will likely want to preserve these. Choose (highlight) the AOL version you want to upgrade and click the Next button to continue.

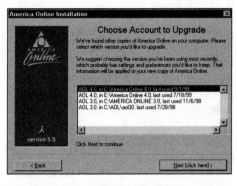

Figure A-18. Choose the version of installed software you wish to update.

The next step is to confirm (or change) the destination directory for your AOL 5.0 software (refer to Figure A-2). Note that upgrading your software still entails adding new software into a new directory on your computer — it doesn't simply modify your existing software. When ready, click Next to tell AOL what to do with your previously downloaded files (see Figure A-19).

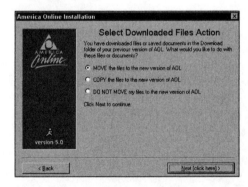

Figure A-19. AOL gives you the option to move, copy, or not move downloaded files.

If you previously downloaded files to the Download directory in your old AOL software, AOL asks you what to do with these. We recommend you move them to your new software, which is the default. Note that only files that are residing in your Download directory are affected by this; files downloaded or later moved to other locations on your hard drive will be untouched. Make your selection and click Next to begin the installation process (refer back to Figure A-3).

Once installed, the AOL software automatically runs. You may be asked if you want this copy of AOL to be your default Internet application for Web pages, newsgroups, and e-mail. We recommend you click Yes. AOL then presents the Sign On screen, completely updated with your screen names and locations from the previous version of AOL. If you look closer, you'll see that AOL transferred your settings and information. Your Address Book, any offline mail in the Personal Filing Cabinet, your list of files to be downloaded (and already downloaded) in your Download Manager, shortcuts, and toolbar icons should all be present.

You can now sign on as usual and begin exploring the new AOL 5.0 software. The Welcome to 5.0 window (refer to Figure A-15) appears for upgrades as well, and you may find it helpful for becoming acquainted with 5.0's new features.

Guest Access

AOL conveniently provides a way for your guests to access their AOL accounts from the installed software on your computer. Better yet, this means *you* can access your AOL account when you're visiting a friend or family member who also has AOL installed. How does it work? Begin by starting the AOL software. At the Sign On screen, click the box below Select Screen Name to reveal the drop-down menu, and then choose Guest from the bottom (see Figure A-20).

Figure A-20. Select the Guest screen name from the Sign On screen.

Now click the Sign On button or just press Enter on your keyboard. AOL connects to the service as usual, and then asks for your screen name and password (see Figure A-21).

Figure A-21. Type your screen name and password carefully.

Pay close attention to the Guest Sign On window. If you mistype either your screen name or your password, you will not be able to sign on. AOL gives you one more try, but if you make a second mistake, AOL will automatically sign you off as a protective measure, and you'll need to repeat the process to try again.

Once signed on with Guest, you can use AOL much as you do on your own computer. There are a couple important differences, however. You cannot use the Switch Screen Names feature or Create New Screen Names option. Additionally, your preferences, Personal Filing Cabinet, Download Manager, favorite places, Address Book, e-mail signatures, shortcuts, and toolbar icons are inaccessible — these features are all running on your own computer's hard disk. However, your Buddy List, mailboxes (New, Old, Sent, and Recently deleted), You've Got Pictures, preferences and signatures for message board and newsgroups, Parental Controls settings, My Calendar, stock portfolios, and news and interest profiles will all work fine.

Another use for the Guest option comes in handy for those with more than one AOL account. For example, you may have a corporate AOL account at work and a personal AOL account at home. If you want to access your personal account at work, you may not be able to install a new copy of the software with the personal account's screen names. But you can still access your personal account at work using the Guest option.

Remote Access

Whether you travel for business or pleasure (or both, as we do), you'll find AOL travels along with you quite easily. There are three main methods of accessing AOL while traveling: via your laptop, via someone else's computer, and via the Internet. Let's look at each method individually.

Laptop Access

If you have a laptop computer with a modem, you can install a copy of the AOL software onto it and access AOL from virtually everywhere. All you need is a phone line and an access number at your destination, and everything else works normally. Phone lines are fairly simple to spot — most hotels provide dataports in their phones these days and virtually every household in America has a phone line.

The first time you install and set up your AOL software, you're asked to choose connection methods and access numbers (refer to Figures A-5 through A-8). This works great for your initial destination. Yet what happens when you travel to a new city? The access numbers you chose won't work outside of the community you chose them for (unless you add the community's area code, in which case you'll be charged long distance fees). To find new access numbers, simply click the Access Numbers button at the bottom of the Sign On screen and follow the on-screen directions (which will look very similar to your initial setup). When you get to the Select AOL Access Phone Numbers (see Figure A-22), you'll need a bit more information to make the right choices.

Any time you return to the Select AOL Access Phone Numbers window after your initial setup, a new field appears on the right side above the selected numbers. If you click the box (which probably reads "Home"), you'll see the Add Location option. This allows you to create a new location set with access numbers for your destination. Select this option to add a new location (see Figure A-23).

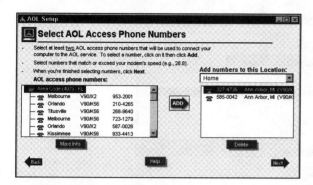

Figure A-22. Note the Add numbers to this Location field now visible on the right side of the window.

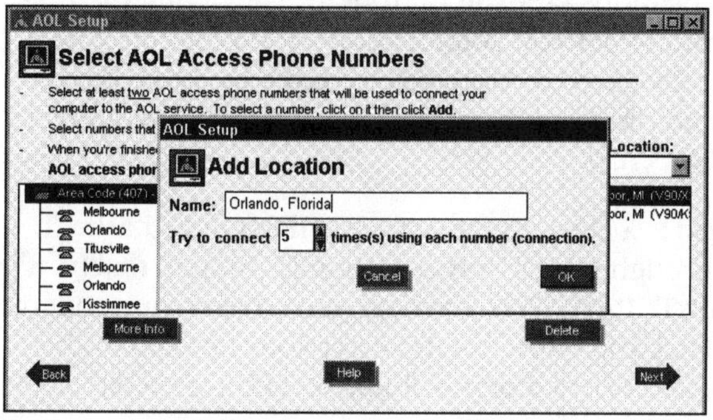

Figure A-23. Name your new location.

Type in a name for your new location, such as "Orlando, Florida," "Beach House," or "Mom's Place." Note that you can increase or decrease the number of times AOL will try to connect at this location. When you're finished, click OK to save your new location and add access numbers to it in the Select AOL Access Phone Numbers window. When you're finished, click the Next button to sign on with the new location. If you don't want to sign on yet, just click the Back button — your location and access numbers are still saved. To use your new location in the future, just select it from the Select Location box on the Sign On screen.

If any of your locations need some tweaking, here's what you can do. First click the Setup button at the bottom of the Sign On screen. Now click the Expert Setup button in the lower-left corner of the resulting window. This opens the Connection Setup window (see Figure A-24).

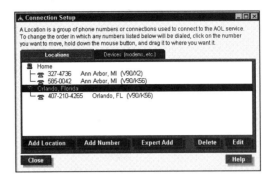

Figure A-24. Connection Setup lets you add, edit, and delete locations and devices.

Connection Setup lists your locations (and their numbers) beneath the Locations tab. The buttons arrayed along the bottom of the window let you add locations, add numbers, add a number manually (Expert Add), delete, and edit. Most are self-explanatory and produce the same or similar setup windows you've already seen.

Note that there is a Devices tab, which when clicked lists the devices through which you can connect to AOL (such as a modem or TCP/IP). This is where you adjust your modem volume. Just click the Devices tab, select your modem in the list, click Edit, and select a new volume level from the Speaker volume drop-down menu.

Guest Computer Access

If you have access to someone else's computer while you're travelling, you generally have two options. The first option is to use the Guest feature in AOL software that may already be installed on the computer (detailed earlier in this appendix). Your second and possibly best option is to install a new copy of the AOL software. If this is your preference, bring along the AOL installation disc and be sure to ask the owner/user of the computer if you can install the software. Regardless of which option you use, any AOL connection charges will be billed to your own account. If there is no a local access number in the area, keep in mind that long distance charges will appear on your friend or family's phone bill; you may want to use the AOL 800 or 888 number instead. If only general Internet access is available, read on.

Internet Access

AOL provides three Internet-based tools that may allow you to access certain aspects of AOL. Use these if you can't connect with your laptop or use another computer that has AOL installed, but you can use a computer with general Internet access. Public terminals found in libraries and airports may have general Internet access, as may a friend or family member who hasn't yet been turned on to AOL (send them a sign-on kit at Keyword: **Friend**).

The first tool is AOL NetMail, which we discuss at the end of Chapter 7. We recently used this at a library to get our AOL e-mail on a camping trip, and it worked like a charm. The second tool is AOL Instant Messenger, which we discuss in Chapter 8. The third tool is Web Boards, which we discuss in Chapter 9. Together, these three tools can give you access to your e-mail, to your friends, family, and coworkers through Instant Messages, and to your message boards.

Preferences are your route to a customized AOL experience. This AOL experience gets richer with every passing year, and the list of options grows right along with it. You can customize your e-mail, chat rooms, downloads, Personal Filing Cabinet, the AOL toolbar, and your Buddy List. The privacy-minded can protect themselves and their families with features such as Parental Controls and Privacy Preferences. And, of course, there's the ever-popular "much, much more!" We hope this appendix helps you discover and adjust all these settings to your taste.

Most of these preferences are accessed by clicking the My AOL icon on the AOL toolbar, and then selecting Preferences

Cross-Reference

Message Board and
Newsgroup Preferences are
described in Chapter 9.

Tip

Although you can access
most of your preferences
while offline, it often pays
to be online to see how
those preferences work.
Many preferences are only
accessible when you're
online.

(see Figure B-1). We've also gathered up information on other
important options and settings with instructions on where to
find them.

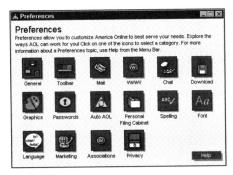

Figure B-1. Your preferences are always within reach under the My AOL icon on
the toolbar.

Whenever suitable, we note the *default* settings, which is the
way AOL comes "out of the box" for a new account. If you
have upgraded to AOL 5.0 from an earlier version of AOL software, your previous preference settings have been copied, for
your convenience.

General Preferences

The General Preferences window, shown in Figure B-2, encompasses a collection of announcement, text, and sound preference settings, which are described here:

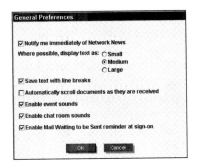

Figure B-2. General Preferences settings control text formats and sounds, among
other things.

Notify me immediately of Network News — If AOL has an announcement (typically regarding a technical problem), it will appear automatically on your screen. (Default: On.)

Where possible, display text as: Small, Medium, Large — This does not affect all text in all AOL windows. *Large* may be easier to read, but can cause the text for some labels and captions to be cut off or overflow its space. (Default: Medium.)

Save text with line breaks — Automatically inserts a hard return at the end of every line of text for any e-mail. Although some Internet users prefer this setting to be on, it can also cause frustration if you expect your text to wrap the way it does in a word processor. (Default: On.)

Automatically scroll documents as they are received — As text enters a document window (such as an e-mail or an online article), the text will scroll as it arrives. This only works well for speed readers or people using very slow network connections. (Default: Off.)

Enable event sounds — Turn on or off sounds such as "You've got mail!," "Welcome," "Goodbye," and the Instant Message chime. (Default: On.)

Enable chat room sounds — People in chat rooms can play sounds in a chat room so that others who have the same sound file installed on their hard disks can hear the sound. Some people love this feature; others are distracted or annoyed by it. (Default: On.)

Enable Mail Waiting to be Sent reminder at Sign-on — If you wrote e-mail offline or used the Send Later feature, this preference setting will remind you to send the e-mail. If you use Send Later to save e-mail "works in progress," you may be annoyed to get this reminder whenever you sign on. (Default: On.)

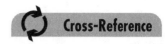

Read more about chat room sounds in Chapter 8.

The Enable chat room sounds option can also be set in the Chat Preferences window described later in this appendix.

Toolbar Preferences

The toolbar at the top of the AOL screen can be customized to your needs (see Figure B-3).

Note

You must be signed on to use the Clear History Now button.

Figure B-3. Change the appearance and functionality of your AOL toolbar with the toolbar preference settings.

Appearance: **Icons and Text** is the normal appearance. **Text Only** removes the icon graphics to supply more space in the main AOL window. (Default: Icons and Text.)

Location: **Move to Top** places the AOL toolbar at the top of the window. **Move to Bottom** places the toolbar at the bottom of the screen, the same place that most people have their Windows taskbar. (Default: Move to Top.)

Navigation: **Use Previous and Next navigation arrows to track open windows only** — When off, you can use the navigation arrows on the toolbar to reopen windows you've recently closed. When this preference is turned on, you can only step through windows that are still on screen. (Default: Off.)

History Trail: Clear History Trail after each Sign Off or Switch Screen Name — The History trail remembers the online areas and Web pages you've visited so you can return again, even if you signed off in the interim. If you share your computer with other members of the family you may prefer to have AOL erase the trail every time someone signs off. On the other hand, as the History Trail can record your children's online activities, some parents may prefer to leave the History Trail on. You can have the best of both worlds (privacy for the parents and a History Trail for the children). Leave the History Trail on, but click the Clear History Now button when you need to obscure your own activities. (Default: Off.)

Mail Preferences

Mail Preferences provide greater control over mail you read, send, and save in your Personal Filing Cabinet (See Figure B-4).

Figure B-4. Get control of your e-mail by setting your Mail Preferences.

Confirm mail after it has been sent — The confirmation message is a reassuring reminder that your e-mail was sent successfully. On the other hand, the OK button, which pops up to tell you your e-mail was sent, is one more button to click when you're in a hurry; disable it if you find it annoying. (Default: On.)

Close mail after it has been sent — This feature reduces screen clutter and helps confirm that your e-mail has been sent successfully. Some people may prefer to keep the e-mail window open so they can modify the text, change the address, and send e-mail to other people. (Default: On.)

Confirm when mail is marked to send later — This is another reassuring reminder, especially if you accidentally clicked Send Later, rather than Send Now. If you use Send Later frequently, this reminder may not be necessary. (Default: On.)

Retain all mail I send in my Personal Filing Cabinet — Saves a copy of all e-mail you send on your hard disk, where you can refer to it long after it disappears from your Online Mailbox. We recommend switching this option on unless you have a shortage of hard disk space or a need for privacy. (Default: Off.)

Cross-Reference

See Chapter 3 for more information on hyperlinks.

Cross-Reference

Read about quoting in e-mail in Chapter 6.

Note

If you receive a lot of e-mail, AOL may delete e-mail you've read in fewer than 7 days regardless of your preference setting. If this is a concern, save e-mail in your Personal Filing Cabinet.

Retain all mail I read in my Personal Filing Cabinet — Saves a copy of all e-mail you read on your hard disk, where you can refer to it long after it disappears from your Online Mailbox. We recommend switching this option on unless you have a shortage of hard disk space or a need for privacy. (Default: Off.)

Perform a spell check before sending mail — Spell checking your e-mail can prevent embarrassment. With this option enabled, clicking the Send button on an e-mail automatically initiates a spell check. When you're in a rush (or if you're an excellent speller), this can be annoying, as you won't be able to send the e-mail until the spell check has been completed. There is spell check button right on the Write Mail form for when you need it. (Default: Off.)

Use white mail headers — If you change the page background color (see "Font Preferences," later), this option makes sure the address information on the e-mail you send is still legible, since you can't change the color of e-mail headers to contrast with the background color. If the page background color contrasts well with black text, the e-mail may look better with this option turned off. (Default: On.)

Show addresses as hyperlinks — E-mail addresses in the e-mail header (not the body of the message) will be displayed as hyperlinks. Click a hyperlink to open a preaddressed Write Mail window with the same subject as the original message. (Default: Off.)

Display next message when current message is deleted — When this option is on, you save some steps (and time), as the next e-mail in your Online Mailbox or Personal Filing Cabinet will open automatically when you delete a message. If you receive a lot of junk e-mail, however, you may prefer to turn this option off so that you don't accidentally add more junk to your Personal Filing Cabinet. (Default: Off.)

Use AOL style quoting/Use Internet style quoting — AOL-style quoting surrounds quoted text with <<double brackets>, whereas Internet-style quoting precedes each line of quoted text with a single > bracket, a convention frequent users of the Internet are accustomed to. This is mostly a matter of personal image, although if you exchange a lot of e-mail with

Internet users, more of them will know what Internet-style quoting means. (Default: AOL-style quoting.)

Keep my old mail online <*number*> days after I read it—AOL automatically deletes your e-mail between 3 to 7 days after you first read it. If you receive a lot of e-mail you may want to set this preference for fewer than 7 days, but most of us will prefer the full 7 days. To change the number of days, type a number between 3 and 7 in the box or use the up and down arrows to increase or decrease the number. You must be online to adjust this setting. (Default: 3 days.)

Tip

You can also access your Microsoft Internet Explorer settings through the Windows Control Panel, but certain AOL-specific settings will not be available, and other options such as connections, programs, and more advanced functions will present themselves.

Web Preferences

Web Preferences are a complex set of tools, just as your Web browser is a complex bit of software. These preferences affect your built-in AOL browser (Microsoft Internet Explorer). If you're using a separate browser (such as Netscape Navigator), you'll have to open your browser to find its preference settings.

Web Preferences are divided into four sections: General, Security, Content, and Web Graphics. Click the tabs at the top of the screen to switch between these sections.

Note

These settings only affect browser windows, which open when you visit Internet addresses or certain AOL-only areas. Other AOL windows will be unaffected.

General Web Preferences

Your General Web Preferences is the first set of options you see when you access your Web Preferences. Options include settings for your home page, temporary Internet files, history trail, colors, fonts, languages, and accessibility (see Figure B-5).

Home page — Determines which page opens when you click the home page icon on the AOL toolbar. Type in the URL of the page you find most useful. The **Use Default** button will restore AOL.com as your home page. (Default: http://www. aol.com, AOL's home page on the Web.)

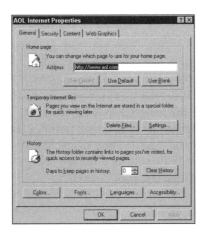

Figure B-5. Web preference settings provide a wide range of control over your Web browser. Note the tabs at the top of the window, which lead to entirely different sets of controls.

Temporary Internet files — Your browser automatically saves Web pages and other Web files on your hard disk. This means you can access them again, offline, and it also speeds access of those pages if you revisit them online. This can use a lot of disk space and may hurt your computer's performance. You can clear out that disk space, which may be the answer to performance problems you were having while browsing the Web. Just click **Delete Files** — the resulting dialog box lets you delete all files in the Temporary Internet Files folder (as well as all offline content if you click the appropriate checkbox). **Settings** helps make sure your browser finds the newest version of a Web page on the Internet, rather than the one that's currently saved on your hard drive. Click the Settings button to produce a dialog box where you can set how often your browser checks for newer versions, as well as determine how much hard disk space your browser will use for temporary Internet files. You can even move the folder that stores the temporary Internet files and view (and selectively delete) files and objects stored on your hard disk with the appropriate buttons at the bottom of the Settings dialog box.

History — Keeps track of your recent travels on the Web. This history trail is a separate function of the Microsoft Internet Explorer browser, unrelated to the History Trail we mentioned in the section "Toolbar Preferences." This History feature has no effect when you browse the Web from within AOL, but is valid if you open Internet Explorer as a separate application, outside of AOL. The AOL History Trail is permanently set to 25 items.

Colors — Affects the text and background color of your browser window and the color of hyperlinks displayed in the browser.

Fonts — Enables you to select the fonts and alphabet you'll see if a Web page's designer did not specify a particular font. (Defaults: Language script — Latin based; Web page font — Times New Roman; Plain text font — Courier New.)

Languages — Some Web pages are available in more than one language. This preference determines your choices, if available, in order of priority. (Default: English - United States.)

Accessibility — If you have trouble reading a computer screen, you may want to override a Web page designer's font and color choices and create a standard style sheet of your own.

Security

The Security Preferences built into Microsoft Internet Explorer are independent of the Parental Controls AOL provides. They can be used to restrict access not only to particular Web sites, but also to various features of Web pages that may be hazardous when used by less-than-scrupulous Web site operators (see Figure B-6).

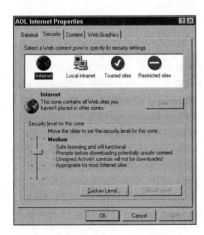

Figure B-6. Your Web Security Preferences let you safeguard yourself, your family, and your computer.

There are so many Web security settings that they fall beyond the scope of this book. *Your Official America Online Internet Guide* by David Peal (AOL Press, 1999) discusses all the ins and outs of these options. However, to get you pointed in the right direction, we will discuss some of them in a general manner.

You can define security settings for each of four zones. The zones are Restricted sites, Trusted sites, Local intranet (most home users won't be connected to an intranet, which is a private computer network that functions like the Web), and Internet (all sites that have not been specified as either Restricted or Trusted). Click the icon for a zone to access the settings for that zone.

Sites — Click this button to create lists of sites that are either Trusted (less-restrictive security settings) or Restricted (highest security settings). This button is grayed-out for the Internet zone, as its settings apply to all sites not otherwise listed as Trusted or Restricted.

Security level for this zone — Move the slider control to adjust the general level of security for Trusted sites and Restricted sites.

Custom level — Access all the various security settings for the zone you're currently adjusting.

Default Level — Restore the "factory" settings if changes to settings have been made.

Content

The name of this group of settings is a bit misleading, as AOL disabled the Content Advisor feature of Microsoft Internet Explorer in favor of its own Parental Controls. The remaining settings in this area relate more to security than the content of Web sites you can visit (see Figure B-7).

Content Advisor — Disabled. See "Parental Control Preferences," later in this chapter.

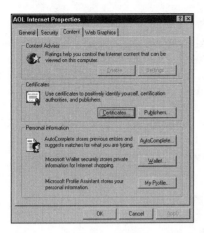

Figure B-7. Web content preference settings give you greater control over the information coming to and going from your computer.

Certificates — *Certificates* are special small files that are exchanged with Web sites. They can either identify you as a trusted visitor, or identify software as coming from a trusted source. Under most circumstances, certificates are automatically installed when you're granted access to sites that require certificates. If you have to manually import, export, or remove certificates, click the Certificates button to reach the Certificate Manager window. Certificates relate to access you've been granted to specific sites, whereas **Publishers** refers to a list of software publishers whose products you have accepted as safe to download and automatically install on your computer without further notice to you. Click Publishers to manually remove publishers from your list.

Personal Information — **AutoComplete** remembers passwords and other entries you have made at Web sites. When you revisit a site, it will "suggest" your previous entries, such as automatically entering your username and password. **Wallet** stores private information that is used for Internet shopping. You must download additional software from Microsoft to use the feature, and it only works at Web sites that incorporate this technology. **My Profile** stores personal information that can be exchanged with Web sites. You must download additional software from Microsoft to use the feature, and it only works at Web sites that incorporate this technology.

Compression is discussed in Chapter 10.

If clicking the reload button on the AOL toolbar doesn't call-up a new, uncompressed graphic, try a "forced reload." Press and hold down the Ctrl key while you click the reload button.

Web Graphics

Graphics files can be large and time consuming to transfer over the telephone lines that nearly all of us use to access AOL. To speed up the process, AOL can "compress" those files as they travel from AOL to your computer. Although the results of this compression technology generally are quite good, the process can seriously degrade the appearance of some images. You can choose to have AOL compress graphics or not through the **Use compressed graphics** option (see Figure B-8).

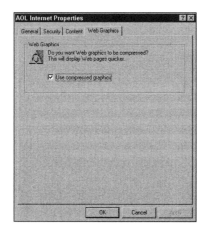

Figure B-8. Choose between compressed or uncompressed graphics on the Web Graphics tab.

If the images you're viewing seem unclear, or the colors are muddy or mottled, disable this preference. You may also have to reload the Web page to receive a new, uncompressed graphic. (Default: On.)

Chat Preferences

Chat Preferences affect features of chat rooms, private rooms, conference rooms, and auditoriums on AOL. They can be accessed by clicking the Preferences button in the chat room or by visiting the Preferences area of My AOL (see Figure B-9).

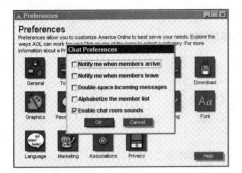

Definition

Online Host is the screen name of AOL's host computer. It is used to send information and is usually seen in chat rooms, conference rooms, and auditoriums.

Figure B-9. Enhance your chats through these chat preference settings.

Notify me when members arrive — The Online Host will announce that a member has entered the chat room. (Default: Off.)

Notify me when members leave — The Online Host will announce that a member has left the chat room. (Default: Off.)

Double-space incoming messages — This may make it easier to read conversations in chat rooms. It also makes the chat conversation scroll twice as fast, so it may be difficult to follow conversations in a busy chat. (Default: Off.)

Alphabetize the member list — Normally, the member list in a chat room displays names in the order members entered the chat room. Alphabetizing that list makes it easier to find a specific member's name so that you can access information about that member or send him or her an Instant Message. (Default: Off.)

Enable chat room sounds — People in chat rooms can play sounds so that others who have the same sound file installed on their hard disks can hear the sound. Some people love this feature, but others are distracted or annoyed by it. (Default: On.)

Download Preferences

Download Preferences affect files you download from AOL's file libraries and forums, and attached e-mail files (see Figure B-10).

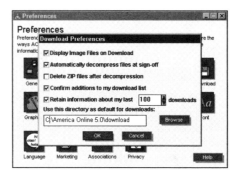

Figure B-10. Control your file downloads with the download preference settings.

Display Image Files on Download — If you download a graphic in GIF, JPG, BMP, or ART format, AOL can start to display the image while it is downloading. The image won't be complete until the download is finished, but you can watch it emerge. If you'd prefer to view the image at a later time, disable this preference. (Default: On.)

Automatically decompress files at sign-off — Files compressed in ZIP format (Windows) or Stuffit format (Mac) can be automatically decompressed when you sign off from AOL. This can save you a lot of time and trouble, but some folks prefer to decompress the files at a different time or using different software. (Default: On.)

Delete ZIP files after decompression — After a file has been decompressed, you will have the original ZIP format, and a new file (or files) in its original, uncompressed format. You may find it handy to keep the original ZIP file, either to share with friends or as a backup, in case you have troubles with the uncompressed file(s). However, you can also waste a lot of hard disk space with old, unneeded ZIP files. If you'd prefer, have AOL delete the ZIP file as soon as it has finished automatically decompressing it. (Default: Off.)

Confirm additions to my download list — When you click the Download Later button, you'll get a message that confirms you've added the file to your Download Manager's download list. If you do a lot of downloading this way, you may prefer to save some time and bypass the message by turning this option off. (Default: On.)

Retain information about my last <*number*> downloads
— This option controls whether your Download Manager will
keep track of the files you've downloaded, and if so, how many
of those downloads will be stored in your Download Manager.
People interested in the privacy of their download information
may prefer to disable this feature. Active downloaders may prefer to increase the number of downloads retained on their list.
(Default: On, 100 downloads.)

Use this directory as default for downloads — By default,
AOL places all downloaded files in a Download directory
(folder) within the America Online software folder. If you prefer to download to another folder, such as the My Documents
folder, click the **Browse** button to select the folder of your
choice. (Default: C:\America Online 5.0\download.)

Graphics Preferences

Graphics Preferences control a variety of features relating to
downloading and displaying images and adding pictures to
e-mail. AOL also speeds your online experience by saving
many graphics, icons, buttons, and other onscreen images on
your hard disk so they don't have to be retransmitted by AOL
over slow telephone lines. Although this is similar to how temporary Internet files work (as we mentioned in "Internet
Preferences" earlier), this particular function only relates to
graphics used by AOL and its forums, not the Web (see
Figure B-11).

Figure B-11. Don't have much hard drive space? Change your graphics viewing
preferences to decrease available disk space for online art, among other settings.

As AOL's forums keep changing and discarding old art, at some point much of the disk space dedicated to online art will be filled with old, unused art. At some point it pays to "squeeze out" the online art files and start collecting art from scratch: Set the maximum disk space to 0 megabytes, sign off and close the AOL software, restart AOL, and set the disk space back to a reasonable figure. For a while every online area you visit will open slowly, as new artwork is transmitted to you, but the payoff will be in less wasted disk space and, perhaps, faster performance.

Maximum disk space to use for online art: <*number*> megabyte(s) — As you visit more and more areas on AOL, you will accumulate more and more artwork on your hard disk. This setting limits the amount of space AOL can use so that it doesn't totally fill your hard disk. When you reach the limit, AOL stops storing new art, which can slow down your online experience. This setting allows your computer to reach a balance between speed and available hard disk space. (Default: 20 megabytes.)

Display image files on download — See "Download Preferences" earlier in this appendix.

Notify before opening mail containing pictures — This safety warning reminds people that an image contained in an e-mail message may turn out to be an objectionable one. If you don't need this warning, you can disable it here. (Default: On.)

Present resizing options when inserting pictures in e-mail — When you insert a large graphic into your e-mail, AOL will offer to resize (shrink) it to fit the e-mail. This is generally a good idea, as it reduces the time needed to send and receive the e-mail. It can also degrade the image quality. Disable this feature to bypass the option window and always insert graphics at full size. (Default: On.)

JPEG compression quality: <*number*> — Graphics in JPEG format (JPG) can be sent to you at higher or lower quality. The trade-off is between download speed and image quality, the higher the number, the better the image quality. If you want more speed, change this setting to a lower number. (Default: 100.)

Set Color Mode — One of the issues affecting the quality of your on-screen image is color depth. Some computers can only display a limited "rainbow" of 256 different colors, whereas others can display thousands or millions of colors. To get the best performance, AOL checks to see what your computer can display and makes appropriate adjustments. Sometimes it can't retrieve that information, and your AOL colors suffer. This option lets you tell AOL which setting to use. (Default: Detect Automatically.)

Password Preferences

These settings let you bypass your password when you sign on or add a password to your Personal Filing Cabinet so that it's more secure. It's unlikely that you'll use both of these options at the same time, since one reduces security and the other enhances it. These settings can only be changed while you're signed on to AOL, and are only available for the screen name you're currently using, which is shown at the lower left of the window (see Figure B-12).

Note

You can't change your sign-on password through the password preference settings. To do that, sign on to AOL and go to Keyword: **Password**. When you change your sign-on password, you must also change the password in the Stored Passwords preference (if you enabled the Sign-On option), or you will get an error when you try to sign on.

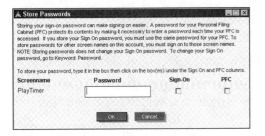

Figure B-12. Use Password Preferences to store your passwords for sign-on and your Personal Filing Cabinet with caution.

Password — If you plan to use the **Sign-On** option, this must be the password you use to sign on to AOL. If you plan to only use the **PFC** option, you may use any password you please. (Default: blank.)

Sign-On — Eliminates the need to enter your password before you sign on to AOL. This reduces the security of your account, as anyone with access to your computer can use your account and screen name. (Default: Off.)

PFC — Adds password protection to your PFC. If this option is off, anyone with access to your computer can access the contents of your PFC. When this option is on, your PFC cannot be accessed without entering the password, whether or not you are signed on. (Default: Off.)

Automatic AOL Preferences

Automatic AOL can send and retrieve your e-mail, file downloads, and message board postings while you're asleep or even out of the country (see Figure B-13).

Figure B-13. Choose the items for Automatic AOL to check when it is enabled.

Send mail from the "Mail Waiting to be Sent" folder — Sends e-mail you wrote offline or specified to be sent later while you were online. (Default: Off.)

Get unread mail and put it in "Incoming Mail" folder — Retrieves unread e-mail from your Online Mailbox and saves it in your Personal Filing Cabinet (Default: Off.)

Download Files that are attached to unread mail — Automatically downloads files attached to e-mail. The Get unread mail preference must be on for this option to be available. This is a security risk, as you may receive attached files from strangers that contain viruses or Trojan Horses. If you prefer, leave this option off and download only the files you want by accessing the Old Mail folder in your Online Mailbox. (Default: Off.)

Send postings from the "Postings Waiting to be Sent" folder — For those message boards and Internet newsgroups that you designated to be read offline, you can also reply to and/or compose new postings offline, via your Personal Filing Cabinet, and send them later, using Automatic AOL. (Default: Off.)

Get unread postings and put in "Incoming Postings" folder — Retrieves unread message board and Internet newsgroup postings for those boards and newsgroups you

designated to be read offline. Postings are stored in your
Personal Filing Cabinet. (Default: Off.)

Download files marked to be downloaded later —
Downloads all files (whether attached to e-mail or in AOL file
libraries) that have been designated to be downloaded later
(a list of which can be found in your Download Manager).
(Default: Off.)

Schedule Automatic AOL — Select the day(s) of the week,
the starting time, and how often during the selected days
an Automatic AOL session will take place. The **Enable
Scheduler** option must be enabled for the scheduled
session(s) to take place. (Default: Off.)

Run Automatic AOL Now — Runs a session for the current
screen name, whether or not you are currently signed on.

Select Names — Select the screen name(s) that will be
included in the Automatic AOL session, and enter the passwords for each of those screen names (see Figure B-14). When
the session is run (either by using Schedule Automatic AOL or
Run Automatic AOL Now), AOL will perform all activities that
have been set in preferences for each screen name that has
been selected. (Default: Off, no passwords.)

Figure B-14. The Select Names window allows you to designate the screen names
(and passwords) checked by Automatic AOL.

Walk Me Through — This feature explains the Automatic
AOL Preferences and options and sets them based on your
response.

Personal Filing Cabinet Preferences

Your Personal Filing Cabinet can take up a lot of hard disk space, so AOL provides settings in the Personal Filing Cabinet Preferences window that limit and manage the hard disk space occupied by your PFC files. You'll also find a couple of settings in the same window that affect file deletions in your PFC, Favorite Places, and Online Mailbox (see Figure B-15).

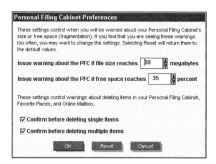

Figure B-15. Configure your saved mail and postings in your Personal Filing Cabinet Preferences.

Issue warning about the PFC if file size reaches <*number*> megabytes — This option helps limit the hard disk space occupied by your PFC. When you reach the preset file size, you'll be advised to either delete items from your PFC or increase the setting. (Default: 10 megabytes.)

Issue warning about the PFC if free space reaches <*number*> percent — When you delete items from your PFC, the empty space cannot be used for other purposes. This warning advises you to compact your PFC, which reduces the size of the PFC and recovers that wasted disk space. (Default: 35 percent.)

Confirm before deleting single items — To prevent accidents, you receive a warning before deleting an item from your PFC, Favorite Places list, or Online Mailbox. Expert users may prefer to forgo the warning. (Default: On.)

Confirm before deleting multiple items — To prevent accidents, you receive a warning before deleting multiple items from your PFC, Favorite Places list, or Online Mailbox. Expert users may prefer to forgo the warning. (Default: On.)

B

Spelling Preferences

The AOL spell checker can fix common grammar, punctuation, and typing errors. Spelling preference settings give you control over which rules will and will not be enforced, and gives you access to your Personal spelling dictionary (see Figure B-16).

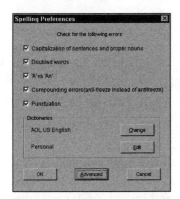

Figure B-16. Fine-tune your spell checker through the Spelling Preferences window.

Check for the following errors — Specify whether you want the spell checker to check the capitalization of sentences and proper nouns, doubled words, *a* versus *an*, compounding errors (anti-freeze instead of antifreeze), and punctuation. (Default: All On.)

Dictionaries (AOL US English and Personal) — The **Change** button permits a switch to a different language dictionary, which must be supplied by AOL. The software supplied to AOL International services such as AOL Canada may come equipped with multiple dictionaries. The **Edit** button allows you to add to or modify the Personal dictionary that is created when you click the Learn button during a spell check.

Advanced — Click this button to bring up the Advanced Spelling Preferences window, which offers a list of over a dozen kinds of grammatical and formatting errors corrected by the spell checker (see Figure B-17). Click a rule in the list to view a full description of that rule. You can disable a rule by clicking the **Current Status On** radio button while that rule is highlighted. (Default: all On.)

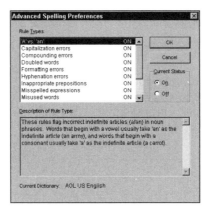

Figure B-17. The Advanced button in Spelling Preferences allows access to the punctuation and grammar settings.

Font Preferences

You can make all your e-mail, chat, and Instant Messages as distinctive as you yourself are by changing your font preference settings. These settings apply to every e-mail, chat, and Instant Message used on your account, regardless of screen name, so there's room for family disagreements. Also note that the fonts you use must also be installed on the computer(s) of those who receive your e-mail and chats, or they will see a common, generic font, rather than the fancy one you selected. AOL provides a sample so you can how things will look (see Figure B-18).

Figure B-18. Spice up your e-mail, chats, and Instant Messages by setting your font preference settings.

The formatting toolbar at the top of the text box includes the following menus and buttons (from left to right). If you allow your mouse pointer to hover over a button, a "bubble help" window containing the button's function name will appear:

▶ **Font name** — Select a font from the drop-down font list. (Default: Arial.)

▶ **Text size** — Select a text size from the drop-down list (Default: 10.)

▶ **Text color** — Click the button and select a color from the palate. (Default: black.)

▶ **Text background color** — Click the button and select a color. (Default: clear.)

▶ **Page background color** — Click the button and select a color for the entire page (Default: white.)

▶ **Text attributes** — Select from any combination of **Bold**, *Italic*, and <u>Underline</u> (Default: none.)

Reset — Returns all settings to the default.

Language Preferences

America Online is available worldwide, and some of AOL's online content is available in more than one language. Select a language (or languages) from the **Available Languages** list and click the **Add** button to state which languages you can choose from when AOL offers you a choice (see Figure B-19).

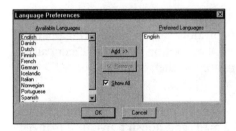

Figure B-19. Broaden your linguistic horizons with your Language Preferences.

Marketing Preferences

Note

When you open each of these preferences, the window always presents both yes and no options. Yet the default selection is always yes, even if you previously set this preference to no. This doesn't mean AOL disregarded your previous setting. Unfortunately, AOL doesn't provide a way to view your current settings. Let's just say that AOL would prefer that you change your preferences back to yes and makes it as easy as possible for you to do that.

AOL is the world's largest online shopping destination and uses many different methods to reach its membership with product and service offers. AOL doesn't want to alienate you with undesired offers or make you feel like your privacy has been breached, so it offers Marketing Preferences to give you a choice in these matters (see Figure B-20). You must be signed on to AOL to set your Marketing Preferences.

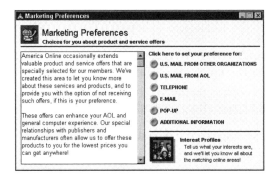

Figure B-20. Protect your personal information with these marketing preference settings.

U.S. Mail from Other Organizations — AOL sells its mailing list (but not your screen name) to other companies. Here's your chance to get off the mailing list. (Default: Yes.)

U.S. Mail from AOL — AOL also sells products and services to its members via U.S. Mail. You can opt out of this mailing list, too. (Default: Yes.)

Telephone — AOL offers products and services to its members via the telephone, too. This option does not affect calls AOL may make that are related to the status of your AOL account. (Default: Yes.)

E-Mail — Although AOL doesn't currently offer goods and services to its members via e-mail (and doesn't give its e-mail list to anyone), it reserves the right to send e-mail of this type to its members. Use this option to let AOL know whether you want this e-mail if and when they do send it. (Default: Yes.)

Pop-up — These are the product offer windows that may appear without warning when you first sign on to AOL or at other times during your online session. These offers are not made to Kids Only, Young Teen, or Mature Teen screen names. (Default: Yes.)

Additional Information — AOL also provides information on how to get off other companys' mailing lists, and provides a link to AOL's Interest Profiles, which give you the option to receive e-mail about areas and activities on AOL that match your personal choices.

Associations Preferences

The Windows desktop can have icons for browsing the Web, sending e-mail, and reading newsgroups. This preference allows you to designate AOL as the application you want to use when you click those icons on the Windows desktop (see Figure B-21). You can also access some of these settings from the Windows Control Panel: Open the Windows Start menu, select Settings and select Control Panel. Double-click the Internet Options icon and click the Programs tab. Select the default E-mail and Newsgroups application by using the drop-down lists for each of those two functions. If you connect to AOL via an Internet Service Provider or local area network you may prefer to retain other programs as your defaults, such as the Netscape Navigator browser or the Microsoft Outlook e-mail reader, and open AOL only when you need it.

Figure B-21. The Association Preferences

Privacy Preferences

You must be signed on to AOL to set these preferences

These preferences relate to Buddy Lists and Instant Messages, and can be accessed either in the Buddy List setup window, or at the Preferences screen (see Figure B-22).

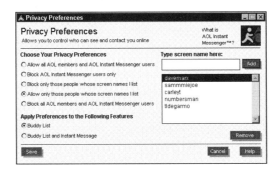

Figure B-22. Privacy Preferences let you designate who can and cannot see you in Buddy Lists and Instant Messages.

You can create a single list of screen names, which can be used in one of the following ways:

Choose Your Privacy Preferences — Select one of the following options:

▶ **Allow all AOL members and AOL Instant Messenger users** — Anyone on AOL (or using AOL Instant Messenger via the Internet) can view you on their Buddy List and send you an Instant message. (This is the default.)

▶ **Block AOL Instant Messenger users only** — AOL members have full Buddy List and/or Instant Message access, but Instant Messenger users (Internet users) do not.

▶ **Block only those people whose screen names I list** — Create a list of the people you never want to hear from, and/or banish yourself from their Buddy Lists. Anyone else can still access you.

▶ **Allow only those people whose screen names I list** — This provides a high level of personal privacy, as only those you place on your list may send you Instant Messages and/or see you on their Buddy Lists.

▶ **Block all AOL members and AOL Instant Messenger users** — This is the maximum privacy setting. Nobody can see you on his or her Buddy List, and/or nobody can send you an Instant Message.

Apply Preferences to the Following Features — You can apply the preceding preferences only to Buddy Lists, or to both Buddy Lists and Instant Messages. Specifically:

▶ **Buddy List**— People you have blocked can't see you on their Buddy List but they can still send you Instant Messages.

▶ **Buddy List and Instant Message** — You won't be seen on Buddy Lists or receive Instant Messages from those whom you have blocked.

Cross-Reference

Read more about Buddy Lists and Instant Messages in Chapter 8.

Parental Control Preferences

Parental Controls give parents the power to tailor their children's access to and use of AOL to activities and information suited to their age and maturity. Parental Controls can only be accessed by screen names with Master Rights. The master screen name that was created when you opened your AOL account automatically has Master Rights, and that screen name may grant those rights to other screen names on the account that have General Access (18+). For this reason, it's important for parents to control access to that master screen name and not share its password with other family members.

Parental control settings can be accessed from the My AOL icon on the AOL toolbar, via Keyword: **Parental Controls** or click the Parental Controls button on the Welcome screen (see Figure B-23).

Parental Controls allow you to create a safe environment for yourself, your family, and your children. A screen name may be placed into one of four age-appropriate categories. These choices are made when a screen name is first created, but can be changed at any time by accessing the Parental Controls window.

Cross-Reference

Parental control settings are described in great depth in Chapter 2.

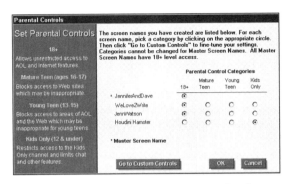

Figure B-23. Set Parental Controls to ensure a safe online experience for your family.

Billing Options and Account Information

Billing and Account information can be modified at Keyword: **Billing**, or by clicking the Billing Center button at AOL Member Services (see Figure B-24).

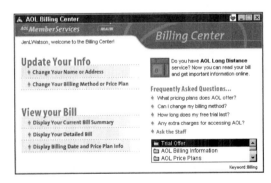

Figure B-24. Change your personal and billing information in the Billing Center.

Through this window you can modify your current payment method, change your AOL price plan, and change your address and telephone number information. You must be signed onto AOL to make these changes, and you must provide your password in order to change price plan or payment method. AOL does not divulge your current settings, so your current information will not be revealed should an unauthorized person obtain access to your account.

Change Your Name or Address — Change the name, address, and/or telephone numbers AOL uses for merchandise and service solicitations and account-related matters.

Change Your Billing Method or Price Plan — Enter your password and select whether you want to change your billing method or price plan.

Update Billing Method — You can pay for your AOL service by credit card, or AOL can receive payment directly from your checking account (there is an extra charge if you pay via a checking account). Make your choice, and provide the information about the account you're planning to use. AOL doesn't tell you which account you are currently paying with.

Update Pricing Plan — AOL lists your current plan and a pending plan, if you recently requested a change to a new plan. You are also presented with a list of other available price plans; use **Display Plan** to receive more details about a particular plan and **Select Plan** when you have made a decision. If you change your mind, press the **Cancel Pending** button.

Connection and Setup Options

Connection and setup options are detailed in Appendix A, but we'll provide a brief description here.

Setup options are accessed while you are offline, from the Setup and Sign On screen. You select connection and setup preferences when you first set up your AOL account. However, you may wish to change these settings if you install new computer hardware, add a new connection method (such as cable modem), or have performance problems with your AOL connection (see Figure B-25).

You may have to change your AOL access number(s) and/or add a new Location if you move or if AOL adds a new access number in your area (see Figure B-26).

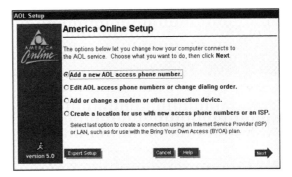

Figure B-25. AOL Setup lets you change your access and connection methods.

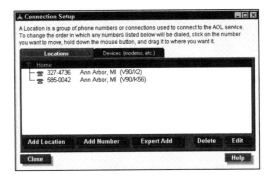

Figure B-26. Set up and edit locations and phone numbers in Connection Setup.

Buddy List Preferences

To access your Buddy List Preferences, click the Setup button on the Buddy List window, and click Buddy List Preferences. Your choices are simple:

Show me my Buddy List(s) immediately after I sign onto AOL — If you don't want to see your Buddy List after signing on to AOL, disable this option. (Default: On.)

Play sound when buddies sign on — You'll hear the default sound (a door opening) whenever one of your buddies signs on if you turn this option on. (Default: On.)

Play sound when buddies sign off — You'll hear the default sound (a door slamming) whenever one of your buddies signs off if you turn this option on. (Default: On.)

Go to Sound Library — This option describes how to install Buddy Sounds and gives you access to a download library with other sounds you can use in place of the default sounds.

Privacy Preferences can also be accessed from the Buddy List Setup screen. They are described in detail earlier in this Appendix.

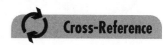

Buddy List setup options are described in detail in Chapter 8.

They say "it's not the destination, it's the journey."
Well, if you've ever clicked on four links, three icons,
two drop-down menus, and a list box in the pursuit of your
destination, you will probably agree that the journey is less
than it's cracked up to be. Instead of click-click-clicking
your way around AOL, use keywords. On America Online,
keywords are shortcuts to thousands of destinations — fast
and easy. Just type the keyword into the toolbar at the top of
your screen, click the Go button (or press Enter), and off you
go. If you're not yet familiar with keywords, refer to Chapter 2
for detailed instructions.

The only problem with keywords is that you need to know
them *before* you can use them. AOL maintains lists of keywords
online at Keyword: **Keyword**. The lists are long, and because
of their length, you may have problems finding the keyword
you're after. To save you the trouble, we've compiled the best
and most useful keywords from the various lists into one
alphabetical list here in this appendix. Do keep in mind that
keywords come and go over time, though the majority of
keywords do stick around. If you encounter a keyword that
no longer works, check Keyword: **Keyword** to see if a new
keyword appears in the list online.

The following list of keywords is organized alphabetically.
Each keyword appears in bold, followed by a description.

@ACTIVE SPORTS
Thrive@active Sports

@AOL SPORTSDOME
Coliseum Auditorium

@BOWL
Bowl Auditorium

@COLISEUM
Coliseum Auditorium

@CYBERPLEX
Cyberplex Auditorium

@CYBERRAP
Cyberrap Auditorium

@DOME
Coliseum Auditorium

@GLOBE
Globe Auditorium

@NEWSROOM
Newsroom Auditorium

@ODEON
Odeon Auditorium

@ROTUNDA
Computing & Software
Rotunda

@SPORTSFAN
Sportsfan Radio Network

@THE NEWSROOM
Newsroom Auditorium

@TIMES
New York Times Online

@TOWER
Tower Records

0S8
Mac Operating System

12TH GRADE
College Bound: Seniors Only

1 800 DOCTORS
1-800 Doctors Web Site

1 800 FLOWERS
1-800-Flowers

1BABY
1baby.com

2 GUYS
Love@AOL: Advice From
Men For Women

3COM
U.S. Robotics

3D HOME
The Learning Channel
SuperStore

3D REALMS
Apogee/3d Realms Games

3RDAGE
Third Age

401 K
Lifestages: Retire In Style

49ERS
San Francisco 49ers

4 STAR
Chefs Catalog Store

4TH
Independence Day@AOL

56K
High Speed Access

777-FILM
Local Showtimes And Movie
Tickets

800 NUMBER
AOL's 800 Number

888 NUMBER
AOL's 800 Number

9
AOL Long Distance

911
Public Safety Center

911 GIFTS
911 Gifts Online Store

9600
High Speed Access

A&R
Addiction & Recovery Forum

A&V
Animation & Video Forums

AA
American Airlines

AAA STORE
AAA Store

AAC
Ask-a-Teacher

AA MEET
Alcoholics Anonymous
Online Meetings

AARP
American Association of
Retired Persons

ABC KIDS
ABC Online: Kids

ABC NEWS
ABC Online: Live News
Broadcasts

ABC WOMEN
ABC Online: Womens Sports

ABI
ABI Yellow Pages

ABL
AOL Pro Basketball

ABOUT CHAT
Chatting Online

ABOUT PLANETOUT
About Planet Out

ABOUT SO
About Special Olympics

ABUSE OF WOMEN
Domestic Abuse: Helping
Men Heal

**ACADEMY OF
ACHIEVEMENT**
Academy Of Achievement

ACCESS
Access Numbers

ACCESS CAMERA
Access Discount Camera
Web Site

ACCESS EXCELLENCE
Access Excellence

ACCESS NUMBER
Accessing America Online

ACCOUNT
AOL Rewards

ACCOUNTANT
AOL WorkPlace: Accounting

ACCOUNTS
Billing Information and
Changes

A CHICAGO MOVIES
Chicago Movies

ACHIEVEMENT
Academy Of Achievement

ACLU
American Civil Liberties
Union

ACTING
The Casting Forum

ACTION GAMES
Antagonist Trivia

ACTION SPORTS
Great Outdoors

ACTIVE TRADER
Active Trader

ACTIVISM
Volunteerism

ACUPUNCTURE
Acupuncture

ADD
Attention Deficit Disorder

ADDICT
Addictions

ADDRESS
Billing Information And
Changes

ADDRESS BOOK
Address Book

AD SDGE
San Diego Energy

AD SIG
Advertising Sig

**ADVANCED
COMPUTERS**
Advanced Computers &
Technology

ADVENTURE
Great Outdoors

ADVENTURE TRAVEL
Adventure and Outdoor
Travel Forum

ADVERTISING SIG
Advertising Sig

ADVICE & PLANNING
Personal Finance: Advice &
Planning

AECSIG
AOL WorkPlace

AEROBICS
AOL Fitness

AERONAUTICS
Aviation & Aeronautics

AFI
American Finance

AFRICAN-AMERICAN
NetNoir

AFRICAN FOOD
African Food

AGES
Ages & Stages

AGGRESSIVE SKATING
Aggressive Inline Miniforum

AGNOSTIC
AOL Religion: Atheism

AH
Better Health

AHA@BETTER HEALTH
The American Heart
Association

AHH
Alternatives: Health and
Healing

AHL
AOL Hockey

AIDS
AIDS & HIV

AIDSLINE
AIDS Line

AIDS QUILT
AIDS Memorial

AIM
AOL Instant Messenger

AIMEE
Travelers Resource Center

AIR
Airlines Center

AIRCRAFT
Aviation & Aeronautics

AIRFARE FINDER
Preview Travel: Farefinder

AIRLINE
Airlines Center

AIRPORT
Airport

AIR RESOURCES
Business Air

AIR TRAVEL
Airlines Center

AIR WARRIOR
Air Warrior

AL
AOL Baseball

ALA
American Lung Assocation

ALARM
Consumer Electronics

ALCOHOL
Alcoholism

AL GORE
Candidate Close-up: Al Gore

ALLAPARTMENTS
Apartment Locators

ALLE JEWELRY
Elan Fine Jewelry

ALLERGIES
Allergy & Respiratory
Disorders

ALL HEALTH
All Health

ALLIED SCHOOLS
Allied Schools

ALLSTATE
Allstate: Lincoln Benefit Life

ALOHABOWL
Aloha Bowl

ALSCOREBOARD
American League
Scoreboard

ALTERNATIVE MEDICINE
Alternative Medicine Forum

ALZHEIMERS
Alzheimer's Disease

AMASSEMBLY
American Assembly

AMAZING
Amazing Trivia Game

AMDOC
America's Doctor

AMERICA
QuickStart: A Guide for New
Members

AMERICA DOCTOR
America's Doctor

AMERICAN DIABETES
American Diabetes

**AMERICAN EDUCATION
WEEK**
American Education Week

AMERICAN FINANCE
American Finance

AMERICAN GREETING
American Greetings

**AMERICAN LEAGUE
SCOREBOARD**
American League
Scoreboard

AMERICA ONLINE
QuickStart: A Guide for New
Members

**AMERICA ONLINE
STORE**
AOL Store

AMERICAS BABY
America's Baby

**AMERICAS DOCTOR
MEDICAL LIBRARY**
America's Doctor Medical
Library

AMERICAS PARKS
America's Parks

AMERICAS PROMISE
America's Promise

AMUSEMENT PARK
Theme Parks

ANCESTOR
Genealogy

ANDERS
Anders CD-ROM Guide

ANDY PARGH
Andy Pargh: The Gadget
Guru

ANEMIA
Anemia

ANGLER
Fishing

ANIMAL
Pets Forum

ANIME
Wizard World Or
Japanimation Station

ANNUAL PLAN
AOL Annual Pricing Plans

ANOREXIA
Eating Disorders

ANSWER
AOL Member Services

ANT CELLAR
The Prize Cellar

ANT GAMES
Antagonist Online Games
Area

ANTHILL
The Ant Hill

ANTIQUE
Collectors Corner Exchange

ANTIQUING
Antiquing

ANTI VIRUS
Virus Information

ANTKIDS
Antagonist: For Kids Only!

ANTONYMS
Merriam-Webster Thesaurus

ANT PC
Antagonist, Inc. Pc Games

ANT PRIZES
The Prize Cellar

ANXIETY
Anxiety & Panic Disorders

AOGIRL
AOL Teens: AOgirl

AOL ACCESS NUMBERS
Accessing America Online

AOL ACCOUNT
Billing Information and
Changes

AOL BASICS
Learn How To Use AOL And
Your Computer

AOL BEGINNERS
Quick Start: A Guide for
New Members

AOL BIKE
Bicycling

AOL BILLING
Billing Information and
Changes

**AOL BUSINESS
DIRECTORY**
AOL Business Directory

AOL CHAT
People Connection

AOL CLASSIFIED
Classifieds

AOL CREDIT ALERT
AOL Credit Alert Area

AOL DIAG
AOL Diagnostic Tool

AOL DIRECT
Great Gifts Ideas

AOL ELSEWHERE
International Access

AOL FAMILIES
Families Channel

AOL FIND
AOL Search

AOL GAMES
Games Channel

AOL GAMES STORE
AOL Games Store/AOL
Store

AOL GLOBALNET
International Access

AOL GLOSSARY
AOL Glossary

AOL HARDWARE SHOP
AOL Store - Computer

AOL HEALTH
Health Channel

AOL HELP
AOL Member Services

AOL HOMETOWN
Hometown AOL

AOL HOT GAMES
AOL Hot Games Collection

AOL INSIDER
AOL Insider Tips

**AOL INVESTMENT
SNAPSHOT**
Quotes & Portfolios

AOL JOBS
Finding A Job

AOL LD BILLING
AOL Long Distance Billing

AOL LINK
Winsock Information Area

AOL LIVE
Today In AOL Live

AOL LIVE QUICK START
AOL Live Quick Start

AOL LOVE
Love@AOL: Personals,
Romance And More!

AOL MARKETDAY
AOL Marketday

AOL MARKET TALK
AOL Market Talk

AOL MFC
Mutual Fund Center

**AOL NEIGHBORHOOD
WATCH**
AOL Neighborhood Watch

AOL NET
Accessing America Online

AOL NETMAIL
AOL Netmail

AOL PERSONALS
The Romance Channel, Your
Area For Love!

AOL PHONE NUMBER
Accessing America Online

AOL PICTURES
You've Got Pictures

AOL PLUGINS
Multimedia Showcase Plugins

AOL PRODUCTS
AOL Shop Direct

AOL QC
AOL Quick Checkout

AOL SECRETS
AOL Secrets

AOL SHOP
Great Gifts Ideas

**AOL SHOP DIRECTS
UPGRADE SHOP**
Upgrade Store / AOL Shop
Direct

**AOL SHOPPERS AD-
VANTAGE**
Shoppers Advantage

AOL SOFTWARE SHOP
AOL Store: Software Shop

AOL SPORTS
AOL Sports Channel

AOL STORE
AOL Shop Director

AOL STORIES
AOL Stories

AOL STUDIOS
AOL Studios

AOL SUPER STORE
Shoppers Advantage

AOL SWITZERLAND
AOL Switzerland

AOL TA
AOL Travelers Advantage

AOL TICKER
AOL News Channel

AOL TIPS
AOL Insider Tips

AOL TODAY
AOL Today

AOL TRAVEL
Travel Channel

AOL UPDATE
AOL System Update

AOL UPGRADE
The Latest AOL Software

AOL US TODAY
AOL Today on America
Online

AOL WEBOPAEDIA
Webopedia

AOL WHITE PAGES
White Pages

AOL YELLOW PAGES
Yellow Pages

APARTMENT
Real Estate Center, Renting
Area

APARTMENTS.COM
Apartments.com Apartment
Locators

APPAREL
Shop@AOL's Apparel
Department

APPLE BIZ
Apple Business Consortium

APPLE CAFE
Apple Cafe Chat Room

APPLE COMMUNITY
Apple Community Live Area

APPLE COMPUTER
Apple Computer, Inc.

APPLE DIRECTORY
Apples Directory Area

APPLE GUIDE
Applescript

APPLE INFO
Apples Info Center

APPLE UPDATE
Mac System Software
Updates

**APPLIANCE
SUPERSTORE**
AOL Netmarket Appliances

AQUARIUMS
Zoos and Aquariums

AQUARIUS
Horoscopes

ARCHAEOLOGY
Archaeology Forum

ARCHITECTURE
House & Home

ARCHIVE PHOTOS
Archive Photos

ARCHY
Archaeology Forum

ARENA
The Colosseum / Arena

ARFA
American Running and
Fitness Assocation

ARMCHAIR
Extreme Fans

AROMATHERAPY
Aromatherapy

**AROUND THE CLOCK
HELP**
Shopping Helper

AROUND THE HORN
NESN Baseball

ART
Arts and Leisure

ART BELL
Artbell

ARTIST
AOL WorkPlace: Artists &
Galleries Community

ARTISTIC SKATING
Artistic Roller Skating
Miniforum Community

ARTS
Arts and Leisure

ART SHOPPING
Image Exchange
Marketplace

ART STUDIO
Kids Only Art Studio

ASHTON-DRAKE
Collectibles Today

ASIAN
Ethnicity

ASTHMA
Asthma

ASTHMA@THRIVE
Asthma@thrive

ASTROLOGY
Astrology & Divination

ASTROLOGY.NET
iVillage Astrology

ASTRONAUT
Astronauts Wife

ASTRONET
Astronet

ASTRONOMY
Astronomy Club

ASYLUM
Entertainment Asylum

AS YOU WISH
Denvers Mental Health

AT
Antagonist Trivia

A TASTE OF FRANCE
A Taste Of France

A TASTE OF ITALY
Italian Food

**ATHLETE DIRECT
FOOTBALL**
Athlete Direct Football

ATHLETE DIRECT TENNIS
Athlete Direct Tennis

ATHLETICS
Oakland Athletics

ATLAS
Geography & Maps

ATTORNEY
Legal Professionals

AUCTION DEALS
Auction Deals

AUDIOA
Audio Adrenaline

AUDIOBOOK
Shop@AOL's Books & Music
Department

AUDIO BOOK CLUB
Audio Book Club

AUDITORIUM
Today In AOL Live

AUG
User Groups Forum

AUTH
Tony Auth Comic Strip On
AOL.com

AUTHOR
Books Community

AUTHORING TOOLS
Home Page Publishing Tools

AUTHORS
Books Community

AUTISM
Autism

AUTO
AOL Auto Center

AUTO & CLASSIFIEDS
Shop@AOL's Auto &
Classifieds Department

AUTO BUYING
Auto Center Buying Guide

AUTOCAD
Cad Resource Center

AUTO CONNECT
Autoconnect On The Web

AUTO DEALS
Auto Deals

AUTODESK
Autodesk

AUTO ENTHUSIAST
Wheels

AUTOGUY
Get The Scoop On Cars
From Bostons Auto Guy

AUTOMOBILE DEALS
Auto Deals

AUTO SHOP
Shopping Channel Auto
Shop

AUTO SOUND
Consumer Electronics

AUTOWEB.COM
Autoweb.com

AV
AOL Autovantage - New Car

AVALAN EVENTS
Southern California Concert
Connection

AVFORUM
Hobbies: Aviation

AVIATION
Aviation & Aeronautics

AVIATION FORUM
Hobbies: Aviation

AVIS
Car Rental

AVON
Avon

AVON CRUSADE
Avons Awareness Crusade
Online

AVON PREFERRED
Avon Preferred

AW
Welcome To AboutWork

AWRT
American Women in Radio &
Television

B&C
Books and Culture

B&N
Barnes & Noble Booksellers

B5
Babylon 5

BABIES
Babies

BABY BOOMER
Baby Boomers

BACKGAMMON
Worldplay Backgammon

BACKPACKER
Backpacker Magazine

BANKING
Personal Finance: Banks

BARGAIN BOX
Bargain Box

BARNES & NOBLE
Barnes & Noble Booksellers

BARRONS
Barrons Booknotes

BASEBALL
AOL Baseball

BASICS
Learn How To Use AOL And
Your

BCREEK
Blackberry Creek

BEGINNER
Help Desk Area

BEST OF AOL
Best Of AOL

BEST TIPS
AOL Insider Tips

BETA APPLY
Apply to be a Beta Tester

BETTER HEALTH
All Health

BETTER LIVING
Better Living

BH
All Health

BIC MAG
Bicycling Magazine Online

BINGO
Rabbitjacks Casino

BISTRO
International Bistro

BIZWEEK
Business Week

BL
Buddy List

BLACK
Net Noir

BLOCK JUNK MAIL
Junk Mail

BLOOMBERG
Bloomberg

BOOK
Books Community

BOOKCENTRAL
Book And Author Information
And Discussion

BOOKMARK
Favorite Places

BOOKNOTES
Barrons Booknotes

BOOKREPORT
The Book Report

BOOKSTORE
Bookstore

BOXER*JAM
Boxerjam Gameshows

BRODERBUND
The Learning Center
Superstore

BUDDY LIST
Buddy List

BUDDY VIEW
View your Buddy List

BUILD YOUR WEB PAGE
Building Home Pages

BUSINESS
AOL Workplace Channel:
Help With Your Business And
Career

BUSINESS KNOW-HOW
The Business Know-how
Forum

BUSINESS NEWS
Business News Center

BUSINESS SENSE
Business Sense

BUSINESS TIPS
Business Tips

BUSINESS TRAVELER
Business Travel Center

BUSY PARENTS
Busy Parents Club

BYOA
Bring Your Own Access

C
Computing Development
Forum

CAD
CAD Resource Center

CALL AOL
AOL Telephone Support

CAMPING
Parks and Camping

CAMPUS LIFE
Campus Life

CANCEL
Account Cancellation
Requests

CANDIDATE
Election 2000

CAR & DRIVER
Car And Driver Online

CAREER
Your Career

CAREER CENTER
Career Center

CAREER CHANGE
Changing Direction

CAREERFINDER
Careerfinder

CARPAL TUNNEL
Carpal Tunnel Syndrome

CARFINDER
Preview Travel: CarFinder

CARTOON
Cartoon Network

CASTING
The Casting Forum

CASTLES
Castles II

CATARACTS
Cataracts

CATHOLIC
Catholic Community

CB
College Board

CBS NEWS
CBS News

CE
Consumer Electronics

CHANNEL GUIDE
Channel Guide

CHARTER
Charter Schools

CHASE
The Chase Manhattan Bank

CHEERLEADER
Cheerleading Forum

CHIC SIMPLE
Chic Simple From
Shop@AOL

CHILD-SUPPORT
Families Going Through A
Separation Or Divorce

CHILDCARE
Family Living

CHILDRENS TV
Family Entertainment

CHRISTIAN
Christianity Spirituality
Department

CHRONIC PAIN
Chronic Pain

CITI
Citibank

CITIZENS BANK
Citizens Bank

CIVIL WAR
Civil War Forum

CL
Campus Life

CLARIS
Claris Corporation

CLASSES
Online Classroom Class
Schedule

CLASSIFIEDS
ClassifiedsPlus

CLOSEDFUNDS
Closed-End Funds

CLOTHING
Shop@AOL: Apparel
Department

CLUB SINATRA
The Official Sinatra Online
Site

CNET
Cnet.com

CNW
Cartoon Network

COLLEGES
College Prep Area

COMING OUT
Coming Out

COMMON COLD
Common Cold

COMMUNITIES
Lifestyles Communitites

COMPAQ
Compaq

COMP DEAL
Computing Deals

COMPOSERS
Composers Coffeehouse

COMPTON
Comptons Encyclopedia Online

COMPUSTORE
Computer Superstore

COMPUTER CAMP
Computing Camp

COMPUTER CLASS
Computing - Online Classroom

COMPUTER GUIDE
New Computer Users Guide

COMPUTER TIPS
Computing Tips

COMPUTING
AOL Computing Channel

COMPUTING COMMU-NITIES
Computing: Communities

CONCERTS
Concerts & Tours

CONTEST
Contest Area

COURSES
Courses Online

CRESTAR
Crestar Bank

CROSS-COUNTRY
Cross Country Travel Tips

CRUISE CRITIC
Cruise Critic

CRYSTAL BALL
Crystal Ball

CSPAN CLASSROOM
CSpan In The Classroom

CULTURE FINDER
Culture Finder

CURRENCY CONVERTER
Currency Converter

CYBERLAW
Cyberlaw/Cyberlex

CYBERSHOP
Cybershop

CYBERVOW
Love@AOL: Cybervows

DAILY BOOK
Book Of The Week

DAILY DOWNLOAD
Computing - Daily Download

DAILY PRESS
Daily Press

DATABASE
Database Computing Forum

DATE DOC
The Date Doctor

DEAF COMMUNITY
Deaf Community

DEALS & STEALS
Shopping Deals & Steals

DELL
Dell Computer Corporation

DEMOCRAT
Democratic National Party

DEPRESSION
Depression

DEPT 56
Dept56

DESKTOP PUBLISHING
Desktop & Web Publishing Forums

DESTINATIONS
AOL Travel: Destinations

DEV
Computing Development Forum

DIABETES
Diabetes

DICTIONARY
M-W Collegiate Dictionary

DIET
Dieting & Weight Loss

DIGITAL CITY
AOL Local Channel

DILBERT
Dilbert Comics

DINNER
What's For Dinner

DISABILITIES
Conditions & Treatments

DISNEY
The Disney Store

DOCTORS
Doctors And Insurance

DOONESBURY
Doonesbury Comic Strip

DRUGSTORE
Online Pharmarcy

DSL
DSL Field Trial Area

DVDEXPRESS
DVD Express

DYSLEXIA
Dyslexia

E
Entertainment Channel

E!
E! Magazine Online

EA
Entertainment Asylum

EARNINGS
Earnings

EBAY
Ebay Online

EDDIE
Eddie Bauer

EMAIL FINDER
E-Mail Finder

ENCYCLOPEDIA
Encyclopedia

ENTERTAINMENT
Entertainment Channel

ENT NEWS
Entertainment News

ETOY
Etoys

ETRADE
E*trade

EXCEL
Spreadsheet Computing Forum

EXPO
Montreal Expos

EXTRA
Extra Online

FACT-A-DAY
Fact-a-Day

FAMILY
AOL Families Channel

FAO
FAO Schwarz

FARE WARS
Fare Wars

FAST FACTS
AOL Fast Facts

FAVORITE PLACES
Favorite Places

FENG SHUI
Feng Shui

FFBN
Fly Fishing Broadcast Network

FFGF
Free Form Gaming Forum

FFL
Fantasy Football

FHL
Fantasy Hockey

FIDELITY
Fidelity Investments

FILE SEARCH
Download Center

FINANCIAL AID
Education Financial Aid

FINANCIALS
Financials

FIND A CHAT
People Connection

FIND A JOB
Find a Job

FIRST TIME SHOPPER
First Time Shopper

FISHING
Fishing

FLEX MAGAZINE
Flex Magazine

FLIGHT TRACKER
Flight Tracker

FLU
Influenza

FOOD
AOL Food

FOOLS
Motley Fool

FOOTBALL
AOL Pro Football

FOREIGN DICTIONARY
Foreign Dictionary

FRIEND
Sign On A Friend

FTN
Family Travel Network

FTP
File Transfer Protocol(ftp)

FUND
Mutual Fund Center

FUNDING FOCUS
RSP Funding Focus

FUNNIES
Funnies

GALLERY
AOL Hometown: The Gallery
Community Center

GAMES
AOL Games Channel

GARFIELD
Garfield Comic Strip

GATEWAY
Gateway 2000

GAY
Gay & Lesbian

GET HELP NOW
AOL Computing: Get Help
Now

GG
Global Gourmet

GIFT REMINDER
Reminder Service

GIFTS
Gifts And Gadgets

GLOBALNET
International Access

GLOSSARY
Glossary

GODIVA
Godiva Chocolatier

GOLF
AOL Golf

GOOD LIFE
The Good Life

GOVERNING
Governing Magazine

GOVERNMENT
Law & Government

GPF HELP
Member Services Error
Messages

GRAD SCHOOL
Graduate School

GRANDSTAND
AOL Grandstand

GRANT A WISH
Grant A Wish

GRAPHICS
Computing Graphic Arts
Forum

GRATEFUL DEAD
The Grateful Dead Forum

GREETING CARDS
Flowers & Cards

GS SOCCER
AOL Grandstand: Soccer

GUARANTEE
AOL Shopping Guarantee

GUERRILLA FORUM
The Guerrilla Marketing
Forum

HAIR LOSS
Baldness & Hair Loss

HAM RADIO
The Ham Radio Forum

HANES
One Hanes Place

HARDWARE
Computing Hardware Forum

HARLEY
Harley Davidson Cafe

HAWKS
Hawks

HBO
HBO.com

HEADHUNTER
Headhunter

HEALTH
Health Channel

HEALTH & VITAMIN
Health & Vitamin Express

HEALTH INSURANCE
Health Insurance

HEALTHY EATING
Healthy Eating

HEART
Heart & Blood Disorders

HELP
AOL Member Services

HELP CLASS
AOL Help Class

HICKORY
Hickory Farms

HIGHSCHOOL
College Bound: Seniors Only

HIGH SPEED
High Speed Access

HISPANIC
Hispanic Online

HIV
AIDS & HIV

HOBBY
Hobby Central

HOCKEY
AOL Hockey

HOLIDAYS
Holidays @ AOL

HOME
House & Home

HOME PAGE
1-2-3 Publish

HOOVER
Hoover

HOROSCOPES
Horoscopes

HOTEL FINDER
Business Travel Center: Hotels

HOW TO DOWNLOAD
How to Download

HP
Hewlett Packard Forum

HURRICANE
AOL Weather: Hurricanes

HYPERTENSION
Hypertension/High Blood
Pressure

IA
Insomniacs Asylum

IBN
International Business News

IC
Internet Connection

IMAGE SCANNING
Image Scanning Resource
Center

INDIANAPOLIS
Digital City Indianapolis

INDIANS
Cleveland Indians

INDUSTRY NEWS
Industry News

I NEED HELP
Notify AOL

INFLUENCE
Influence Channel

INFO CENTER
Download Info Center

INQUEST
Inquest Magazine

INSIDER
AOL Insider Tips

INTEREST PROFILES
AOL Interest Profiles

INTERESTS
AOL Interests Channel

INTERNATIONAL
AOL International Channel

INTERNATIONAL GRANDSTAND
AOL International: Grandstand

INTERNATIONAL LOVE
Passport to Love

INTERNET
Internet Connection

INTL
AOL International Channel

INTL BUSINESS
International Business

INTL CULTURE
International Cultures

INTL FUN
International Fun & Games

INTL NEWS
International News

INTL TRAVEL
International Travel

INTOON
Mike Keefe Editorial Cartoons

INVESTING
Personal Finance: Investing Forums

INVESTING BASICS
Investing Basics

IQVC
iQVC

ISDN
Future Connectivity Options

IVILLAGE
Ivillage

JAVA
Java Forum

JAYS
Toronto Blue Jays

JAZZ
Jazz

JCP
JCPenney

JENX
JenX: A Twentysomething Perspective

JEWISH
Jewish Community Online

JUNK MAIL
Junk Mail

KAUFMANN
The Kaufmann Fund

KEYWORD
Keyword List

KIDS
Kids Only Channel

KIDS BIZ
Kids Biz

KIDS DICTIONARY
Kids Dictionary

KO HELP
Kids Only Help

KO PARENT
Kids Only Feedback

KO SEARCH
Kids Only Search

LATE SHOW
The Late Show Online

LATINONET
Latinonet

LAW
Law & Government

LAW RESOURCES
Legal Resources

LEADERS
AOL Community Leaders

LEARN AUTO AOL
Learn Automatic AOL

LEARN CHAT
Learn People Connection

LEARN DOWNLOAD
Learn Downloading

LEARN EMAIL
Learn E-Mail

LEARN GETTING AROUND
Learn Getting Around

LEARN KEYWORD
Learn Keywords

LEARN PARENT
Learn Parental Controls

LEARN QUOTES
Learn Quotes

LESBIAN
Gay & Lesbian

LIFESTAGES
Personal Finance: Advice & Planning

LIFESTYLES
AOL Lifestyles Channel

LIFETIME
Lifetime Television For Women

LILLIAN
Lillian Vernon

LIVE
Today In AOL Live

LIVING WILL
Wills

LOAN CENTER
Loan Center

LOCAL
AOL Local Channel

LOCAL NEWS
AOL News: Local

LOTTERY
Lottery

LOVE@AOL
Love@AOL

MAC
Macintosh Computing & Software

MAIL CENTER
Post Office

MAIL CONTROLS
Mail Controls

MAIL EXTRAS
Mail Extras

MANIC
Bipolar Disorder/Manic Depression

MARKETDAY
AOL Marketday

MARKETING PREFS
Marketing And Telephone Preferences

MARKET NEWS CENTER
Market News Center

MAYO
Mayo Clinic Database Information

MB CD
Music Boulevard

MCAFEE
Mcafee Associates

MCO
Military City Online

MEDICAL DICTIONARY
Medical Dictionary

MEMBER OPINIONS
AOL Travel: Member Opinions

MEMBER PERKS
AOL Member Perks

MEMBERS
AOL Member Directory

MEMPHIS
Digital City Memphis

MENOPAUSE
Menopause

MHM
Members Helping Members

MISS AMERICA
Here She Is... Miss America!

MMA
Metropolitan Museum Of Art

MNC
Market News Center

MO
Moms Online

MODEM HELP
Modem Help

MONTESSORI
Montessori Education

MOS
Mac Operating System
Forum

MOVIEFONE
Local Showtimes And Movie
Tickets

MOVIE SHOWTIMES
Local Movie Info

MS ACCESS
Microsoft Access Resource
Center - Us

MTV
MTV Online

MUSIC BLVD
Music Boulevard

MUSICSPACE
MusicSpace

MY BOARDS
Manage Your Message
Boards

MY FTP SPACE
FTP Space

MY HOMEPAGE
Personal Publisher

MY PORTFOLIOS
Portfolios

NAMES
Screen Names

NASA
National Space Society

NEA
NEA Online

NEIGHBORHOOD
AOL Neighborhood Watch

NETFIND
AOL Search

NETMAIL
AOL Netmail

NETSCAPE
Netscape Navigator

NEW
What's New on AOL

NEW PC
New Computer Users Guide

NEWS
AOL News Channel

NEWS SEARCH
Search the News

NEWSGROUPS
Internet Newsgroups

NEWSGROUP SCOOP
Newsgroup Scoop

NEWSLETTERS
Newsletters

NEWSSTAND
The Newsstand

NEW YORK
Digital City New York

NFL
AOL Pro Football

NHL
AOL Hockey

NOTIFY AOL
Notify AOL

NTN
NTN Trivia

NUL
National Urban League

NYO
New York Observer

NYT
New York Times Online

ODDBOX
Odd Box.com

OFFICE DEPOT
Office Depot

OFFICEMAX
Officemax

ONE HANES PLACE
One Hanes Place

ONLINE INVESTOR
Online Investor

ONLINE PSYCH
Online Psych

ONLINE WEDDINGS
Love@AOL Cybervows

ONLY ON AOL
Only On AOL

ONQ
onQ - Gay and Lesbian
Community Forum

ON THE LINE
On The Line - Teen Channel
Chat

OPERATING SYSTEMS
The Operating Systems Area

OUT ONQ
onQ: Coming Out

OUTDOOR ADVENTURE
Outdoor Adventure Online

OUTDOORFUN
Outdoor Fun

OUTDOORS
Great Outdoors

OUTDOOR TRAVEL
Adventure And Outdoor
Travel Forum

OWL
Owl Magazine

OXFORD
Oxford Health Plans

OYXGEN
Oxygen: Womens Forums

PAPERSTUDIO
Paperstudio.com

PARENTAL CONTROLS
Parental Controls

PARENTING
Families Main Screen

PARENT SOUP
Parent Soup Main Screen

PARKS
Americas Parks

PARLOR
The Game Parlor

PASSWORD
Change Your Password

PC HELP
Computing PC Help Area

PC SOUND
Pc Music & Sound Forum

PDA
Personal Digital Assistants
Forum

PEOPLE
People Magazine

PEOPLE CONNECTION
People Connection

PERKS
AOL Member Perks

PERSONAL FINANCE
Personal Finance Channel

PET CARE
Pet Care Forum

PETERSONS
Petersons Online

PETS
Pets

PET WAREHOUSE
Pet Warehouse

PF
AOL Personal Finance

PHILADELPHIA
Digital City Philadelphia

PHOENIX
Digital City Phoenix

PICTURE HELP
You've Got Pictures Help

PICTURES
You've Got Pictures

PITTSBURGH
Digital City Pittsburgh

PLANET OUT
Planet Out

PLANET RX
Planet RX Online Pharmacy

PLANO STAR COURIER
Plano Star Courier

PLAY-BY-MAIL
Play-by-mail Forum

PLAYBILL
Playbill Online

PNO
Planet Out

POKEMON
Kids Only Pokemon Special

POPULAR PHOTOGRAPHY
Popular Photography

POPULAR SCIENCE
Popular Science

PORTFOLIOS
Stock Portfolio

POSTMASTER
AOL Postmaster

POST OFFICE
AOL Mail Center

POWERTOOLS
Powertools For AOL By Bps Software

PREFERRED MAIL
Preferred Mail

PREFERENCES
My AOL

PREMIERE
Premiere Magazine Online

PREVIEW TRAVEL
Preview Travel

PRICING PLANS
New Pricing Plans

PRINTER
Printer Resource Center

PRODUCTIVITY
Productivity Forum

PROFILE
Change Profile

PROGRAMMER U
Programmer University

PROGRAMMING
Computing Development Forum

PULSE
Pulse Magazine Online

PURINA
Ralston Purina Home Page

PUZZLES
Puzzle Zone: Interactive Puzzles

QUARTERLY REVIEW
Mutual Fund Quarterly Review

QUICKEN
Quicken Financial Network

QUICKSTART
AOL New Members Quick Start

QUILL
Quill In AOL Shopping

RABBITJACKS
Rabbitjacks Casino

RACING
Auto Racing

RAILROADING
Model Planes/trains

RANDOM
Keyword Roulette!

READ MY BOARDS
Manage Your Message Boards

REAL ESTATE
AOL Personal Finance: Real Estate

RECIPES
Whats For Dinner

REDBOOK
Hearst Home Arts Redbook Magazine

REFUND
AOL Access Refund Policy

RELIGION
Religion & Beliefs Channel

REMINDER
Reminder Service

RESEARCH
Research And Learn

RESERVATIONS
AOL Travel Reservation Center

RESUME
Post A Resume Feature Package

ROAD & TRACK
Road & Track Online

ROADMAPS
Maps And Directions

ROCK AND ROLL
Rock And Roll

ROOTS
Genealogy Forum

ROSIE
Rosie O'Donnell Online

ROYALTY
Royalty Forum

RPG
Roleplaying Games Forum

RSP FUNDING
RSP Funding Focus

SAGE
Sage Personal Finance Investing

SAILING
Boating and Sailing Forum

SALON
Salon Magazine

SBA
US Small Business Administration

SCANNING
Image Scanning Resource C

SCIFI CHANNEL
The Scifi Channel

SCOREBOARD
AOL Sports Scoreboards

SCOUTS
Scouting

SCREEN NAMES
Screen Names

SCUBA
AOL Scuba Forum

SCUDDER
Scudder Investments

SEARS
Wishbook.com

SENIORGOLFER
Senior Golfer

SENIORS HEALTH
Seniors Health

SERVICE MERCHANDISE
Service Merchandise

SEVENTEEN
Seventeen Online

SEWING
Sewing

SHARPER IMAGE
Sharper Image

SHEET MUSIC PLUS
Sheet Music Plus Online

SHORTHAND
Mail Extras

SHOWTIMES
Local Showtimes And Movie Tickets

SIGN ON AFRIEND
Sign On A Friend

SIM
The Simming Forum

SKI
Skiing

SKINSTORE.COM
Skinstore.com In AOL Shopping

SMITHSONIAN
Smithsonian Online

SOAP OPERA DIGEST
Soap Opera Digest

SOFTWARE
Download Software

SOFTWARE STORE
AOL Store - Computer

SOFTWARE SUPER-STORE
AOL Nm Computers & Software

SOHO
Home Office Computing Magazine

SONGS
Music

SOUND
Pc Music & Sound Forum

SPACE
National Space Society

SPACE WARS
Space Wars Sim Forum

SPADES
Play Spades

SPAM
E-Mail Spam Information

SPEAK OUT
AOL News: Speak Out

SPELLING
M-W Collegiate Dictionary

SPIRITUALITY
Spirituality

SPORTS
AOL Sports Channel

SPORTS CHAT
Sports Chat

SPORTS INVESTOR
What Smart Sports Fans Do
On AOL

SPORTS LIBRARIES
Sports Libraries

SPORTS LIVE
Sports Live

SPORTS NEWS
Sports News Front Page

STAMPS
Stamp Collecting

**STARTING YOUR
BUSINESS**
Getting Started

STARTUP
Start-Up Businesses

STOCK INDICES
Stock Indices Part Of Market
News

STOCK REPORTS
Stock Reports

STOCKS
Quotes & Portfolio

STRATEGIES
The Business Know-how
Forum

STREP THROAT
Strep Throat

STRESS
Emotional Well-being

STRIKE-A-MATCH
Play Strike A Match

SUGGESTIONS
Suggestion Boxes

SUPERMAN
DC Comics

SUPERSTORE
Computer Superstore

SURFLINK
Surflink

SYNONYMS
Merriam-Webster Thesaurus

SYSTEM RESPONSE
System Response Report

TAX
Tax Forum

TECH LIVE
Member Services

TECH SUPPORT
Member Services

TERMS OF SERVICE
Terms Of Service

THE ASYLUM
Entertainment Asylum

THEATER
Arts And Leisure

THE MOTLEY FOOL
Motley Fool

THE NEW YORK TIMES
New York Times Online

THE POST
New York Post

THESAURUS
Merriam-Webster Thesaurus

THE SHARPER IMAGE
Sharper Image

THE WALL
The Wall

THINGS TO DO
Things To Do

THIRD AGE
Third Age

THRIVE
Thrive@AOL

TIME FOR KIDS
Time For Kids

TIMER
Online Clock

TIMES
New York Times Online

TNC
The Nature Conservancy

TODAY IN HEALTH
Today in Health

TODAYS NEWS
Todays News

TOOLS & REFERENCE
Tools & Reference

TOOTH DECAY
Tooth Decay & Cavities

TOS SPAM
Junk Mail

TOTN
National Public Radio
Outreach

TOUR DATES
Concerts & Tours

TOUR DE FRANCE
Tour De France

TOWER
Tower Records

TO YOUR HEALTH
To Your Health Newsletter

TOY S RUS
Toys 'R' Us

TPO
Time - Warners Teen People
Magazine Online

TP REALITYCHECK
Teen People: Reality Check

TP SHOUTOUT
Teen People: Virtual
Dedicator

TP SS
Teen People: Stars & Stuff

TRACK
Road & Track Online

TRANSWORLD
Transworld Snowboarding

TRAVEL
Travel Channel

**TRAVEL MESSAGE-
BOARDS**
Travel Messages & Chat

TRAVEL NEWS
Travel News & Features
Department

TRAVEL NEWSLETTER
Travel Channel Newsletter

TRAVEL ONQ
Travel onQ

TRAVEL OPINIONS
Travel News & Features
Department

TRIBUNE
Chicago Tribune

TRIVIA
Trivia

TROY
Digital City Albany

TRUCKS
AOL Auto Center

TRUE TALES
True Tales

TSHIRT
Shop@AOL's Apparel
Department

TSN
The Sporting News

TTALK
Teachers Forum

TUBERCULOSIS
Tuberculosis

TUTORIAL
Quick Start: A Guide To New
Members

TV LAND
Nick At Nite

TV SATIRES
TV Spoofs

TV SHOWS
TV Shows

TWANG
Twang This!

TWOLVES
Timberwolves

TWS
Transworld Snowboarding

TY
Beanie Babies

TY BEANIE BABIES
Beanie Babies

UCAOL
Univ of California Extension

UPGRADE
The Latest AOL Software

USER GROUPS
User Groups Forum

US WORLD
Us World News

UTAH
Utah Forum

V.90
V.90 Connections

VACATIONS
Travel

VANGUARD
Vanguard Funds

VEGATARIAN
Vegatarians Online

VIEWERS
Recommended Viewers

VIRUS
Virus Information

VIRUS INFO
AOL Virus Info Area

WARCRAFT
Warcraft II

WASHINGTON
Digital City Washington

WATCHES
Shop@AOL's Apparel
Department

WAV
Music & Sound Software

WB KIDS
Kids Wb! Online

WB NET
The WB Network

WEATHER
Local Weather Reports

WEATHER.COM
Weather.com Website

WEATHER CHANNEL
The Weather Channel

WEB
World Wide Web

WEB BUSINESS
Doing Business Online

WEB CENTER
AOL.com Web Centers

WEB HELP
Member Services: Net Help

WEB HOST
Verio, Inc.

**WEB PAGE PUBLISHING
TOOLS**
Home Page Publishing Tools

WEB PAGES
Hometown AOL

WEB PUBLISHING
Building Home Pages

WEB QUICKSTART
World Wide Web Features

**WEBSTERS MEDICAL
DICTIONARY**
Medical Dictionary

WEB TUTORIAL
Web Tutorials

WEDDING
Weddings

WEDDING PLANNER
Digital City Wedding
Handbook

WEEKLY FILES
New Files

WEIGHT
Dieting & Weight Loss

WELCOME
Welcome Screen

WHATS NEW
Whats Hot / Whats New On
AOL

WHEELS
Wheels

WHITE HOUSE
Investigating the President

WHITE PAGES
White Pages

WINDOWS 95
Windows 95 Computing
Forum

WINDOWS 98
Windows 98 Computing
Forum

WINDOWS UPGRADE
Windows 98 Upgrade

WINDOW TIPS
Computing Tips

WINE & DINE ONLINE
Food and Drink Network

WIN FORUM
Windows Forum

WIN MAG
Windows Magazine

WIN NT
Windows NT Computing
Forum

WINSOCK
Winsock Information Area

WIN ZIP
Utility Software

WIRED
Wired Magazine

WIRELESS
Wireless Communication

WOMANS DAY
Womans Day

WOMEN
Womens Channel

WORK FUN
The Lighter Side Of Work

WORKING WEB
Your Business: Working The
Web

WORKOUT
AOL Fitness

WORKPLACE
AOL Workplace Channel:
Help With Your Business And
Career

WORLD CRISIS
World Crisis Network

WORLDLY INVESTOR
Worldly Investor

WORLDPLAY
Worldplay Games

WORLD WIDE WEB
World Wide Web

WORTH
Worth Magazine

WRESTLING
Wrestling

WRITER
The Writers Club

**WRITERS CLUB
MARKETPLACE**
Writers Club Marketplace

WRITERS RESOURCE
Grammar And Style

WRITING
Reading & Writing

WWF
World Wrestling Federation

WWW
World Wide Web

WWW HELP
Member Services: Net Help

X-FILES
X Files Area

XTREME
Xtreme Games

Y2K
Year 2000

Y2K SHOP
Millennium Store

Y2K TRAVEL
Millennium Travel

YACHTING
Boating Selections

YEAR 2000
Year 2000

YELLOW PAGES
Yellow Pages

YGP
You've Got Pictures

YGP HELP
Help for You've Got Pictures

YOUR BUSINESS
Your Business

YOUR CAREER
Your Career

YOUR CHURCH
Your Church

YOUR INDUSTRIES
Professional Forums

YOUR JOB
Your Career

YOUR MONEY
Personal Finance: Advice &
Planning

YOUR WEB PAGE
Learn How to Create Your
Web Page

YOUTH NET
Youth Net

YOUTH TECH
Youth Tech

YOUVE GOT PICTURES
You've Got Pictures

YP
Yellow Pages

ZEALOT
Zealot: Sci-fi and Fantasy Fun

ZIP
Utility Software

ZIP CODE
Zip Code Directory

ZOO
Zoos and Aquariums

Glossary

800 and 888 numbers

America Online provides 800 and 888 numbers, at a modest hourly rate, to U.S. and Canadian members who are without local access numbers. Additional information on these numbers is at Keyword: **Access**. For more information on their use, see Appendix A. See also *access number* and *AOLNET*.

A

access number

A phone number (usually local) your modem uses to access America Online. To find an access number online, go to Keyword: **Access**. If you aren't able to sign on to America Online, see Appendix A. See also *800 and 888 numbers*, and *AOLNET*.

Address

1. An e-mail address that allows you to send an e-mail to anyone on America Online or anywhere on the Internet. You can look up addresses for America Online members at Keyword: **Members**, and addresses for Internet denizens at various places on the World Wide Web (World Wide Web). More information is available in Chapter 5.

2. A location address for information on America Online or the Web, which is better known as an URL. An example of an address on America Online is `aol://1722:help`, which takes you to Member Services when entered into the keyword window. On the Web, the address `http://members.aol.com/jennifer/` takes you to Jennifer's home page. See also *e-mail*, *e-mail address*, *Internet*, *URL*, and *World Wide Web*.

Address Book

An AOL software feature that allows you to store e-mail addresses for easy access. Your Address Book may be created, edited, or used through the Address Book icon available when composing mail. You can also create or edit them with the Edit Address Book or Address Book option under the Mail Center button on the toolbar. See Chapter 5.

America Online, Inc. (AOL)

The nation's leading online service, headquartered in Virginia. Founded in 1985 and formerly known as Quantum Computer Services, America Online has grown rapidly in both size and scope. America Online has over 18 million members and hundreds of alliances with major companies. America Online's stock exchange symbol is AOL. To contact America Online headquarters, call 1-703-448-8700 or use 1-800-827-6364 to speak to a Member Services representative. Contrast with *CompuServe*, *Microsoft Network*, and *Prodigy*.

AOL

Abbreviation for America Online, Inc. Occasionally abbreviated as AO. See also *America Online, Inc.*

AOL Instant Messenger (AIM)

Software that allows people with Internet accounts to send and receive Instant Messages from America Online members. Once a person has downloaded, installed, and registered the AOL Instant Messenger software, America Online members can add that person to their Buddy List and send Instant Messages to them. More information is available online at Keyword: **AIM**. See also *IM*.

AOL Mail

A new member of the AOL family that lets Palm organizer owners to check their AOL e-mail. AOL Mail connects members directly to AOL using their regular screen names and passwords. Using AOL's global network of access numbers, AOL Mail allows members to connect with the service from just about anywhere. More information is available at Keyword: **AOL Mail**. See also *PDA*.

AOL Radio

An upcoming feature on America Online similar to Progressive Network's RealAudio. AOL Radio will allow members to listen to real-time broadcasts of news, music, and advertisements.

AOL Search

America Online's exclusive Internet directory and search service available at http://www.aol.com or at Keyword: **AOL Search**. It was created through America Online's partnership with Excite, Inc. See Chapter 14 for more information. Formerly known as AOL NetFind.

AOL Slideshow

An America Online exclusive presentation consisting of a series of images, animation, and sound. AOL Slideshows takes advantage of streaming technology to begin playback without having to wait for the entire slideshow to download. Slideshows are only available for AOL software version 3.0 or later. See Keyword: **Slideshows** for examples and more information.

AOL.com

America Online's home page on the Web located at http://www.aol.com.

AOLNET

America Online's own packet-switching network that provides members with up to 56,600 bps local access numbers. For members who do not have a local access number, there is also an 800 number that is more affordable than most long-distance fees. Another alternative is to sign on to America Online through an Internet or ISP (Internet service provider) connection. To find AOLNET local access numbers, go to Keyword: **AOLNET**. See also *800 and 888 numbers, access number,* and *packet-switching network.*

archive

1. A file that has been compressed with file compression software. See also *file, file compression, WinZip,* and *StuffIt.*

2. A file that contains message board postings that may be of value, but have been removed from a message board due to their age, inactivity of topic, or lack of message board space. These messages are usually bundled into one document and placed in a file library for retrieval later. See also *file* and *library*.

attached file

A file that hitches a ride with e-mail. Whether the file is text, sound, or pictures, it is said to be attached if it has been included with the e-mail for separate downloading by the recipient (whether addressed directly, carbon copied, or blind carbon copied). E-mail that is forwarded will retain any attached files as well. Files are usually attached because the information that they contain is either too long to be sent in the body of regular e-mail or is impossible to send via e-mail, such as with software programs. Multiple files may be attached by compressing the files into one archive and attaching the archive to the piece of e-mail with the Attach File icon. More information is available in Chapter 6. See also *archive*, *download*, *e-mail*, and *file*.

auditorium

Auditoriums are specially equipped online "rooms" that allow large groups of America Online members to meet in a structured setting. More information on auditoriums can be found at Keyword: **AOL Live** or Chapter 8. Contrast with *chat room*.

Automatic AOL (Auto AOL)

An automated feature that can send and receive your e-mail and files, as well as receive newsgroup postings. Auto AOL can be set up to run at any time, including while you are online. It is accessible under your Mail menu. More information is available in Chapter 7 and Chapter 10. See also *e-mail*, *file*, and *newsgroup*.

B

baud rate

A unit for measuring the speed of data transmission. Technically, baud rates refer to the number of times the communications line changes states each second. Strictly speaking, baud and bits per second (bps) are not identical measurements, but most nontechnical people use the terms interchangeably. See also *bps* and *V.90*.

beta test

A period in a new product or service's development designed to discover problems (or "bugs") prior to its release to the general public. America Online often invites members to beta test its new software. If you are interested in beta testing AOL software, you may be able to apply at Keyword: **Beta Apply**. See also *bug*.

blind courtesy copy (bcc)

A feature of the America Online e-mail system that allows you to send e-mail to a member or members without anyone other than you being aware of it. See Chapter 6 for more information. See also *e-mail*; contrast with *courtesy copy*.

board

An abbreviated reference to a message board or bulletin board service (BBS). See also *message board*.

boolean search

A search that uses logical operators from boolean algebra to narrow the number of matches. For example, a search in the classifieds for "car" would yield many matches, but not exactly what you want. A search for "car and brown and (Firebird or TransAm)" would help you find exactly what you are looking for. Most searches on America Online are boolean searches and use the following boolean operators: *and*, *or*, *not*.

bounce

Something that is returned, such as e-mail. For example, e-mail sent to recipients outside America Online may bounce and never make it to its intended destination, especially if it was not addressed correctly. Sometimes members who are disconnected will refer to themselves as bounced. See also *e-mail*.

bps (bits per second)

A method of measuring data transmission speed. Currently, speeds up to 56K are supported on America Online (see Keyword: **AOLNET** for more information). See also *baud* and *V.90*.

browser

A component of your AOL software that allows you to access the World Wide Web. See also *favorite place*, *Internet*, *page*, *site*, and *World Wide Web*.

Buddy List

A special list that stores your "buddies" (screen names of friends, family members, coworkers, and so on) and informs you when they sign on or off America Online. You add (or remove) buddies yourself, and can define several groups of buddies as you like. See also *buddy* and *invitation*.

bug

A problem or glitch in a product, be it software or hardware. A bug may be referred to jokingly as a "feature." You can report a problem with AOL software or services by going to Keyword: **Help**, clicking Error Messages, and clicking the Ask The Staff button.

C

cache

A portion of a data storage device, RAM, or processor set aside to temporarily hold recently accessed or frequently accessed information. By saving the information locally, performance is improved because it is quicker to receive the information from the cache than from the original source. See Appendix B for details on resizing and emptying your cache.

channel

This is the broadest category of information into which America Online organizes its content. See Keyword: **Channels** for an interactive list or **Channel Guide** for listings of the areas within each channel. See Chapters 12 and 13 for a description of AOL's Channels.

chat

To engage in real-time communications with other members. America Online members that are online at the same time may chat with each other in a number of ways: Instant Messages (IMs), chat/conference rooms, and auditoriums. Chatting provides immediate feedback from others; detailed discussions are better suited toward message boards, and lengthy personal issues are best dealt with in e-mail if a member isn't currently online. Chapter 8 has more information on chatting. See also *IM*, *chat room*, and *auditorium*; contrast with *message board* and *e-mail*.

chat room

An online area where members may meet to communicate and interact with others. There are two kinds of chat areas: public and private. Public chat areas can be found in the People Connection area (Keyword: **People**) or in the many forums around America Online (see Keyword: **AOL Live** for schedules). See Chapter 8 for more information. See also *private room*, *chat*, *host*, *TOS*, and *People Connection*; contrast with *auditorium*.

chat sounds

Sounds played in chat areas. You can play and broadcast sounds to others in chat areas by typing {**S** <*sound*>} (<*sound*> refers to the name of the sound you wish to play) and pressing Enter. For example, {S Welcome} will play America Online's "Welcome" sound in a chat area. See also *chat room* and *library*.

Community Leader

America Online members who volunteer in the various forums and areas online. They usually participate from their homes, not America Online headquarters; hence they have been known as *remote staff* in the past. They serve as Guides, Hosts, Forum leaders/assistants/consultants, and so on. To learn more, see Keyword: **Leaders**. See also *host*.

compression

See *file compression*.

CompuServe

A large established commercial online service now owned by America Online. information is available at Keyword: **CS**. Contrast with *America Online*, *Microsoft Network*, and *Prodigy*.

courtesy copy (cc)

A feature of the America Online e-mail system that allows you to address e-mail to a member for whom the e-mail is not directly intended or is of secondary interest. The primary addressee(s) are aware that the copy was made, similar to the carbon copy convention used in business correspondence. As such, the members copied are not usually expected to reply. See also *e-mail*; contrast with *blind courtesy copy*.

Customer Relations

The number for America Online's Customer Relations Hotline is 1-800-827-6364. The billing and technical assistance departments are open 24 hours a day. The Terms of Service, Community Action Team, and screen name departments are open 9 a.m. to 12 a.m. Eastern time, seven days a week.

D

database

A collection of information, stored and organized for easy searching. A database can refer to something as simple as a well-sorted filing cabinet, but today most databases reside on computers because they offer better access. Databases are located all over America Online, with a prominent example being the Member Directory (Keyword: **Members**). See the AOL Research & Learn channel (Keyword: **Research**) for a large collection of databases. See also *AOL Search*, *boolean search*, *Member Directory*, and *searchable*.

Delete

An America Online e-mail system feature that allows you to permanently remove a piece of mail from any and all of your mailboxes. The Delete feature is useful for removing unneeded mail from your Old Mail box. Do not confuse this feature with the Unsend option, which will remove mail you've sent from the recipient's mailbox. Chapter 5 contains more information. See also *e-mail* and *status*; contrast with *Unsend*.

domain

Used in Internet addresses and analogous to a city in a postal address. In e-mail addresses, usually everything to the right of the @ symbol is referred to as the domain. For example, the domain name for America Online member addresses is *aol.com*. See also *address*, *e-mail*, *e-mail address*, and *Internet*.

download

The transfer of information stored on a remote computer to a storage device on your personal computer. This information can come from America Online via its file libraries, or from other America Online members via attached files in e-mail. Usually, downloads are files intended for review once you're offline. More information on downloading is available in Chapter 10. See also *archive*, *attached file*, *download count*, *Download Manager*, *FileGrabber*, and *library*.

download count

The download count refers to the number of times a file has been downloaded. This is often used as a gauge of the file's popularity. While this may not be too significant for a new upload, it is a good indication of the popularity of files that have been around for

a while. More information is available in Chapter 10. See also *file*, *library*, and *download*.

Download Manager

An AOL software feature that allows you to keep a queue of files to download at a later time. You can even set up your software to automatically sign off when your download session is complete. You can schedule your software to sign on and grab files listed in the queue at times you specify. See Chapter 10 for more information. See also *Automatic AOL, download, file,* and *Personal Filing Cabinet*.

E

e-mail

Short for electronic mail. One of the most popular features of online services, e-mail allows you to send private communications electronically from one person to another. E-mail is usually much faster and easier to send than ordinary mail; the shortcomings are that not everyone has an e-mail address to write to and your mail resides in electronic form on a computer system, although e-mail is considered as private and inviolable as regular U.S. Mail. See Keyword: **Mail Center** or Chapters 5, 6, and 7 for more information. See also *attached file, blind courtesy copy, courtesy copy, Delete, e-mail address, gateway, Ignore, Keep As New, Personal Filing Cabinet, return receipt* and *status*; contrast with *message* and *IM*.

e-mail address

A cyberspace mailbox. On America Online, your e-mail address is simply your screen name; for folks outside America Online, your address is your screen name with

@aol.com after it. For example, if our friend Tracy wants to e-mail us from her Internet account, she can reach us as *jenniferanddave@aol.com*. See also *address*, *e-mail*, and *screen name*.

emoticon

Symbols consisting of characters found on any keyboard that are used to give and gain insight into emotional states. For example, the symbol :) is a smile — just tilt your head to the left and you'll see the : (eyes) and the) (smile). The online community has invented countless variations to bring plain text to life, and you'll see emoticons used everywhere from chat rooms to e-mail. Emoticons, like emotions, are more popular in "face-to-face" chat. Some people consider them unprofessional or overly cute in correspondence. Regardless, they are one of the best methods of effective communication online. Emoticons may also be referred to as smileys, and collectively with other chat devices as shorthands.

encryption

The manipulation of data in order to prevent any but the intended recipient from reading that data. There are many types of data encryption, and they are the basis of network security.

ET (EST or EDT)

Abbreviation for eastern time. Most times are given in this format, as America Online is headquartered in this time zone.

F

FAQ

Short for Frequently Asked Questions. FAQs may take the form of an informational file containing questions and answers to common concerns/issues. These are used to answer questions that are brought up often in message boards or discussions. These files may be stored online in an article or archived in a file library. See also *message board* and *library*.

favorite place

A feature that allows you to "mark" America Online and World Wide Web sites you'd like to return to later. These favorite places are stored in your Favorite Places list. Any World Wide Web site can be made a favorite place, as well as any America Online window with a red heart in the upper-right corner of the window. See Chapter 3 for more details.

file

Any amount of information that is grouped together on a computer as one unit. On America Online, a file can be anything from text to sounds and can be transferred to and from your computer via America Online. Collections of files are available in libraries for downloading, and files may be attached to e-mail. See also *download*, *library*, and *software file*.

file compression

A programming technique by which files can be reduced in size without changing their content. Files are usually compressed so that they take up less storage space, can be transferred quicker, and/or can be bundled with others. Files must be decompressed before they can be used, but the AOL software can be set to automatically decompress most files (check your Preferences). More information is available in Chapter 10. See also *file*, *download*, *Stuffit*, and *WinZip*.

file library

See *library*.

File Transfer Protocol

See *FTP*.

forum

A place online where members with similar interests may find valuable information, exchange ideas, share files, and get help on a particular area of interest. Forums (also known simply as areas or clubs) are found everywhere online, represent almost every interest under the sun, and usually offer message boards, articles, chat rooms, and libraries, all organized and accessible by a keyword. See also *keyword*.

FTP

Abbreviation for File Transfer Protocol. A method of transferring files to and from a computer that is connected to the Internet. America Online offers FTP access via the Keyword: **FTP**, as well as personal FTP sites at Keyword: **My Place**. More information is available in Chapter 10. See also *Internet*, *World Wide Web*, and *home page*; contrast with *library*.

G

GIF (Graphic Interchange Format)

A type of graphic file that can be read by most platforms; the electronic version of photographs. GIFs can be viewed with your AOL software or with a GIF viewer utility, which are located at Keyword: **Viewers**.

Gopher

A feature of the Internet that allows you to browse huge amounts of information. The term implies that it will "go-pher" you to

retrieve information. It also refers to the way in which you "tunnel" through the various menus, much like a gopher would. See also *WAIS* and *Internet*; contrast with *newsgroup* and *World Wide Web*.

GPF

Abbreviation for General Protection Fault. If you get a GPF error, it means that Windows (or a Windows application) has attempted to access memory that has not been allocated for its use. GPFs are the scourge of Windows AOL software everywhere. If you experience a GPF while using Windows AOL software, write down the exact error message, then go to Keyword: **GPF** help for assistance. See also *bug*.

H

hacker

Hackers are self-taught computer gurus who take an unholy delight in discovering the well-hidden secrets of computer systems. Blighted by a bad reputation of late, hackers are not necessarily those who intend harm or damage. There are those, however, who feed upon the pain inflicted by viruses. For more information, see Chapter 2. See also *virus*.

header

The information at the top (or bottom) of e-mail received from the Internet, which contains, among other things, the message originator, date, and time. Headers can also be found in newsgroup postings. See also *e-mail*, *Internet*, and *newsgroup*.

history

In the context of AOL software version 4.0 and 5.0, this refers to the last 16 to 25 places you visited. This history list is found under the small arrow next to the keyword-entry box on the toolbar. You can clear your history list in your Toolbar preferences, described in Appendix B. More information on using the history list is available in Chapter 3. See also *toolbar.*

home page

1. The first "page" in a World Wide Web site.

2. Your own page on the Web. Every member on America Online can now create his or her own home page — see Keyword: **My Home Page**.

3. The page you go to when you first enter the Web.

See also *browser, favorite place, page, site, URL,* and *World Wide Web.*

host

1. The America Online computer system.

2. An AOL community leader who facilitates discussion in chat rooms. These are usually chat-fluent, personable individuals with particular expertise in a topic. See also *chat room.*

html

Acronym for Hypertext Markup Language. This is the language used in creating most Web pages and is interpreted by the AOL Web browser to display those pages.

http

Acronym for Hypertext Transport Protocol.

I

icon

A graphic image of a recognizable object or action that leads to somewhere or initiates a process. For example, the icons in the Compose Mail window may lead you to the Address Book, allow you to attach a file, send the mail, or look up help. Icons are activated by clicking on them with a mouse; some may even be used with keyboard shortcuts. More information is available in Chapter 3. See also *keyboard shortcuts.*

Ignore

1. A way of blocking a member's chat from your view in a chat/conference room window. Ignore is most useful when the chat of another member becomes disruptive in the chat room. Note that the Ignore button does not block or ignore IMs from a member — it only blocks the text from your own view in a chat or conference room. For details, see Chapter 8.

2. An AOL software e-mail system feature that allows you to ignore mail in your New Mail box, causing it to be moved to your Old Mail box without having to read it first. To use, simply select and highlight the piece of mail you wish to ignore in your New Mail box and then click on the Ignore button at the bottom of the window. Mail you have ignored without reading first will appear as "(ignored)" in the Status box. See also *e-mail* and *status.*

IM (Instant Message)

America Online's equivalent of passing notes to another person during a meeting, as opposed to speaking up in the room (chat) or writing out a letter or memo (e-mail). Instant Messages (IMs) may be exchanged between two America Online members signed on at the same time and are useful for conducting conversations when a chat room isn't appropriate, available, or practical. For details, see Chapter 8. Internet users can also send and receive Instant Messages if they download and install the free AOL Instant Messenger program (see Keyword: **AIM**).

insertion point

The blinking vertical line in a document marking the place where text is being edited. The insertion point may be navigated through a document with either the mouse or the arrow keys. Also called a "cursor."

Instant Messenger

See *AOL Instant Messenger*.

Internet

The mother of all networks is not an online service itself, but rather serves to interconnect worldwide computer systems and networks. The Internet, originally operated by the National Science Foundation (NSF), is now managed by private companies (one of which is America Online). America Online features the Internet Connection, which includes access to USENET Newsgroups, Gopher & WAIS Databases, FTP, and the World Wide Web, plus help with understanding it all. To obtain more information about the Internet, use the Keyword: **Internet**. See also *address, browser, domain, FTP, gateway, Gopher, header, newsgroup, page, site,* and *URL*.

Internet Explorer

See *Microsoft Internet Explorer*.

invitation

A request by another member to join a chat or visit an area on America Online, service made possible by the Buddy List feature in your AOL software. To invite someone, add them to your Buddy List, select their name, and click the Invite button. You will then be prompted to fill in the information regarding the invite. Note that you may need the address (or URL) or an area in order to invite someone to it. For more information see Chapter 8. See also *address, buddy, Buddy List,* and *URL*.

ISDN

Acronym for Integrated Services Digital Networks. ISDN is a relatively new type of access offered by local telephone companies. You can use an ISDN to connect to other networks at speeds as high as 64,000 bps (single channel). See also *TCP/IP*; contrast with *packet-switching network*.

ISP

Acronym for Internet Service Provider. An ISP generally provides a point to which you can connect and access various Internet-based services such as Web sites, FTP, e-mail, gopher, and newsgroups. Some ISPs also provide more advanced services that range from hosting Web sites and servers to wide area networking. See also *FTP, gopher, newsgroups,* and *World Wide Web*.

J

Java

A computer language developed by Sun Microsystems. Java is similar to C++ and is used to develop platform-independent applications commonly known as *applets*. Java programs are safely downloaded to your computer through the Internet and immediately run without fear of viruses or other harm to your computer or files. You may encounter a "Javascript error" while browsing the Web; if you do, this simply means your browser was unable to successfully run the Java applet for one reason or another.

K

Keep As New

An America Online e-mail system feature that allows you to keep mail in your New Mail box, even after you've read or ignored it. To use, simply select and highlight the piece of mail you wish to keep (in either your "New Mail" or "Old Mail" list [a.k.a. "Mail You Have Read" list]) and then click the Keep As New button at the bottom of the window. Returning read mail to your New Mail box with the Keep As New button will not change the time and date that appears in the Status box of the sender. See also *e-mail*.

keyboard shortcuts

The AOL software provides you with keyboard command equivalents for menu selections. For example, rather than selecting Instant Message from the People button on the toolbar, you can press Ctrll+I on Windows or Command+I on the Mac to achieve the same results.

keyword

1. A fast way to move around within America Online. For example, you can go directly to the Games channel by using the Keyword: **Games**. To use a keyword, type it directly into the entry field in the toolbar (the long, white box) and click the Go button. You can also press Command+K on the Mac or Ctrl+K on the PC, type the keyword, and press the Return or Enter key. Keywords are communicated to others in a standard format: Keyword: **Name**. The name of the keyword is shown in all caps to distinguish it from other words around it, but it does not need to be entered that way. Currently, there are over 15,000 public keywords. An updated list of most public keywords is available online at Keyword: **Keyword**. There is also a book listing all the keywords, including several hundred left out from the online list. It is titled *AOL Keywords* and was authored by Jennifer Watson. See Chapter 3 for more information on keywords.

2. A single word you feel is likely to be included in any database on a particular subject. A keyword is usually a word that comes as close as possible to describing the topic or piece of information you are looking for. Several of America Online's software libraries, mainly those in the AOL Computing channel, can be searched for with keywords.

L

library

An area online in which files may be uploaded to and downloaded from. The files may be of any type: text, graphics, software, sounds, and so on. These files can be downloaded from America Online's host computer to your personal computer's hard disk or floppy disk. Some libraries are searchable, whereas others must be browsed. You may also upload a file that may interest others to a library. A library is the best way to share large files with other America Online members. To search libraries available for your platform, go to Keyword: **Download Center** and click Shareware. See also *file*, *download*, *upload*, and *search*; contrast with *FTP*.

link

A pointer to another place that takes you there when you activate it (usually by clicking it). America Online has literally thousands of links that criss-cross the service, but they can't compare to the millions of links on the Web (often called hyperlinks) that can cross continents without your knowing it. See also *address*, *browser*, *favorite place*, *page*, *URL*, and *World Wide Web*.

M

mail controls

A set of preferences that enable the master account holder to control who you receive mail from. It can be set for one or all screen names on the account. Changes can be made by the master account screen name at any time. To access controls, go to

Keyword: **Mail Controls**. You can also block junk mail from your e-mailbox at Keyword: **Preferred Mail**.

mailing list

A group of e-mail addresses that receive e-mail on a regular basis about a topic in which they have a mutual interest. Mailing lists can be as simple as a few friends' addresses that you often e-mail, or as complex as a daily digest of news delivered to the e-mailboxes of millions of addresses. See also *address* and *e-mail*.

member

An America Online subscriber. The term "member" is embraced because we consider ourselves members of the online community. There are currently over 18 million member accounts on America Online, each of which may have up to seven different screen names. See also *online community*.

Member Directory

The database of America Online member screen names that have profiles. To be included in this database, a member need only create a Member Profile. Note that profiles for deleted members are purged periodically; therefore, it's possible to have a Member Profile for a deleted screen name. You can search for any string in a profile. Wildcard characters and boolean expressions also may be utilized in search strings. The Member Directory is located at Keyword: **Members**. More information is available in Chapter 15. See also *member*, *member profile*, *database*, and *searchable*.

member profile

A voluntary online information document that describes oneself. Name, address information, birthday, sex, marital status, hobbies, computers used, occupation, and a personal quote may be provided. This is located at Keyword: **Members**. See also *member* and *Member Directory.*

message

A note posted on a message board or newsgroup for others to read. A message may also be referred to as a post. See also *message board*.

message board

An area where members can post messages to exchange information, ask a question, or reply to another message. All America Online members are welcome and encouraged to post messages in message boards (or boards). Because messages are a popular means of communication online, message boards are organized with "topics," wherein a number of messages on a specific subject (threads) are contained in sequential order. Members cannot create new topics, so they should try to find an existing topic folder before requesting a new one. There are two kinds of message boards in use on America Online right now: regular and response-threaded. Message boards may be grouped together in a Message Center to provide organization and hierarchy. Message boards are occasionally called bulletin boards. See Chapter 9 for more information. See also *message*, *Message Center*, and *thread*.

Message Center

A collection of message boards in one convenient area. See also *message board*.

MHM (Members Helping Members)

A message board in the free area where America Online members can assist and get assistance from other members. Located at Keyword: **MHM**.

Microsoft Internet Explorer

The Web browser software integrated in all America Online 3.0 and higher clients. See also *Netscape Navigator*.

Microsoft Network (MSN)

An online service by the Microsoft Corporation. See also *America Online*, *CompuServe*, and *Prodigy*.

MSIE

See *Microsoft Internet Explorer*.

MSN

See *Microsoft Network*.

N

'Net

Abbreviation for the Internet. See *Internet*.

NetFind

See *AOL Search*.

netiquette

'Net manners. Cyberspace is a subculture with norms and rules of conduct all its own; understanding of these will often make your online life more enjoyable and allow you to move through it more smoothly. Online etiquette includes such things as proper capitalization (don't use all caps unless you mean to shout). Basically, the most important rule to keep in mind is one we learned offline and in kindergarten of all places: Do unto others as you'd have them do unto you (a.k.a. The Golden Rule). See Chapter 2 for a primer in America Online etiquette.

Netscape Navigator

An Internet browser produced by the
Netscape Corporation, which is owned
by America Online. You can use Netscape
Navigator in place of America Online's
built-in browser with AOL software 3.0 or
later. See also *Microsoft Internet Explorer*
and *TCP/IP*.

network

A data communications system that
interconnects computer systems at various
different sites. America Online could be
considered a network.

newsgroup

Internet's version of a public message
board. Available on America Online at
Keyword: **Newsgroups**. See also *header*
and *Internet;* contrast with *FTP*, *gopher*,
and *World Wide Web*.

online

The condition of a computer when it is
connected to another machine via modem.
Contrast with *offline*, the condition of a
computer that is unconnected.

online community

A group of people bound together by
their shared interest or characteristic of
interacting with other computer users
through online services, BBSs, or
networks. Because of the pioneer aspects
of an online community, established
onliners will welcome newcomers and
educate them freely, in most cases. On
America Online, elaborate conventions,
legends, and etiquette systems have
developed within the community.

P

packet-switching network (PSN)

The electronic networks that enable you to
access a remote online service by dialing a
local phone number. Information going to
and from your computer is segmented into
packets, which are given an address. The
packets are then sent through the network
to their destination similar to the way a
letter travels through the postal system,
only much faster. America Online uses a
variety of PSNs to supply local nodes (local
telephone numbers) for members' access.
See also *access number* and *AOLNET;*
contrast with *ISDN*.

page

A document on the World Wide Web,
presented in the Browser window. Web
pages can contain any combination of links,
text, graphics, sounds, or videos. A set of
pages is often referred to as a site. See also
browser, *favorite place*, *home page*, *html*,
link, *URL*, and *World Wide Web*.

palmtop

See *PDA*.

Parental Controls

Parental Controls enable the master
account holder to restrict access to
certain areas and features on America
Online (such as blocking Instant Messages
and chat rooms). It can be set for one or
all screen names on the account. Once
Parental Controls are set for a particular
screen name, they are active each time
that screen name signs on. Changes can
be made by the master account holder
at any time. To access controls, go to
Keyword: **Parental Controls**. See

Chapter 2 for more information. Contrast with *ignore*.

password

The secret 6-to-8 character code word that you use to secure your account. Never reveal your password to anyone, even those claiming to be America Online employees. More information on passwords is available in Chapter 2.

PDA

Short for Personal Digital Assistant. A handheld computer that performs a variety of tasks, including personal information management. PDAs are gaining in popularity and variety. A limited version of the AOL software, called AOL Mail, can be run on any Palm device with a Palm snap-on modem. See Keyword: **AOL Mail**. PDAs may also be referred to as palmtops. For more information, check out the PDA Forum at Keyword: **PDA**. See also *AOL Mail*.

People Connection (PC)

The America Online channel dedicated to real-time chat. Many different rooms can be found here: AOL-created rooms, member-created rooms, and private rooms. You can access this area with Keyword: **People**. Feel free to surf PC. More information on the People Connection is found in Chapter 8. See also *channel* and *chat room*.

Personal Filing Cabinet (PFC)

A special feature of the AOL software that organizes your e-mail, as well as message board and newsgroup postings. Note that everything in your Personal Filing Cabinet is stored on your hard disk. You can set your Personal Filing Cabinet preferences by choosing My AOL from the toolbar, selecting Preferences, and selecting Personal Filing Cabinet. See Chapter 7 for more information. See also *e-mail*, *favorite place*, *file*, and *newsgroup*.

post

1. The act of putting something online, usually into a message board or newsgroup.

2. A message in a message board or newsgroup. See also *message board* and *message*; contrast with *upload*.

postmaster

The person responsible for taking care of e-mail problems, answering queries about users, and other e-mail-related work at a site. America Online's postmaster can be reached at, you guessed it, screen name *Postmaster*. You can also reach other postmasters by simply adding the @ symbol and the domain name you wish to reach, such as *postmaster@msn.com*. See also *domain* and *e-mail*.

private room

A chat room that is created by a member via an option in People Connection where the name is not public knowledge. See Chapter 8 for information on creating private rooms. See also *chat room*; contrast with *auditorium*.

Prodigy

An information service founded as a joint venture between IBM and Sears. In the past, it was one of the larger competitors that America Online faced. Contrast with *America Online*, *CompuServe*, and *Microsoft Network*.

profile

America Online allows each screen name to have an informational file (a profile) attached to it. You may search profiles through the Member Directory. See also *member*, *Member Directory*, and *screen name*.

R

real time

Information received and processed (or displayed) as it happens. Conversations in Instant Messages and chat rooms happen in real time.

RealAudio

A streaming audio data format that allows Internet users and America Online members to listen to music and events in real time. The basic RealAudio player is available free for individual use from Progressive Networks at http://www.realaudio.com. AOL Radio is similar to RealAudio. See also *AOL Radio*.

release

To make something available to the general public, such as a file in a file library. See also *file* and *library*.

return receipt

A feature available with the AOL software that returns a piece of e-mail acknowledging that mail you sent to another America Online member (or members) has been received. Return receipts should be used sparingly as they can clutter up your mailbox. More information is available in Chapter 6. See also *e-mail*, *courtesy copy*, *blind courtesy copy*, and *status*.

S

screen name

The names (actually pseudonyms more often than not) that identify America Online members online. Screen names may contain no fewer than three and no more than sixteen characters, and must be unique. Any individual account may have up to seven screen names to accommodate family members or alter-egos, and each can (and should) have its own unique password. Either way, you cannot replace the original screen name created when you set up the account, and the person that established the original screen name and account is responsible for all charges incurred by all seven screen names. To add, delete, or restore deleted screen names, sign on with a master screen name and go to Keyword: **Names**. More information is available in Chapter 1. See also *address*, *e-mail address*, and *member*.

scroll

The movement of incoming text and other information on your computer screen. See *scroll bar*.

scroll bar

The bar on the right-hand side of a window, which allows you to move the contents up and down, or the bar on the bottom of a window for moving things to the left or right. The area on the scroll bar between the up and down arrows is shaded if there is more information than can fit in the window, or white if the entire content of the window is already visible. See also *scroll*.

search

Typically used in association with libraries and other searchable databases, the term refers to a specific exploration of files or entries themselves. More information is available in Chapters 10, 14, and 15. See also *searchable*, *database*, *file*, and *library*; contrast with *browse*.

searchable

A collection of logically related records or database files, which serve as a single central reference; a searchable database accepts input and yields all matching entries containing that character string. The Members Directory is an example of a searchable database. See also *search*, *database*, and *Members Directory*.

self-extracting archive

A compressed file that contains instructions to automatically decompress itself when opened; the software that decompressed it originally is not needed. On the Mac, these files can be decompressed simply by double-clicking on the icon. Self-extracting archive files are usually identifiable by the .sea extension. On the PC, these are often identified by an .exe extension. See also *file compression* and *StuffIt*.

server

A provider of resources, such as a file server. America Online uses many different kinds of servers, as do several of their partners.

sig

Short for signature. A block of text that some folks include at their end of the newsgroup postings and/or e-mail. You can designate a sig for your e-mail, message board posts, and newsgroup posts through their respective preferences. More information on using signatures in e-mail is available in Chapter 6, and more information on message board and newsgroup signatures is in Appendix B. See also *newsgroup* and *post*.

sign-on kit

The free software, registration codes, and directions for creating a new America Online account. If a sign-on kit didn't come with this book, there are a number of ways to obtain sign-on kits. Online, go to Keyword: **Friend** and follow the directions there to have kit sent via snail mail. Offline, you can always find a "free offer" card in a magazine. You may also find the sign-on kits themselves bundled with commercial software, modems, and computers. Sign-on kits can also be ordered via phone (1-800-827-6364If you simply need new AOL software but not an entirely new account, you can download the latest software for your platform at Keyword: **Upgrade**.

slideshow

See *AOL Slideshow*.

SLIP

An acronym for Serial-Line Internet Protocol. The SLIP protocol specifies how computers connect to the Internet through a dial-up connection. SLIP is used by some ISPs to connect their members to the Internet. See also *PPP*.

sounds

See *chat sounds*.

spam

To barrage a message board, newsgroup, or e-mail address with inappropriate, irrelevant, or simply numerous copies of the same post. Not only is this annoying, but it is also exceedingly bad netiquette. Members who spam will often have their posts removed (in message boards), find their mailbox full of e-mail from angry persons (if in a newsgroup), or even have their account terminated. See also *e-mail address*, *message board*, and *newsgroup*.

status (of e-mail)

An AOL software feature that allows you to check whether e-mail has been read and, if read, when. The status for an e-mail message may be "(not yet read)," "(ignored)," "(deleted)," or show the precise date and time when the mail was read. Status information includes recipients who were carbon copied (and even those who were blind carbon copied, if you were the sender). See Chapter 6 for more information. See also *e-mail*, *courtesy copy*, *blind courtesy copy*, and *return receipt*.

streaming

A method whereby information, usually in the form of audio or video, is delivered to your computer and becomes available for immediate playback. Information that is delivered through streaming technology differs from normal file or download because you don't have to wait for the entire file to download before it becomes usable. See also *AOL Radio*, *AOL Slideshow*, *download*, and *RealAudio*.

StuffIt

A popular compression program for the Apple Macintosh currently published by Aladdin Software and written by Raymond Lau. Files compressed with StuffIt can be automatically "unstuffed" when downloaded from Mac AOL software or when opened using the Mac AOL software. Programs to extract stuffed files are free and exist both for the IBM and Mac. See also *archive*, *file compression*, *self-extracting archive*, and *download*; contrast with *WinZip*.

surf

To cruise in search of information not readily evident in the hope of discovering something new. Usually paired with another word to describe the type of information being sought. Examples are room surfing and keyword surfing.

T

TCP/IP

Acronym for Transmission Control Protocol/Internet Protocol. The protocol language that Internet machines use to communicate. Windows AOL software 2.5 and Mac AOL software 2.6 and higher allow you to sign on via TCP/IP, and you can use other TCP/IP-capable applications through Mac AOL software 3.0 and higher at the same time. See also *Internet*.

thread

In general terms, a discussion that travels along the same subject line. More specifically, a thread refers to a group of posts in a message board under the same subject and topic. See also *message board*.

timeout

1. This happens when you've got two computers connected online and one gets tired of waiting for the other (that is, when the hourglass (PC) or beachball (Mac) cursor comes up and the "host fails to

respond"). You can report problems with frequent time-outs at Keyword: **System Response**.

2. The result of remaining idle for a certain amount of time while signed on to America Online. This timeout time is about ten minutes or so, but may vary at different times of the day.

toolbar

The row of buttons in the AOL software, usually found at the top of your screen. In AOL software version 4.0 and 5.0, many of the buttons have menus and portions of the toolbar are customizable. Navigational buttons and a keyword-entry box are also a part of the toolbar. See Chapter 3 for more information.

topic

Groupings of messages by subject within message boards are termed "topics" on America Online. You cannot create topics. See also *message* and *message boards*.

TOS

Short for America Online's Terms of Service — the rules everyone agrees to when registering for and becoming a member of America Online. These terms apply to all accounts on America Online. You can read these terms at Keyword: **TOS**.

Trojan Horse

A destructive program that is disguised within a seemingly useful program. A Trojan Horse is only activated by running the program. If you receive a file attached

to e-mail from a sender you are not familiar with, you are advised not to download it. If you ever receive a file you believe could cause problems, forward it to screen name *TOSEmail* and explain your concerns. Contrast with *virus*.

U

Unsend

An America Online e-mail system feature that allows you to retrieve mail that has been sent but not yet read. To use, simply select and highlight the piece of mail you wish to unsend from the Mail Sent window and click the Unsend button at the bottom of the window. The mail will be permanently deleted and cannot be retrieved. Note that only mail sent to other America Online members can be "unsent" or retrieved; Internet e-mail cannot be retrieved. See also *e-mail*.

upload

The transfer of information from a storage device on your computer to a remote computer, such as America Online's host computer. This information may be uploaded to one of America Online's file libraries or it may be uploaded with a piece of e-mail as an attached file. More information is available in Chapter 10. See also *file*, *file compression*, and *library*; contrast with *download*.

URL

An address for an online resource, such as a World Wide Web site or an America Online page. URL stands for Uniform Resource Locator, and the acronym is pronounced "earl." You can enter an URL address directly into the keyword box in the toolbar or the keyword window. There is no list of URL addresses as they are constantly changing and growing, but you can save your favorites by clicking the heart in the upper-right corner of a window. America Online's home page URL is `http://www.aol.com`. See also *address*, *browser*, *favorite place*, *page*, and *World Wide Web*.

V.90

The technical standard for 56K modems. If you have an older 56K modem that uses X2 or K56flex protocols, you should use a local access number that supports the V.90 standard *and* your modem's protocol. AOL has upgraded most of its network to take advantage of the V.90 standard. More information on V.90 connections is available at keyword: V.90. See also *baud* and *bps*.

virus

Computer software that has the capability to attach itself to other software or files, does so without the permission or knowledge of the user, and is generally designed with one intent — to propagate itself. A virus may also be intentionally destructive; however, not all virus damage is intentional. Some benign viruses suffer from having been poorly written and have been known to cause damage as well. Virus prevention software and information may be found at Keyword: **Virus**. Contrast with *Trojan Horse*.

WinZip

A shareware compression utility for Windows. WinZip is used to compress one file, or multiple files, into a smaller file (called an archive). Compression makes for shorter uploading and downloading. Windows AOL software 2.5 and Mac AOL software 2.6 (and higher) can automatically decompress archives compressed with WinZip. For more information, see `http://www.winzip.com`. See also *archive*, *download*, *file*, *file compression*, and *StuffIt*.

World Wide Web (WWW)

One of the more popular aspects of the Internet, the World Wide Web is actually an overarching term for the many hypertext documents that are displayed and linked together via a special protocol called Hypertext Transfer Protocol (or HTTP). World Wide Web information is available on America Online, using URL addresses to get to various Web sites or pages, much like you use keywords on America Online. Chapters 14 and 15 have several tips on searching the Web. See also *browser*, *favorite place*, *home page*, *Internet*, *page*, and *URL*.

Z

ZIP
See *WinZip*.

Index

A

About America Online command, 61
Academic Assistance Center, 274–275
access levels, 19
accounts, screen names in, 8
Add Top Window to Favorite Places
    command, 61
Address Book, 8, 97–99
    adding entries, 98
    Delete button, 99
    Edit button, 99
    New Group button, 99
    New Person button, 98
    Notes field, 98
    Picture tab, 98
    Save/Replace button, 99
    saving for export, 99
ads, classifieds, 244–247, 258
Ages & Stages, 296
Aim Instant Messenger (AIM), 156–157
AIM Web site, 157
air fares. *See* Travel Channel
albums, photo, 221–224. *See also*
    Buddy albums
allHealth.com, 299
Alt key, 52
America Online. *See* AOL 5.0
American Greetings Online Greetings
    store, 132

Anti-Virus Center, 272
antivirus programs, 213–214
AOL 5.0
    accessing, 7
    changing nature of, 5
    community nature of, 5–6
    customer service, 236–237
    growth of, 5
    information available on, 6
    and the Internet, 5–6
    national services, 259
    new features of, 8
    new members, number of, 5
    notifying, 28–29, 31–33
    online store, 247
    as shopping destination, 10–11. *See also*
        Shopping Channel
    via Broadband, 8
AOL Canada, 167
AOL Companion (Watson), 73
AOL E-mail (Watson and Marx), 72–73
AOL for Dummies (Kaufeld and
    Kaufeld), 73
AOL Foreign Services, 260
AOL Help, 75–77
AOL icon, 18, 54, 56
AOL in a Nutshell (Degenhart and
    Muehlbauer), 73
AOL Insider Tips, 75
AOL Instant Messenger (AIM), 156–158

AOL Keywords (Watson), 12–13, 64, 73, 317

AOL Live, 170

AOL members, finding, 325–327

AOL NetMail, 7, 143–145

AOL News, 11–12

AOL 101 Downloading Files course, 206

AOL Progress icon, 63

AOL Screen Names window, 18

AOL Search, 311–313

AOL Search window, opening, 63

AOL Tips, 75

AOL Today, 11

AOL window, 59–63
  menus of, 60–61
  navigation bar, 62–63
  toolbar, 62
  Welcome screen, 59–60. *See also* Welcome screen

AOL.com home page, NetMail link, 144

appointment book, electronic. *See* My Calendar

Appointment Details window, 173

appointments. *See also* My Calendar
  adding to My Calendar, 173
  tracking, 8

Arrange Icons command, 61

arrow keys, navigating menus with, 52, 58

Ask-A-Teacher, 274–275

Ask the Staff buttons, 76

asterisks, in Buddy List, 160

at (@) symbol, 14, 94, 96

attachments. *See* file attachments

auctions, online, 249

auditoriums, 170–171

Auto AOL, 8, 216–217
  and downloading safety, 217
  e-mail services, 130
  Schedule Automatic AOL button, 217

Auto Center, 293

B

Back button, 62

banking online, safety reassurances, 28

behavior, inappropriate, notifying AOL of, 31–33

beta testers, 12

Beyond.com, 211–212

billing help, 77

The Bistro, 263

blind courtesy copies, 44, 111–112

BMP format, 140

Boolean operators, 211, 310

bots, 319

Brokerage Center, 267

browsing
  in AOL Search, 313
  through files, 212–213

buddies, 158

Buddy Albums, 221, 223–224

Buddy Chat window, 160

Buddy List, 9, 157–160
  asterisks in, 160
  blocking names in, 45

Buddy Chat feature, 168
  creating new, 158
  deleting, 158
  editing, 158
  parentheses in, 160
  setting up, 158–159
  using, 159–160
Buddy List Setup window, 158
  Buddy List Preferences, 159
  Privacy Preferences button, 159
  View button, 158–159
Buddy List window
  Buddy Chat button, 160
  Locate button, 159
  Setup button, 158
business etiquette, 261
Business Know-How forum, 269
business news, 256, 260
businesses, searching for, 327–329
buttons, 53–54

C

Calendar icon, 62
Capture Picture command, 61
car rentals. *See* **Travel Channel**
carbon copies, blind, 44, 111–112
Career Center, 269–270
carets, in e-mail quotes, 115
Cascade command, 61
Case, Steve, 87
CBS news, 255
Certified Merchant Guarantee, 237–238

**Certified Merchants Program, 11,
    236–238**
chain letters, 30, 44–45
Chamber of Commerce Directory, 273
Change Your Password dialog box, 17
Channel Guide, 316–317
channel windows, close box, 254
channels, 7
  Computing, 270–273
  Entertainment, 287–289
  Families, 300–302
  Games, 289–292
  Health, 298–300
  Interests, 292–295
  International, 259–263
  Kids Only, 303–304
  Lifestyles, 295–297
  Local, 276–277
  navigating, 254
  News, 254–258
  Personal Finance, 265–268
  Research & Learn, 273–275
  Search & Explore feature, 264
  searching, 313–315
  Shopping, 298. *See also* Shopping
    Channel
  Sports, 281–282
  Teens, 304
  Travel, 283–287
  WorkPlace, 268–270
Channels icon, 62, 254
**Chat button, message board links
    on, 180**
chat hosts, 163–164

chat lobby, 163

chat logs, 169

chat rooms, 9, 161

  capacity of, 164

  categories of, 163

  chat box, 165

  chat logs, 169

  Chat Preferences button, 165

  chat sounds in, 167

  chatting in, 166–167

  versus conference rooms, 166

  creating, 168

  hyperlinks in, 167

  Ignore feature, 165

  interactive help in, 77–78

  international, 263

  netiquette guidelines for, 45

  Notify AOL button, 162, 165

  offensive behavior in, 162

  Parental Control settings for, 37

  people lists, 165

  separate screen name for, 136

  for sports, 282

  text entry box, 165

chat sounds, 167

chatting, 166–167

Check Spelling window, 130–131

Chic Simple, 236

children, 29. *See also* **Kids Only**
    Channel; Parental Controls;
    Teens Channel

city guides, 276–277

classified ads, online, 258

ClassifiedPlus, 243–247

  creating ads, 245–246

  searching through, 244–245

ClassifiedPlus Newsletter, 244–245

classrooms, online, 271

clicks, mouse, 51

Close All Except Front command, 61

Close Box, 55

CNET, 271

collaboration tools. *See* **Instant**
    Messages (IM)

colleges, online listings, 275

.com extension, 97

communities, 8–9

  finding, 162–164

  finding for message board exchanges,
    180–181

  finding for newsgroup exchanges,
    191–192

  variety of, 180

Community Action Team, 33

Community Leaders, 80

Compton's Encyclopedia Online, 273

Computer Protection Center, 214

computers

  help and information on, 81, 271

  safety settings for, 28

Computing Channel, 205, 270–273

  Chats & Messages, 272

  CNET, 271

  Communities, 272

  Download Center, 272–273. *See also*
    Download Center

  file libraries in, 208

  Help and Education, 271

help topics in, 79–80

searching through libraries, 211

The Concise Columbia Electronic Encyclopedia, 273

conference rooms, 160, 166

  capacity of, 166

  versus chat rooms, 166

  netiquette guidelines for, 45

Connecting to AOL window, 57

consumer tips, for shopping online, 248

content, AOL rights to, 30

context menu, 51, 117

control boxes, 54

control menu, 56

copying, 32

copyrights

  on photographs, 140, 224

  respecting, 218

country codes, for e-mail, 97

country profiles, 262

Courses Online, 275

courtesy copies, 110–111

Create Signature window, 139

credit card transactions, 241

  purchase protections benefits for, 248

  saving information, 239–240

  security of, 238–239, 241

Cruise Critic, 285

culture information, 261–262

Custom Search window, 184

customer service, for online shopping, 236–237

D

dates, tracking, 8. *See also* My Calendar

decompressing, 216

Desktop Publishing Community, 272

dictionaries, online, 274

Dictionary command, 61

Digital City, 276–277

Dogpile, 320

domains, 36, 96–97, 135

double-clicks, 51

Download Center, 209–213, 272–273

  Buy Software area, 211, 213

  Download Catalogue, 212

  Top Ten Picks, 213

download count, 208

Download folder, 207

Download Manager, 207, 214–215

  Download button, 214

  filename preservation in, 8

  Show Files Downloaded button, 215

downloading. *See also* Download Center; Download Manager; downloads

  attached files, 29

  defined, 205

  games, 290–291

  how to, 205–207

  picture files, 222–223

  resuming, 215

  viruses and Trojan Horses and, 214

downloads, 205

  accessing, 215

Continued

downloads *(continued)*

blocking, 39–40

descriptions of, 208–209, 218

location of, 206

Dr. Solomon's antivirus programs, 214

drop-down lists, 58

drop-down menus, 58

E

e-mail, 9, 86–87. *See also* **Write Mail window**

attachments, 117–120

background color, 137

blind courtesy copies, 44, 111–112

blocking, 29, 134–136

checking for new mail, 87–88

colors and styles for, 132–133

context menu for, 117

courtesy copies, 110–111

for Customer Service, 237

deleted, accessing, 8

deleting, 90, 101

expiration dates on, 93

font selection, 137

forwarding, 94–95

getting help through, 76–77

graphics in, 89, 140–143

hyperlinks in, 133, 138

ignoring, 117

information resources on, 72–73

junk mail, 93–95

keeping as new, 9189

letterhead options, 133

as message board reply, 190

netiquette guidelines for, 44

opening, 90

opening in PFC, 127

Parental Control settings for, 36

photographs in, 133, 140–143

printing, 90

quoting, 114–115, 190

reading new mail, 89–92

reading offline, 130

remote access to, 143–145

replying to, 112–115

return receipts, 110

safety settings for, 28

saving, 90, 125

sending, 108

sending, delayed, 110

sent mail status, 116–117

signatures for, 108, 138–140

spell checking, 130–132

styled text in, 89, 136–137

subject line, 108

text alignment, 137

text color, 137

text size, 137

text style, 137

unsending, 117

viruses in, 28, 94

writing, 107–110

writing offline, 129

e-mail addresses, 14, 95–99

at (@) symbol in, 94, 96

Address Book for, 97–99

case sensitivity, 111

country codes, 97

searching for, 330–331

spaces in, 16

viewing as hyperlinks, 114

E-mail Finder, 330–331

e-mail signatures, 8. *See also* **sigs
(signature files)**

e-mail window

Add Address button, 90, 97

closing, 90

Delete button, 89

Forward button, 89, 115

Help button, 90

New Mail tab, 87

Next button, 89–90

Old Mail tab, 87–88

Reply All button, 90

Reply button, 89–90, 112

Reply to All button, 113

Send Later button, 129

Sent Mail tab, 87–88

Edit Hyperlink window, 138

Edit menu, 61

Check Spelling, 189

Copy, 32

Find in Top Window, 197

Paste, 32

Spell Check, 130

editorials, online, 256

.edu extension, 97

Education Resources department, 275

Electronic Library, 273–274

emoticons, 133

emotional health, 299

encyclopedias, online, 273

Enter key, 52

Entertainment Asylum, 289

Entertainment Channel, 287–289

AOL MovieFone, 288–289

Entertainment Asylum, 289

entertainment news, 257

Entrepreneur Magazine, 269

Esc key, 52, 63

etiquette

for international business, 261

netiquette, 43–45, 138

events

reminders for, 243

sharing with friends, 174

tracking, 8

.exe extension, 222

Exit command, 61

F

F1 key, 71

Fair Credit Billing Act, 248

Families Channel, 300–302

Genealogy Forum, 302

Moms Online, 301

Parent Soup, 301

family members, screen names for, 15

FastFacts, 74

Favorite icon, 54, 62, 65

Favorite Places, 65–66

adding one, 65–66

editing list, 66

exchanging in chat rooms, 167

message boards as, 182

private chat rooms, 168–169

Favorites menu, AOL Top Picks, 244

Federal Trade Commission, shopping tips from, 248

file attachments, 117–120

blocking, 36, 120, 136

downloading, 29

editing list of, 118

size of, 120

file compression, 119–120, 207

file libraries, 207–209, 218

File menu, 60–61

Open Picture Gallery, 142

Save As, 125

filenames, preserving, 8

files

browsing, 212–213

defined, 205

deleting, 128

descriptions of, 208–209, 218

download count, 208

downloaded, finding, 206

exchanging, 12

FTP transport, 225–227

searching for, 210–212

uploading, 217–218

Files You've Downloaded screen, 216

Filing Cabinet window

Add Folder button, 127

Compact PFC button, 128

PFC Find, 128

filters

for message board posts, 187

for newsgroups, 196

finances, managing with AOL, 10–11.
See also Personal Finance
Channel

Financial Centers, 267–268

financial market news, 11

Find in Top Window command, 61

Find Setup Wizard, 72

finding people, 325–327

fitness. See Health Channel

5 Minute Guide to AOL, 74

floppy disks, downloading files to, 214

food, international, 261

Food forum, 294–295

foreign language dictionaries, online, 262

Forget Window Size and Position command, 61

formatting

for chat text, 165

for e-mail text, 136–137

forums, 180

Business Know-How, 269

on entertainment, 289

Food, 294–295

Home & Garden, 293

Oxygen, 296

Pets, 294

searching through, 315–316

on wellness, 299–300

Forward button, 62

forwarding, 115–116

friends, meeting new, 8–9

FTP (File Transfer Protocol), 225–227

public sites, 226

storage space, 226–227

FTP window, 226

fun and games, 262. See also Games Channel

G

Game Parlor, 290–291
Game Shows Online, 291–292
games
  blocking access, 291
  international, 262
Games Channel, 289–292
  Game Parlor, 290–291
  Game Shows Online, 291–292
  Xtreme Games, 291
gardening, forum on, 293
Gay & Lesbian area, 297
Genealogy Forum, 302
General Access setting, 19
Get Help Now window, Expert Live
    Help link, 80
GIF format, 140
Global Gourmet, 261
Global Meeting Place, 263
Global Message Board Preferences
    window, 185–188
  Offline Reading, 186
  Posting tab, 186
  Threading area, 186
Global Newsgroup Preferences
    window, 194–196, 198
Go2Net Metacrawler, 320
.gov extension, 97
graphics
  copyrights on, 140
  in e-mail, 140–143
  storage of, 60
grayed-out selections, 58
greeting cards, creating, 141
groups, 113–114, 158

H

hand pointer, 53
hard disk, saving e-mail on, 125
hardware reviews, 271
headers
  for e-mail, 89
  for newsgroups, 195
Health Channel, 298–300
  allHealth.com, 299
  Thrive Online, 299–300
health news, 257
heart icon, 54
help
  offline, 61, 71–73
  online, 73–81
help classes, 79
Help Illustrated, 80–81
Help menu, 57, 61
  Member Services Online Help, 75
  Offline Help, 71
Help window
  Tell Me About AOL 5.0 button, 73
  What's New in AOL 5.0, 73
History Trail, 63
hobbies. *See* Interests Channel
holidays
  adding to My Calendar, 172
  reminders for, 242–243
Home & Garden forum, 293
Home Page button, 62
home pages, 12
hotel reservations. *See* Travel Channel
How to Download window
  How to Download link, 206
  Take a Class link, 206

human interest news, 257

hyperlinks, 53–54

in chat rooms, blocking, 37

checking location of, 94

customizable, 8

descriptions of, 54

in e-mail, 133, 138

e-mail addresses as, 114

in Instant Messages, 154–155

in sigs, 187

hypertext links. *See* **hyperlinks**

I

icons, 53, 58

Independent Traveler, 284–285

Instant Messages (IM), 9, 151–157

deceitful, 152

hyperlinks in, 154–155

ignoring, 151

Parental Control settings for, 37–38

sending and receiving, 152–155

sending to Buddy List members, 159

turning off and on, 155–156

Instant Messenger, 6–7, 156–157

Buddy List capabilities of, 158

insurance, shopping for, 267

Interest Profiles, 74–75

Interests Channel, 292–295

Auto Center, 293

Food, 294–295

Home & Garden, 293

Pets, 294

International Channel, 259–263

Business, 260

Country Information, 262

Cultures, 261–262

Fun & Games, 262

Global Meeting Place, 263

News, 260

Travel, 262

International Etiquette Guide, 261

international news, 260

Internet, 309

AOL as part of, 5–6

blocking e-mail from, 135

e-mail addresses from, 96

information resources on, 72

netiquette for, 45

Internet icon, 62

FTP, 225

Newsgroups, 191

White Pages, 329

Yellow Pages, 327

Internet Newsgroups window, 191

Add Newsgroups button, 193

Expert Add button, 193

Newsgroups Etiquette article, 197

Read My Newsgroups button, 193

Search All Newsgroups button, 191–193

Set Preferences button, 194

investing. *See* **Personal Finance**
            Channel

Investing Basics, 267

J

jenuine.net, 65

job listings, online, 270

Johnson, Kim, 236

JPG format, 140
junk blocks, 195, 197
junk mail, 93–95, 134–136, 195

K

keyboard shortcuts, 51–53, 62
Keyword button, 63
keyword searches, 316–317
Keyword window, 64
keywords, 63–65
  AAC, 274
  Ages, 296
  AH, 299
  AOL Search, 198
  AOL Tips, 75
  Auto, 293
  Beyond, 211
  Billing, 225, 291
  Bistro, 263
  Bookstores, 73
  Buddy List, 158
  Business News, 267
  Calendar, 171
  Call AOL, 72
  Career Center, 269
  CBS News, 255
  Channel Guide, 314, 316
  Channels, 253
  Chic Simple, 236
  CITY + DEPARTMENT, 277
  city names, 276
  Classifieds, 244, 258
  cnet, 271
  Computing, 270

  Computing Communities, 272
  Countries, 262
  Courses, 275
  Cruise Critic, 285
  Daily Download, 206
  Destinations, 283
  Dictionary, 274
  Digital City, 276
  Download Center, 210
  Download Manager, 215
  EA, 289
  Email Finder, 330–331
  ENT, 287
  Ent News, 257
  Entertainment, 287
  Family, 300
  Fast Facts, 74
  File Search, 120, 273
  Find a Job, 270
  Food, 295
  Fools, 267
  Foreign Dictionary, 262
  Friend, 175
  FTP, 225
  Game Shows, 292
  Games, 290
  Gay, 297
  Get Help Now, 80, 271
  GG, 261
  Global Citizen, 261
  Global Meeting, 263
  GS, 282
  GS Soccer, 181
  Guarantee, 238
  Hardware, 214

Continued

keywords *(continued)*

  Health, 298

  Help, 45, 75

  Help Class, 79

  Home, 293

  How to Download, 205–206

  I Need Help, 162

  Instant Messenger, 156, 175

  Interest Profiles, 75, 102

  Interests, 292

  INTL, 259

  INTL Business, 260

  INTL Cultures, 261

  INTL News, 256, 260

  INTL Travel, 262

  Investing Basics, 267

  Junk Mail, 93

  Keyword, 64, 317

  Kids Only, 303

  KO, 303

  KO Help, 304

  KO Parent, 304

  Leaders, 80

  Lesbian, 297

  Life News, 257

  Lifestyles, 295

  Live, 170

  Local, 276

  Local News, 258

  Mail Center, 102

  Mail Controls, 29, 134

  Marketing Prefs, 238

  Member Opinions, 284

  Members, 111

  MHM, 78, 180, 182, 188

MNC, 267

MO, 301

Moviefone, 288

Movies, 287

My FTP Space, 227

My Portfolios, 266

Names, 18, 21

Neighborhood Watch, 27, 162

Netfind, 192

New, 305

New Files, 212

News, 254

News Search, 255

Newsgroup Scoop, 192, 197

Newsgroups, 191, 217

Newsletter, 102

Newsstand, 257

Notify AOL, 29, 31

Online Classrooms, 271

Out OnQ, 297

Oxygen, 296

Parental Controls, 34

Parlor, 290

Password, 17, 29

Petersons, 275

Pets, 294

PF, 265

Picture Help, 229

Pictures, 219–220

Politics, 257

Preview Travel, 286

PS, 301

Quick Checkout, 239

Quickstart, 74

Quotes, 265

Real Estate, 267
Reminder, 242
Roots, 302
Royalty, 262
Scoreboard, 281
Shop Direct, 247
Shopping, 233, 298
Shopping Customer Service, 236
Speak Out, 256
Sports, 281
Startup, 268
Teens, 304
Thrive, 300
Today in Health, 257
TOS, 30
Travel, 283
Traveler, 179, 284
UCAOL, 275
US World, 256
Virus, 213, 272
Virus Info, 214
Weather, 257
White Pages, 329
Women, 296
Workplace, 268
Worldly Investor, 260
Yellow Pages, 327
Kids Help, 42–43
Kids Only Channel, 41–43, 303–304
  adults in, 304
  Buddy Album restrictions, 224
  Instant Messages controls, 151
Kids Only setting, 19
Kodak, 219

L

language dictionaries, 262
Lasky, Jane, 261
The Learning Company, 38
lesbianism, links for, 297
letterhead, for e-mail, 133
libraries. *See* file libraries
Lichty, Tom, 12–13
Lifestyles Channel, 295–297
  Ages & Stages, 296
  Gay & Lesbian, 297
  Women, 296
links. *See* hyperlinks
list boxes, 57–58
live events, 9
Live One-on-One Help button, 77
Local Channel, 276–277
local news, 258
local searches, 316
locked out status, 219
Logging window, Chat log, 169
Look Up Answers, 274
Love@AOL personal ads, 246
lurking, 165, 167

M

Macintosh, games for, 292
Mail Center icon, 62
  Address Book, 97
  Mail Extras, 167
  Mail Waiting to be Sent, 129
  Run Automatic AOL, 217
  Set up Automatic AOL, 216

Continued

Mail Center icon *(continued)*

Set up Signatures, 139

Write Mail, 107

Mail Center menu, 99–102

Address Book, 100

Mail Center, 100

Mail Controls, 100

Mail Extras, 100

Mail Preferences, 100

Old Mail, 100

Read Mail, 100

Read Offline Mail, 101

Recently Deleted Mail, 100–101

Sent Mail, 100, 116

Set up Mail Signatures, 100

Write Mail, 100

Mail Center window, 99, 101–102

Mail Controls, 29, 36, 134–136

Mail Extras, 132–133

mail headers, 89

Mail Preferences, 91

caret style, choosing, 115

Retain all mail I read/send in my
Personal Filing Cabinet, 126, 130

Mail Waiting to be Sent window, 130

mailbox, 87–88, 91

Delete button, 92

Keep As New button, 91–93

locking, 29

Old Mail tab, 92–93

Read button, 89, 92

refreshing, 93, 109

Status button, 92

mailbox icon, 87

Major Tom, 13

Market News Center, 267

marketing preferences, 238

Marx, Dave, 12–13

Master Rights, 20

master screen name, 34–35

assigning status of, 39

privileges of, 39

Mature Teen setting, 19

Maximize Box, 55

McAfee's antivirus programs, 214

meeting people, with Instant Messages, 151

member chats, 168

Member Directory, 111, 153, 325–327

member profiles, 8, 153, 326–327

member rooms, 161

Member Services, 17, 75–77

Members Help Interactive Live, 13

Members Helping Members, 78–79, 199

menu bar, Sign Off, 22

menus, 60–61

ellipsis following item name, 57

grayed-out selections in, 58

navigating with keyboard shortcuts, 52

selecting items on, 57

merchants, certified, 236–238

Merriam-Webster Collegiate Dictionary, 274

Message Board Reply window, 190

message boards, 9, 179–190

creating subjects, 188

as Favorite Places, 182

Find by drop-down menu, 182

finding communities, 180–181

finding messages, 183–185

for help topics, 78–79

List All button, 182

List Unread button, 182

Mark Read button, 182

netiquette guidelines for, 44–45

offline reading, 198

offline reading for, 217

posting on, 180, 188–190

posts, 183

preferences for, 185–188

Read Offline button, 182

reading messages, 181–183

sigs for, 186–187

for sports, 282

subject display window, 182

topic creation, 181

for travel information, 285

meta search engines, 320

Metacrawler, 320

mini-icons, 58

Minimize Box, 56

Moms Online, 301

More About Screen Names button, 16

More Help button, 75

The Motley Fool, 267

mouse, 51

mouse clicks, 51

mouse pointer

as double-headed arrow, 56

as hand, 53

MovieFone, 288–289

movies

local show times, 288–289

online information, 287–289

MTV, 288

music, online information, 287–288

My AOL icon, 62

Buddy List, 158

Mail button, 114

My Member Profile, 153

Passwords, 17

Preferences, 155, 216

Select Preferences, 91

My Calendar, 8, 11, 171–175

appointment creation, 173

Day and Week tabs, 173

default view of, 173

Event Directory, 11, 172, 174

flipping pages, 172

hyperlinks in, 174

Idea List, 172, 174

remote access to, 175

sharing events, 174

My Calendar icon, 174

My Files icon, 62

Download Manager, 207, 215

Log Manager, 169

Offline Newsgroups, 217

Personal Filing Cabinet, 126

My Places, 8, 60

My Portfolios screen, Help button, 266

My Shortcuts, 62

N

Name That Flag, 262

national anthems, 262

navigation, information resources on, 73

Navigation Bar, 62–63

Neighborhood Watch, 27
  Computer Safety, 28
  E-mail Safety, 28
  Notify AOL button, 28
  Parental Controls, 27
  Shopping and Banking button, 28
  Suggested Safeguards, 28
.net extension, 97
NetFind, Search Newsgroups link, 192
netiquette, 43–45
  for newsgroups, 197
  for sigs, 138
NetMail, 143–145
**Netscape Navigator, Instant Messenger
    software, 157**
Netscape Netcenter, 318–319
New command, 60
news
  business, 256
  international, 260
News Channel, 254–258
  automatic clipping service, 11
  Business News, 256
  CBS News, 255
  Classifieds, 258
  Entertainment News, 257
  Health News, 257
  Life, 257
  Local, 258
  News Search, 255
  News Ticker, 258
  Newsstand, 257
  Politics, 257
  Speak Out, 256
  time of last update, 255

  U.S. and World, 256
  Weather, 257
News Profiles, 11
news ticker, 258
newsgroups, 190–197
  addresses of, 193–194
  filtering preferences, 196
  finding communities, 191–192
  finding messages, 197
  headers for, 195
  name style, 195
  netiquette guidelines for, 44–45
  offline reading, 196, 198, 217
  opening, 194
  posting messages, 197
  posting preferences, 195
  preferences for, 194–196
  reading, 194
  reading messages, 193–194
  restricting access to, 40
  subscribing to, 192–193
  unsubscribing, 193
  viewing preferences, 195
newsletters, subscribing to, 102
newsstands, 257
Notify AOL, 31–33, 165
nutrition. *See* **Health Channel**

O

*The Official America Online Tour
    Guide* **(Lichty), 12**
Offline Help, 61, 71–73
  Contents tab, 71

Find tab, 71

Index tab, 71

Offline Mail, 126, 128–130

Old Mail, 91–93

1-2-3 Shop, 235

Online Campus, 275

online communications, privacy of, 31

online help, 73–81

online safety, 27–29

online scams, 29

online storage, for pictures, 219, 223

Open command, 60

Open Picture Gallery command, 60

.org extension, 97

Oxygen, 296

P

Parent Soup, 301

Parental Controls, 14–15, 19, 27, 33–41

    for Buddy Album access, 224

    categories of, 41

    category window, 35

    changing, 35

    chat controls, 37

    customized settings for, 20, 34–35

    download controls, 39–40

    e-mail controls, 36

    IM controls, 37–38

    Kids Only category, 41–43

    for member profile creation, 153

    newsgroup controls, 40

    premium services controls, 41

Recommend or Report Web sites buttons, 38

    slideshow on, 34

    Web controls, 38–39

parentheses

    in Buddy List, 160

    in Copy To field, 111

parenting tips, 301–302

Passport to Love, 263

passwords

    changing, 17, 29

    for children, 22

    creating, 28

    for deleted screen names, 21

    entering, 18–19

    protecting, 28

    for Quick Checkout accounts, 240

    safeguarding, 15

    setting, 17

    for shopping sites, 248

    storing, 22

pasting, 32

PC Games FTP site, 226

PDAs & Palmtops, 272

people

    finding, 325–327

    meeting, 8–9

People Connection, 12, 78, 160–161

    chat areas, blocking, 37

    Chat Schedule, 164

    hosts for, 164

People Connection screen

    Chat Now!, 163

    Find a Chat, 163

People icon, 62

AOL Live, 170

Chat Now, 163

Find a Chat, 163

Get a Member's Profile, 153

Instant Message, 152

Start Your Own Chat, 168

Perks icon, 62

personal ads, 246

Personal Filing Cabinet (PFC), 8

cleaning and organizing, 127

downloading posts to, 198

folders, creating, 127

Incoming/Saved Mail folder, 127

password for, 22, 128

saving e-mail in, 90–91, 126–128

Personal Finance Channel, 10, 265–268

Departments, 266–267

Financial and Brokerage Centers,
267–268

Online Stock Portfolios, 266

Quotes, Charts, News & Research, 265

personal information, divulging, 29

Peterson's LifeLongLearning.com, 275

Pets forum, 294

phone support, 72

photo developing prices for, 219–220.
See also You've Got Pictures

photographs. *See also* **You've Got**
Pictures

for classified ads, 247

copyrights on, 140, 224

digital versions of, 219

downloading, 222

in e-mail, 133, 140–143

editing, 142–143, 222

exchanging, 12

qualities (resolution) of, 222

viewing, organizing, and sharing, 8

Picture Gallery, 60, 142–143

pictures. *See* **photographs; You've Got**
Pictures

politics, news items on, 257

portfolios, online, 265–266

Post New Message window, 188–189

posts, 183. *See also* **message boards**

filtering, 187

to newsgroups, 197

replying to, 188–190

searching for, 183–185

sending via e-mail, 190

Pre-Pregnancy Community, 301

preferences

for Buddy List, 159

for chatting, 165

for mail, 91, 100, 114–115, 126

for marketing your address, 241

for message boards, 185–188

for newsgroups, 194–196

for privacy, 28, 155–156

Preferences window, Privacy button,
155

premium services, blocking, 41

Preview Travel, 286–287

Print command, 60–61

Print icon, 62

Print Setup command, 60–61

privacy, online, 29, 44

Privacy Preferences, 28, 155

private chats, 168

private rooms, 161, 168–169

Professional Forums, 269

ProFusion, 320

punctuation marks, in screen names, 16

pyramid schemes, 30

Q

Quick Checkout, 239–241

QuickStart, 73–75

Quotes icon, 62

R

Raise Your Cultural IQ, 262

Read icon, 62

Read My Newsgroups window, 193–194

  Internet Names button, 194

  Mark All Newsgroups Read button, 194

Receive Live One-on-One Help button, 77

recipes, online, 261, 294–295

references, 273–274

Regents College, 275

Reload button, 62

Remember Window Size and Position command, 61

Remember Window Size command, 61

Reminder Service, 242–243

remote control, for channels, 254

Remove from Toolbar command, 63

Research & Learn Channel, 273–275

  Ask-a-Teacher, 274–275

  Education and Courses, 275

  Explore a Subject, 274

  References, 273–274

resources, online, 309

Restore Box, 56

return receipts, 110

right-click, 51

Rolling Stone Online, 288

Royalty Forum, 262

S

safety, online, 27–29

Save As command, 60

Save command, 60

Save to Personal Filing Cabinet command, 60

schoolwork, help with, 274–275

Scoreboard, 281

screen names, 13–15, 44

  for children, 34

  choosing, 15–16

  creating, deleting, and restoring, 18–21

  deleting, 21

  forgotten, 95

  General Access, 19–20

  length of, 8

  limitations on, 16

  number of, 8

  Parental Controls settings for, 34–35

  passwords for, 17

  privacy of, 220

  private, 45

  rights and privileges of, 14–15

  signature files for, 139

  spelling help, 107

Screen Names area, 18

  Create Screen Name button, 18

Continued

Screen Names area *(continued)*
  More About Screen Names button, 16
  Restore Screen Name button, 21
scroll bars, 54–55
Search & Explore, 264
Search button, 63, 311
search capabilities, of AOL 5.0, 8
search engines, 309–311, 319–320
Search Results window, 185, 312–313
Search Shop @ AOL, 234
search tools, 313
searching
  within AOL, 311–317
  AOL Search, 311–313
  channel searches, 313–315
  for downloadable files, 210–212
  for help topics, 71
  keyword searches, 316–317
  local searches, 315–316
  matching categories, 312
  matching sites, 312–313
  in message boards, 183–185
  for news items, 255
  in newsgroups, 197
  outside of AOL, 318–320
  for people, 325–327
  tips and techniques, 310
security, for shared accounts, 22
Send Instant Message window, 152
settings, grayed out, 38
sexual health, 299–300
shared accounts, 21–22
shareware files, searching for, 211
Shop @ AOL, 233, 235

Shop Direct, 247
ShopHelp, 237
shopping carts, electronic, 234–235
Shopping Channel, 10–11, 233, 298.
       See also **shopping online**
  Auctions & Outlets button, 249
  Customer Service button, 236
shopping online, 10–11, 233–236
  browsing, 234
  Certified Merchant Guarantee, 237–238
  checking out, 235
  ClassifiedPlus, 243–247
  customer service for, 236–237
  Internet shopping, 247–248
  money for, 241
  Quick Checkout, 238–241
  Reminder Service for, 242–243
  safety issues, 28, 238–239
shorthands, 167
Sign Off command, 61
Sign Off menu, 62
sign on, delayed, 21
Sign On screen, Screen Name menu, 95
sigs (signature files), 138–140
  default, 140
  for message boards posts, 186–187
  for newsgroup posts, 195
slider, 55
smileys, 133, 167
software
  downloadable, 227–228, 273
  help with, 71–72
  reviews of, 271
  searching for, 211, 213

sounds, for chats, 167

spam, 93–95

spell checking, 44

   e-mail, 130–132

   Instant Messages, 155

spiders, 319

SPIN Online, 288

Sports Channel, 281–282

   Grandstand, 282

   Scoreboard, 281

sports news, 11

SSL (Secure Sockets Layer) encryption, 241, 247

Start-Up Businesses department, 268–269

stationery, for e-mail, 133

stock indices, tracking, 266

stock market. *See* **Personal Finance Channel**

stock portfolios, online, 265–266

stock ticker, 256

Stone, Jeff, 236

Stop button, 62

Stored Passwords, 22

StuffIt file compression, 120

styled text, 136–138, 140

submenus, 57

Switch Screen Name command, 21, 61

Symantec's antivirus programs, 214

symbols, in screen names, 16

T

Tab key, navigating with, 59, 107

Teach Yourself America Online (Bowen and Watson), 73

TechLive, 13

technical help, 77

Teens Channel, 304

telephone support, 72

Tell Me About AOL 5.0 button, 73

Terms of Service (TOS), 30–31

   e-mail violations, 95

   violations of, 33

Terms of Service window

   Ask the Staff button, 31

   Questions? button, 31

text

   copying, 32

   netiquette for, 43

   pasting, 32

   styled, 136–138, 140

text entry boxes, 58–59

text insertion mark, 58

theaters, 288–289

Thesaurus command, 61

threading, 186

Thrive Online, 299–300

thumbnail images, 142

Tile command, 61

tiling, 141

title bar, 54

   color of, 55

   controls on, 55–56

toolbar, 62, 63

travel, international, 262

travel advisories, 28–29

travel agency, online, 286–287

Travel Channel, 283–287

   Cruise Critic, 285

   Independent Traveler, 284–285

   Preview Travel, 286–287

Trojan Horses, 213–214

   defined, 213

   safety settings against, 28

TTY Service, for member support, 72

U

universities, online listings, 275

University of California Extension
      Online, 275

uploading, 208, 217–219

Uploading form, 218

URLs (Universal Resource Locators), 65

V

viruses, 213–214

   antivirus programs for, 213–214

   contracting, 28

   defined, 213

   from e-mail, 94

   eliminating, 214

   safety settings against, 28

W

Watson, Jennifer, 12–13, 64, 164

weather forecasts

   current, 11

   in My Calendar, 171

weather updates, 257

Web browsers, security features, 247

Web publishing, 227

Web sites

   opening, 63

   personal, 12

   recommendations on, 38

Weekly New Files area, 212

Welcome screen, 6–7, 11, 59–60, 253

   AOL Help button, 75

   AOL logo, 254

   customizable links to, 8

   for Kids Only, 42

   mailbox icon, 87

   My Calendar icon, 171

   Set My Places button, 60

   Shopping button, 233

   You've Got Pictures icon, 219–220

Welcome to AOL 5.0 window, 73

What's New in AOL 5.0 guide, 61

What's New in AOL 5.0 slideshow, 73

White Pages, 329–330

Window menu, 61

windows, 54–55

   bringing to front, 55

   closing, 55

   frames around, 54

   interrupting loading, 63

maximizing, 55

minimizing, 56

moving, 56

resizing, 55–56

Windows Community, 272

Windows menu

Remember Window Size, 56

Remember Window Size and Position, 56

Women area, 296

words, spell checking, 132

WorkPlace Channel, 268–270

Career Center, 269–270

Start-Up Businesses, 268–269

World Wide Web

information resources on, 309

Parental Controls for accessing, 38

publishing on, 12

Worldlyinvestor.com, 260

Write icon, 62

Write Mail window, 58–59, 107

Address book button, 110

Attachments button, 110, 117–118

Copy To field, 107, 110–111

Finish Later button, 120

formatting bar, 136–137

Help button, 110

Insert a Picture, 140

Insert Signature File button, 140

Mail Extras button, 110, 132

in NetMail, 144

Request "Return Receipt" button, 110

Send Later button, 110

Send Now button, 108

Send To field, 107

Sign Off After Transfer, 119

Sign on a Friend button, 110

Spell Check button, 130

Subject field, 107–108

X

Xtreme Games, 291

Y

Yellow Pages, 327–329

Young Teen setting, 19

Buddy Album restrictions, 224

Instant Messages controls, 151

***Your Official America Online Internet Guide, 3rd Edition* (Peal), 72, 227**

You've Got Mail announcement, 93, 109

You've Got Pictures, 8, 219–225

Albums feature, 223–224

guidelines, 225

Roll Viewer, 221

You've Got Pictures Quick Start screen, 220–221

Z

.zip extension, 207

ZIP file compression, 119–120

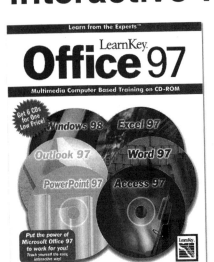

AOL Selects the Best

Express Yourself with an Electronic Smile :)

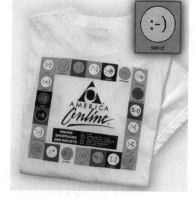

Order Today!
1-888-299-0329

Emoticon Mug and Mousepad
$12.95 (s&h $5.50)
#0010473N00011757

Emoticon T-shirt
XL only.
$14.95 (s&h $5.30)
#0010470N00011400

AOL Emoticon Book Binder
$19.95 (s&h $6.10)
#0010471N00011645

Emoticon Picture Frame
$12.95 (s&h $4.10)
#0010472N00011753

AMERICA Online

So easy to use, no wonder it's #1

AOL *Selects the* **Best**

Increase Your Computer's Productivity!

Order Today!
1-888-299-0329

AOL's PowerSuite Deluxe

Seven powerful utilities to help you work smarter and make your computer work harder for you! The programs on these CD-ROMs will help you perform tests and diagnostics to help your computer work at peak performances, give your computer more open space safely and easily, keep your software up-to-date with the help of AOL and the Internet, index Web sites quickly and easily, and stay organized and on schedule!

$39.95 (s&h $5.60)   #0010372N00010141

AMERICA
Online

So easy to use,
no wonder it's #1

Save time. Get organized. Work smart.

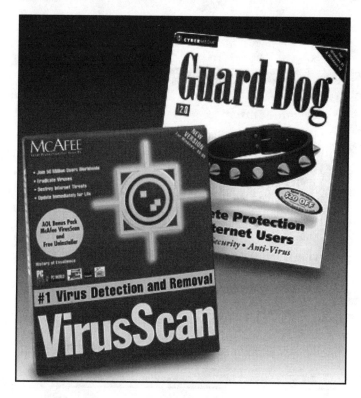

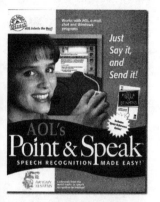